DUMBARTON OAKS TEXTS

X

NIKEPHOROS
PATRIARCH OF CONSTANTINOPLE
SHORT HISTORY

CORPUS FONTIUM HISTORIAE BYZANTINAE

CONSILIO SOCIETATIS INTERNATIONALIS
STUDIIS BYZANTINIS PROVEHENDIS DESTINATAE
EDITUM

VOLUMEN XIII

NICEPHORI PATRIARCHAE CONSTANTINOPOLITANI BREVIARIUM HISTORICUM

EDIDIT, ANGLICE VERTIT,
COMMENTARIO INSTRUXIT
CYRILLUS MANGO

SERIES WASHINGTONIENSIS
EDIDIT IHOR ŠEVČENKO

In aedibus Dumbarton Oaks
Washingtoniae, D.C.
MCMXC

NIKEPHOROS
PATRIARCH OF CONSTANTINOPLE
SHORT HISTORY

TEXT, TRANSLATION, AND COMMENTARY

by

CYRIL MANGO

Dumbarton Oaks
Research Library and Collection
Washington, D.C.
1990

Manufactured in the United States of America by
Sheridan Books, Inc., 450 Fame Avenue, Hanover, PA 17331 | (717) 632-3535

LIBRARY OF CONGRESS CATALOGING IN PUBLICATION DATA
Nicephorus, Saint, Patriarch of Constantinople.
[Breviarium historicum. English]
Short history / Nikephoros, Patriarch of Constantinople
text, translation, and commentary by Cyril Mango.
Translation of: Breviarium historicum.
(Dumbarton Oaks texts ; 10) (Corpus Fontium Historiae Byzantinae ; 13)

Includes bibliographical references.

ISBN 978-0-88402-184-1 (hardcover: alk. paper)
ISBN 978-0-88402-450-7 (paperbound: alk. paper)
LCCN permalink: https://lccn.loc.gov/89017058

1. Byzantine Empire—History—527–1081.
I. Mango, Cyril A. II. Title. III. Series.
IV. Series: Corpus fontium historiae Byzantinae ; v. 13.
DF57.N513 1990
949.5—dc20 89-17058

In accordance with the rules adopted by the
International Commission
for the Edition of Sources of Byzantine History,
the text and translation of this volume have been verified
by Ihor Ševčenko

EU GPSR Authorised Representative
LOGOS EUROPE, 9 rue Nicolas Poussin, 17000, La Rochelle, France
E-mail: Contact@logoseurope.eu

CONTENTS

PREFACE

The idea of producing this edition stems from two courses on the historical work of Patriarch Nikephoros I gave at the University of Oxford in 1975/6 and 1979/80. For teaching purposes I made then an English translation of the *Breviarium*. It occurred to me that its usefulness would be enhanced if it were to accompany a re-edition of the Greek text that would combine the versions of the Vatican and London manuscripts. Indeed, most historians are content to consult the former in C. de Boor's excellent edition of 1880; not many go to the trouble of examining at the same time L. Orosz' publication of the latter (part edition, part collation), which happens, furthermore, to be somewhat difficult of access. As might have been expected, my collation of the two manuscripts did not produce any great surprises. The process of relying on both, and not on the Vaticanus alone, has yielded, however, for the portion they have in common a somewhat more satisfactory text than de Boor's.

If it has taken me longer than I had anticipated to complete what appeared at first sight a fairly straightforward task, that is due, among other reasons, to the Commentary, which the editors of the Series Washingtoniensis deemed indispensable. In view of the fact that the *Breviarium* is one of the two most important Greek texts for our knowledge of Byzantine history of the seventh and eighth centuries, the information it contains has been the subject of endless discussion. An exhaustive commentary would, therefore, have become extremely bulky. After some hesitation I adopted the expedient of a succinct commentary to match the succinctness of the *Breviarium* itself. Readers and critics please take note. Given sufficient time I could have multiplied tenfold my bibliographic references and discussed at length a number of speculative theories that have been advanced about this or that passage or aspect of the work. I thought it would be more useful to restrict my comments to essentials, having in view the needs of historians rather than those of philologists. As for the latter, the time has not yet come to study in detail the patriarch's handling of the Greek language and his knowledge of the classics. To do so properly we would need to have an edition of his principal and as yet unpublished work, the *Refutatio et eversio* (as P. J. Alexander has christened it) and a better text of his other theological writings than is available in Migne's Patrology.

I should like to thank Professor Ihor Ševčenko, who has gone through the entire text and made a number of felicitous emendations; Dr. Jeffrey Featherstone for communicating to me the text of the *Refutatio et eversio*, which he edited in part in his Harvard Ph.D. thesis; Miss Claudia Rapp for a preliminary description of the Vaticanus; Professor P. Speck for allowing me to read prior to publication his *Das geteilte Dossier* (ΠΟΙΚΙΛΑ ΒΥΖΑΝΤΙΝΑ 9); Dr. Frances Kianka for her meticulous editing; and, as usual, my wife for her support and help with the intractable computer.

July 1988

LIST OF ABBREVIATIONS

A.G.: Anno Graecorum (Seleucid era)

Agapios: Agapius of Menbidj, *Kitāb al-ʿUnvān*, ed. A. Vasiliev, PO 7–8

A.H.: Anno Hegirae

Alexander, *Nicephorus*: P. J. Alexander, *The Patriarch Nicephorus of Constantinople* (Oxford, 1958)

A.M.: Anno mundi

Anastasius: Anastasius Biliothecarius, *Historia tripertita*, ed. C. de Boor in vol. II of his ed. of Theophanes

AnBoll: *Analecta Bollandiana*

Artamonov, *Istorija*: M. I. Artamonov, *Istorija Khazar* (Leningrad, 1962)

BCH: *Bulletin de correspondance hellénique*

Beševliev, *Protobulg. Periode*: V. Beševliev, *Die protobulgarische Periode der bulgarischen Geschichte* (Amsterdam, 1980)

BMGS: *Byzantine and Modern Greek Studies*

BNJ: *Byzantinisch-neugriechische Jahrbücher*

BSl: *Byzantinoslavica*

Bury, *Admin. System*: J. B. Bury, *The Imperial Administrative System in the Ninth Century* (London, 1911)

Bury, *LRE*: J. B. Bury, *A History of the Later Roman Empire from Arcadius to Irene* (London, 1889)

Butler, *Conquest*: A. J. Butler, *The Arab Conquest of Egypt*^{2} (Oxford, 1978)

ByzF: *Byzantinische Forschungen*

BZ: *Byzantinische Zeitschrift*

Cameron, *Circus*: A. Cameron, *Circus Factions* (Oxford, 1976)

Cer.: Constantinus Porphyrogenitus, *De cerimoniis aulae byzantinae*, ed. J. J. Reiske, I (Bonn, 1829)

Chr. 724: *Chronicon ad AD 724 pertinens*, trans. J.-B. Chabot, *Chronica minora*, II, CSCO, Scr. syri 4 (1904)

Chr. 846: *Chronicon ad AD 846 pertinens*, trans. J.-B. Chabot, ibid.

Chr. 1234: *Chronicon anonymum ad AD 1234 pertinens*, trans. J.-B. Chabot, CSCO, Scr. syri 56 (1937)

LIST OF ABBREVIATIONS

Chr. Altinate: *Origo civitatum Italie: Chronicon Altinate*, ed. R. Cessi, *Fonti per la storia d'Italia* (Rome, 1933), 102ff.

Chr. Pasch.: *Chronicon Paschale*, ed. L. Dindorf, I (Bonn, 1832)

Chr. Seert: *Chronique de Séert*, ed. A. Scher and R. Griveau, PO 13

Christensen, *Iran*: E. A. Christensen, *L'Iran sous les Sassanides*[2] (Copenhagen, 1944)

CRAI: *Comptes rendus des séances de l'Académie des Inscriptions et Belles-lettres*

CSCO: Corpus scriptorum Christianorum orientalium

DAI: Constantine Porphyrogenitus, *De administrando imperio*, ed. Gy. Moravcsik, trans. R. J. H. Jenkins (Washington, D.C., 1967)

DHGE: *Dictionnaire d'histoire et de géographie ecclésiastique*

Doctr. Iacobi: *Doctrina Iacobi nuper baptizati*, ed. N. Bonwetsch, Abh. Kön. Ges. d. Wiss. Gött., Phil.-hist. Kl., NF XII/3 (1910)

Donner, *Conquests*: F. McG. Donner, *The Early Islamic Conquests* (Princeton, 1981)

DOP: *Dumbarton Oaks Papers*

ΕΕΒΣ: Ἐπετηρὶς Ἑταιρείας Βυζαντινῶν Σπουδῶν

EHR: *English Historical Review*

Elias Nisib.: *Eliae metropolitae Nisibeni opus chronologicum*, trans. E. W. Brooks, CSCO, Scr. syri 23 (1910)

EO: *Echos d'Orient*

Georg. Mon.: *Georgii Monachi Chronicon*, ed. C. de Boor (Leipzig, 1904)

GRBS: *Greek, Roman and Byzantine Studies*

Grumel, *Chronologie*: V. Grumel, *La Chronologie*. Traité d'études byzantines, I (Paris, 1958)

Haldon, *Praetorians*: J. F. Haldon, *Byzantine Praetorians*, ΠΟΙΚΙΛΑ ΒΥΖΑΝΤΙΝΑ 3 (Bonn, 1984)

Hunger, *Hochsprachliche Lit.*: H. Hunger, *Die hochsprachliche profane Literatur der Byzantiner* (Munich, 1978)

Ioann. Ant.: Ioannes Antiochenus

IRAIK: *Izvestija Russkogo Arkheologičeskogo Instituta v Konstantinopole*

Janin, *CP*: R. Janin, *Constantinople byzantine*[2] (Paris, 1964)

Janin, *Eglises*: R. Janin, *La géographie ecclésiastique de l'Empire byzantin*, I/3. *Les églises et les monastères* (de Constantinople)[2] (Paris, 1969)

Janin, *Grands centres*: R. Janin, *Les églises et les monastères des grands centres byzantins* (Paris, 1975)

JDAI: *Jahrbuch des Deutschen Archäologischen Instituts*

JHS: *Journal of Hellenic Studies*

JÖB: *Jahrbuch der Österreichischen Byzantinistik*

LIST OF ABBREVIATIONS

John of Nikiu, Charles: *The Chronicle of John . . . Bishop of Nikiu*, trans. R. H. Charles (London, 1916)

John of Nikiu, Zotenberg: *Chronique de Jean évêque de Nikiou*, trans. H. Zotenberg, *Notices et extraits des manuscrits de la Bibliothèque Nationale*, 24 (Paris, 1883)

JTS: *Journal of Theological Studies*

Kaegi, *Unrest*: W. E. Kaegi, Jr., *Byzantine Military Unrest, 471–843* (Amsterdam, 1981)

Kedr.: Georgius Cedrenus, ed. I. Bekker (Bonn, 1838–39)

Khuzistan Chr.: *Chronicon anonymum*, trans. I. Guidi, *Chronica minora*, I, CSCO, Scr. syri 2 (1903)

Kulakovskij: J. U. Kulakovskij, *Istorija Vizantii*, 3 vols. (Kiev, 1913–15; repr. London, 1973)

Leo gramm.: *Leonis grammatici Chronographia*, ed. I. Bekker (Bonn, 1842)

Lilie: R.-J. Lilie, *Die byzantinische Reaktion auf die Ausbreitung der Araber*, Misc. byz. Monac. 22 (Munich, 1976)

Lombard, *Constantin V*: A. Lombard, *Constantin V, empereur des Romains* (Paris, 1902)

Mansi: J. D. Mansi, *Sacrorum Conciliorum nova et amplissima collectio*

Mich. Syr.: *Chronique de Michel le Syrien*, ed. and trans. J.-B. Chabot, 4 vols. (Paris, 1899–1924)

Mir. S. Artemii: *Miracula S. Artemii*, ed. A. Papadopoulos-Kerameus, *Varia graeca sacra* (St. Petersburg, 1909)

Mir. S. Demetrii: P. Lemerle, *Les plus anciens recueils des Miracles de S. Démétrius*, I (Paris, 1979)

Moravcsik, *Byzantinoturcica*: Gy. Moravcsik, *Byzantinoturcica*², 2 vols. (Berlin, 1958)

Müller-Wiener, *Bildlexikon*: W. Müller-Wiener, *Bildlexikon zur Topographie Istanbuls* (Tübingen, 1977)

Nik.: Nikephoros

Oikonomides, *Listes*: N. Oikonomidès, *Les listes de préséance byzantines des IXᵉ et Xᵉ siècles* (Paris, 1972)

Orosz, *London MS*: L. Orosz, *The London Manuscript of Nikephoros' 'Breviarium,'* Magyar-Görög Tanulmányok 28 (Budapest, 1948)

Parastaseis: *Parastaseis syntomoi chronikai*, ed. Th. Preger, *Scriptores originum Constantinopolitanarum*, I (Leipzig, 1901), 19–73

Patria: *Patria Konstantinoupoleos*, ibid., II (Leipzig, 1907)

PG: J.-P. Migne, Patrologia graeca

Pisides: A. Pertusi, ed., *Giorgio di Pisidia. Poemi*, I, Studia patristica et byzantina 7 (Ettal, 1959)

LIST OF ABBREVIATIONS

PLRE: A. H. M. Jones et al., *Prosopography of the Later Roman Empire*, I–II (Cambridge, 1971, 1980)

PO: Patrologia Orientalis

Ramsay, *Hist. Geogr.*: W. M. Ramsay, *The Historical Geography of Asia Minor* (London, 1890)

RE: Pauly-Wissowa, *Realencyclopädie der classischen Altertumswissenschaft*

REB: *Revue des études byzantines*

RSBS: *Rivista di studi bizantini e slavi*

Sebeos: *Histoire d'Héraclius par l'évêque Sebéos*, trans. F. Macler (Paris, 1904)

Severus of Eschmounein: Severus of Eschmounein, *History of the Patriarchs of the Coptic Church of Alexandria*, ed. and trans. E. Evetts, PO 1

Simok.: *Theophylacti Simocattae Historiae*, ed. C. de Boor (Leipzig, 1887)

Speck, *Artabasdos*: P. Speck, *Artabasdos, der rechtgläubige Vorkämpfer der göttlichen Lehren*, ΠΟΙΚΙΛΑ ΒΥΖΑΝΤΙΝΑ 2 (Bonn, 1981)

Speck, *Dossier*: P. Speck, *Das geteilte Dossier*, ΠΟΙΚΙΛΑ ΒΥΖΑΝΤΙΝΑ 9 (Bonn, 1988)

Strategios Georg.: *La prise de Jérusalem par les Perses en 614*, ed. and trans. G. Garitte, CSCO 203, Scr. iber. 12 (1960)

Stratos: A. N. Stratos, Τὸ *Βυζάντιον στὸν ζ´ αἰῶνα*, 6 vols. (Athens, 1965–77)

Suda: *Suidae Lexicon*, ed. A. Adler (Leipzig, 1928–38)

Synax.CP: *Synaxarium ecclesiae Constantinopolitanae*, ed. H. Delehaye, Propylaeum ad Acta Sanctorum Nov. (Brussels, 1902)

Synk.: Georgius Syncellus, *Ecloga chronographica*, ed. A. A. Mosshammer (Leipzig, 1984)

TAPA: *Transactions of the American Philological Association*

Theod. Synk.: Theodorus Syncellus, ed. L. Sternbach, *Analecta Avarica*, Rozprawy Akad. Umiejętności, Wydz. Filol., ser. II, t. 15 (Cracow, 1900), 298–320

Theoph.: *Theophanis Chronographia*, ed. C. de Boor (Leipzig, 1883)

TM: Centre de Recherche d'Histoire et Civilisation Byzantines. *Travaux et Mémoires*

V. Anast. Persae: *Vita S. Anastasii Persae*, ed. A. Papadopoulos-Kerameus, Ἀνάλεκτα ἱεροσολυμιτικῆς σταχυολογίας, IV (St. Petersburg, 1897), 126–48

Van Dieten, *Patriarchen*: J. L. van Dieten, *Geschichte der Patriarchen von Sergios I. bis Johannes VI.* (Amsterdam, 1972)

VizVrem: *Vizantijskij Vremennik*

V. Theod. Syk.: *Vie de Théodore de Sykéôn*, ed. A.-J. Festugière, Subsidia hagiographica 48 (Brussels, 1970)

LIST OF ABBREVIATIONS

Zacos-Veglery: G. Zacos-A. Veglery, *Byzantine Lead Seals*, I (Basel, 1972)
Zlatarski, *Istorija*: V. Zlatarski, *Istorija na Bŭlgarskata dŭržava prez Srednite vekove*, I/1 (Sofia, 1970)
ZDMG: *Zeitschrift der Deutschen Morgenländischen Gesellschaft*
ZRVI: *Zbornik radova Vizantološkog Instituta*

INTRODUCTION

THE AUTHOR

The life of Nikephoros has been surveyed by several scholars, most fully by P. J. Alexander.[1] For the present purpose it will be sufficient to recall its main landmarks.

Nikephoros was born at Constantinople in or about 758 in the reign of the iconoclastic emperor Constantine V (741–775). His father, Theodore, belonged to a prominent family and held the post of imperial secretary (*asekretis*); being, however, of an iconophile persuasion, he was denounced to the authorities and exiled to Pontos, probably some time in the 760s. Recalled to the palace, he did not abandon his religious convictions and was once again banished, this time to Nicaea, where he died six years later.

Nikephoros received a normal education (*enkyklios paideia*) and followed his father's footsteps by joining the civil service, also in the capacity of imperial secretary. He probably did so in the reign of Leo IV (775–780), who was nominally, though not aggressively, an iconoclast. He served as the subordinate of the first secretary Tarasios, who, in 784, was elevated to the patriarchal throne. At the Second Nicene Council (787) Nikephoros made a brief appearance to read aloud a Greek translation of the pope's letter addressed to the reigning emperors Constantine VI and Eirene. For some years thereafter Nikephoros seems to have remained at his post. His subsequent retirement to a life of quietude somewhere in the Asiatic suburbs of the capital is not dated exactly, but may have been occasioned by the assumption of supreme power by Eirene and the blinding of Constantine VI in 797. Probably after the overthrow of Eirene in 802 Nikephoros was brought back to Constantinople and made the administrator of the biggest poorhouse (unnamed).

In February 806 Patriarch Tarasios died. In naming his successor Emperor Nikephoros I consulted many prominent churchmen, but found no unanimity of opinion. He decided to confer the appointment on his namesake Nikephoros, though

[1] *Nicephorus*.

the latter was as yet a layman. Rushed at a few days' interval through the grades of monk, deacon, and presbyter, Nikephoros was ordained patriarch on Easter Sunday, 12 April 806.

In the exercise of his functions Nikephoros appears to have been docile to his emperor, who was killed in Bulgaria five years later. He lent his support to the appointment of the next emperor, Michael I (1 Oct. 811), and when Michael was overthrown after the defeat at Versinicia, Nikephoros approved the elevation of Leo V, from whom he requested but did not obtain a formal affirmation of orthodoxy.

When the worst of the Bulgarian threat had been averted by the sudden death of the Khan Krum (14 April 814), the new emperor appointed a committee to inquire afresh into the justification of banning religious images. In December Leo asked Nikephoros to yield to popular demand by removing icons; Nikephoros refused. An open clash between emperor and patriarch took place on Christmas day, and early the following year Nikephoros was forced to abdicate. He was succeeded by Theodotos, son of the patrician Michael Melissenos, and, after Easter 815, the iconoclastic doctrine was reaffirmed by a council held in St. Sophia.

Nikephoros retired to the monastery *τὰ 'Αγαθοῦ*, north of Chrysopolis, which he may have built himself. Soon thereafter he was moved by the emperor's order to the more distant monastery of St. Theodore, another of his foundations. He had a chance of resuming patriarchal office under Michael II on condition of keeping silent about the issue of images, but refused. He died in 828.

HISTORICAL WORKS

The major part of Nikephoros' literary output is devoted to theological controversy and was composed between 814 and some time after 820. Among his theological works two contain a certain amount of historical information designed to demonstrate that the period of iconoclasm and, in particular, the reign of Constantine V was a time, not of success and prosperity, but of calamity: these are the *Third Antirrheticus* (PG 100, 493D ff.) and the as yet unpublished *Refutatio et eversio*.[2] The relevant passages found in them are discussed below, pp. 9–11.

In addition, Nikephoros is credited with two historical works, namely:

1) the *'Ιστορία σύντομος* or *Breviarium*, edited here; and

2) the *Χρονογραφικὸν σύντομον*, of which a few words ought to be said.

[2] Analyzed ibid., 242–62. For a transcription of the complete text I am greatly indebted to Dr. J. Featherstone.

This is no more than a set of chronological tables and consists in de Boor's standard edition of the following elements:

a) An Old Testament chronology from Adam to the Babylonian captivity.

b) The kings of Persia from Cyrus to Alexander's conquest.

c) The Ptolemies down to Cleopatra.

d) The emperors of Rome from Julius Caesar to Michael II.

e) Roman empresses, starting with Theodora and Helena, wives of Constantius Chlorus.

f) The kings of the ten tribes of Israel in Samaria.

g) The high priests of the Jews from Aaron to the sack of Jerusalem by the Romans.

h) The bishops of Constantinople from the apostle Andrew[3] to the iconoclast Theodotos.

i) The popes of Rome.

j) The bishops of Jerusalem.

k) The bishops of Alexandria.

l) The bishops of Antioch.

m) A list of the canonical, dubious, and apocryphal books of the Old and New Testaments with the number of verses in each.

It should be noted that de Boor failed to take account of the Slavonic versions[4] and of the four oldest Greek manuscripts, which are:

1) British Library, *Add. 19390* of the early tenth century, which also contains the *Breviarium*. It is limited to items a–d and h, and, as regards the Χ*ρον. σύντομον*, appears to have been copied from an original dating soon after 821. For further details see below, pp. 23–24.

2) Oxford, Christ Church, *Wake 5*, of the late ninth century, which contains

---

[3]It should be noted that in the *Lond. Add. 19390* the list starts with Metrophanes, omitting the 22 mythical bishops from Andrew to Probus.

[4]Namely, (1) The *Letopisec vskore*, preserved in many variant versions. Ed. from Novgorod Kormčaja by N. V. Stepanov, *Izv. Otd. Russk. Jaz. i Slov. Akad. Nauk* 17/2 (1912), 250–93; 17/3 (1912), 256–320 (Slavonic and Greek texts in parallel columns, pp. 293 ff.). Items a–d down to the murder of Michael III (867). For the Greek text Stepanov has added variants from two Moscow MSS, viz. Synodal Library (now Historical Museum) *Vladimir 318* and *439*. Cf. E. K. Piotrovskaja, *Trudy Otd. Drevnerussk. Lit.* 29 (1974), 170–77; eadem, *VizVrem* 36 (1974), 147–53. (2) A list of Roman emperors from Augustus to 920 in Svjatoslav's *Izbornik* of 1073, after the colophon, on fols. 264^r–266^v. Ed. E. K. Piotrovskaja in *Izbornik Svjatoslava 1073 goda* (Moscow, 1977), 317–31. (3) The *Istorikii za Boga v'krat'ce*, dated 893/4 and ascribed to Constantine of Preslav. It is a list from Adam to Leo VI, but the last two reigns, those of Basil I and Leo VI, given in rounded numbers (i.e., without indication of months and days), appear to have been added. Ed. V. N. Zlatarski, *Spisanie BAN* 27 (1923), 132–82. Cf. B. S. Angelov, *Byzantinobulgarica* 2 (1966), 83–105.

part of the Chronicle of Synkellos (from Julius Caesar to the end)[5] and the Chronicle of Theophanes.[6] Items a–e, h–m only. The list of Roman emperors ends with the accession of Basil I (867), for whom no length of reign is given, and the list of empresses likewise with Basil's wife Eudokia. The bishops' lists are given in the order: Jerusalem, Rome, Constantinople, Alexandria, Antioch. The Constantinople list ends with Ignatios (847–858), with no indication of years, but the same applies to his predecessors.

3) Former Dresden, *Da 12*, now reunited with its parent, Moscow, *Hist. Museum 231* (Vladimir), written for Arethas in 932.[7] Items a–d only. The series of emperors ends with the accession of Constantine VII (913). Some additional comments have been incorporated into the text.

4) Jerusalem, *Patriarch. cod. 24* (several hands of the 10th century).[8] Items a–d (to Leo VI) and h (to Antony II Kauleas, 893–901).

It is questionable whether the concept of authorship can be applied to an almanac like the *Χρον. σύντομον*. Its archetype does appear to have been put together before Nikephoros' death, and he may have had a hand in its compilation; alternatively, it may have been found among his papers. Not all manuscripts attribute it to him: in the London and Dresden copies it appears anonymously. Furthermore, it is difficult to determine which items the archetype may have contained.

Another consideration that ought to be borne in mind is that the *Χρον. σύντομον* is but one of several similar compilations that seem to have circulated at about the same time. A set of chronological tables certainly underlies the Chronicle of Synkellos (not later than 811) and another set the Chronicle of Theophanes (completed by 814). A third set (including also the kings of Persia and the Arab caliphs) exists in *Vat. gr. 2210* (10th century).[9] It appears to have been put together out of disparate material toward the middle of the ninth century and, strangely enough, presents the bishops in the order: Rome (down to Paschal I, 817–824), Alexandria, Antioch, Jerusalem, Constantinople (down to Methodios, 843–847).

The *Χρον. σύντομον* deserves to be reedited on the basis of a fuller manuscript tradition than was utilized by de Boor, but that can only be profitably done in the context of the other cognate compilations we have mentioned.

---

[5] See Synk., pp. XII–XIII.

[6] For a description of the MS, see N. G. Wilson, *DOP* 26 (1972), 357–58.

[7] See L. G. Westerink, *Byzantion* 42 (1972), 197, 199, 204.

[8] A. Papadopoulos-Kerameus, *Ἱεροσολυμιτικὴ βιβλιοθήκη*, I (St. Petersburg, 1891), 89–96. Wrongly dated ca. 900 by K. and S. Lake, *Dated Greek Minuscule Manuscripts*, I (Boston, 1934), No. 1, pls. 1–2. See also V. Beneševič, *BNJ* 5 (1927), 109–10 (early 10th century); N. Oikonomides, *Listes*, 239–43 (11th century).

[9] Ed. A. Schoene, *Eusebii Chron. liber prior*, I (Berlin, 1875), App. IV, 81–83. Lake, op. cit., IX (1938), No. 331 and pl. 604 with a date of "ante AD 886 (?)."

THE NATURE OF THE *BREVIARIUM*[10]

As transmitted in the Vatican MS (V), the *Breviarium* is a condensed historical account of the Byzantine Empire from Phokas (602) to the marriage of Leo IV to Eirene (769). The reign of Phokas is, however, dismissed in one sentence, and the narrative really starts with the revolt against him in Africa. It then proceeds to October 641, leaves out entirely the reign of Constans II (641–668), then carries on from the accession of Constantine IV (668) to the end. The London MS (L) also starts in 602 but breaks off in 713.

L was not known to de Boor, and when it first came to the attention of interested scholars the view was expressed, in spite of the attribution to Nikephoros in the title, that it was the work of an earlier author, or rather of two earlier authors (the first allegedly to fol. 30^r, corresponding to the marriage of Herakleios to Martina, the second from 30^v to the end), which Nikephoros later copied.[11] On closer study, this theory proved to be untenable, and L came to be regarded as the descendant of a first draft, of which V represents a reworking. This appears to be the simplest solution of what is admittedly a very complicated puzzle (see below, pp. 25–29).

The existence of two redactions by the same author represents a rare case in Byzantine historiography[12] and leads to some interesting observations. Setting aside a number of minor omissions and additions (some of them being of a scribal nature), the differences between L and V are purely stylistic and do not concern the substance of the narrative. Furthermore, it is apparent that the first eleven paragraphs of L (in our numeration) were subjected to a thorough revision, but from paragraph 12 to the end of L only small changes were made. Another historian, in going over his first draft, might have wished to make substantive alterations by correcting any errors he may have committed or introducing evidence he had overlooked. Not so Nikephoros: his concern was merely with the literary presentation of his work.

It has been claimed[13] that the termination of L with the overthrow of Philippikos

---

[10] For a partial discussion of what follows see my "The *Breviarium* of the Patriarch Nikephoros," *Byzance: Hommage à A. N. Stratos* (Athens, 1986), II, 539–52. Previous bibliography in Moravcsik, *Byzantinoturcica*, I, 458–59; Hunger, *Hochsprachliche Lit.*, I, 346–47.

[11] A. Burckhardt, *BZ* 5 (1896), 465–77.

[12] The view of C. de Boor concerning two author's versions of the Chronicle of George the Monk, one represented by *Coislin 305*, the other by all the other MSS (in his ed. of same, I, pp. lxviii ff.) has been disproved by M.-A. Monégier du Sorbier, *Recherches sur la tradition manuscrite de la Chronique de Georges le Moine*, Thesis, Ecole des Hautes Etudes en Sciences Sociales (Paris, 1985), 483 ff.

[13] This was first stated by Burckhardt, op. cit., 468 because of the scribe's pious formula at the end of L and the fact that fol. 55^v of the same MS has been left blank. Often repeated, e.g., by E. Honigmann, *Nouvelle Clio* 4 (1952), 290 note 1; Moravcsik, *Byzantinoturcica*, I, 457, 532; C. Head, *Justinian II of Byzantium* (Madison, Wisc., 1972), 16. I shall not discuss here the highly complex problem of the

Bardanes (713) was deliberate, but on closer examination that turns out not to be the case. L breaks off, if one may say so, in the middle of a paragraph. Of course, the division of the text into paragraphs by modern editors is somewhat arbitrary, and one may wish to start a new paragraph with the words *τῇ ἐπαύριον*, just after the end of L. That, however, does not alter the fact that the flow of the narrative is continuous over the point of the break, as it is also in the parallel text of Theophanes, which is based on the same source.

It may be that the ending of L is due to accidental mutilation of its model, but it is equally possible that Nikephoros, for whatever reason, stopped at that point and laid his work aside. The scribe's pious formula at the end of L, *Χριστῷ τελειώσαντι δόξα καὶ χάρις*, does not appear to me to favor one alternative over the other. In the absence of any clear evidence, let us assume that the first draft extended only to A.D. 713. On picking it up again Nikephoros felt dissatisfied with its literary form and proceeded to rewrite the first eleven paragraphs, the biggest change he made being in Shahīn's speech (c. 6), which was expanded into a kind of mini-oration in the manner of Thucydides. He even felt compelled to "improve" some proper names.[14] On reaching c. 12, he either became tired of such extensive revision or found his draft nearly acceptable as it stood, and so made only minor changes to his earlier text. He then carried the narrative forward to 769. A close reading of the added section (A.D. 713–769) shows, however, clear signs of progressive weariness. As we shall see, what Nikephoros did, to all intents and purposes, was to paraphrase into ancient Greek a small number of chronicle sources written in "vulgar" Greek. In the first part of his History he went to some trouble to camouflage the "chronicle element" and even suppressed (to our great regret) nearly all dates.[15] In the final part, on the other hand, individual chronicle entries are barely disguised.[16] This circumstance suggests that the History is unfinished as it stands and that it was not necessarily intended to stop in 769, a date that cannot

---

so-called *Epitome*, the first version of which (also ascribed by some scholars to Traianos Patrikios) is thought to have extended to the reign of Justinian II. See D. Serruys, *BZ* 16 (1907), 1–51. The *Epitome* in its redactions A (= Theodosius Melitenus), B1 (represented by *Paris. gr. 854*, negligently edited by J. A. Cramer, *Anecdota graeca e codd. mss. Bibl. Reg. Paris.*, II [Oxford, 1839], 243ff.), and B2 (namely, the Va tradition of George the Monk and *π*, the common source of *Paris. gr. 1712* and Kedrenos) does not appear to me to throw much light on the source of Nikephoros.

[14] He changed *Δομνητζιόλος* to *Δομεντιόλος*, *Βουνοῦσος* to *Βονόσσος* (c. 1), *Βιζουλῖνος* to either *Βουτηλῖνος* or *Βιτουλῖνος* (c. 4). I am not sure whether the change of *Φάβιος* to the incorrect *Φλαύιος* (c. 11) is deliberate or scribal.

[15] Down to A.D. 641 the only chronological indications are: arrival of the True Cross at Constantinople (c. 18); death of Patriarch Sergios (c. 26); length of reign of Herakleios (c. 27); length of reign of Constantine III (c. 29); ordination of Patriarch Paul II (c. 32).

[16] Cc. 78, 79, 82, 84, 85, 86, 87, 88.

be regarded as particularly significant. The fact, however, that Photios (*Bibl.*, cod. 66) read it in the same form as that represented by V proves that we possess the final text.

Here a small problem presents itself. Granted that L is manifestly not the author's autograph, why is it that a first and, indeed, incomplete draft of the History was copied into a manuscript of fine quality? Of course, we do not know the answer. It may be that Nikephoros himself gave a copy of his first version to a friend (say for the purpose of criticism), or it may have been found among his papers after his death. In either case we can be reasonably certain that the scribe of L was unaware of the existence of the V text.

Although in L the *Breviarium* is entitled *Χρονογραφικόν*—a neutral and imprecise term—there can be no doubt that Nikephoros intended to write a "history" in the technical sense of that word. This is shown not only by the title in V (confirmed by Photios), but also by the author's style and his deliberate use of a vocabulary derived, directly or indirectly, from ancient historiography.[17] And if he did so, the chances are that there existed no "history" of the events after 602, that is, until Nikephoros took up his pen. It has already been observed[18] that his purpose was probably to provide a continuation of Theophylact Simokatta, who stopped in 602: this is corroborated by the fact that in V the *Breviarium* follows Theophylact's text[19] and Photios, too, read them in the same order (*Bibl.*, codd. 65, 66). Yet the *Breviarium*, apart from its self-confessed brevity, fails to meet one essential requirement of the genre in not being based on autopsy. In 769, his terminal date, Nikephoros was about eleven years old. He could not have had personal knowledge of any of the events he describes, and it is highly unlikely that he had recourse to living witnesses. The significance of his *démarche* should be sought in the context of the Byzantine "renaissance." Alongside the revival of grammar, epistolography, and other antique literary forms, Nikephoros sought to produce a "history" that would bridge the gap of nearly two centuries that separated his time from the Roman world of the early seventh century. As far as we know, he was the only one to have done so: indeed, no other "history" was produced until the reign of Constantine Porphyrogenitus.

---

[17] As far as we have been able to ascertain, his borrowings are lexical and do not comprise whole phrases. Among his affectations we may note the use of *ὡς* (prep.), not always confined to cases where the object is a person (also frequent in Simok.); *ἤθη* = "abodes of men" (as, e.g., in Herodotus); *ὄνομα* = "by name" (as in Xenophon, etc.), which V^2 studiously altered to *ὀνόματι*. On the rhythmic structure of Nikephoros' prose see W. Hörandner, *Der Prosarhythmus in der rhetorischen Literatur der Byzantiner* (Vienna, 1981), 131.

[18] Alexander, *Nicephorus*, 157–58.

[19] Even if the two parts of V were written in different scriptoria. See below, pp. 19–20.

THE DATE OF THE *BREVIARIUM*

There is no decisive evidence to determine the date when Nikephoros composed the *Breviarium*. He may have done so in the earlier part of his career when he was in imperial service (say ca. 780–797) or during his first retirement from the capital (ca. 797–802) or while he was *ptochotrophos* (ca. 802–806) or after he had been expelled from patriarchal office (815–828). It is not likely that he would have had the leisure for such pursuits while serving as patriarch.

A number of hypothetical dates have, however, been advanced on the basis of internal indications. Bury thought that the *Breviarium* was earlier than 796 (when the Avars were subjugated by Charlemagne) because in c. 34 Nikephoros refers to Pannonia as being still under Avar rule (τῇ νῦν ὑπὸ Ἀβάροις κειμένῃ).[20] Alexander suggested that it was earlier than 787, "as the author shows no knowledge of the official restoration of image-worship."[21] Ohnsorge[22] and Speck[23] saw a contemporary reference in the words of the people of Constantinople addressed to Empress Martina: "Nor can you, O Lady, receive barbarian or other foreign emissaries who come to the palace or hold converse with them. May God forbid that the Roman State should come to such a pass!" (c. 28). If, as these scholars believe, the passage in question is directed against Empress Eirene, a date in 790 or later would necessarily follow. As far as I know, K. N. Uspenskij stands alone in assuming a date after 800,[24] but he did not justify his opinion.

How much weight we may wish to attribute to any of the above arguments will depend on two considerations:

1) In view of the fact that Nikephoros wrote his History not at first hand but on the basis of earlier sources that are unavailable to us, it would be helpful to know which of his statements are personal and which are derived from his sources. To this question there is, alas, no answer. Thus, when Nikephoros says that Pannonia is "today" under Avar rule, he is either copying his source or expressing contemporary reality (assuming he had knowledge of it). I would suspect the former, but cannot prove it. The same applies to the passage about Martina: the natural assumption would be that Nikephoros found it in his source, in which case it is not directed against Eirene. Another remark that deserves to be considered concludes

---

[20] *LRE*, II, 450 note 1.

[21] *Nicephorus*, 162.

[22] *Saeculum* 14 (1963), 225–26; repr. in *Konstantinopel und der Okzident* (Darmstadt, 1966), 57–58.

[23] *Kaiser Konstantin VI* (Munich, 1978), II, 638 note 233; *Artabasdos, der rechtgläubige Vorkämpfer der göttlichen Lehren* (Bonn, 1981), 110ff.

[24] To be more precise, in the second decade of the 9th century: *VizVrem* 3 (1950), 421.

the account of the civil war between Constantine V and Artabasdos (c. 65): "What terrible things are wont to happen in such conditions . . . is, indeed, known to many from experience." If this is a personal aside, it may well be thought to refer to the revolt of Thomas the Slav (821–823), the only internecine war that Nikephoros himself experienced. But again we cannot be certain that it is a personal observation.

2) A related question concerns the amount of bias (*Tendenz*), hidden or overt, that may be detected in the *Breviarium*. Being, as we are, keenly sensitive to political motivation, we should be on our guard in ascribing a similar attitude to a medieval author. We should also bear in mind that the style and literary conventions of historiography which Nikephoros adopted forced on him an appearance of detachment if not complete impartiality. Certainly, he is anti-iconoclastic, though less stridently so than Theophanes. But then there is reason to believe that his source was also anti-iconoclastic.[25] Is the relative moderation of his anti-iconoclasm due to the fact that he is writing "history" or to some other reason? Here and there Nikephoros expresses censure, for example, of Emperor Herakleios on the grounds of the latter's incestuous marriage with Martina. The censure was probably present in Nikephoros' source, but was he trying to make a point by repeating it? Was he perchance thinking of the irregular marriage of Constantine VI? It has been claimed that Nikephoros shows a strong sense of loyalty to the imperial government (of whatever complexion) and that he deliberately omits events that wounded his patriotism.[26] That, too, is a subjective interpretation. The omissions, in particular, can be explained on other grounds, and Nikephoros' silence about the disastrous reign of Constans II is due either to the fact that he knew nothing about it or to accidental loss in the archetype, not to his unwillingness to relate events he found distasteful (see below, pp. 14–15).

We should inquire next whether any chronological deduction may be drawn from a comparison of the *Breviarium* with the two polemical works of Nikephoros, which, as we have said, contain historical information on the reign of Constantine V, namely, *Antirrheticus* III (composed after 815 or in 818–820 according to Alexander)[27] and the *Refutatio et eversio* (after 820). There can be no doubt that there is a significant overlap among all three and that the polemical works provide a number of details that are absent in the *Breviarium*, as the following examples show:

1) Monasteries converted to profane use, turned into stables or sold for cash, among them those of Floros and Kallistratos. The piles of refuse (?) left from that period can still be seen today (*ὧν τὰ περιττώματα καὶ ἐφ' ἡμῶν αὐτῶν διήρκεσαν ἐπιχρονίσαντα*): *Antirrh.* III, 493D; cf. *Refut.*, *Cod. Paris. gr. 1250*,

[25] Alexander, *Nicephorus*, 159–62.

[26] E. E. Lipšic, *VizVrem* 3 (1950), esp. 97 ff.

[27] *Nicephorus*, 188.

fol. 195r. Not in the *Breviarium*, but corresponds loosely to Theoph., 443.1 ff., who mentions the monasteries of Dalmatos, Kallistratos, Dios, and Maximinos, not that of Floros.

2) The plague (*Brev.*, c. 67): *Antirrh.* III, 496B–D adds the information that Constantine V, out of fear for his own safety, departed to the suburbs of Nicomedia and even farther away, and kept informed by letter of the number of victims; that three or five corpses would be piled on the same bier; that the gravediggers would sometimes die in the exercise of their task; that the names and number of future victims would be supernaturally announced. These details are also lacking in Theoph., 422.29 ff., who is fuller than the *Breviarium*. Only a brief reference in the *Refut.*

3) Earthquakes: *Antirrh.* III, 496D–497A; cf. *Refut.*, fol. 195v. Collapse of fine houses, especially on high ground; their ruins may still be seen at Constantinople. Not in *Brev.* or Theoph.

4) Falling stars (*Brev.*, c. 71; brief mention in Theoph., 435.5): *Antirrh.* III, 497A adds that this happened in winter, χειμῶνος ὥρᾳ (March in Theoph.). Cf. *Refut.*, fol. 196r in terms similar to *Brev.*: *καὶ γὰρ ἐδόκει τοὺς ἀστέρας ἅπαντας τοῦ οὐρανίου, ἐν ᾧ ἐπεπήγεσαν, χώρου ἀπορρηγνυμένους ῥαγδαίως κατὰ γῆς φέρεσθαι.*

5) Famine (not in *Brev.*), no less severe than any recorded in olden times or the one that is prevailing today: *λιμῶν γὰρ ἦν ὁ δεινότατος . . . οὔτε τοῦ νῦν ἐντεῦθεν ἐναρξαμένου, οὔτε τῶν πάλαι μνημονευομένων . . . ἐλαττούμενος*: *Antirrh.* III, 500B.

6) Raid into Armenia (Melitene), *Brev.*, c. 70; Theoph., 427.14 ff. *Antirrh.* III, 508D–509A adds that Constantine took advantage of a civil war among the Arabs and that he captured forts by the surrender of the local inhabitants, who were Armenians and Christian Syrians. When the Arabs heard of this, they sent against him a force of five thousand men, but he fled with his whole army.

7) Severe winter: fairly short reference in *Refut.*, fols. 195v–196r in terms similar to *Brev.*, c. 74.

8) Spurious abundance of foodstuffs (*Brev.*, c. 85; Theoph., 443.18): *Antirrh.* III, 513C–516A has the same comparison as the *Brev.* and Theoph. of Constantine V to Midas,[28] and adds that some farmers were forced to sell their entire holdings for one gold piece; others hanged themselves from trees, "as I have seen myself" (εἶδον ἔγωγε).

Some of the above items (1, 3, 8 in part) may be based on personal recollection. Elsewhere, in speaking of Constantine's beastly life, his infirmities, nightmares, cruelty, etc., he invokes the testimony of the emperor's servants, some of

[28] Ibid., 159–60.

whom were still alive (*Antirrh.* III, 504D). Items 2, 4, 6, 7 and (in part) 8 are, however, clearly based on written evidence, which, being fuller than the *Brev.* (except 7) was, in all probability, the latter's source. In fact, in the *Antirrh.*, 496A Nikephoros explicitly refers to historical writings of eyewitnesses (*τῶν τότε παρόντων τινές, εὐκαίρως καὶ εἰς δέον χρώμενοι, ἱστορίᾳ παραδοῦναι ἄξιον ᾠήθησαν* with reference to the various catastrophes and, in particular, the plague) and, further down (508B), states that he had also read Constantine's boastful dispatches regarding his Bulgarian victories (*καθά γε ἡμῖν ἐκ τῶν γεγραμμένων αὐτῷ πρὸς τοὺς ἐνηυλισμένους κατὰ τὴν βασιλεύουσαν ἀναλεξαμένοις ἔγνωσται*). One may conclude from the above that after he had gone into banishment in 815 Nikephoros had access to one of the historical sources utilized (and abbreviated) in the *Brev.* and, possibly, to the *Brev.* itself. That he went over this material in ca. 820 does not, however, preclude the possibility that the *Brev.* had been composed considerably earlier.

One further consideration to which I recently called attention[29] concerns Nikephoros' unexpectedly sympathetic attitude toward Patriarch Pyrrhos (638–641). It should be remembered that Pyrrhos was a heretic, who had been duly condemned by the Sixth Ecumenical Council. How he was viewed in Orthodox circles is made clear by Theoph., 330–31: Pyrrhos, together with Martina, poisoned Emperor Constantine III; he was expelled from his see by the Senate because of his impiety; he proceeded to Africa, where he was confuted by St. Maximos, then dishonestly assured Pope Theodore of his orthodoxy, but when he had reached Ravenna, returned, like a dog to his vomit, etc. Indeed, the collapse of the Roman Empire and the successes of the Arabs were the direct consequence of the Monothelete heresy, of which Pyrrhos was a prominent champion. When we turn to the *Brev.* we are told a very different story: Pyrrhos is represented as a loyal friend of Herakleios (c. 26); he does not poison Constantine III, toward whom, on the contrary, he behaves very correctly; he is forced out of office by the worst elements of the city rabble, including Jews and other *κακόδοξοι*; after embracing the sacred objects of his cathedral, he lays his pallium on the altar table and departs peacefully; is given shelter by a pious woman, then sails away to Carthage, where he holds a discussion with Maximos and other monks concerning the two wills of Christ (c. 31).

Doubtless, Nikephoros drew the above details from the source he was following, a source that was favorable to Pyrrhos. The question is why he reproduced it without any change or comment. I cannot believe that he had himself any Monothelete sympathies—indeed, the whole issue had long been dead. The only possible explanation is that Nikephoros did not realize that Pyrrhos was a heretic. Such a

---

[29] "The *Breviarium*" (as in note 10 above), 544–45.

lapse may be understandable if, at the time of writing, he was a young layman, not too well versed in ecclesiastical history; it would be much more difficult to account for in an aging prelate who had written several tomes about Orthodox doctrine.

In the light of the last argument I would tentatively conclude that the *Brev.* is an *oeuvre de jeunesse*, datable, perhaps, to the 780s.

It remains to note a final point that has some bearing on chronology. The *Brev.* and Theophanes, while they draw on the same source(s) for the period 668–769, are entirely independent of one another. This is rather odd: the two authors were not only exact contemporaries, they also belonged to the same ecclesiastical party. George Synkellos, to whom Theophanes owed the bulk of his documentation, held high office under Patriarch Tarasios and must have been personally known to Nikephoros. It may well be asked, if the *Brev.* was written in the 780s, why Theophanes was unaware of it. By the same token, if the *Brev.* was written in ca. 820, why did Nikephoros not consult the Chronicle of Theophanes (completed by 815), from which he could have drawn a wealth of pertinent information? The answer, I suspect, is that both works were kept out of circulation for a fairly long time, perhaps until after the defeat of Iconoclasm in 843, and that communication between men of letters was not as close as we may suppose.

SOURCES OF THE *BREVIARIUM*

The *Breviarium* falls into two parts, the first from 602 to 641, the second from 668 to 769. It is virtually certain that each of them is based on a different source or sets of sources.

Part I

In the light of the detailed comparison made in our Commentary between Nikephoros and other extant Greek historical texts, the following conclusions may be drawn:

a) The only source that can be identified with reasonable certitude is John of Antioch for c. 1.

b) There is no significant convergence with the Paschal Chronicle.

c) Points of contact with Theophanes are very slight (see cc. 1, 10, 32).

d) The theory, advanced by Orosz,[30] that Nikephoros made use of certain lost

[30] *The London MS*, 11–12.

poems by George of Pisidia and has preserved *disiecta membra* of iambic verse has little to recommend it.[31] Phrases such as *καὶ ἱππικοῦ ἀγῶνος ἐπιτελουμένου* or *ἐν μέσοις τοῖς δημόταις* or Νικήτα *τοῦ πατρικίου* may scan, but show no trace of poetic diction or imagery such as we find in George's fragments that are imbedded in Theophanes.

The probable dependence of Nikephoros on a single paragraph ascribed to John of Antioch raises problems that appear at present incapable of solution. It is generally accepted that the genuine fragments of John of Antioch are those contained in the *Excerpta* of Constantine Porphyrogenitus,[32] namely, one series of extracts imbedded in the *Exc. de virtutibus et vitiis*,[33] another, and more important, in the *Exc. de insidiis*,[34] plus one truncated fragment in the *Exc. de legationibus*.[35] Down to the end of the reign of Anastasios (518) these extracts are in classical Greek. In the *Exc. de virtutibus* there are no entries later than Anastasios except for the final one (c. 75), which may be rendered: "Phokas had a girlfriend, Kallinike, a former prostitute. The same Phokas was bloodthirsty (*αἱμοπότης*)." As far as one can judge from so small a sample, the language is here colloquial. After c. 75 is written the note:

τέλος τῆς ἱστορίας Ἰωάννου *μοναχοῦ*
περὶ ἀρετῆς καὶ κακίας

In the *Exc. de insidiis* we find a similar situation. The longer extracts in classical Greek end with the reign of Anastasios (c. 103). The reign of Justinian is represented by a single laconic entry (c. 104) and that of Justin II by another (c. 105). There follow three fairly circumstantial entries about Maurice (cc. 106–8) and two about Phokas (cc. 109–10), all of them in colloquial Greek. It is the last (c. 110) that concerns us here.

From the above facts it appears reasonably certain that the MS which Constantine's excerptors had before them consisted of two disparate parts: a main section in classical Greek down to A.D. 518 and a continuation in "vulgar" Greek. Whether John of Antioch was the author of the first or the second or merely the compiler who put the two together is not altogether clear; nor is it easy to explain the near absence of material for the period extending from Anastasios to Maurice, which would certainly have yielded many suitable instances of virtue and vice as

---

[31] See A. Pertusi, *Giorgio di Pisidia, Poemi*, I (Ettal, 1959), 22.

[32] For bibliography see Moravcsik, *Byzantinoturcica*, I, 315; Hunger, *Hochsprachliche Lit.*, I, 326–28. Add A. Markopoulos, Ἡ *Χρονογραφία τοῦ Ψευδοσυμεὼν καὶ οἱ πηγές της*, Diss. (Ioannina, 1978), 66ff. We are not here concerned with the so-called *Excerpta Salmasiana*, which extend to A.D. 455. The latter are edited by Cramer, *Anecdota graeca Paris.*, II, 383–401.

[33] Ed. Th. Büttner-Wobst, I (Berlin, 1906), 164–206.

[34] Ed. C. de Boor (Berlin, 1905), 58–150.

[35] Ed. C. de Boor (Berlin, 1903), 6.

well as many conspiracies. The final note in the *Exc. de virtutibus* has been taken to indicate that John of Antioch ended in 610, but even that is not certain, for it may equally well mean that the reign of Phokas constituted the limit of the extracts drawn from John on the specific topic of virtues and vices.

Confining ourselves to the continuation of John of Antioch down to 610, at least two possibilities may be envisaged: (a) it was the original composition of an author who was writing soon after 610; (b) it was excerpted from another work, namely, a chronicle in "vulgar" Greek, which need not have ended in 610. If we accept the first alternative, we shall have to suppose that Nikephoros had at least two sources for the period 602–641: John of Antioch for his c. 1 and another for 610–641. If we accept the second, he could have had only one source. Whichever turns out to be the correct answer, the source(s) in question broke off in October 641. This is suggested by the fact that the events after the death of Herakleios are related in considerable detail, leaving a number of loose threads. The reference to the disputation between Pyrrhos and Maximos (July 645) could be explained, say, on the assumption that it was mentioned in a later note appended to the MS of the source.

Everything goes to show that the source of Part I was a Constantinopolitan chronicle. This is indicated by the disconnected character of the entries, some of them being rather trivial in content, by the prominence given to events in the capital, and the lack of exact information about distant developments, such as military campaigns. If this is granted and if the chronicle source was written soon after 641 (by a Monothelete sympathizer, as we have seen), it would follow that its entries were probably in correct sequence. The historical implications of this remark cannot be discussed here in detail in view of the extreme complexity of the chronology of the reign of Herakleios, but it is proper to draw attention to them. It will suffice to consider briefly cc. 8–11.

8. Famine and plague at Constantinople: these appear to refer to 618 or 619.

9. Baptism of Huns: no recorded date.

10. Avar surprise: if the sequence is correct, the date advanced by N. H. Baynes, viz. June 617, would have to be abandoned.

11. Herakleios marries Martina. The accepted date is 613/4. Could this have happened as late as 623, that is, after the Avar surprise as dated by *Chr. Pasch.*?

The Gap of 27 Years

Part I breaks off *in medias res*. Heraklonas and Martina are still in power, Valentinos is still encamped at Chalcedon. Paul is ordained patriarch of Constantinople in October 641. Then, without any transition, the text goes on with *Κωνσταντῖνος οὖν* . . . , "Constantine, therefore (*or* indeed), was treacherously murdered by his own servants," i.e., in 668. The presence of the adverb οὖν led Lilie[36] and Speck[37] to suppose that one folio had dropped out at that point. Personally, I would not have placed so much emphasis on the οὖν, which need not imply a logical connection with the preceding narrative and which Nikephoros himself sometimes uses in contexts where another author would have preferred δέ (e.g., 13.35, 30.3). The question remains, however, why Nikephoros, even if he knew nothing about the reign of Constantine (i.e., Constans II), did not at the very least inform us that Heraklonas and Martina were deposed and that Constantine was given supreme power, as does Theophanes, A.M. 6133.

The hypothesis of a lost folio removes one difficulty while at the same time creating another. In two pages Nikephoros could well have rounded off the story of Martina and Heraklonas, placed Constans on the throne, and even told us a little about the reign of the latter. Yet the gap is common to both V and L and so must go back to their common archetype, which we call ω (see below, pp. 25ff.). *Ex hypothesi* ω must have corresponded to the unrevised version of the *Breviarium*. When Nikephoros set about revising his text the folio was already missing (otherwise something of its content would have been included in V), so we have to suppose that he showed no awareness of the gap! That would be as big a paradox as the one we are trying to account for.

Unfortunately, neither Theophanes nor George the Monk is of any help in this matter. Practically everything Theophanes records in the reign of Constans is drawn from his Oriental (Syriac) source and George is dependent on Theophanes. We can hardly avoid the conclusion that there was almost no "Byzantine" historical material for that period.

Part II

From 668 to the end, the *Breviarium* and Theoph. run in parallel channels and are quite clearly derived from the same sources. To be more precise, there is very little in Nikephoros that is not also in Theoph., whereas the latter includes a considerable body of other material, some of it of Near Eastern origin. The sources our two authors had in common may have been no more than two. The earlier one, it may be argued, was written in the first quarter of the eighth century. Indications of near contemporaneity with the events described can be detected in cc. 35 (settlement of the Bulgars), 42 (return of Justinian II), 45 (downfall of Justinian II), 48 (fall of Philippikos), 54 (siege of Constantinople), and 56 (birth of Constantine V). Possibly

---

[36] *BSl* 45 (1984), 31 note 22.

[37] *Dossier*, 205.

this source extended to c. 58 (coronation of Constantine V), that is, to A.D. 720, after which date there occurs in both Theoph. and Nikephoros a hiatus as regards Constantinopolitan information. The source was certainly a chronicle composed in the capital, and it appears to have been favorable to Leo III. Theoph. preserves it more fully than does Nikephoros both as regards factual content and language, and where our two texts differ among themselves preference can usually be given to Theoph. The one notable exception is c. 57 (plot of Artemios to regain the throne), for which a tentative explanation is offered in the Commentary. As a working hypothesis we may, therefore, be allowed to postulate a "Chronicon ad a. 720 pertinens."

A second source, likewise a Constantinopolitan chronicle, appears to have been composed toward the end of the reign of Constantine V, and may have ended where Nikephoros ends, viz. in 769. The last event recorded by him (the coronation of Eirene) is related in considerable detail by Theoph. (A.M. 6261), after which there occurs in Theoph. no Constantinopolitan material for a space of four years, that is, down to the Bulgarian expedition of 773 (A.M. 6265). This second chronicle source appears to have been iconophile (above, note 25). Once again, Theoph. reproduces it more faithfully than does Nikephoros, although in some cases Nikephoros records certain events that are not in Theoph., and these have been noted in the Commentary.

The foregoing hypothesis is, I believe, the most economical. It is, of course, possible to postulate a greater number of sources and to argue, for example, that where Nikephoros tells us something that is lacking in Theoph. he must have had access to another document and not, as I have assumed, that Theoph. simply left out certain entries or facts. In view of the dearth of historical writing in the eighth century a multiplicity of lost sources is, to my mind, unlikely in itself and should not be advanced without sufficient reason.

Traianos Patrikios

Among the sources that have been mentioned in learned literature as underlying the *Brev.* figures the enigmatic patrician Trajan. As we shall have occasion to note, E. Honigmann has even suggested (wrongly) that the text of L was the work of that author.

All we know about Trajan can be said in a few words. According to the *Suda*,[38] he lived at the time of Justinian II, wrote a *χρονικὸν σύντομον, πάνυ θαυμάσιον*, and was "very Christian and most orthodox." Theoph., too, with reference to the Gothic wars of Theodosios I, says, "Trajan the patrician in his History

[38] S.v. Τραϊανός, ed. Adler, IV, 582.

says that the Scythians are called Goths in their native language" (66.2). A Trajan, elsewhere mentioned by Theoph. (62.10), was, indeed, a prominent general, who was killed at the battle of Adrianople (378) and was known as a zealous Catholic.[39] De Boor is certainly right in suggesting that the designation "very Christian and most orthodox" would apply better to an author of the fourth century than to one of ca. A.D. 700.[40] Did the compiler of the *Suda* confuse the general Trajan with another Trajan, who flourished under Justinian II and also wrote a historical work (so de Boor), or was there only one Trajan, viz. the earlier one?

However that may be, a *χρονικὸν σύντομον* could have been either a bare list of names and years (like the *χρονογραφικὸν σύντομον* attributed to Nikephoros) or a narrative chronicle. If the former, it does not concern us in this context. If it was a proper chronicle, the chances are that it would have covered a fairly long span of time prior to the reign of Justinian II. Yet we have seen that neither Nikephoros nor Theoph. had knowledge of any Byzantine material for the period 641–668. From this we would have to draw the further conclusion that Trajan's hypothetical chronicle started no earlier than 668 and ended less than half a century later. Such a possibility cannot be excluded; indeed, the name of Trajan may be attached to our postulated Chronicle of 720, but little is to be gained by so doing.

The Megas Chronographos

Another source that has been postulated for the *Brev.* is the "Great Chronographer," represented by fifteen extracts, added by an eleventh-century hand to the unique MS of *Chr. Pasch., cod. Vat. gr. 1941*.[41] These extracts concern various disasters, both natural and political, ranging in date from the reign of Zeno to that of Constantine V. Of the fifteen, three (Nos. 2, 3, and 10) have no known source; one (No. 13) is paralleled by *Brev.*, c. 71; the rest are shared by Theoph. and other chronicles. We must, therefore, consider No. 13, which reads as follows: *Ἐπὶ τῆς γενέσεως Λέοντος τοῦ υἱοῦ Κωνσταντίνου τοῦ Κοπρωνύμου τοῦ οὐρανίου χώρου ἐδόκουν οἱ ἀστέρες πάντες μετακινεῖσθαι καὶ καταφέρεσθαι δι' ὅλης τῆς νυκτός· οἱ δὲ περίγειοι γινόμενοι ἀθρόον διελύοντο. φασὶ δὲ πολλοὶ ὅτι διὰ πάσης τῆς οἰκουμένης τὸ τοιοῦτον ἐξαίσιον διεδείκνυτο θέαμα.*

As I have pointed out elsewhere,[42] it seems evident to me that this extract is not the source of *Brev.*, c. 71, but is derived from the latter. The same conclusion may be drawn by comparing a number of parallel passages in Theoph. and the

---

[39] *PLRE*, I, Traianus 2.

[40] *Hermes* 17 (1882), 489–92.

[41] Ed. P. Schreiner, *Die byzantinischen Kleinchroniken*, I (Vienna, 1975), 37ff. (who breaks it down into 18 fragments); L. M. Whitby, *BMGS* 8 (1982–83), 17–20.

[42] "The *Breviarium*" (as in note 10), 547–48.

Megas Chronographos: it is Theoph. who preserves the more original text. From this it follows that the *Megas Chronographos* was a compilation no earlier than the mid-ninth century and should be ruled out of consideration as one of the sources of Nikephoros.

DIFFUSION AND INFLUENCE OF THE *BREVIARIUM*

Unlike the Chronicle of Theoph., which exerted an enormous influence on later historiography in both East and West, the impact of the *Breviarium* was more limited and exercised not so much directly as through the Chronicle of George the Monk (after 871)[43] who, in addition to utilizing Theoph. and other sources, made numerous borrowings from the *Brev.* (identified in de Boor's edition of George, 665 ff.). It may be noted that George (780.13 ff.) also quotes a lost work by Nikephoros dealing with the origin, impiety, and grievous death of Emperor Leo V (813–820). Judging by the violent tone of the passage (which appears to extend to 792.5), its rhetorical amplification, and the introduction of theological arguments, this must have been a polemical pamphlet: it was certainly not a work of history.[44]

Toward the middle of the ninth century the *Brev.* was read by Photios, who expresses a highly favorable judgment regarding its style: its only shortcoming, he says, lies in its extreme concision (*Bibl.*, cod. 66). It seems, indeed, that the *Brev.* was appreciated more for its literary qualities than as a work of reference. An alphabetical glossary of about 150 notable words found in it was copied into *cod. Barocc. 50* (10th century),[45] considered by some scholars to be of south Italian origin.[46] The author of this word list was not a good hellenist: he explains *ἀμφιλαφῆ* by *ἀμφοτέρωθε δάση*, *ἐσκευαγώγουν* by *ἐδωροφόρουν*, *εὐζώνους* by *ἀνδρείους*, etc., and even finds it necessary to gloss *ἄστυ* (*πόλιν*), *ἀστῶν* (*πολιτῶν*), and *ὕπερθεν* (*ἐπάνωθεν*).

---

[43] So A. Markopoulos, *Σύμμεικτα* 6 (1985), 223–31. It is not clear to me, however, why George, if he was writing after 871, should have laid so much stress in his Preface (de Boor, 3.27) on the revolt of Thomas the Slav, an event that had happened fifty years earlier.

[44] Alexander, *Nicephorus*, 179–80 suggests that this work may have been a homily, but it is unlikely that Nikephoros had occasion to do any preaching after his deposition.

[45] Fols. 293^{r-v}, 295^{r}, 298^{v}, 299^{r}, 303^{v}, 305^{v}, 307^{r}, 311^{r}, 312^{r-v}, 313^{v}, 314^{v}, 315^{r}, 316^{r-v}, 317^{r-v}, 318^{r-v}, interspersed with words from the Psalter and *τῆς γραμματικῆς*. Negligently edited by Cramer, *Anecdota graeca Oxon.*, II (Oxford, 1835), 427 ff. See de Boor's corrections and comments in his edition of Nikephoros, pp. XVII ff.

[46] In particular J. Irigoin, *JÖB* 18 (1969), 37–55 and note 49. Disputed by N. G. Wilson, *Scholars of Byzantium* (London, 1983), 211; idem, *GRBS* 23 (1982), 369–71.

As we have said, the *Brev.* provided some material for the *Megas Chronographos*. Seven extracts from it were included in the *Suda* (s.v. Ἀρτέμιος, βρύχιος, ἐνώτια, Ἡράκλειος, Ἰουστινιανὸς ὁ Ῥινότμητος, πυρεῖον, Φιλιππικός), of which four are of a historical and three of a lexical character. There is no direct evidence that it was pilfered for the *Excerpta* of Constantine Porphyrogenitus.

In the twelfth century the *Breviarium* in its L recension was used by Zonaras. This can be demonstrated, for example, with regard to the funeral of Empress Eudokia (c. 3), where Zonaras (Bonn ed., III, 205) reproduces L's distinctive κόρη τις . . . βάρβαρος, and by his reference to Herakleios' son Fabius (so in L; Flavius in V), whom he mistakenly identifies with Heraklonas. Cf. our Commentary *ad* 11.8. In the thirteenth century an extract concerning the Holy Cross, corresponding to 18.9–21, was copied into *cod. Sabait. 366* (a miscellany).[47]

MANUSCRIPTS

Vat. gr. 977[48]

Tenth century; parchment; 209 folios (excluding *feuilles de garde*); 225 × 295 mm. Consists of two separate MSS of roughly the same date bound together. First part (fols. 1–184): rulings similar to Lake I 2e or Leroy 20 A 1, with prickings. Inscribed surface 125 × 220 mm; 30 lines per page. Medium brown ink. Second part (fols. 185–209): rulings similar to Lake I 16a or Leroy 11 C 1bn; no prickings. Inscribed surface 155 × 235 mm; 35 lines per page. Medium to dark brown ink. Binding with arms of Pope Paul V (1605–21).

Contents:

Feuilles de garde: I–II paper, with two separate tables of contents in Latin. III–IV and I′–II′ (at the back), parchment taken from a Sienese account book.

1) History of Theophylaktos Simokatta (fols. 1–2ᵛ, Dialogue between Philosophy and History; 2ᵛ–10ᵛ, Title and table of contents; 11 ff. text). On fol. 184ᵛ a scholion in the same hand derived from a lost work by a St. Isaac explaining why the eldest son of Emperor Maurice was called Theodosios. Ed. P. Maas, *BZ* 21 (1912), 29n.1.

2) Fol. 185 to the end: *Breviarium* of Nikephoros. The original scribe left

---

[47] A. Papadopoulos-Kerameus, Ἱεροσολυμιτικὴ Βιβλιοθήκη, II (St. Petersburg, 1894), 482–83.

[48] For bibliography see P. Canart and V. Peri, Studi e Testi 261 (1970), 519. Add T. Olajos, *Revue d'histoire des textes* 9 (1979), 261–66 and esp. P. Schreiner, *JÖB* 37 (1987), 1–29.

many gaps which have been filled by a later hand (V^2). The latter also added corrections either above the line or over erasures in the text, very rarely in the margin.

A note on fol. 93ᵛ (reproduced in de Boor's edition of Theophylaktos, p. VI) records that in 1417/8 the MS was given by Arsenios bishop of Samos to John *chorepiskopos* of Kos.

In a recent study devoted to the *Vaticanus*,[49] P. Schreiner has established or suggested the following points:

a) The Theophylaktos part of the MS can be dated to the early tenth century.

b) The Nikephoros part is roughly of the same period.

c) The marginalia in the Theophylaktos part (hands C and D) were in all probability added with a view to identifying suitable passages for the *Excerpta* of Constantine VII.

d) The presence of a few marginalia by hand D in the Nikephoros part indicates that both parts were united when the excerptors set to work, that is, by the middle of the tenth century.

The Corrector (V^2)

The total number of corrections and supplements made by a person other than the main scribe is, if I am not mistaken, 117 and, although in some cases it is not certain that they are by the same hand, most of them may be attributed to V^2. The best specimen of his writing (an inclined minuscule) may be seen in the outer margin of fol. 204ᵛ, where he has added several words that had been omitted in the text.

As noted above, the main scribe left a considerable number of small lacunae. De Boor, in his lengthy discussion of the MS (Praefatio, pp. v ff.), is probably right in arguing that these were due not to a damaged archetype but to the scribe's inability to read abbreviations. This conclusion is indicated by the following considerations:

1) A high percentage of lacunae filled by V^2 occur in the endings of words.

2) More than half (38 out of 55) of the evident corrections made by V^2 also concern endings.

3) Twice the word *λίτραι*, which is normally abbreviated, has been left out (20.18, 30.5), although it is written out in full at 76.24.

4) The main scribe himself avoids abbreviations except in the most usual *nomina sacra*.

If that is granted, two further conclusions appear to follow: (1) the model of V was also in minuscule; and (2) V^2 must be nearly contemporary with V, since it is not likely that the lacunae would have been left unfilled for any length of time.

De Boor's further contention that all of V^2's corrections were made by him *ex*

---

[49] As in note 48.

ingenio suo and should, therefore, be treated as conjectures is invalidated by L. In some cases, it is true, V² seems to have been guided by his own judgment, for example, in needlessly changing *ὄνομα* to *ὀνόματι* nine times or altering the correct *ἦγεν* to *ἤγαγεν* at 19.3. In many more cases, however, there can be no doubt that he had before him a MS of the L tradition as proved by the following examples:

1.11 *τοὺς υἱεῖς* V: V² adds the redundant *ἑαυτῶν*, which is supported by L.

13.12 V and Georg. Mon. have the correct *τὰ τῆς 'Ασιάτιδος μοίρας*: *τάς* V²L.

15.14 *ἡσυχάζειν* V: *ἐφ' ἡσυχάζειν* L: *ἐφ'* written above the line V².

20.2 V has the perfectly unexceptionable *εὐθύς*: *εὐθέως* V²L.

20.17 *ἐμπορεύεσθαι* V²L, the former altered from *ἐκπορεύεσθαι*—by no means an obvious correction.

26.15 *ἐπητιᾶτο* correctly in V: *ἐπαιτιᾶτο* V²L.

28.6 *διελογίζετο* V: *διελέγετο* V²L.

35.18 *τῇ νῦν ὑπὸ 'Αβάροις κειμένῃ* edd.: *τῆς . . . κειμένης* L: *τῆς . . . κειμένης* from *τῆς . . . κοιμένοις* V².

36.19 *περαιωθέντες δὲ τὸν "Ιστρον* edd.: *περαιωθέντ[ων] δὲ το[ῦ] "Ιστρ[ου]*, the endings being written in by V²: *περαιωθέντων τὸν "Ιστρον* L.

V²'s marginal addition at 66.27–29, *πλείσταις δὲ πληγαῖς . . . κατεδικάσθησαν*, is also deserving of note. De Boor's contention (Praefatio, p. XI) that the supplement was invented by V² is surely unconvincing, the more so as Theoph., 420.22 has the nearly equivalent *πολλοὺς δὲ καὶ ἄλλους συμμαχήσαντας 'Αρτανάσδῳ τῶν προυχόντων ἀνεῖλεν, ἀναριθμήτους δὲ ἐτύφλωσεν, καὶ ἄλλους ἐχειροκόπησε καὶ ἐποδοκόπησεν*. But where did V² obtain it from? If he collated V against *one* other MS only, we would have to conclude that L did not terminate in A.D. 713. The other possibility is that he collated V against *two* other MSS, namely, the model of V and the model of L.

Marginalia

Setting aside textual corrections, the marginalia are in two hands. The first, by the main scribe, are in a mixture of uncial and minuscule and consist largely of headings. Their distribution is very uneven, as shown by the following table:

Against	1.1	Περὶ τῆς τοῦ Φωκᾶ ἀναδείξεως
	1.20	Περὶ Κρίσπου
	1.35	Περὶ Φωτίου
	1.43	'Αναίρεσις Φωκᾶ
	1.48	Περὶ Δομεντιόλου
	2.7	'Αναγόρευσις 'Ηρακλείου

2.58	Περὶ Φιλιππικοῦ
8.3	Σημ(είωσαι) ὅτι ἕως Ἡρακλείου ἡ Αἴγυπτος τῇ μεγαλοπόλει ἐπεσίτιζεν
9.1	Σημ(είωσαι) τὰ περὶ Οὔννων
10.1	Σημ(είωσαι) τὰ περὶ Ἀβάρων
37.5	The numeral $\bar{\text{S}}$ referring to the 6th General Council
46.2	Περὶ τῆς $\bar{\text{S}}$ συνόδου
46.6	Ση(μείωσαι) περὶ τοῦ θείου Γερμανοῦ
48.14	Ση(μείωσαι) τύφλωσις Φιλιππικοῦ
48.18	Ἀρτέμιος ὁ καὶ Ἀναστάσιος
50.23	Ση(μείωσαι) with reference to the elevation of Theodosios
51.3	Θεοδοσίου
51.16	Περὶ Γερμανοῦ
52.13	Παραίτησις Θεοδοσίου βασιλέως
52.19	Λέων ὁ Ἴσαυρος
53.1	Σαρακηνοὶ τὴν Πέργαμον
56.1	Περὶ Κωνσταντίνου καὶ Αὐγούστου $\overline{\text{ιε}}$ with reference to the birth of Constantine V and the departure of the Arab armament from Constantinople on 15 August 718
57.1	Περὶ Ἀρτεμίου
58.1	Περὶ Γερμάνου (sic) καὶ Κωνσταντίνου βασιλέως
59.1	Περὶ Θήρας καὶ Θηρασίας
60.4	Περὶ καθαιρέσεως τῶν σεπτῶν εἰκόνων
62.3	Περὶ Γερμανοῦ
63.2	Περὶ Χαζάρου
64.1	Λέοντος ὑδέριος θάνατος
64.4	Περὶ Ἀρταβάζου
80.4	Σημ(είωσαι) οἷα κατὰ τῶν μοναχῶν ἔδρα ὁ ἄθεος Κωνσταντῖνος
83.22	Σημ(είωσαι) τὰ κατὰ Κωνσταντίνου τοῦ ἀρχιερέως
83.26–28	Ση(μείωσαι)

In addition, there are a number of marginalia in a different hand (Schreiner's hand D), written in minuscule and confined to the reign of Herakleios:

14.5	μονομαχία Ἡρακλείου βα(σιλέως)
15.9	Χοσρόου διὰ λιμοῦ θάνατος καὶ ἀνάρρησις βα(σιλέως) Σειρόου υἱοῦ αὐτοῦ
16.1	Σειρόου τελευτὴ καὶ Καβόου ἀναγόρευσις· θάνατος τε τούτου καὶ Ὁρμίσδα ἀναγόρευσις
17.9	ἀναίρεσις υἱοῦ Ὁρμίσδα βασιλέως Περσῶν καὶ προβολὴ παρὰ Ἡρακλείου Σαρβάρου ἐπὶ τὸ βασιλεύειν Περσῶν

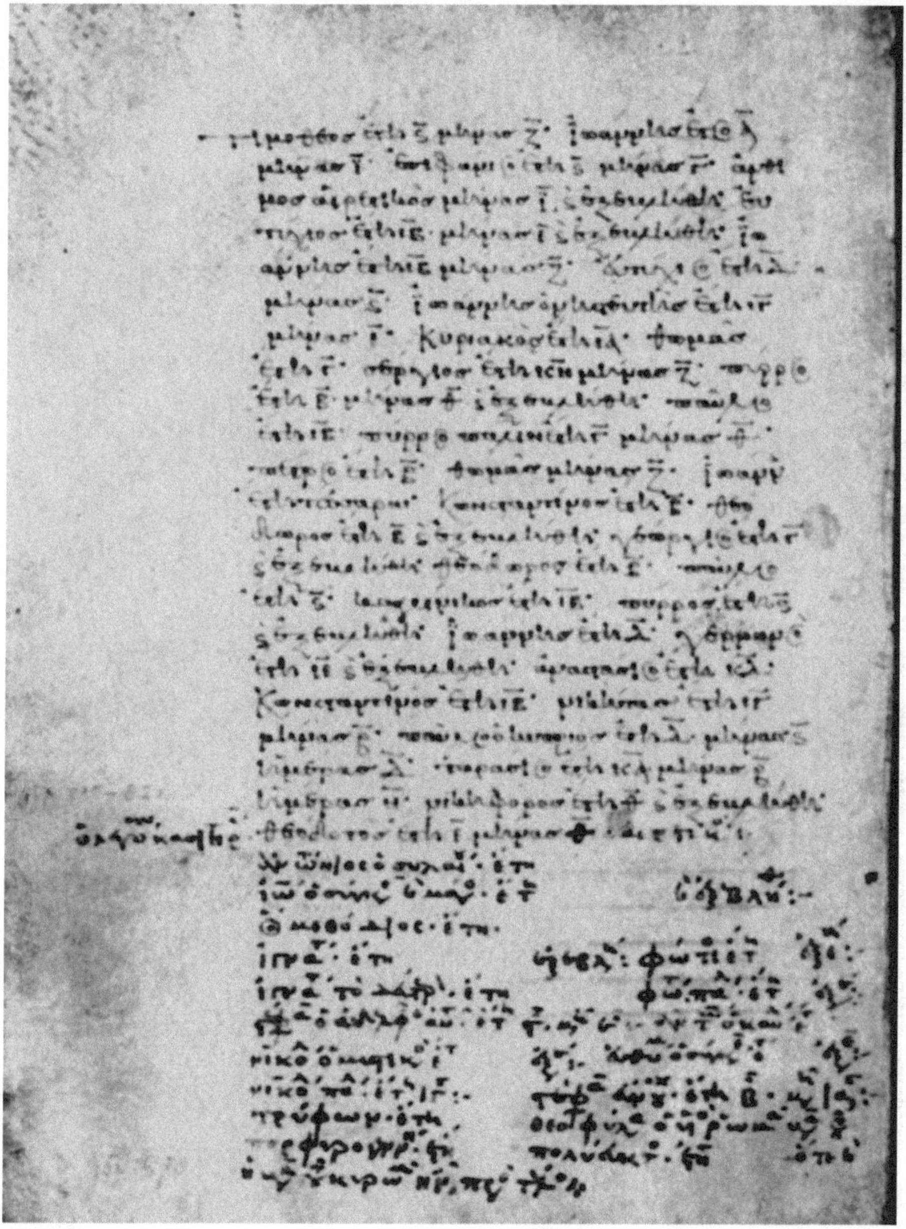

British Library, Add. MS 19390, fol. 23 (verso). Last page of *Chronographikon syntomon* (photo: British Library)

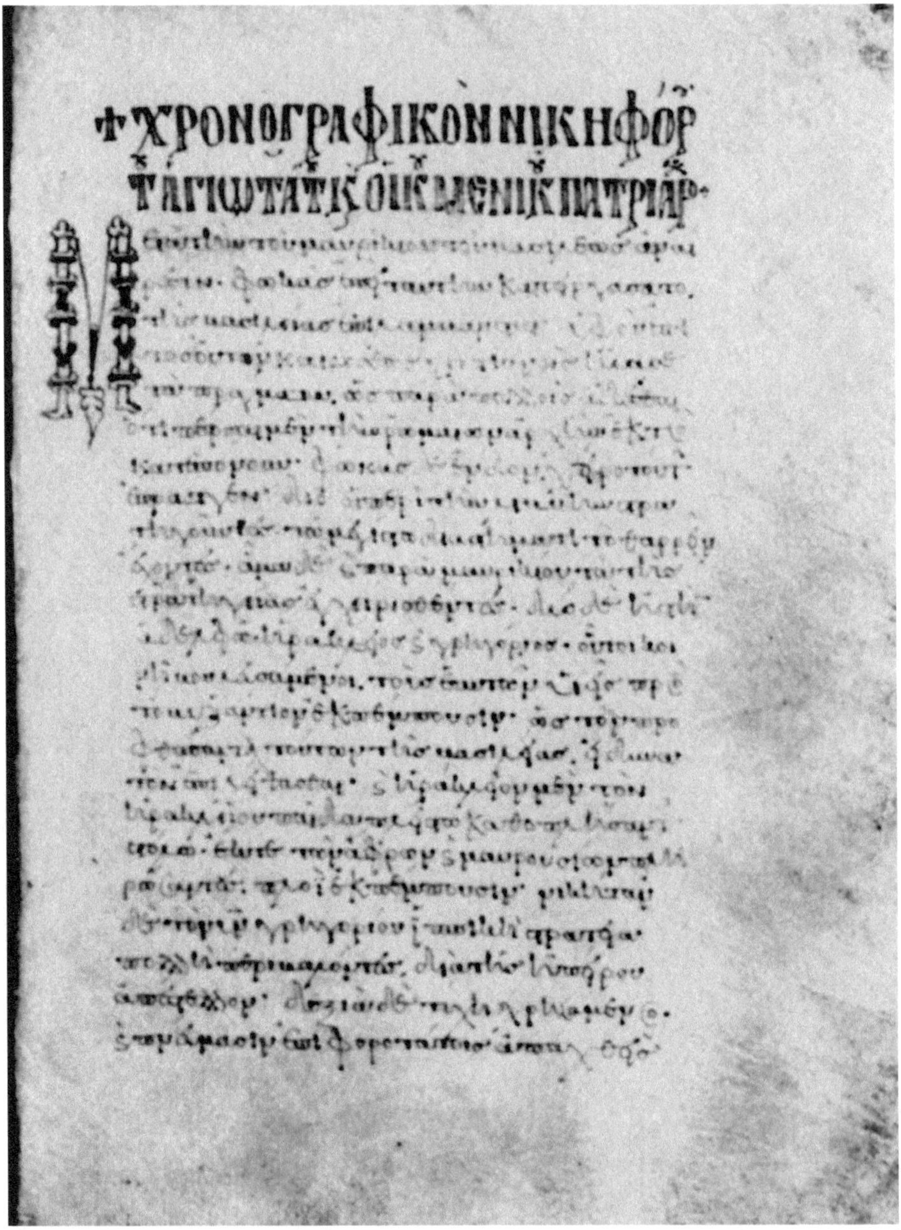

British Library, Add. MS 19390, fol. 24 (recto). First page of *Breviarium* (photo: British Library)

18.7 ὅτι διάγοντ(ι) Ἡρακλείῳ ἐν Περσίδι παῖδες ἐγεννήθ(ησαν) αὐτῷ ἐξ ὧν ἐτελεύτησαν ἐκεῖσε ἄρ⟨ρεν⟩ες μὲν β′ καὶ θήλειαι δὲ δύο. This adds an item of information to what is in the text. See below, Commentary, *ad* 18.4.

British Library, *Add. 19390*[50]

Commonly described as being of the late ninth century but more probably of the first half of the tenth; parchment; 55 folios; 145 × 205 mm. Rulings similar to Lake I 2c or Leroy 20 C 1. Writing mostly above ruled lines. Inscribed surface 76 × 145 mm, 27 lines per page. One scribe. Light brown ink. Minuscule with occasional uncial letters, especially N, but also Γ, H, and K. Illuminated initials in bright blue, red, and yellow on fols. 1, 17, 23, and 24. Smaller initial letters colored blue and/or yellow. Spelling rather erratic. Corrections by main scribe and by another hand (L^2) in a darker brown ink. Last two folios stained and full of worm holes. 19th-century binding.

Not a complete MS, but less than one fifth of the original codex, which, according to a note on fol. 55ᵛ (+εἰσὶ τ(ῆς) βίβλου ταύτ(ης) φύλλ(α) σπε′) contained 285 folios. The quires are numbered λ′ (barely visible) on fol. 1, λα′ on fol. 9 (in a more recent hand), and, in an old hand, λγ′ on fol. 25, λδ′ on fol. 33, λε′ on fol. 41, λS′ on fol. 49. Twenty-nine quires corresponding to 230 folios are, therefore, missing at the beginning.

On fol. 54ᵛ a few Hebrew letters are written in the margin.

On the last page, in addition to various scribblings, is a large "monocondyle" mark of ownership, which may be read as +Βίβλος μονῆς τῆς Θ(εοτό)κου.

Contents:

1) Fol. 1: (Pseudo-) John Damascene, *De dormientibus in fide* (PG 95, 248 ff.). Marginal scholia in a later (11th/12th century) hand, among them the following one (fol. 9): Ἀπὸ τοῦ Τραϊανοῦ παρῆλθον πολλοὶ βασιλεῖς, καὶ πάλιν μανθάνομεν ὅτι ὁ εἰκονομάχος Θεόφιλος ἠξιώθη ἐλέους. ἀλλὰ καί τινα εἶχεν ὁ Τραϊανὸς προτερήματα ὡς καὶ ὁ εἰκονομάχος Θεόφιλος.

2) Fol 17: Χρονογραφικὸν ἀπὸ Ἀδὰμ μέχρι τοῦ παρόντος, being part of the Χρον. σύντομον ascribed to Nikephoros, ed. de Boor, 81–101.16. List of Roman emperors ending with Theophilos, whose length of reign, ἔτη ιβ′, is in the same light brown ink as the original scribe's but in a different hand. A thirteenth-century hand (black ink) has added μήνας γ′ ἡμέρας κ′ and continued the list of

---

[50] *Catalogue of Additions in the Years 1848–1853* (London, 1868), 228; *Palaeographical Society* (Original Series), I, 231.

emperors down to the capture of Constantinople by the Latins. A few scholia in brown ink by the same hand that has added *ὁ λεγόμενος Κασιτηρᾶς* on fol. 23ᵛ and marginal additions in black ink by the same hand that completed the list of emperors on fol. 22ᵛ.

Fol. 23: *Ἔτη πατριαρχῶν Κωνσταντινουπόλεως* = de Boor, 114.10–120.4, inc. *Μητροφάνης ἔτη ι'* down to *Θεόδοτος ἔτη ε' μῆνας θ'* (the *θ'* reinforced in brown ink) *αἱρετικός* (this word not by the main scribe). A later hand has added *ὁ λεγόμενος Κασιτηρᾶς* next to the name *Θεόδοτος* and continued the list of patriarchs, in most cases leaving the length of their tenure blank, down to Polyeuktos (956–970), *Πολύευκτος ἔτη* blank *ὅτε καὶ ἡ βασιλεία τοῦ κὺρ Ῥωμανοῦ ἦν πρὸς τέλος*. Since Romanos II died in 963, the addition to the patriarchal list would appear to have been close to that date.

While it cannot be argued that L itself is of the early ninth century, there is every reason to believe that the original from which the *Χρονογραφικόν* was copied dated from shortly after 821 and that the scribe of L made no attempt to bring it up to date.

3) Fol. 24 to end: *Breviarium* of Nikephoros.

L was purchased, as noted on the flyleaf, from C. Simonides on 12 March 1853. This refers to the notorious adventurer and forger Constantine Simonides (?1820–67), who sold eight other MSS to the British Museum (genuine, but mostly imperfect). The fact that L is merely a fragment raises the possibility of its remainder being still in existence. Simonides himself claimed that the MSS he supplied to the British Museum as well as to other institutions (the latter being mostly forgeries) came from Mount Athos,[51] which may well have been so, although he is said to have also visited the libraries of Jerusalem, Mount Sinai, and other centers.

---

[51] This is stated in a pamphlet by one Charles Stewart (probably composed by Simonides himself) entitled *A Biographical Memoir of Constantine Simonides, Dr.Ph. of Stageira* (London, 1859), 36ff. as proof of the genuineness of all his MSS. The Bodleian Library copy I have consulted (No. 25796.e.b) is particularly informative because it has been copiously annotated by Sir Frederic Madden, who was at the time Keeper of Manuscripts at the British Museum. Simonides remained about two years on Mount Athos (1839–40) under the aegis of his maternal uncle Benediktos, described as abbot of the Rossikon monastery, although, according to G. Smyrnakes, Τὸ *Ἅγιον Ὄρος* (Athens, 1903), 663–64, the last Greek abbot of that establishment was called Gerasimos and remained in office from 1832 to 1875. Benediktos (Stewart, op. cit., 4) is said to have acquired many MSS, "the greater portion of which he took from the monastery of Esphygmenos (sic)." From Athos Simonides proceeded to Constantinople, Odessa, Athens, Thessaly, the Black Sea coast of Asia Minor(?), Athos again, Constantinople, Athos for the third time (1851 for a whole year), the Aegean islands, Egypt, and England. His chances of purloining MSS were thus very numerous. On his career see A. Lykurgos, *Enthüllungen über den Simonides-Dindorfschen Uranios* (Leipzig, 1856), who also states (pp. 56, 59) that Simonides' MSS came from Mount Athos; the unsigned article (by D. Chaviaras) in S. I. Voutyras, *Λεξικὸν ἱστορίας καὶ γεωγραφίας*, VII (Constantinople, 1889), 580–83; A. R. Rangabes in Πανδώρα 1 (1850–51), 551–55, 595–602; A. Papadopoulos-Kerameus, *BZ* 14 (1905), 268–69; and Ch. A. Kalliga, Τὸ *πατρικὸ σπίτι τοῦ* Κ. *Σιμωνίδη* in Ἐπώνυμα *ἀρχοντικὰ τῶν χρόνων τῆς* Τουρκοκρατίας, Ἐθνικὸ

In view of the impenetrable veil of mendacity that surrounds Simonides' career, the Athonite origin of L cannot be taken for granted. A search for its missing portion cannot, furthermore, be undertaken on the basis of the existing catalogues of the monasteries of Mount Athos, which are insufficiently detailed.

TRANSMISSION OF THE TEXT

Two attempts have hitherto been made to construct a stemma of the textual tradition of the *Breviarium*, the first by Orosz, the second by Speck. Orosz accepted the hypothesis that L was the descendant of the author's first draft and V that of a completed and stylistically improved second draft. He went on to argue, among others, the following points:

1) The frequent agreement of V^2 with L proves, contrary to de Boor's view, that V^2 was guided by MS tradition, namely, by a MS that shared characteristics of both the L and the V branches.

2) In several cases L and V agree in error. It being unlikely that both branches were independently corrupt in the same places, the corruptions must have arisen in one branch (probably that of L) and then affected the other.

3) Where the *Breviarium* and Theoph. share a common source, Theoph. is more often than not closer to L, but occasionally closer to V.

4) Likewise, the borrowings from Nikephoros in George the Monk are sometimes closer to L and at other times closer to V.

These propositions led Orosz to a contaminated stemma. To avoid confusion we shall change his symbols as follows:

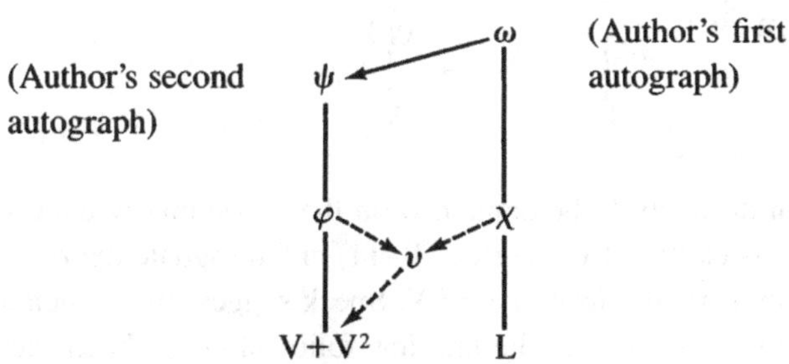

Μετσόβιο Πολυτεχνεῖο, Σπουδαστήριο Ἱστορίας τῆς Ἀρχιτεκτονικῆς (Athens, 1986), 247–54. Note that the 3 folios of the Shepherd of Hermas, sold by Simonides to the University Library of Leipzig, were taken from cod. 96 of the Gregoriou monastery, as shown by S. P. Lambros, *A Collation of the Athos Codex of the Shepherd of Hermas* (Cambridge, 1888), 5–6.

That is a possible reconstruction if one is willing to ascribe to contamination the presence of some twenty-five common errors in both branches of the tradition. Incidentally, I am not convinced (but that is a minor point) of the alleged agreement of Theoph. with V against L, it being limited to the spelling of a few proper names, two cases of omission (which could have occurred in the process of copying L from χ), and a few other, equally indecisive examples.

Speck's reconstruction[52] stems from his analysis of c. 28. He believes that the sentence order has been disturbed, that is, that *ἐξαίρετον . . . προχειρισθέντι* was meant to follow *καὶ κατήρχοντο ἀνευφημοῦντες τοὺς βασιλεῖς*. He explains the disturbance by the supposition that Nikephoros in his autograph made two marginal additions, one being *ἐξαίρετον . . . προχειρισθέντι* and the other *οὐδὲ γὰρ βαρβάρων . . . ἐλθεῖν πολιτείαν*, with appropriate reference signs, and that the intended order was confused by a copyist. The "disturbed" sequence occurs, however, in both L and V. That means, according to Speck, that the archetype (ω) could not have been produced under Nikephoros' direction: it was made after his death. Hence the following stemma:

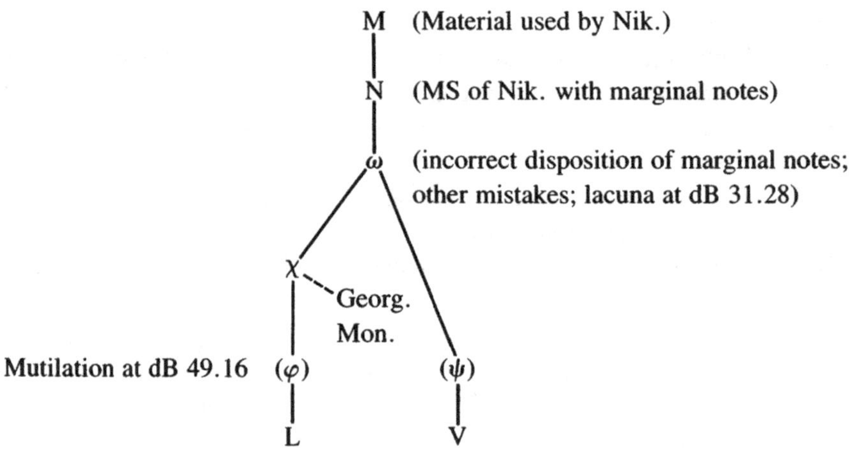

The main difficulty to be explained on the above theory concerns the beginning of L—let us call it L1 (= our cc. 1–11) and designate the rest of L by L2—which differs so markedly from that of V. Speck suggests that when a second copy of ω was made (presumably χ) the first few folios of ω had been accidentally lost. The distraught copyist consulted the patriarch's Nachlass and, finding N (or does he mean M?), supplied the beginning from that MS. An unlikely solution, but not an impossible one.

[52] *Dossier*, 195 ff.

Two main objections can be made to Speck's stemma. First, its point of departure is questionable. The existing sentence order in c. 28, though perhaps less clear than Speck's rearranged order, is by no means impossible, and several generations of scholars have accepted it without demur. Furthermore, Nikephoros was not so much composing an original text as paraphrasing a source, perhaps sentence by sentence: the sequence may well be that of his source. Second, according to Speck's stemma, the divergences between L and V (setting aside L1) should all be of a scribal or accidental nature (misreading, inattention, or damage). But they are not all of that nature: a fair number are what one would call redactional, for example, the following:

15.25 *ἅπερ αὐτῷ κατάφορα γένοιντο* L: *εἴπερ αὐτῷ κατάφορα γένοιτο* V
17.11 *ἐζήτει* L: *ἐξαιτεῖ* V
18.12 *ἐπέγνωσαν* L: *ἐπεγίνωσκον* V
22.5 *φυλάξει* L: *ἐφύλαξαν* V
23.19 *γάρ* L: *δέ* V
26.2 *ἐπειδὴ δὲ Πύρρῳ προσέκειτο Ἡράκλειος* L: *ἐπειδήπερ προσέκειτο Ἡράκλειος Πύρρῳ* V
26.15 *ἀλλ' ἄλλους ταῦτα ἐπαιτιᾶτο* L: *ἄλλους τε ταῦτα ἐπητιᾶτο* V (*ἐπαιτιᾶτο* V[2])
26.16 *περὶ τούτων* L: *ὑπὲρ τούτων* V
34.8 *ἀντιπαρατάσσεται* L: *ἀντιπαρατάττεται* V
34.27 *πρὸς τὰ Σαρακηνῶν ἤθη γενόμενος* L: *πρὸς τὰ τῶν Σαρ. γεν. ἤθη* V
35.4 *λεγομένη* L: *καλουμένη* V
36.11 *κατασχεθείς* L: *συσχεθείς* V
37.13 *ἀποτίθεται* L: *κατατίθεται* V
38.2 *ἑξκαιδέκατον* (sic) L: *ἑκκαιδέκατον* V
38.7 *κατὰ τῶν Σκλαβίνων ἐθνῶν ὥρμησεν* L: *κ. τ. Σκλαβηνῶν εὐθέως ὥρμησε* V
38.16 *ἐκστρατεύσας* L: *ἐκστρατεύει . . . καί* V
44.13 *θαρσαλαιώτεροι* L: *θαρραλεώτεροι* V
44.15 *πρὸς βραχὺ ἀπειπόντες* L: *τῶν πρὸς μάχην ἀπειπόντες* V
45.7 *Στέφανον τὸν πατρίκιον* L: *Σ. δέ τινα πατρίκιον* V.

Whoever made these and other changes in tense, word order, vocabulary, in introducing Attic forms, and even changing the sense was not simply a scribe: he was either Nikephoros himself or another learned redactor.

If we are to suggest a different stemma without recourse to arbitrary or farfetched suppositions, we have to be guided by two considerations that affect the direct tradition.

1) The presence of common errors already noted by Orosz (pp. 13–14). Set-

ting aside misspellings and one vulgarism (42.75 *ἀπὸ Χαζαρίαν*), I have counted eighteen obvious errors, six more that are arguable, plus two redundant words that have been bracketed by editors. The obvious errors are:

12.29	*ἅμα καὶ στολὴν βασιλικήν* VL: *στολῇ βασιλικῇ* edd.
12.31	*τοῖς . . . ἄρχουσι* VL: *τοὺς . . . ἄρχοντας* edd.
12.32	*παρ' ἐκείνῳ* VL: *παρ' ἐκείνου* edd.
13.7	*Εὐτρόπιον* VL: *Εὐτροπίου* edd. Admittedly, this mistake could have been easily overlooked.
13.11	*ἑκάτερος* VL: *ἑκάτεροι* edd.
13.24	*ἀναφανέντος* VL: *ἀναφανέντες* edd.
13.33	*εἰς μέσους* VL: *εἰς μέσον* edd.
28.11	*καὶ τὴν ἡλικίαν* VL: *κατὰ τὴν ἡλικίαν* edd.
29.6	*διωθουμένην* VL: *διωθουμένη* edd.
35.29	*ὑπὸ . . . λεγόμενον* VL: *ἀπὸ . . . λεγομένης* edd.
35.31–32	Corrupt passage in VL
36.23	VL read *τῶν ἐγγιζόντων πανωκημένων* (sic), followed in V by *Σκλαβηνῶν ἐθνῶν*, the latter two words being omitted in L. Editors print [*ἐγγιζόντων*] *παρῳκημένων Σ. ἐθνῶν* and note that Theoph. has *παρακειμένων*. Whatever may be the origin of the corruption of *παρῳκημένων* to *πανωκημένων*, it is a near synonym of *ἐγγιζόντων*.
38.11	*στρατεύει ἄχρι καὶ ἕως τριάκοντα χιλιάδας* (*χηλιάδας* V) *λαόν* VL: *ἄχρι καὶ εἰς* edd. It appears that *ἕως* was meant to be an alternative reading.
39.10	*τοῖς* VL: *τούς* edd.
40.23	*σκεδαννύμενοι* VL: *σκεδαννυμένους* edd.
40.38	*Θεοδόσιον* VL: *Θεόδοτον* edd.
45.77	*αὐτούς* VL: *αὐτός* edd.
47.6	*αὐτῶν* VL: *αὐτοῖς* edd.

The six cases where I have maintained traditional corrections whereas another editor might have preferred to follow the MSS are:

12.56	*σκεψάμενος* VL: *σκηψάμενος* edd. Cf. 2.30.
18.5	*κατεγγυῆσαι* VL: *κατεγγυήσας* edd.
18.6	*ἀναιρεῖτο* VL: *ἀνῄρητο* edd.
36.16	*συντόμως* VL: *συντόνως* edd.
40.19	*πραίτωρος* VL: *πραιτωρίου* edd., admittedly, not an entirely satisfactory emendation.
45.61	*ἐπιπεσόντων* V, *ἐπεισπεσόντων* L: *ἐπιπεσόντος* edd.

Finally, the redundant words shared by V and L are:

12.6	*μέχρις*
30.9	*τά*

2) As we have seen, however, all of L was revised in V.

It follows that the errors were present in the common archetype and survived the revision. We are then left with at least two alternatives. The simpler one may be expressed by the following stemma:

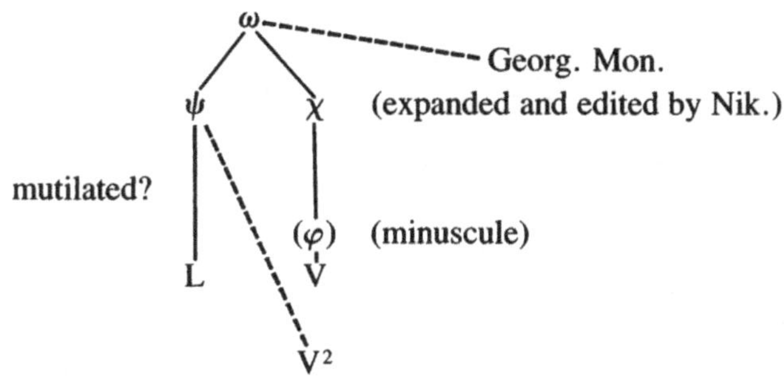

According to this scheme, Nikephoros' personal draft incorporating the unedited beginning (L1) would have been copied in ω. It does not particularly matter whether it extended to 713 or 769. The archetype ω then gave rise to two further copies, and one of these (χ) was revised by Nikephoros. The weakness of this solution (I readily admit it) is that it makes Nikephoros appear as a singularly absent-minded redactor: he neglected to correct a series of obvious mistakes and did not even try to patch up the gap between cc. 32 and 33. The second alternative is that the redactor was a person other than Nikephoros. But would such a person have taken upon himself the task of improving the patriarch's prose and, in particular, of rewriting L1? Furthermore, if he was a man of some literary ability, why did he miss so many errors? The truth of the matter may have been more complex, but I see no way of attaining it with the evidence at our disposal.

EDITIONS AND TRANSLATIONS

Editio princeps by D. Petavius, *S. Nicephori patriarchae Constantinopolitani Breviarium historicum* (Paris, 1616) from an apographon made from V and brought from Rome by Sirmond (ibid., p. 9); repr. in Paris Corpus, vol. I (1648) and Venice Corpus (1729). New edition by I. Bekker in Bonn Corpus (1837) without recourse to MS, but improved through a number of felicitous emendations. Repr. Migne, PG 100 (1865), 876–994. Critical edition from V by C. de Boor (Leipzig, 1880).

Text of L edited from photographs by L. Orosz (Budapest, 1948) in full to c. 11 (as also by us), variants only to the end. The edition is on the whole very accurate, but many routine emendations have been made tacitly.

Translations: Latin by Petavius; French by Moret, *Abrégé de l'Histoire byzantine de Saint Nicéphore, patriarche de Constantinople* (Paris, 1684); Russian by E. E. Lipšic, *VizVrem* 3 (1950), 349–87. For partial translations into other languages see Moravcsik, *Byzantinoturcica*, I, 457. Add I. S. Čičurov, *Vizantijskie istoričeskie sočinenija* (Moscow, 1980), 159–67 (extracts).

LIST OF SIGNS

MANUSCRIPTS

L = *cod. Londinensis, Add. 19390*
L^1 = manus prima
L^2 = manus secunda
V = *cod. Vaticanus graecus 977*
V^1 = manus prima
V^2 = manus secunda
Sab = *cod. Sabaiticus 366*, fol. 22^v
gloss. Barocc. = glossae quae in *cod. Barocc. 50* continentur (vide p. 18)

EDITIONS

B = coniecturae Bekkeri
dB = coniecturae Caroli de Boor
Or = correctiones Oroszii
P = coniecturae Petavii
vulg. = correctiones editionum tacite factae

*	lacuna
[ ]	secludenda. In apparatu autem critico uncis quadratis includuntur quae a V^2 in lacunis vel rasuris codicis addita sunt.
⟨ ⟩	addenda
†	locus corruptus

See also Abbreviations, pp. ix ff.
The apparatus as a rule is negative.

TEXT AND TRANSLATION

ΤΟΥ ΕΝ ΑΓΙΟΙΣ ΠΑΤΡΟΣ ΗΜΩΝ ΝΙΚΗΦΟΡΟΥ ΠΑΤΡΙΑΡΧΟΥ ΚΩΝΣΤΑΝΤΙΝΟΥΠΟΛΕΩΣ ΙΣΤΟΡΙΑ ΣΥΝΤΟΜΟΣ ΑΠΟ ΤΗΣ ΜΑΥΡΙΚΙΟΥ ΒΑΣΙΛΕΙΑΣ

V185ʳ dB3

1. *Μετὰ τὴν Μαυρικίου τοῦ βασιλέως ἀναίρεσιν Φωκᾶς, ἐπεὶ ταύτην διειργάσατο, τῆς βασιλείου ἀρχῆς ἐπιλαμβάνεται· οὗ δὴ ἄρξαντος ἐπὶ τοσοῦτο κακώσεως Χριστιανοῖς ἤλασε τὰ πράγματα ὡς παρὰ πολλοῖς ᾄδεσθαι ὅτι Πέρσαι μὲν τὴν Ῥωμαίων ἀρχὴν ἐκτὸς κατεπήμαινον, Φωκᾶς δὲ ἔνδον χείρω τούτων ἔπραττε. ταῦτα οὐκ ἀνεκτὰ Ῥωμαίοις ἐγίνετο· διὸ οἱ περὶ τὴν Λιβύην τηνικαῦτα ἡγεμονεύοντες, ἅτε τῷ μεγίστῳ διαστήματι τὸ θαρσεῖν ἔχοντες καὶ ἅμα παρὰ Μαυρικίου τὰ τῆς στρατηγίδος ἀρχῆς ἐγκεχειρισμένοι (δύο δὲ ἤστην ἀδελφώ, Ἡράκλειος καὶ Γρηγόριος), οὗτοι κοινῇ βουλευσάμενοι τοὺς υἱεῖς πρὸς τὸ Βυζάντιον ἐκπέμπουσιν ἄστυ, ἀλλήλοις συνθέμενοι ὡς τὸν προφθάσαντα τούτων τῆς βασιλείας, εἰ δύναιτο, ἐπιλήψεσθαι. καὶ Ἡράκλειον μὲν τὸν Ἡρακλείου παῖδα πλείστῳ καθοπλίσαντες στόλῳ ἔκ ⟨τε⟩ τῶν Ἄφρων καὶ Μαυρουσίων ἀνδρῶν πληρώσαντες πλοῖ ἐξέπεμπον, Νικήταν δὲ τὸν Γρηγορίου υἱὸν ἱππικῇ στρατιᾷ πολλῇ περιβαλόντες διὰ τῆς ἠπείρου ἀπέστελλον. δεξιᾷ δὲ τύχῃ* dB4 *χρησάμενος Ἡράκλειος καὶ πνεύμασιν ἐπιφορωτάτοις ἀναχθεὶς φθάνει Νικήταν εὐπλοΐσας εἰς Βυζάντιον, καὶ ἤδη τῇ πόλει προσεσχηκὼς ἐπέλαζε. Κρίσπος δέ (τοῦ Φωκᾶ δὲ ἦν οὗτος γαμβρός, ὃς τηνικάδε τὸν τοῦ ὑπάρχου τῆς πόλεως θρόνον διέπειν ἔλαχε, καὶ μεγάλα ἐν τοῖς βασιλείοις δυνάμενος), ἐπεὶ ἀπηχθάνετο Φωκᾷ ὡς δὴ περιυβρισμένος ὑπ' ἐκεί-*

1: 2 διειργάσ*το ex *διειργάσατο* V² una littera deleta in *διείργαστο* fort. ut mutetur ‖ 11 post *υἱεῖς* V² add. *ἑαυτῶν* ‖ 14 *πλεῖστον . . . στόλον* dB ‖ *τε* addidi ex L ‖ 19 *εὐπλοΐσας* V¹ ex *εὐπλοίας* ‖ 23 *ὑπ' ἐκείνου* vulg. *ἐπ' ἐκ.* V

SHORT HISTORY
⟨STARTING⟩ AFTER THE REIGN OF MAURICE
BY
OUR FATHER WHO IS AMONG THE SAINTS, NIKEPHOROS, PATRIARCH OF CONSTANTINOPLE

1. After the murder of Emperor Maurice, Phokas, who had committed this ⟨deed⟩, seized the imperial office. When he had assumed power the situation of the Christians came to such a pitch of misfortune that it was commonly said that, while the Persians were injuring the Roman State from without, Phokas was doing worse ⟨damage⟩ within. Wherefore, the men who at that time were governing Libya, emboldened as they were by being so far away—they were two brothers, Herakleios and Gregorios, who had jointly been appointed to their military command by Maurice—made common counsel and sent forth their sons to the city of Byzantium on the understanding that the one who arrived first would take possession of the imperial office if he was able to do so. And after equipping a great fleet, manned by Africans and Moors, they sent off ⟨at its head⟩ Herakleios, the son of Herakleios; as for Niketas, the son of Gregorios, they invested him with ⟨the command of⟩ a numerous force of cavalry and dispatched him by land. By good chance, Herakleios was carried by favorable winds and, overtaking Niketas, sailed easily to Byzantium, where he reached shore in front of the city. Now Krispos[1] (this man, who enjoyed great power in the palace, was Phokas' son-in-law and at the time happened to occupy the post of city prefect), because he hated Phokas, by whom he had been insulted on account of the removal of his own image

[1] *Recte* Priskos.

νου τυγχάνων τῆς οἰκείας εἰκόνος καθαιρέσεως ἕνεκεν, ἥν ποτε οἱ τῶν ἀντιθέτων χρωμάτων δημόται τῇ τοῦ Φωκᾶ συμπαρέγραψαν εἰκόνι, δόλῳ αὐτὸν μετήρχετο, καὶ πονεῖν μὲν ὑπὲρ αὐτοῦ πλαττόμενος ἔπειθε καὶ Ἡράκλειον ἐπ' ἀπωλείᾳ ἑαυτοῦ ἥκειν ἀπισχυρίζετο, συνήργει δὲ ὅμως Ἡρακλείῳ καὶ τῷ ὄντι τὰ ὑπὲρ αὐτοῦ εἰς τὰ μάλιστα ἔπραττεν. οἱ οὖν περὶ Φωκᾶν θεασάμενοι καὶ ὅσον πολιτικὸν ἐξ αὐτῶν ἐστασίαζον (ἤδη γὰρ οἱ τοῦ πρασίου χρώματος δημόται τοῖς περὶ τὴν Καισαρίου τὸ πῦρ ὑφῆπτον καὶ τὸν ἔπηλυν βασιλέα ἀνευφήμουν), ἐπικειμένους δὲ αὐτοῖς καρτερώτατα καὶ τοὺς ἐκ τῶν Ἡρακλείου στρατευμάτων εἰσιδόντες, καταλιπόντες αὐτὸν ἐφ' ἑαυτοῖς γίνονται. Φώτιος δέ τις τοὔνομα, ὃς παρ' αὐτοῦ εἰς τὴν σύζυγον ἐπιβουλευθείς ποτε | καθυβρίζετο, εἰς τὰ βασίλεια V185v *σὺν πλήθει στρατιωτῶν ἐπιὼν Φωκᾶν αὐτίκα κατέσχε, καὶ τῆς βασιλικῆς αὐτὸν ἀπαμφιέσας ἐσθῆτος, περίζωμα μέλαν αὐτῷ περιθέμενος, τὰς χεῖρας περιηγμένας εἰς τοὐπίσω ἀποδεσμήσας καὶ πλοίῳ ἐμβαλὼν πρὸς Ἡράκλειον δεσμώτην ἀπήγαγεν. ὃν ἰδὼν Ἡράκλειος ἔφη "οὕτως, ἄθλιε, τὴν πολιτείαν διῴκησας;" ὁ δὲ "σὺ μᾶλλον" εἶπε "κάλλιον διοικεῖν μέλλεις". εὐθὺς οὖν αὐτοῦ τὸν διὰ ξίφους ἔτι πρὸς τῷ πλοίῳ ὄντος καταψηφίζεται θάνατον, ἔπειτα ἀκρωτηριάζεσθαι, χεροῖν τε δεξιὰν ἄνωθεν ἐκ τοῦ ὠμιαίου ἄρθρου ἐκκόπτεσθαι* dB5 *καὶ τῶν αἰδοίων ἐκτέμνεσθαι καὶ κοντοῖς ἀναρτᾶσθαι, οὕτω τε τὸ σῶμα συρὲν κατὰ τὴν τοῦ Βοὸς λεγομένην ἀγορὰν τῷ πυρὶ καταπίμπρασθαι, Δομεντιόλον τε τὸν Φωκᾶ ἀδελφὸν καὶ Βονόσσον καὶ Λεόντιον τὸν τῶν βασιλικῶν χρημάτων ταμίαν τὸν αὐτὸν τῷ Φωκᾷ συνδιαφέρειν κίνδυνον προσέταττε. καὶ δὴ ταῦτα οὕτως ἀπέβαινε.*

2. *Σέργιος δὲ αὐτίκα ὁ τῆς πόλεως πρόεδρος καὶ ὁ λοιπὸς ταύτης ὅμιλος σὺν πάσῃ εὐγνωμοσύνῃ Ἡράκλειον ἐντὸς εἰσδέχεται. καὶ αὐτὸς Κρίσπον εἰς τὴν βασίλειον ἀξίαν προὔτρεπε· μηδὲ γὰρ τῆς βασιλείας ἕνεκεν αὐτὸς ἐληλυθέναι ἔφασκε, τίσασθαι μᾶλλον Φωκᾶν τῆς εἰς Μαυρίκιον καὶ τὰ Μαυρικίου τέκνα παρανομίας. ὁ δὲ οὐκ ἐδέχετο. τέλος ὑπὸ τῆς συγκλήτου βουλῆς καὶ τοῦ δήμου Ἡράκλειος βασιλεὺς ἀνακηρύσσεται καὶ τὸν βασίλειον παρὰ τοῦ προέδρου περι-*

---

25 *δημῶται* V ‖ 29 *εἰς τὰ μάλιστα* V²: *τὰ* om. V¹ ‖ 30 *ἐξ αὐτῶν* dB: *ἑαυτῶν* V ‖ 31 post *γὰρ* V² add. *καὶ* ‖ *δημῶται* litt. *β*, *χρώματος* litt. *α* superscripta V ‖ 36 *ποτὲ* V ‖ 37 *ἐπιὼν* dB *ἐπὶ τὸν* V ‖ 43 *μέλλ[εις]* V ‖ 44 *ὄντος* B *ὄντι* V ‖ 46 *τὸ αἰδεῖον* dubitanter coni. dB ‖ 49 *τῶν τὸν* V

(which on one occasion the partisans of the competing colors had put up alongside that of Phokas), behaved treacherously toward him; and, while he pretended to be striving on his behalf and alleged that Herakleios had come to destroy him, he yet cooperated with Herakleios and indeed helped him most actively. When, therefore, the men around Phokas saw how many citizens among them were rioting (for already the partisans of the green color were setting fire to the surroundings of ⟨the house⟩ of Kaisarios and were proclaiming the newcomer emperor) and perceived that Herakleios' soldiers, too, were pressing upon them with great force, they abandoned Phokas and went home. Now a man called Photios, whom Phokas had once disgraced by seducing his wife, entered the palace with a throng of soldiers and straightaway arrested Phokas, whom he stripped of the imperial robes and, after putting a black tunic on him and tying his arms behind his back, cast him in a boat and brought him prisoner to Herakleios. On seeing him Herakleios said: "Is it thus, O wretch, that you have governed the state?" He answered: "No doubt, you will govern it better." Immediately, while Phokas was still in the boat, Herakleios decreed that he be put to the sword and then that he be mutilated, namely, that his right arm should be amputated at the shoulder joint and his genitals be cut off and ⟨these members⟩ be affixed to poles, and that his body should be dragged in this condition to the so-called marketplace of the Bull and be consigned to the fire. He also ordered that Domentiolos, the brother of Phokas, Bonossos, and Leontios, the imperial treasurer, should undergo the same penalty as Phokas. These matters, then, happened in this manner.

2. Straightaway, Sergios, the bishop of the city, and the rest of its inhabitants received Herakleios within ⟨the walls⟩ with much gratitude. Now Herakleios urged Krispos to assume the imperial office, saying he had come not to take the empire, but to punish Phokas for his unlawful ⟨murder⟩ of Maurice and his children; but Krispos would not accept it. At length, Herakleios was proclaimed emperor by the senate and the people and was invested by the bishop with the imperial crown. And he appointed Krispos com-

βάλλεται στέφανον· Κρίσπον δὲ στρατηγὸν ἀποστέλλει χειροτονήσας τῶν ἐν Καππαδοκίᾳ ἐκστρατευμάτων. ἐπεὶ δὲ ἡ φήμη διέθεεν ὡς Πέρσαι ἐπὶ Ῥωμαίους στρατεύουσιν, Ἡράκλειος ἐκ Βυζαντίου ἄρας παρὰ Κρίσπον κατὰ τὴν Καίσαρος πόλιν τηνικαῦτα τυγχάνοντα προσπορεύεται ὡς δὴ αὐτῷ [περὶ] τῶν κοινῶν ἕνεκεν βουλευσόμενος. καὶ ὃς μὲν νοσεῖν προσεποιεῖτο καὶ τὸν βασιλέα συχνῶς παραγινόμενον ἐν σχήματι ἀρρώστου κατακλινόμενος ἀηδῶς καὶ μόλις ἐδέχετο· εἶτα ἠκούετο ὡς καὶ διελοιδορεῖτο αὐτῷ· Ἡράκλειος δὲ τὸ δρᾶμα συνῆκε καὶ τὴν ὕβριν ὅμως ἤνεγκε καὶ ἤδη ἐκαιροφυλάκει. ἀλλ' ἔδοξε τέως γνησιώτερόν πως διαλέγεσθαι περὶ τοῦ δεῖν πονεῖν ὑπὲρ ἀλλήλων τῆς πολιτείας χάριν. ὁ δὲ οἷα ἐπιτωθάζων οὐκ ἐξὸν βασιλεῖ ἔφασκε καταλιμπάνειν βασίλεια καὶ ταῖς πόρρω ἐπιχωριάζειν δυνάμεσιν. ἐν τούτοις τίκτεται παῖς τῷ βασιλεῖ Ἡράκλειος, ὃν δὴ καὶ Κωνσταντῖνον ὠνό|μασε. τότε δὴ παραγίνεται καὶ Νικήτας ὁ τὴν ἀξίαν πα- V186[r] τρίκιος πρὸς τὸ βασίλειον ἄστυ. διὰ τοῦτο Ἡράκλειος εἰς τὸ dB6 Βυζάντιον ἐπάνεισι καὶ Νικήταν σὺν τιμῇ μεγίστῃ καὶ περιφανείᾳ ὥσπερ ἀδελφὸν γνήσιον καὶ ὁμότιμον δέχεται, καθὰ ἦν αὐτοῖς ἤδη συντεταγμένον ἐκ Λιβύης ἀπαίρουσι. καὶ Κρίσπος δὲ εἰς Βυζάντιον ἧκεν ὡς τῇ εἰσόδῳ Νικήτα συνησθησόμενος. σκήπτεται δὲ Ἡράκλειος τῷ θείῳ λουτρῷ τὸν υἱὸν καθαγνίζειν, υἱοθετεῖσθαι δὲ αὐτὸν ὑπὸ Κρίσπου. ὁ δὲ ἐπὶ τούτοις εἰσέρχεται εἰς τὰ βασίλεια. Ἡράκλειον δὴ ἀθροίσαντα τοὺς ἐκ τῆς συγκλήτου βουλῆς ἅπαντας καὶ τὴν ἄλλην πληθὺν τοῦ ἄστεως ἅμα τῷ προέδρῳ Σεργίῳ εἰπεῖν λέγεται πρὸς αὐτούς "ὁ βασιλέα ὑβρίζων τίνι προσκρούει;" τοὺς δὲ φάναι "τῷ θεῷ τῷ ποιήσαντι αὐτὸν βασιλέα". καὶ Κρίσπον προτρέπειν, καὶ αὐτὸν ἀποφαίνεσθαι τὸ δοκοῦν ὀρθῶς· τὸν δὲ οὐκ εἰδότα τὸ δραματούργημα λέξαι μηδὲ φιλανθρώπου τυχεῖν δίκης τὸν ἐπὶ τοιούτῳ ἁλόντα τολμήματι. καὶ τὸν βασιλέα ἀναμιμνήσκειν αὐτὸν οἷα ἐν Καισαρείᾳ ἐπὶ τῇ νόσῳ κατεσχηματίσατο, καὶ ὡς τὸ τῆς βασιλείας κατευτελίζειν ἀξίωμα ᾤετο, καὶ ὡς εἰς τὴν βασίλειον ἀρχὴν προὔτρεπε. καὶ ἅμα λαβόντα τόμον κατὰ κόρρης τοῦτον παίειν, καὶ εἶτα λέγοντα "ὡς γαμβρὸν οὐκ ἐποίησας, φίλον πῶς ἂν ποιήσειας;"

2: 14 *περὶ* secl. dB || 16 *ἀειδῶς* V || 23 Ἡράκλειος ex Ἡρακλείῳ corr. V^1 vel V^2 || 33 *τοὺς* V^2 *τῆς* V || 39 *τοιούτῳ* ex *τοιοῦτῳ* V^1 vel V^2

mander of the expeditionary forces in Cappadocia and sent him ⟨thither⟩. Since, however, a rumor was afoot that the Persians were mounting an expedition against the Romans, Herakleios went forth from Byzantium to meet Krispos at Caesarea (where he happened to be at the time) so as to take counsel with him concerning public affairs. Krispos pretended to be ill and, lying down in the manner of an invalid, received the emperor, who paid frequent calls on him, with displeasure and unwillingly. It was also reported that he railed at him. Herakleios understood the plot, but he bore the insult and bade his time. He decided meanwhile to have a more sincere conversation on the necessity of mutual striving on behalf of the state. But the other man, as if in mockery, said it was not proper for an emperor to abandon his palace and to be tarrying among distant armies. At this juncture a son was born to Emperor Herakleios, whom he named Constantine. At the same time Niketas, who had the dignity of patrician, arrived at the imperial city. For this reason Herakleios returned to Byzantium and received Niketas with great honor and distinction as he would his own brother and equal as they had previously agreed when they were departing from Libya. Krispos, too, came to Byzantium so as to join in celebrating the arrival of Niketas. Now Herakleios pretended that he was about to purify his son in the sacred font and would have him adopted by Krispos. On this pretext Krispos entered the palace. After assembling all the members of the senate and the remaining people of the city together with their bishop Sergios, Herakleios is reported to have asked them: "When a man insults an emperor, whom does he offend?" They answered: "He offends God who has appointed the emperor." And he urged Krispos also to express his honest opinion. The latter, not understanding the play that was being acted, said that a man convicted of such a daring deed should not even have the benefit of a lenient sentence. Then the emperor reminded him of his feigned illness at Caesarea, and how he thought of degrading the imperial dignity, and how he ⟨Herakleios⟩ had offered him the empire. And picking up a book, he struck him on the head and then he said: "You have not made a ⟨good⟩ son-in-law. How will you make a friend?" And straightaway he directed that his head

εὐθὺς δὲ ἐπιτρέψαι εἰς κληρικοῦ σχῆμα την κεφαλὴν ἀποκείρασθαι, καὶ τὸν ἱεράρχην τὰ νενομισμένα ἐπὶ τῇ ἀποκάρσει ἐπιφθέγξασθαι. ἐξελθόντα δὲ αὐτὸν τοῖς μετὰ Κρίσπου στρατιώταις ἐπὶ λέξεως ὧδε εἰπεῖν "ὁ παπᾶς Κρίσπος ὑπουργοὺς ὑμᾶς ἕως τοῦ νῦν εἶχεν, ἡμεῖς δὲ σήμερον οἰκειακοὺς τῆς βασιλείας ὑπηρέτας". προσθεῖναι δὲ αὐτοῖς τὸ ἐξ ἔθους σιτηρέσιον, πρώτους τε καλεῖσθαι καὶ ἐν τοῖς στρατιωτικοῖς τάγμασιν· αὐτούς τε ἀσμενέστατα δεξαμένους τὸν βασιλέα ἐπευφημῆσαι ἅμα τῇ ἄλλῃ πληθύϊ. μετὰ δὴ ταῦτα Κρίσπον εἰς τὸ λεγόμενον τῆς Χώρας περιεῖρχθαι σεμνεῖον, ὃς ζήσας dB7 ἐνιαυτὸν αὐτοῦ ἐτελεύτησεν. Ἡράκλειος δὲ Θεόδωρον τὸν ἑαυτοῦ ἀδελφόν, τὴν μετὰ βασιλέα πρώτην ἀρχὴν κεκτημένον (κουροπαλάτην δὲ αὐτὸν οἱ περὶ τὰ βασίλεια καλεῖν εἰώθασιν), ἔτι καὶ Φιλιππικὸν τὸν Μαυρικίου τοῦ βασιλέως γαμβρὸν ἐπ' ἀδελφῇ γεγονότα, τηνικαῦτα δὲ εἰς κληρικοῦ σχῆμα ἀποκεκαρμένον τὴν κόμην, ἡγεμόνα τῆς ὑπὸ Κρίσπου πρῴην ἰθυνομένης ἀρχῆς ἐξέπεμπε. Φιλιππικὸς δὲ ἐπιβιοὺς χρόνον ὕστερον ἐτελεύτα, καὶ πρὸς τῷ ὑπ' αὐτοῦ δωμηθέντι περικαλλεῖ ἄγαν καὶ σεβασμίῳ ἱερῷ τῷ κατὰ Χρυσόπολιν ὄντι ταφῇ παραδίδοται.

3. Ὀλίγου δέ χρόνου διιπ|πεύσαντος νόσῳ ἐπιληψίας ἡ V186[v] τοῦ βασιλέως γαμετὴ Εὐδοκία ληφθεῖσα ἐτελεύτησεν. ἐν ᾧ δὲ τὸ ταύτης σῶμα ἐξεκομίζετο, καὶ πολλῶν ὡς τὸ εἰκὸς ἐπὶ τῇ θέᾳ συρρεόντων, συνέπεσε κόρην τινὰ ὕπερθεν τῶν ὑπερῴων διακύψασαν (θεράπαινα δὲ ἦν αὕτη τῶν ἀστῶν τινος) ἀποπτύσαι ὡς τὸν ἀέρα ἀφύλακτα καὶ τὸ περίττωμα κατὰ τῆς πολυτελοῦς ἐκείνης ἐσθῆτος περιενεχθῆναι ἣ τὸ τῆς βασιλίδος νεκρὸν περιέστελλεν· ἐφ' ᾧ οἱ περὶ τὴν ἐκφορὰν περιοργεῖς γενόμενοι συλλαμβάνουσί τε αὐτὴν καὶ τὸν διὰ πυρὸς κατεδίκασαν θάνατον, ἐντάφιον οὐκ εὐαγές, βαρβαρικῷ νόμῳ χρησάμενοι, τῇ ἐκδημίᾳ τῆς βασιλίσσης ἀθέσμως συμπαραπέμψαντες οἱ ἀνόσιοι. περιεζήτουν δὲ οἵγε καὶ τὴν δέσποιναν τῆς οἰκέτιδος, ὡς καὶ αὐτῇ τὸν ἴσον διάθοιντο κίνδυνον· ἡ δὲ δήπου αἰσθομένη τὸν ὄλεθρον διαπέφευγεν, οὔτι ὁραθεῖσα

---

45 δὲ del. B δὴ coni. dB ‖ 47 *ἐπιφθέγξασθαι* V[1] ex *ὑποφθέγξασθαι* ‖ 49 *ὑμᾶς* ex *ἡμᾶς* V ‖ 50 *τ[ῆ]ς* V ‖ 52 *δεξαμένους* V[1] ex *δεξαμενος*

3: 8–9 *περὶ ὀργῆς* V corr. B

should be shorn in the manner of a clergyman and that the bishop should recite the customary ⟨prayers⟩ over the act of tonsure. He then went out to meet the soldiers of Krispos and said to them these exact words: "The Reverend Krispos had you as his assistants until now, but today we ⟨make you⟩ the emperor's own servants." ⟨He ordered⟩ that they should receive the usual allowance and should have first place among the military contingents. They assented with great pleasure and acclaimed the emperor together with the rest of the crowd. After this, he confined Krispos in the monastery of the Chora, as it is called, where he died a year later. Now Herakleios sent out as commanders in the post previously held by Krispos his own brother Theodore, who held the second highest rank after that of emperor (which in the language of courtiers is habitually called *curopalates*), as well as Philippikos, the brother-in-law of Emperor Maurice, who at that time had his head shorn in the manner of a clergyman. Philippikos survived for a time, but then he died and was consigned to burial in the very beautiful and venerable church he had built at Chrysopolis.

3. A short time had gone by when the emperor's wife Eudokia was seized by the illness of epilepsy and died. And while her body was being carried out to burial and, as usual, a great many people gathered for the spectacle, it happened that a girl (she was the servant of one of the citizens) leaned out from an upper floor and spat unguardedly into the air. Her secretion landed on the splendid vestment in which the empress' corpse was enveloped. Whereupon, those taking part in the funeral became incensed: they apprehended the girl and condemned her to death by fire, thus, in the manner of barbarians, attaching to the demise of the empress an unholy burial rite, sacrilegious men that they were. They also searched all around for the mistress of the servant girl so as to inflict on her the same punishment. But she, doubtless sensing the danger, escaped and was never seen again. Such were the events surrounding

εἰς τὸ ἔπειτα πώποτε. καὶ ταῦτα μὲν ἀμφὶ τὰ βασίλεια ὧδέ πως ἔσχε.

4. Τὰ δ' αὖ ἑτέρωσε ὡς ἐτελεῖτο οὕτω συνέβαινεν. ἔν τινι τῶν† ἐπιχωρίων† (χώρα δὲ ἥτις ποτέ ἐστιν, οὐδαμῇ ἐς τὸ νῦν παραδέδοται) ἦν τις ⟨τῶν⟩ ἐν ἐκείνῃ περιφανείᾳ κομώντων dB8 εὐπορίᾳ τε βίου λαμπρός, οὗ τὸ ἐπώνυμον Βουτηλῖνος ἐτύγχανε, τὴν δὲ ἀξίαν ἣν κανδιδάτον Ῥωμαίοις κικλήσκειν ἔθος. τούτῳ γυνή τις χήρα ἐν γειτόνων διῳκημένη χαλεπῶς ἔφερε τὸ γειτόνημα· ἀμφισβητήσεως γὰρ αὐτοῖς μεθορίων γῆς ἕνεκεν συμβαινούσης ὁ Βουτηλῖνος τοῖς παισὶ τοῖς αὐτοῦ ἐνεκέλευε μάχῃ ἐπιέναι τοῖς ὁμοροῦσι, καὶ οἵγε ῥοπάλοις ἕνα τῶν τῆς χήρας υἱέων ἀναιροῦσιν. αὕτη ἀνελομένη τοῦ ἤδη τεθνηκότος υἱοῦ ᾑμαγμένον τὸ ἄμφιον ἐς Βυζάντιον ὡς Ἡράκλειον ἵκετο, καὶ ἐπεὶ προϊόντα εἶδε, εἰσδραμοῦσα τοῦ χαλινοῦ τοῦ ἵππου ἐφ' οὗ ἐπωχεῖτο ἐφάπτεται, καὶ ἅμα τὸ τοῦ παιδὸς ἔσθημα ἐπιδεικνῦσα σὺν βοῇ πρὸς αὐτὸν ἀνεφθέγγετο "οὕτω γένοιτο τοῖς σοῖς τέκνοις, ὦ βασιλεῦ, εἰ μὴ τὸ αἷμα τοῦτο, ὅ σοι δείκνυμι, αὐτίκα ἐνδίκως τιμωρήσειας". τῶν δ' οὖν περὶ τὸν βασιλέα δορυφόρων ἐπιόντες πλήττειν ἠπείγοντο· βασιλεὺς δὲ διεκώλυσε, καὶ τῇ γυναικὶ μηκέτι τολμᾶν προσιέναι παρηγγύησεν, ἐπεξιέναι δὲ τὰ τῆς δίκης ὁπηνίκα ἂν αὐτῷ δεδογμένα εἴη. ᾤχετο εὐθὺς μὴ δίκης τυχὸν ὀλολύζον τὸ γύναιον. χρόνος δὲ διήρχετο, καὶ δὴ ὁ τὸν φόνον ἐπιτρέψας, δεδιὼς καὶ αὖθις τὴν γυναῖκα τοῦ ἀνῃρημένου εἵνεκεν βασιλεῖ ἐπικαλεῖν, ταύτῃ τοι εἰς Βυζάντιον εἴσεισι καὶ δὴ ἐς τὸ δημοτικὸν ἑαυτὸν ἐγκαταμίγνυσι. καὶ ἱππικοῦ | ἀγῶνος τελουμένου τοῦτον βασιλεὺς ἐν μέσοις δημόταις κα- V187r τιδὼν τῷ ὑπάρχῳ ἐπιτρέπει τῆς πόλεως φρουρᾷ καθειργνύναι τὸν ὕποπτον. εἶτα τὸ γύναιον μεταπέμπεται καὶ τὰ τῆς μιαιφονίας ἀσφαλέστερον ἀνηρεύνα. κελεύει τοίνυν τὸν Βουτηλῖνον ὑπὸ τῶν παίδων τῶν αὐτοῦ ἴσην ὑποσχεῖν τῷ ἀνῃρημένῳ τὴν τιμωρίαν, καὶ αὐτοὺς ἐκείνους ὡσαύτως κτείνεσθαι.

5. Ἡράκλειος δὲ τὸν υἱὸν Ἡράκλειον, ταὐτὸν δὲ εἰπεῖν dB9 Κωνσταντῖνον (διώνυμος γὰρ ὢν ἐτύγχανεν), παρὰ τοῦ ἱεράρ-

---

4: 2 *ἐπιχωρίων*] *ἐπαρχιῶν* B *τῶν ἐπὶ Θρᾴκης χωρίων* (fort. recte) vel *τῶν περιχωρίων* coni. dB ‖ 3 *τῶν* addidi *τῶν ἐκείνῃ* coni. dB ‖ *κωμώντων* V ‖ 4 Βιτουλῖνος V ‖ 6 *ἐν* ex *ἓν* . . . *διωκειμένη* V ‖ 9 *οἵγε* B *οἵδε* V ‖ 10 *ὕεων* V corr. vulg. ‖ 11 *ἄμφιον* gloss. Barocc. f. 293r *ἀμφί** νον* V ‖ 12 *ἥκετο* V corr. B ‖ *προιέντα* V. corr. vulg. ‖ 24 *δημωτικὸν* V ‖ 25 *δημώταις* V ‖ 30 *αὐτοὺς ἐκείνους* coni. dB *αὐτῆς ἐκείνης* V *ὑπ' αὐτῆς ἐκείνης* B

the palace.

4. As to what happened elsewhere, here is an account of it. In a certain rural district[2] (which village this was has not been recorded anywhere) there lived a man called Boutelinos,[3] who prided himself on his nobility and was conspicuous by his riches; his rank was that which the Romans are wont to call *candidatus*. A neighbor of his, who was a widow, was distressed by their propinquity. For there was a dispute between them concerning the boundaries of their lands, and Boutelinos ordered his slaves to make an armed attack on his neighbor; and these men clubbed to death one of the widow's sons. Taking up the bloodstained garment of her dead son, the woman came to Byzantium to see Herakleios; and catching sight of him in a procession, she rushed in and caught the bridle of his horse. Showing him her son's garment, she cried to him: "May the same fate, O emperor, befall your children if you don't immediately avenge in a just manner the blood I am showing you." Some of the imperial bodyguard came forward to strike her, but the emperor stopped them and ordered the woman not to dare come into his presence again, but to pursue the legal process at the time of his choosing. So the woman straightaway went off lamenting without having obtained justice. Some time passed and the perpetrator of the murder, fearing that the woman would again appeal to the emperor on account of the killed man, followed her to Byzantium and mingled among the members of the demes. When the hippodrome races were being held the emperor noticed him among the fans and directed the city prefect to imprison the suspect. He then summoned the woman and made a more thorough inquiry into the murder. He ordered that Boutelinos should suffer at the hands of his slaves the same penalty as the man who had been killed, and that his slaves likewise should kill one another.

5. Now Herakleios, after having his son, who was called both Herakleios and Constantine (for he had a double name), sanctified by the bishop in the

---

[2]Or perhaps "in a village of Thrace"; see Commentary.

[3]Classicized from L's Bizoulinos.

χου τῷ θείῳ λουτρῷ καθαγνίσας ἀγκάλαις ⟨ἐκ⟩ τῆς ἱερᾶς κολυμβήθρας ἐδέξατο. αὐτίκα δὲ αὐτῷ τῆς βασιλείου ἀξίας τὰ σύμβολα τἆλλά τε καὶ τὸ διάδημα περιθέμενος ἐταινίωσε καὶ βασιλέα ἀνεῖπε. τὴν θυγατέρα δὲ Γρηγορίαν τοὔνομα Νικήτα τοῦ τὴν ἀξίαν πατρικίου εἰς γαμετὴν κατηγγύησεν· οὗ δὴ καὶ ταύτῃ τῷ βασιλεῖ μειζόνως οἰκειωθέντος τὸν ἀνδριάντα κεχρυσωμένον καθύπερθε κιόνων ἔφιππον κατὰ τὴν τοῦ Φόρου λεγομένην ἀγορὰν ἀνέστησεν. καὶ οὕτω μὲν ταῦτα ἐπράττετο.

6. Χοσρόης δὲ ὁ Περσῶν βασιλεὺς στρατιὰν ὡς πλείστην ἀθροίσας ἐπὶ Ῥωμαίους ἐξέπεμψεν, ἡγεμόνα τῶν Περσικῶν Σάϊτον χειροτονήσας δυνάμεων. οὗτος ἐπὶ τὴν Ἀλεξάνδρου ἐφορμισθεὶς ταύτην ἀνὰ κράτος εἷλε καὶ τὴν ὅλην Αἴγυπτον ἠνδραπόδιζε καὶ τὴν ἑῴαν ἅπασαν μοῖραν κατεδῄου καὶ δοριαλώτους ὡς πλείστους ἦγε καὶ ἄλλους ἀνῄρει, οὐδεμιᾷ φειδοῖ εἰς αὐτοὺς χρώμενος. ταῦτα τοίνυν οὕτω διαθέμενος εἰς τὸ ἔπειτα πανστρατιᾷ κατὰ τὴν Χαλκηδόνος πόλιν ᾔει καὶ περιεκάθητο ταύτην χρόνον ἐπὶ συχνόν, ἠξίου τε βασιλέα εἰς ὁμιλίαν οἱ λόγων ἱκέσθαι. καὶ δὴ βασιλεὺς εἰσήκουε καὶ ὡς αὐτὸν διεπεραιοῦτο, βασιλικῇ δορυφορίᾳ τε καὶ πομπῇ χρώμενος. καὶ αὐτὸν ἰδὼν Σάϊτος ἐξανέστη τε τῆς καθέδρας καὶ πρὸς τοὔδαφος ἑαυτὸν ἀπορρίψας προσεκύνει· αὐτός τε ἐκ τοῦ ἀκατίου, ἐν ᾧ ἐπέπλει, τὸ χαῖρε αὐτῷ προσεφώνει καὶ δωρεαῖς ἠμείβετο. ὧδε πρὸς αὐτὸν Σάϊτος ἔλεξεν. "ἔδει μέν, ὦ βασιλεῦ, τοὺς Ῥωμαίων τε καὶ Περσῶν βασιλέας μήτε διίστασθαι ταῖς γνώμαις μηδ' ὁπωστιοῦν ἀλλήλοις dB10 ἀντικαθίστασθαι, ἐς φιλίαν τε καὶ συμβάσεις ἰέναι ὡς προθυμότατα· (ὅπερ ἥδιστόν τε καὶ εὔχαρι ἀνθρώποις τοῖς πάλαι καὶ νῦν τυγχάνει ἅπασιν, ἅτε ζωῆς τε τῆς εὐκτέας καὶ εὐνομουμένης αἰτιώτατον·) καὶ τῷ περιόντι τῆς ἐξουσίας συμπαραμένειν καὶ τὸ τῆς συμβάσεως μέγεθος. | καὶ γὰρ ἴσμεν V187v ὡς ἥκιστα ταῖς ἐξουσίαις δὴ ταύταις ἐφάμιλλος πολιτεία φανείη ἂν πώποτε. οὐ γὰρ ὅσιον, παρὸν ἐπιφροσύνῃ καὶ

5: 3 *ἐκ* add. dB cf. L ‖ 5 *ἐτενίωσε* V *ἐτενίωσεν* gloss. Barocc. f. 298v corr. vulg. ‖ 7 *Νικήτα τοῦ . . . πατρικίου* P coll. **17.**19 *Νικήτα τῷ . . . πατρικίῳ* V ‖ 8 *ταύτην* V corr. vulg.

6: 4 *ἐφορμισθεὶς* coni. dB *ἀφορμισθεῖς* V *ἀφορμηθεὶς* B ‖ post *ταύτην* V² add. *τε* ‖ *ἀνακράτως* V corr. vulg. ‖ 9 *ἐπισυχνὸν* V ‖ 10 *οἱ* vulg. *οἵ* sequente rasura duarum litterarum V ‖ 15 *ὧδε* ex *ὡδὲ* V¹ ‖ 16 *τοὺς* corr. ex *τῆς* vel *τοῖς* V² ‖ 17 *μηδ'*] *μηθ'* coni. dB ‖ 20–21 *εὐνομουμένης* dB sec. gloss. Barocc. f. 298v *εὐνομούμενος*: *εὐγνωμουμένης* V ‖ 23 *δεῖ* V corr. P ‖ 24 *παρ' ὃν* V corr. vulg.

holy bath, received him in his arms out of the sacred font. And straightaway he invested him with the diadem and the other tokens of the imperial office, and so crowned him and declared him emperor. And he betrothed to him the daughter of the patrician Niketas, called Gregoria. Niketas became in this way so intimate with the emperor that the latter erected a gilded equestrian statue of him on top of some columns in the marketplace which is called the Forum. So much for these matters.

6. Now Chosroes, king of Persia, collected a numerous army and sent it against the Romans after appointing Saitos[4] commander of the Persian forces. This man came up to Alexandria, which he took by main force, and he captured all of Egypt. He devastated the entire oriental part ⟨of the empire⟩, taking many prisoners and killing others without any pity. Having done these things, he proceeded with his whole army against the city of Chalcedon, which he invested for a long time, and requested that the emperor should come and parley with him. Indeed, the emperor assented and crossed over to meet him, surrounded by the imperial bodyguard and his retinue. Upon seeing him, Saitos rose from his seat and prostrated himself on the ground to do obeisance, while ⟨the emperor⟩ addressed to him a greeting from the boat he was sailing in and gave him gifts. Saitos spoke these words to him:

"It would have been desirable, O emperor, that the kings of the Romans and the Persians neither disagreed among themselves nor opposed each other in any way, but established friendship and concord with all willingness; for such a state of affairs has been most pleasant and enjoyable to men of old as it is to all of us now, inasmuch as it is conducive to a desirable and orderly life. This concord should be as profound as our empires are great; for we know that no other state will ever appear to rival these our empires. Indeed, it is not

[4] Shahīn: see Commentary.

εὐβουλίᾳ χρωμένους τὸ εὔνουν καὶ φίλιον εἰς ἀλλήλους κρατύνασθαι, ὅπλα κατ' ἀλλήλων αἴρεσθαι καὶ πημαίνειν οὐκ ἐν δίκῃ καὶ κακοῦν τὸ ὑπήκοον. ἐξ ὧν τί συμβαίνει; εἰ μὲν τὸ ὁμόγνωμον καὶ εἰρηνικὸν θήσεσθε, εὐδαίμονά τε ἑκάτερον ὑμῶν τῶν ἄλλων ἀνθρώπων μᾶλλον ὑπάρξαι, ζηλωτούς τε καὶ ἀξιαγάστους ἐς τὸν ἅπαντα βίον δείκνυσθαι· εἴς τε τὸ ἄμοχθον καὶ εὔθυμον ὁ πόνος ὑμῖν καὶ ἡ φροντὶς περιστήσεται. εἰ δ' αὖ γε ταυτὶ μεθιέμενοι καὶ ἡλίκον οἷον ἀγαθὸν τὴν εἰρήνην ἐκποδὼν ποιήσασθαι ἕλοισθε, καὶ οὐδὲν ὅτι ὀνησιφόρον λογίσασθαι ὑμῖν οἶσον, δυσμένειαν δὲ τὴν εἰς ἀλλήλους καὶ τὸ ἔχθιστον ἀνθῃρημένοι, πολέμων μὲν ὡς πλείστων, ὅπερ ἀπηχὲς καὶ ἀπώμοτον, παραίτιοι γενήσεσθε, ἱδρῶτάς τε καὶ πόνους ὡς τὸ εἰκὸς ἀνελέσθαι μεγίστους, πολλὰ δὲ σώματα προϊέμενοι δαπανήσετε χρημάτων τε ἀνάλωσιν ὡς πλείστην ποιήσεσθε· καὶ ἁπαξαπλῶς εἰς μέγα κακοῦ τὸ τοῦ πολέμου ὑμῖν πέρας ἥξει. οἷα δὴ καὶ νῦν ὁρᾶν ὑμῖν πάρεστιν, ἀφ' ὧν ἔγωγε εἰς τὴν Ῥωμαίων εἰσβαλὼν γῆν, τὰ δεινότατα εἶδε καὶ πέπονθεν. ἐντεῦθεν οὖν λελείψεται τὰ τῶν πολιτειῶν οἰκτρότατα καὶ ἀθλιώτατα διακείσεσθαι". ταῦτα διώμνυτο λέγων αὐτὸς καὶ ὡς ἐν σπουδῇ τίθεσθαι τὰς πολιτείας Ῥωμαίων τε dB11 καὶ Περσῶν εἰς τὸ τὰ συμβατήρια ἥκειν. ταῦτα ἐπιτελῆ ποιήσειν ὅγε ἐπήγγελτο, καί, ὡς τῶν ὀμωμοσμένων τὰ πιστὰ δοίη, προσέφερεν, ὅτι γε δὴ ταῦτα καὶ Χοσρόῃ βουλομένῳ [αἱρετέα] εἴη. "εἴ τι οὖν μοι" φησὶ "πείθεσθαι ἔχοιτε, αὐτίκα δὴ μάλα τοὺς ὡς Χοσρόην πρεσβευσομένους τούτων ἕκατι ἅμα ἐμοὶ ἐκπέμποιτε. πεισθείη δ' ἄν μοι καὶ αὐτός, εὖ οἶδα, εἰς τοῦτο γνώμης καθιστάμενος σπείσεσθαι μεθ' ὑμῶν καὶ τὴν εἰρήνην τὸ λοιπὸν εἰς τὸν ἅπαντα χρόνον βεβαίαν τε καὶ ἀκραιφνῆ καταστήσεσθαι".

7. Βασιλεὺς δὲ Ἡράκλειος, ἐπεὶ τοῦτ' οὖν ἐπέπυστο, τῷ προσηνεῖ καὶ θελκτηρίῳ τῶν λόγων συνηδόμενός τε καὶ κατακηλούμενος, ὑπέσχετο εἰς ἅπαντα πράσσειν ἑτοιμότατά τε καὶ σπουδαιότατα. καὶ οἷς ἐβουλεύετο τούτων πέρι συνέπραττόν τε μάλιστα καὶ συνήνουν ὁ ἱερομύστης τε καὶ οἱ ἐν τέλει.

---

28 *ἑκατέρων* V corr. vulg. || 31 *ὑμῖν* in mg. V || 33 *ἐκ ποδῶν* V || *ἕλοισθε* ex *ἕλυσθε* V[1] vel V[2] || 34 *δὲ*] *δὴ* coni. dB || 45 *ἐπὶ τέλει* V corr. P || 48 *αἱρετέ*α* V secl. dB || [*εἴη*] V || *πείθεσθε. ἔχοιτε. αὐτίκα* V *πείθεσθαι* B || 51–53 *σπείσεσθαι . . . καταστήσεσθαι* scripsi *σπείσεσθε . . . καταστήσεσθε* V dB ita interpunxit: *ἐκπέμποιτε (ποισθείη . . . καθιστάμενος) σπείσεσθε . . . καταστήσεσθε*

proper—given the possibility of strengthening our mutual good relations and friendship by exhibiting wisdom and prudence—that we should take up arms and unjustly injure each other to the detriment of our subjects. For what would be the consequence of that? If you choose concord and peace, each one of you will be the happiest of men and will appear as long as he lives to be worthy of envy and admiration: your toil will become painless and your cares will yield to joy. If, on the other hand, you let go of this course and choose to banish peace (a great boon though it may be), believing it to bring you no benefit, and take up mutual hostility and enmity instead, you will become responsible for many wars (a discordant and hateful action), with the natural result that you will undergo much sweat and toil, suffer many casualties, and expend an enormous amount of money: in a word, the effect of the war will be to bring you great distress. This you can see already from the terrible experiences and sufferings of the Roman land since my invasion of it. As a consequence, our states will be reduced to a wretched and miserable condition."

In uttering these words he swore that he would do his utmost for the Roman and Persian states to come to an agreement. He undertook to accomplish these things and, by way of confirming his sworn statements, he added that they were also agreeable to Chosroes. "If, therefore, you believe me," he said, "you will immediately dispatch in my company your ambassadors who will treat these matters with Chosroes. I am sure he will be persuaded by me, since he is also minded to make an accord with you and to establish for all time to come a sure and inviolate peace."

7. When Emperor Herakleios heard these things, pleased and charmed as he was by the appealing gentleness of the speech, he promised to act most readily and strenuously in all respects. His views on these matters were supported and approved by the high priest[5] and the dignitaries. The ambassadors

[5] I.e., the patriarch Sergios.

καὶ ὅτι τάχιστα οἱ διαπρεσβευσόμενοι ἐξελέγοντο, Ὀλύμπιος μὲν ὁ τὴν τῶν ὑπάρχων τῶν πραιτωρίων διέπων ἀξίαν, Λεόντιος δὲ ὁ τῆς πόλεως ὕπαρχος, Ἀναστάσιός τε ὁ τὴν οἰκονομίαν τοῦ μεγίστου ἱεροῦ, ᾧ Σοφία ὁ θεῖος λόγος ἐπώνυμον, τῶν πραγμάτων πεπιστευμένος. τούτους παραλαβὼν | Σάϊτος καὶ ἄρας ἐκ Χαλκηδόνος ὀπίσω ἀπήλαυνε καὶ πρὸς τὰ (V188r) Περσικὰ ἤθη ἐχώρει· καὶ ἕως μὲν τῆς Ῥωμαίων ἐπέβαινε γῆς, διὰ τιμῆς ἦγε καὶ θεραπείας ἠξίου, τῇ Περσικῇ δὲ ἐμβαλὼν πέδας τὰς ἐκ σιδήρων αὐτοῖς περιθέμενος δεσμώτας παρὰ Χοσρόην ἐκόμισε. Χοσρόης δὲ ἐπεὶ ἔγνω ὡς Σάϊτος Ἡράκλειον ὡς βασιλέα εἶδέ τε καὶ τετίμηκεν, ἀλλ' οὐ δοριάλωτον ἑλὼν ὡς αὐτὸν ἤγαγεν (ἐν τούτῳ γὰρ αὐτῷ τὰ τῆς ἐλπίδος ὠνειροπολεῖτο καὶ ἔκειτο), μεγάλα τε ἐπ' αὐτῷ ἠγανάκτει καὶ τέλος εἰς ἀσκὸν αὐτῷ ἀπέδειρε τὴν δοράν, πικρὸν αὐτῷ καὶ βίαιον καταστήσας τὸν θάνατον. (dB12) Ῥωμαίων δὲ τοὺς πρεσβευτὰς ἰδίᾳ διαστείλας ὡς ἕκαστον φρουραῖς ἀσφαλεστάταις ἀπέθετο καὶ ἐκάκου τὰ μέγιστα.

8. Ταῦτα οὐ μικρῶς ἠνία τὸν βασιλέα καὶ ἐπετάραττεν. ἐφ' οἷς καὶ λιμὸς τηνικαῦτα τῇ πολιτείᾳ ἐπεφύη βαρύτατος· οὐ γὰρ ἡ Αἴγυπτος αὐτοῖς τὸ λοιπὸν ἐπεσίτιζεν, ἐξ οὗ καὶ τὰ πλεῖστα τῶν βασιλικῶν ἐπελελοίπει σιτηρεσίων. ἐν τούτοις καὶ νόσος λοιμώδης τοῖς ἐν τῇ πόλει ἐνσκήψασα θανάτῳ τὰ πλήθη τὰ ἐν αὐτῇ διέφθειρεν. ὧν ἁπάντων ἕνεκεν πολλὴ δυσθυμία καὶ ἀπορία τῷ κρατοῦντι περιεκέχυτο. καὶ οἴχεσθαι διὰ ταῦτα πρὸς Λιβύην βουλομένῳ ἦν. καὶ αὐτόθι χρήματα τέως πλεῖστα χρυσόν τε καὶ ἄργυρον καὶ λίθων τοὺς τιμιωτάτους προὔπεμπεν· ὧν οὐκ ὀλίγιστα καταίροντα κλύδωνι μεγίστῳ περιπεπτώκει καὶ τοῖς ποντικοῖς ῥείθροις βρύχια γέγονε. ταῦτα τοίνυν τῶν πολιτῶν αἰσθόμενοι, ὡς δυνατὰ ἦν αὐτοῖς, διεκώλυον. ὁ γοῦν ἱεράρχης ἐπὶ τοῦ ἱεροῦ τοῦτον καλέσας ὅρκοις ἐνταῦθα περιεδέσμει ὡς ἥκιστα τῆς βασιλευούσης ἐξίστασθαι. οἷς εἴξας τὰς μὲν παρούσας τύχας ἀπωλοφύρετο, τὰς δὲ γνώμας τὰς αὐτῶν καὶ οὐκ ἐθελοντὴς ἔστεργε.

9. Χρόνος δέ τις παρῴχετο, καὶ ὁ τῶν Οὔννων τοῦ ἔθνους κύριος τοῖς ἀμφ' αὐτὸν ἄρχουσι καὶ δορυφόροις ἅμα εἰς Βυ-

---

7: 9 ᾧ] ὃ V corr. vulg. || 15 Σάϊτος ex Σάϊτον V[1]

8: 8–12 cf. Sudam s.v. Βρύχιος

were chosen with all speed, namely, Olympios, who held the office of praetorian prefect, Leontios, prefect of the city, and Anastasios, who was entrusted with the administration of the property of the Great Church, which bears the name of Sophia, the divine Logos.[6] Taking these men along, Saitos set out from Chalcedon and retreated toward the abode of the Persians. As long as he was on Roman soil he treated ⟨the ambassadors⟩ honorably and took good care of them, but when he entered Persia he put iron fetters on them and brought them captive to Chosroes. When Chosroes learned that Saitos had seen Herakleios and had honored him like an emperor, instead of taking him prisoner and bringing him before him (for such was his hope and dream), he was greatly incensed and, finally, had Saitos flayed and made his skin into a bag—a painful and violent death. As for the Roman ambassadors, he separated them one from another and confined them to secure prisons where they underwent great hardship.

8. The emperor was greatly distressed and troubled by these things. In addition, a severe famine developed at that time in the state: for Egypt was no longer providing grain, as a result of which the imperial *annonae* gave out. Furthermore, a plague fell on the inhabitants of the City and a multitude died of it. On account of these circumstances the emperor was overwhelmed by despondency and despair, and decided accordingly to depart to Libya. He sent thither an advance shipment of a great quantity of money, gold and silver and precious stones; which, on its way, was overtaken by a violent storm and a good part of it sank in the waters of the sea. On becoming aware of these ⟨moves,⟩ some of the citizens tried to prevent them as best they could. The archpriest, too, invited Herakleios to the church and bound him there by an oath that he would not by any means abandon the Imperial City. He yielded to them and, against his will, acquiesced in their views while lamenting the misfortunes that were upon them.

9. After a lapse of time the chieftain of the Hunnic nation came to Byzantium in the company of his noblemen and bodyguard and requested the

[6] He was in other words *oikonomos* of St. Sophia.

ζάντιον εἰσῄει, μυεῖσθαι δὲ τὰ Χριστιανῶν βασιλέα ἐξῄτει. ὁ δὲ ἀσμένως αὐτὸν ὑπεδέχετο, καὶ οἱ Ῥωμαίων ἄρχοντες τοὺς Οὐννικοὺς ἄρχοντας καὶ τὰς ἐκείνων γαμετὰς αἱ τούτων αὐτῶν τῷ θείῳ λουτρῷ ἐτεκνώσαντο σύζυγοι. οὕτω τε τὰ θεῖα μυηθεῖσι δώροις βασιλικοῖς καὶ ἀξιώμασιν ἐφιλοτιμήσατο· τῇ γὰρ ἀξίᾳ τοῦ πατρικίου τὸν ἡγεμόνα τούτων τετίμηκε καὶ πρὸς τὰ Οὐννικὰ ἤθη φιλοφρόνως ἐξέπεμπε.

10. *Μετὰ δὴ ταῦτα καὶ ὁ τῶν Ἀβάρων τοῦ ἔθνους ἡγεμὼν ἐπὶ συμβάσεσιν ὡς Ἡράκλειον ἐπικηρυκεύεται. ἐφ' ᾧ λίαν* dB13 *ὑπεραγάμενος δώροις αὐτὸν ἠμείβετο καὶ δὴ καὶ ἔπεμπεν ὡς αὐτὸν ἀγγελιαφόρους, Ἀθανάσιον τὸν πατρίκιον, εἶτα μετ' αὐτὸν καὶ Κοσμᾶν τὴν ἀξίαν ἣν δὴ κυαίστορα καλοῦσι, τὰ τῆς βασιλέως | γνώμης αὐτῷ ἀπεροῦντας. ὁ Ἄβαρος δὲ τὰ* V188v *πρὸς φιλίαν ὑποκρινόμενος αἱμύλα τε καὶ ἐπαγωγὰ πρὸς αὐτοὺς ἀποφθεγγόμενος ὑπήγετο, ὡς φίλος εἴη Ῥωμαίοις, καὶ ἥκειν ὡς βασιλέα ἐπὶ σπονδαῖς ἐπήγγελτο. οἳ δὴ καὶ ἀναζεύξαντες τὰ τῆς εὐνοίας ἐκείνου ἔνδηλα βασιλεῖ ἐποίουν. οἷς ἄγαν ὑπερηδόμενος βουλεύεται εἰς τὴν πόλιν Ἡράκλειαν, καθ' ἃ ἦν αὐτοῖς συγκείμενον, τῷ Ἀβάρῳ συμβαλεῖν. τὴν θυμελικὴν σκευὴν προύπεμπε, καὶ ἱππικὴν ἀγωνίαν ἐπὶ τῇ δοχῇ αὐτοῦ τελεῖν εὐτρέπιζε, στολήν τε αὐτῷ λαμπρὰν καὶ τοῖς συνομαρτοῦσιν ἐκόμιζεν. εἶτα κατὰ τὴν Σηλυμβρίαν πόλιν ἀφιγμένος ηὐλίζετο. τρισὶ δὲ ὕστερον ἡμέραις ὁ χαγάνος σὺν πλήθει πολλῷ τῶν Ἀβάρων ἀμφὶ τὴν Ἡράκλειαν παρῄει. ἀποδασμὸν δέ τινα τῶν οἱ ἑπομένων, οἳ ἄλκιμοί τε καὶ μαχιμώτατοι ἐτύγχανον, ἀπολεξάμενος, κατὰ τὰ ὑπερκείμενα τῶν Μακρῶν λεγομένων Τειχῶν λοχμώδη τε καὶ ἀμφιλαφῆ ἐκπέμψας, σκεδάννυσι κρύβδην κατὰ τῶν ἐκεῖ ὀρῶν χωρήσειν τὰ λάσια, ὡς ἂν κατὰ νώτου τοῦ βασιλέως γενόμενοι, αὐτόν τε μέσον καὶ τοὺς περὶ αὐτὸν ἀποληψόμενοι, σχοῖεν εὐχείρωτον. τούτους Ἡράκλειος αἰσθόμενος καὶ οὐ μετρίως τῷ παραλόγῳ καταπλαγείς, τὸ ἁλουργὸν ἀπαμφιέννυται ἔσθημα· οἰκτρὸν δέ τι καὶ πενιχρόν, ὡς ἂν ἰδιώτης τοῖς ἐντευξομένοις φαίνοιτο, περιβαλόμενος ἔνδυμα τόν τε στέ-*

9: 4–5 *τοὺς Οὐννικοὺς* corr. ex *τῆς Οὐννικῆς* V[2] ‖ 8 *τούτων* B *τοῦτον* V *αὐτῶν* L

10: 6 *ἀπαιροῦντας* V ‖ 8 *ὑπείγετο* V corr. vulg. ‖ 15 *Σιλυμβρίαν* V corr. vulg. ‖ 16–17 *χαγᾶνος* V ‖ 18 *οἱ*] *οἵ* V ‖ 21 *ὁρῶν* V ‖ 25 *καταπλαγὲν* V corr. V[2]

emperor that he be initiated in the Christian ⟨faith⟩. The latter received him gladly: the Roman noblemen became baptismal fathers of the Hunnic noblemen, and the wives of the former ⟨did the same⟩ to the spouses of the latter. After they had thus been initiated in things divine, ⟨the emperor⟩ presented them with imperial gifts and dignities: for he honored their chief with the rank of patrician and so dismissed him graciously to the abode of the Huns.

10. After this, the chief of the Avar nation, too, sent a message to Herakleios with a view to ⟨concluding⟩ a treaty. The latter was greatly pleased at this and rewarded him with gifts. Furthermore, he sent ambassadors to him, namely, the patrician Athanasios and, in addition, Kosmas, who held the post of quaestor (as they call it), to make a statement of imperial policy. Putting on a mask of friendship, the Avar ⟨chief⟩ spoke to them wily and alluring words, pretending to be a friend of the Romans, and announced that he would meet the emperor so as ⟨to conclude⟩ a treaty. The ambassadors returned and reported to the emperor that man's friendly attitude. Greatly pleased at this, he decided to meet the Avar ⟨chief⟩ in the city of Herakleia as had been agreed. He sent in advance some theatrical equipment and made preparation for chariot races to be held at the reception; he also brought along splendid vestments for him ⟨the Chagan⟩ and his companions.[7] He then arrived at Selymbria and lodged there. Three days later the Chagan arrived before Herakleia with a great throng of Avars. After picking among his followers a contingent of the bravest fighting men, he sent them to the overgrown and wooded heights overlooking the so-called Long Walls and scattered them secretly in the bushy hills that are there so that, taking the emperor in the rear, they might encircle him and make an easy prey of him and his retinue. Upon becoming aware of them, Herakleios, greatly astonished at this unexpected event, took off his purple robe and, putting on instead some mean and miserable clothes so as to appear like an ordinary man to anyone he encountered; hiding, furthermore, his imperial crown

[7] Or possibly "for himself," if we make the slight alteration of *αὐτῷ* to *αὑτῷ*.

φανον τὸν βασίλειον τῇ ὠλένῃ περιαψάμενος, ἀγεννῶς παραχρῆμα εἰς φυγὴν ἐτράπετο καὶ μόλις πρὸς τὸ Βυζάντιον διεσώζετο. οἱ δὲ Ἄβαροι σὺν θυμῷ κατὰ τὴν δίωξιν ἐπετίθεντο, καὶ πρὸς τὸ πεδίον τὸ πρὸ τῆς πόλεως ὃ Ἕβδομον καλοῦσι dB14 καταλαβόντες ἱδρύσαντο. ἐνθένδε τε σκεδάννυνται ἄχρι καὶ εἰς τὴν τοῦ Βαρβύσσου παταμοῦ γέφυραν καὶ τὰ τῇδε χωρία πικρῶς κατεληΐζοντο καὶ τὸν Ῥωμαίων ὅμιλον ἀφειδῶς ἐκεράϊζον, τήν τε βασιλικὴν ἐσθῆτα καὶ τὰς στολὰς παραλαμβάνουσι, πρὸς δὲ καὶ τὰ θυμελικὰ ὄργανα καὶ τοὺς διακομίζοντας ἅπαντας. πλεῖστον δὲ ὅσον λαὸν ἀνδραποδισάμενοι δοριάλωτον ἄγοντες πρὸς τῇ σφετέρᾳ ἀπεκόμισαν· εἰς ἑβδομήκοντα δὲ καὶ διακοσίας χιλιάδας ἀνδρῶν τε καὶ γυναικῶν, καθάπερ ἔνιοι τῶν ἁλόντων διαδράντες ἀλλήλοις συνῳδὰ ἔφασαν, ὁ ἀριθμὸς αὐτοῖς ἅπας συνήνεκτο.

11. Ἡρακλείῳ δέ, καίτοι τῶν κοινῶν αὐτῷ πραγμάτων ἐπὶ τοσοῦτο δυσχερείας καὶ ἀνωμαλίας ἡκόντων, οὐ μὴν οὐδὲ τὰ οἰκεῖα εὖ θέσθαι φροντὶς ἐγεγόνει, ἀλλ᾽ ὅγε πρὸς πρᾶξιν ἄθεσμον καὶ ἣν Ῥωμαίων ἀπαγορεύουσι νόμοι ἰδών, τὸ πρὸς τὴν ἀνεψιὰν Μαρτῖναν | ἠσπάσατο κῆδος. θυγάτηρ αὕτη Μα- V189^r ρίας τῆς αὐτοῦ ἐτύγχανεν ἀδελφῆς, πατρὸς δὲ Μαρτίνου, ὃν Μαρία πρὸ Εὐτροπίου γαμέτην ἐκέκτητο. καὶ δὴ δύο υἱεῖς ἐξ αὐτῆς τίκτει, ὧν τὸν μὲν Φλάυιον τὸν δὲ Θεοδόσιον προσηγόρευσεν. ἡ δίκη δὲ ἐθριάμβευε τὸ ἀθέμιτον, καὶ τοῦ μὲν πρεσβυτέρου παρειμένον ἐδείκνυ τὸν αὐχένα ὡς μηδ᾽ ἑτέρωθι ἐπιστρέφεσθαι οἷόν τε εἶναι, τοῦ δ᾽ αὖ νεωτέρου τὴν ἀκουστικὴν ἀφῄρητο αἴσθησιν καὶ κωφὸν ἤδη ἀπέφαινε. διήλεγχον δὲ αὐτοῦ μάλιστα τὸ ἄσεμνον συνοικέσιον ἐπὶ ταῖς ἱππικαῖς ἁμίλλαις καὶ οἱ τοῦ πρασίου δημόται χρώματος, ⟨οἱ δὲ τοῦ ἀντικειμένου χρώματος⟩ συνῄνουν τε [ἐπὶ ταύτῃ] καὶ συνέπραττον. Σέργιος δὲ ὁ τῶν Βυζαντίων ἱεράρχης γράμμασιν αὐτὸν λιπαρῶς ἐγκείμενος ἐνουθέτει τὴν πρὸς τὸ γύναιον τοῦτο κοινωνίαν ἀνήνασθαι. ὁ δὲ αὐτῷ ἀπελογεῖτο ὡς "εὖ μὲν ἔχει τὰ παρὰ σοὶ λεγόμενα· ὃ γάρ σοι χρέος ὡς ἀρχιερεῖ καὶ dB15 φίλῳ, ἤδη ἀποδέδωκας· ἐφ᾽ ἡμῖν δὲ τὸ λοιπὸν κείσεται τὰ τῆς

28–29 *περιαψάμενος ἀγεννῶς, παραχρῆμα* interpunxit V || 39 *χιλιάδας ο'* Georg. Mon. 669.19

11: 5 post *θυγάτηρ* V^{2} in mg. add. *γὰρ* || 7 *γαμετὴν* V corr. vulg. || 7–8 *ὑεῖς . . . ὃν* V corr. vulg. || 14 *δημῶται* V || *οἱ δὲ . . . χρώματος* addidi ex L || 15 *ἐπὶ ταύτῃ* seclusi: v. comment. || 19 *ἔχει* B *ἔχοι* V

under his arm, immediately turned to ignominious flight and barely escaped to Byzantium. The Avars set out in hot pursuit and reached the plain in front of the City that is called Hebdomon, where they encamped. Spreading out from there as far as the bridge of the river Barbysses, they grievously devastated the settlements that are there and pitilessly slaughtered the Roman people. They also seized the imperial vestments, the theatrical equipment, and all the men who were transporting ⟨those items⟩. After taking a great many captives, they carried them off to their own country: the total number amounted to 270,000 men and women, as was mutually confirmed by some of the prisoners who escaped.

11. Now Herakleios, even though matters of state had come to such a sorry and abnormal pass, did not even take care to put his private affairs in order; instead, he committed an unlawful deed, one that is forbidden by Roman custom, by contracting a marriage with his niece Martina. She was the daughter of his sister Maria; her father was Martinos, who was Maria's husband before Eutropios. ⟨Herakleios⟩ begot two sons by her, the first of whom he called Flavius[8] and the second Theodosios. Justice, however, proclaimed the unlawfulness ⟨of the deed⟩ by causing the elder to have a paralyzed neck which he could not turn in any direction, and depriving the younger of the sense of hearing—indeed, he proved to be deaf. This unseemly marriage was strongly denounced at the chariot races even[9] by the partisans of the Green color, ⟨and those of the opposing color[10]⟩ concurred and cooperated with them. Sergios, the archpriest of Byzantium, also put earnest pressure on him by letter and admonished him to repudiate his connection with this woman, but he excused himself as follows: "What you say is very well. The obligation you owe me as high priest and friend you have already paid. For the rest, the

[8] *Recte* Fabius, as in L.

[9] Because Herakleios was a supporter of the Greens.

[10] I.e., the Blues.

πράξεως". | L30v κατὰ δὲ τὸν αὐτὸν καιρὸν διεπιπράσκοντο τὰ τῶν ἐκκλησιῶν κειμήλια καὶ εἰς ὑπαγωγὴν φόρων τοῖς βαρβάροις ἐξενεμήθη.

12. Αὖθις οὖν ἐπιστρατεύει Χοσρόης ὁ τῶν Περσῶν βασιλεὺς κατὰ Ῥωμαίων, Σάρβαρον ἡγούμενον τῆς στρατιᾶς ἐκπέμψας, ὃς κατεδῄου πᾶσαν τὴν ἀνατολικὴν χώραν. καταλαμβάνει δὲ τῶν ἁγίων τόπων τὰ ζῳοποιὰ ξύλα τοῦ σωτηρίου σταυροῦ, Μωδέστου τηνικαῦτα Ἱεροσολύμων προεδρεύοντος. παρεσκευάζοντο δὲ οἱ Πέρσαι καὶ ἠπείγοντο [μέχρις] ἐλθεῖν εἰς Χαλκηδόνα. ὁ οὖν Ἡράκλειος ἔκ τε Περσῶν καὶ Ἀβάρων θορυβούμενος ἅμα καὶ λιμῷ πιεζομένης τῆς Ῥωμαϊκῆς πολιτείας καὶ λοιμικῷ θανάτῳ φθειρομένης, προσεκαλεῖτο Σέργιόν τε τὸν τῆς πόλεως πρόεδρον, ἔτι τε καὶ ἄρχοντας καὶ τὸ λοιπὸν τοῦ λαοῦ μέρος, καὶ παρατίθεται αὐτοῖς τοὺς παῖδας, καὶ Βῶνον τὸν πατρίκιον ἐγχειρίζει τὰς τῶν πραγμάτων διοικήσεις, καὶ ἀπάρας διὰ τοῦ Εὐξείνου ἐπειρᾶτο διὰ Λαζικῆς εἰς τὴν Περσικὴν εἰσβαλεῖν· καθ' ἣν τίκτεται αὐτῷ υἱὸς ἐκ Μαρτίνης τῆς γυναικός (μεθ' ἑαυτοῦ γὰρ ταύτην ἤγετο), ὃν καὶ ἐπωνόμασεν Ἡράκλειον. ἐντεῦθεν ἀποστέλλει δῶρα πρὸς τὸν Τούρκων | L31r κύριον, ἐπὶ συμμαχίᾳ τῇ κατὰ Περσῶν συγκαλούμενος· ὁ δὲ δεξάμενος ὑπέσχετο συμμαχήσειν. ἐν τούτῳ ἡσθεὶς Ἡράκλειος ὥρμησε καὶ αὐτὸς πρὸς αὐτόν, κἀκεῖνος τὴν τοῦ βασιλέως παρουσίαν ἀκηκοὼς σὺν πλήθει Τούρκων πολλῷ τῷ βασιλεῖ ὑπηντίαζε, καὶ ἀποβὰς τοῦ ἵππου τῷ βασιλεῖ κατὰ γῆς προσκυνεῖ. ἐποίει δὲ τοῦτο καὶ ὁ σὺν αὐτῷ πᾶς ὄχλος. ὁ δὲ βασιλεὺς τὸ ὑπερβάλλον τῆς τιμῆς θεασάμενος ἐδήλου αὐτῷ ὡς εἰ τὰ τῆς | V189v φιλίας αὐτῷ βέβαια εἴη, (dB16) καὶ ἐποχούμενον πλησιάζειν, καὶ ἅμα τέκνον ἴδιον ἀποκαλῶν. οὕτως οὖν οὗτος ἀσπάζεται τῷ βασιλεῖ. ὁ δὲ ὃν περιέκειτο στέφανον τῆς κεφαλῆς λαβὼν τῇ τοῦ Τούρκου κεφαλῇ περιέθετο, συμποσιάσας τε αὐτῷ πάντα τὰ εἰς ὑπηρεσίαν τοῦ συμποσίου σκεύη ἅμα καὶ στολῇ βασιλικῇ καὶ ἐνωτίοις ἐκ μαργάρων κεκοσμημένοις δωρεῖται αὐτῷ. ὡσαύτως

---

22 *φόρων* L *φόρον* V

12: 2 *στρατειᾶς* L ‖ 3 *κατεδίου* VL corr. vulg. ‖ 6 *ὑπείγοντο* V *ὑπήγοντο* L corr. vulg. ‖ *μέχρις* secl. dB ‖ 7 *Χαλκιδόνα* L ‖ rasura inter *ἔκ* et *τε* L ‖ 8 *λιμῷ* ex *λιβῷ* V ‖ 11 *καὶ*[2] om. V ‖ 12 *Βόνον* L ‖ 17 *τὸν τῶν Τούρκων . . . συμμαχεία* L ‖ 21 *πολλῷ* L *πολλῶν* V ‖ 24 *ὡς εἰ* L *ὡσεὶ* V ‖ 28–29 *τὴν ὑπηρεσίαν* L ‖ 29 *στολὴν βασιλικὴν* VL corr. P ‖ 29–30 cf. Sudam s.v. *ἐνώτια*

responsibility shall lie on me." During this period the plate of the churches was being sold and expended to raise tribute to the barbarians.

12. Once again Chosroes, king of Persia, made war on the Romans, having placed his army under the command of Sarbaros, who devastated all the eastern lands. This man seized in the Holy Places the life-giving relic of the Cross of redemption, Modestos being at that time bishop of Jerusalem. Finding himself troubled by both the Persians and the Avars, and the Roman State hard pressed by famine and decimated by plague, Herakleios called in Sergios, the bishop of the City, along with the noblemen and the rest of the people, and placed his children in their care. He entrusted the administration of affairs to the patrician Bonos and, setting out by way of the Black Sea, he attempted to invade Persia through Lazica. At this juncture a son was born to him by his wife Martina (for he had taken her along), and he named him Herakleios. From there ⟨Lazica⟩ he sent gifts to the chieftain of the Turks, whom he urged to enter on an alliance against the Persians. The latter accepted ⟨the gifts⟩ and promised to be an ally. Herakleios was pleased at this and set forth in his direction; and he, on being informed of the emperor's presence, met him with a great multitude of Turks and, dismounting from his horse, prostrated himself on the ground before the emperor, while his entire host did the same. On perceiving this exceedingly great honor, the emperor declared to him that if their friendship was steadfast, he could draw nigh even on horseback; and he called him his own son. Taking off the crown from his head, he placed it on the Turk's and, after serving a banquet, presented to him all the utensils of the table as well as an imperial garment and earrings adorned

12

δὲ καὶ τοὺς περὶ αὐτὸν ἄρχοντας τοῖς ὁμοίοις ἐνωτίοις αὐτοχειρίᾳ ἐκόσμει. εἶτα δεδιὼς μὴ τὰ αὐτὰ τῷ Ἀβάρῳ καὶ παρ' ἐκείνου πείσεται, ἐπικρατέστερα δ' αὐτῷ καὶ τὰ τῆς συμβάσεως ἀπεργάζεται, παραδείκνυσιν αὐτῷ τῆς θυγατρὸς Εὐδοκίας εἰκόνα ἔφη τε πρὸς αὐτὸν ὡς "ἥνωσεν | ἡμᾶς ὁ θεός, σὲ L31v τέκνον ἐμὸν ἀπέδειξεν. ἰδοὺ δὴ αὕτη θυγάτηρ μού ἐστι καὶ Ῥωμαίων Αὐγούστα. εἰ οὖν συναίρεις μοι καὶ βοηθεῖς κατὰ τῶν ἐχθρῶν, εἰς γυναῖκα δίδωμί σοι αὐτήν". ὁ δὲ τῷ κάλλει τῆς εἰκόνος καὶ τῷ περὶ αὐτὴν κόσμῳ τρωθεὶς ἔρωτι τοῦ ἀρχετύπου ἔτι μᾶλλον ἐπὶ τῇ συμμαχίᾳ ἐπέκειτο. εὐθὺς οὖν ἄρχοντα καὶ πλῆθος Τούρκων τῷ βασιλεῖ παραδίδωσι· σὺν αὐτοῖς τε εἰς τὴν Περσικὴν εἰσβαλὼν τάς τε πόλεις καθῄρει καὶ τὰ πυρεῖα διέστρεφεν. ἐφ' ἑνὸς δὲ τούτων εὕρηται, ὡς Χοσρόης ἑαυτὸν θεοποιήσας ἐν τῇ τούτου στέγῃ ἑαυτὸν καθήμενον ὡς ἐν οὐρανῷ ἀνεστήλωσεν, ἄστρα καὶ ἥλιον καὶ σελήνην συγκατασκευάσας, καὶ ἀγγέλους περιεστῶτας αὐτῷ, καὶ βροντὴν διὰ μηχανῆς ποιεῖν καὶ ὕειν ὁπότ' ἂν θελήσειεν. τοῦτο τὸ βδέλυγμα θεασάμενος Ἡράκλειος εἰς γῆν κατέρριψε καὶ ὡς κονιορτὸν διέλυσε. Χοσρόης τοίνυν ἀκούσας τά τε ἄλλα πάντα καὶ ὡς Τοῦρκοι συμμαχοῦσιν Ἡρακλείῳ, δῆλα ἐποίει dB17 πάντα διὰ γραφῆς τῷ Σαρβάρῳ, καὶ ὡς ταχέως πρὸς αὐτὸν ἐκ τῆς Ῥωμαϊκῆς ἀναζευγνύναι καὶ Ἡράκλειον ἀμύνασθαι· μηδὲ γὰρ δύνασθαι τῷ πλήθει τῷ ἐκείνου ἀντικαθίστασθαι. | τὸ δὲ γράμμα περιτραπὲν Ἡρακλείῳ ἐγχειρίζεται. ὁ δὲ τοῦτο L32r ἀναγνοὺς ταῦτα μὲν ἐξηφάνισεν, ἑτέραν δὲ γραφὴν ὡς ἀπὸ Χοσρόου σκηψάμενος τῷ Σαρβάρῳ ἐκτίθεται, τῇ ἐκείνου σφραγῖδι σημηνάμενος, ἔχουσαν οὕτως "ὁ Καῖσαρ Ῥωμαίων φιλίαν μετὰ Τούρκων ἐσπείσατο καὶ εἰσῆλθε μέχρι τοῦ Ἀδορβαδιγάνου καλουμένου τόπου, καὶ ὅτι πέμψας στρατιὰν κατ' αὐτοῦ αὐτόν τε καὶ τοὺς Τούρκους διώλεσα, οἱ δὲ περιλειφθέντες ἔφυγον. μὴ οὖν ἀπάρῃς ἐκ τῆς Ῥωμαίων γῆς, ἀλλὰ τῇ Χαλκηδόνι προσέ|δρευε, Ῥωμαίους αἰχμαλωτεύων καὶ ληϊζό- V190r

31 τοῖς . . . ἄρχουσι VL corr. P || 32 δεδειῶς L || τὰ αὐτῶ L || Ἀβάρῳ] prima littera in ras. ex βαρ– sive σαρ– V || 32–33 παρ' ἐκείνω VL corr. vulg. || 33 πήσεται V corr. vulg. || δὲ αὐτῶ omisso καὶ L || 36 ταύτη L || 39 τρωθεὶς ex τρωθὲν V² || 40 συμμαχεῖα L || 42 Περσικὴν γῆν L || 43 πυρία L cf. Sudam s.v. πυρεῖον || ὡς L erasum in V rest. dB || 45 ἄστρα L cf. Georg. Mon. 671.18 ἀστραπὰς V || 46 καὶ ante ἀγγέλους om. V || ἀγγ. περ. αὐτῷ σκηπτούχους Georg. Mon. 671.19–20 || 49 τοίνυν V τε L || 54 τὸ δὲ V τὸ γὰρ L || 55 ἐξηφάνησεν L || 56 σκεψάμενος VL corr. vulg. || 58 μετὰ Τούρκων φιλίαν ἐσπήσατο L || 60–61 περιλιφθέντες L

with pearls. He likewise decorated with his own hand the noblemen of ⟨the Turk's⟩ suite with similar earrings. Fearing, however, lest he suffer the same fate as with the Avar ⟨chief⟩, and with a view to making the agreement more binding, he showed him the portrait of his daughter Eudokia and said to him: "God has joined us and has made you my son. Behold, this is my daughter, the Roman Augusta. If you espouse my cause and help me against my enemies, I shall give her to you in marriage." ⟨The Turk⟩ was so struck by the beauty of the picture and its adornment that he fell in love with the person represented and held fast to the alliance all the more. Straightaway he delivered to the emperor a multitude of Turks under a commander. Taking these along, ⟨Herakleios⟩ invaded Persia and set about destroying cities and overturning the fire temples. In one of these temples it was discovered that Chosroes, making himself into a god, had put up his own picture on the ceiling, as if he were seated in heaven, and had fabricated stars, the sun and the moon, and angels standing round him, and a mechanism for producing thunder and rain whenever he so wished. Upon seeing this abomination, Herakleios threw it down and ground it into dust. Now Chosroes, when he had heard all these things and the fact that the Turks were fighting on the side of Herakleios, made everything known to Sarbaros in writing and ⟨directed him⟩ to return from the Roman country with all speed so as to ward off Herakleios, since he himself was unable to oppose the latter's numerous host. This letter was intercepted and delivered to Herakleios who, after reading it, erased the contents and forged a different message to Sarbaros as if it were from Chosroes, whose seal he affixed to it. It ran as follows: "The Roman Caesar has concluded an alliance with the Turks and has marched in as far as the country called Adorbadigan. I have sent an army against him and have destroyed him along with the Turks, and the remainder have fled. Do not, therefore, depart from the Roman country, but go on investing Chalcedon, taking Roman captives and devastating

μενος". καὶ Σάρβαρος μὲν τὸ γράμμα δεξάμενος τῆς προσεδρίας εἴχετο.

13. Οἱ δὲ Ἄβαροι ἐπεὶ τὰς σπονδὰς διέλυσαν (καὶ γὰρ Ἡράκλειος πρὶν πρὸς Πέρσας ἐκστρατεῦσαι δώροις πρὸς αὐτοὺς ταύτας ἐβεβαίου, ὑποσχόμενος παρέχειν αὐτοῖς νομισμάτων μυριάδας εἴκοσι, ὁμήρους αὐτοῖς δεδωκὼς ἕνα τῶν υἱῶν Ἰωάννην τοὔνομα, ὃν δὴ καὶ Ἀταλάριχον ἐκάλεσε, νόθος δὲ ἦν αὐτῷ ἐκ παλλακῆς, καὶ Στέφανον ἀνεψιὸν αὐτοῦ, υἱὸν Μαρίας τῆς ἀδελφῆς αὐτοῦ καὶ Εὐτροπίου, ἔτι δὲ καὶ Ἰωάννην ἕτερον, υἱὸν Βώνου τοῦ πατρικίου, καὶ αὐτὸν ἐκ παλλακῆς αὐτῷ γεγονότα), | καὶ αὐτοὶ ἐκστρατεύοντες τῷ τείχει (L32v) τοῦ Βυζαντίου πελάζουσιν, εὐθύς τε πάντα ἐνεπίπρων τὰ προάστεια. καὶ ὥσπερ ἀναμερισάμενοι ἑκάτεροι τὸν Θρᾳκικὸν Βόσπορον Πέρσαι μὲν τὰ τῆς Ἀσιάτιδος μοίρας καθῄρουν, Ἄβαροι δὲ τὸν ἐπὶ Θρᾴκης διέφθειρον χῶρον. ἀλλήλοις τε λόγοις οἱ βάρβαροι συνετίθεντο συμφωνήσαντες (dB18) ἑλεῖν τὸ Βυζάντιον. οἱ οὖν Ἄβαροι μηχανήματα τειχομάχα ἐτέκταινον· πύργοι δὲ ἦσαν ξύλινοι καὶ χελῶναι τὰ κατασκευάσματα. καὶ ἐπεὶ προσῄεσαν τῷ τείχει τὰ ὄργανα, θεία δύναμις ἐξαπιναίως ταῦτα διέλυσε καὶ τοὺς ἐν αὐτοῖς τῶν Ἀβάρων μαχητὰς διώλεσεν. ἐπειδὴ δὲ καὶ Σκλαβηνὰ πλήθη οἱ Ἄβαροι ἐπεφέροντο καὶ εἰς συμμαχίαν ἐχρῶντο, δεδώκεσαν δὲ αὐτοῖς σημεῖον ὡς ἡνίκα ἂν ἴδοιεν πυρσοὺς ἀναφθέντας εἰς τὸ Βλαχερνῶν προτείχισμα, τὸ καλούμενον Πτερόν, εὐθὺς ἅμα τοῖς μονοξύλοις ἀκατίοις κἀκεῖνοι ἐπεξίοιεν, ὡς πλοΐμῳ ἀναφανέντες τὴν πόλιν κραταιῶς θορυβήσωσιν αὐτοί τε ἀδείας λαβόμενοι ἐκ τῶν τειχῶν ἀνατρέχοντες ἐντὸς τῆς πόλεως γένωνται. δῆλα οὖν ταῦτα Βώνῳ τῷ πατρικίῳ ἐγένοντο, καὶ αὐτὸς διήρεις μὲν καὶ τριήρεις ἁρμόσας, εἰς τὸν | (L33r) χῶρον ἐν ᾧ τὸ σημεῖον ἐδέδοτο καθοπλίσας προσώρμισεν,

63–64 *προσεδρίας* L *προεδρίας* V

13: 2 *πρὸς* om. V ‖ 3 *αὐτοῖς* om. L ‖ 4 *ὁμείρους* L ‖ 7 Εὐτροπίου P Εὐτρόπιον VL ‖ 8 Βόνου L ‖ 9 *αὐτοῖ* lit. ex *αὐτοῖς* V ‖ 10 *ἐνεπίμπρων* L ‖ 11 *ἑκάτερος* VL corr. vulg. ‖ 12 *τὰ* V Georg. Mon. 671.1 *τὰς* V^2 L ‖ Ἀσίτιδος V ‖ 14 *βάρβαροι* L Ἄβαροι V ‖ *συνετίθοντο* L ‖ 15–16 *τειχομάχια ἐτέκτενον* V ‖ 17 *προσίεσαν* L ‖ 18 *ἐξαπηνέως* V *ἐξαπηναῖος* L ‖ 19 δὲ om. L ‖ *Σκλάβινα πλήθει* L ‖ 20–21 *συμμαχεῖαν . . . δεδώκασι* L ‖ 24 *πλοῖμον* L ‖ *ἀναφανέντος* VL corr. vulg. ‖ *θορυβήσουσιν* V ‖ 26 *γένονται* L ‖ Βόνω L ‖ 27 *ἁρμώσας* L ‖ 28 *καθοπλήσας* L ‖ *προσώρμησεν* VL corr. B

⟨their land⟩." On receipt of this letter Sarbaros continued the siege.

13. The Avars, for their part, broke the treaty which Herakleios, before taking up arms against Persia, had confirmed by means of gifts—indeed, he promised to pay them 200,000 solidi and gave them as hostages one of his own sons, John by name, whom he had also called Atalarichos (he was a bastard born of a concubine), as well as his nephew Stephen (the son of his sister Maria and Eutropios) and, furthermore, another John, son of the patrician Bonos (also a bastard son born of a concubine). So they took up arms and drew near the walls of Byzantium, and straightaway they set fire to all the suburbs. Dividing, as it were, between themselves the Thracian Bosporos, the Persians destroyed the Asiatic part, while the Avars devastated the Thracian side, and they made a mutual agreement to capture Byzantium. Now the Avars constructed siege engines, namely, wooden towers and "tortoise shells"; but when these machines approached the walls, a divine force undid them and destroyed the Avar soldiers who were inside. Furthermore, the Avars had brought along a multitude of Slavonic allies and gave them the following signal, namely, that when the latter saw pyres kindled by the forward wall of the Blachernai (the one called Pteron), they would immediately set out in their hollowed-out canoes with a view to producing a mighty disturbance in the City by their sea-borne sortie, while ⟨the Avars⟩, seizing this opportunity, would climb up the walls and so get inside the City. When these moves became known to the patrician Bonos, he, too, fitted out biremes and triremes, which he armed and stationed at the spot where the signal was to be given; he

ὡσαύτως καὶ πρὸς τὴν ἀντιπέρα ἀκτὴν τὰς διήρεις ἐπέλασεν διαφρυκτωρεῖσθαί τε εὐθέως ἐπέτρεψεν. ὅπερ δὴ οἱ Σκλάβοι θεασάμενοι ἐκ τοῦ ποταμοῦ τοῦ καλουμένου Βαρβύσσου *ἀφώρμων καὶ κατὰ τῆς πόλεως ᾔεσαν. αἱ δὲ ἐπεκδραμοῦσαι καὶ εἰς μέσον αὐτοὺς ἀπολαβοῦσαι ἐκ τοῦ εὐθέως ἔκτεινον, καὶ αἵματι πολλῷ τὸ θαλάσσιον ὕδωρ ἐφοινίσσετο. ἐν τοῖς πτώμασιν οὖν τῶν ἀναιρεθέντων καὶ γυναῖκες* Σκλαβηναὶ *κατεφαίνοντο. ἀλλὰ ταῦτα οἱ* Ἄβαροι *θεασάμενοι καὶ τῆς προσεδρίας ἀπειπόντες πρὸς τὴν αὐτῶν ἀνεζεύγνυον. ὁ δὲ ἀρχιερεὺς τῆς πόλεως σὺν* Κωνσταντίνῳ *τῷ βασιλεῖ εὐχαριστηρίους λιτὰς τῷ θεῷ προσέφερον ἐν τῷ ναῷ τῆς θεομήτορος, τῷ* | [V190v] *ἐν* Βλαχέρναις *ἱδρυμένῳ ἀφικόμενοι· τεῖχος δὲ εὐθὺς δωμησάμενοι τοῦ ἱεροῦ ἐκείνου ναοῦ φρούριον κατέστησαν.* [dB19] *καὶ τὰ μὲν* Ἀβάρων *οὕτω πῃ ἔσχε.*

14. Μαθὼν δὲ Χοσρόης Ἡράκλειον *πλησιάσαντα τοῖς βασιλείοις* Περσῶν *ἐκπέμπει κατ᾽ αὐτοῦ στρατηγόν τινα* Ῥαζάτην *ὄνομα, γενναῖον ὄντα καὶ ἔμπειρον τὰ πολέμια. οὗτος ἐλθὼν τῷ βασιλεῖ παρατάσσεται, καὶ τῆς οἰκείας ἀφορμῶν φάλαγγος μόνος* | [L33v] *πρὸς μόνον προυκαλεῖτο διαμάχεσθαι.* Ἡράκλειος *δὲ ἐπεὶ οὐδένα τοῦ οἰκείου στρατοῦ προθυμούμενον ἐπεγίνωσκεν, αὐτὸς ἐξῄει κατὰ τοῦ βαρβάρου. ὁ δὲ ὡς τὴν τοξικὴν ἔμπειρος ὀϊστὸν ἠφίει καὶ ἄκρων χειλέων τοῦ βασιλέως καθήπτετο· εἶτα καὶ ἄλλον ὀϊστὸν ἐξέπεμψε καὶ τὸ σφυρὸν τοῦ ποδὸς ἐπέξυσεν. αὐτὸς δὲ* Ἡράκλειος *τῷ ἵππῳ ἐπῄει, καί τις τῶν αὐτοῦ δορυφόρων προφθάσας τὸν ὦμον* Ῥαζάτου *ξίφει ἀπέτεμε, καὶ αὐτὸν πεσόντα ὁ βασιλεὺς κατηκόντισε καὶ εὐθὺς τὴν τούτου κεφαλὴν ἀπέτεμεν. ἐπὶ δὲ τῇ νίκῃ ταύτῃ προθυμίας ὁ τῶν* Ῥωμαίων *στρατὸς πλησθείς, αἰσθόμενος τὴν τοῦ βασιλέως παρρησίαν, κατὰ* Περσῶν *ἐχώρουν συντονώτατα, καὶ ἀνὰ κράτος ἡττηθέντας ἐδίωκον καὶ πλῆθος αὐτῶν πολὺ ἀπέκτειναν.*

---

29 *ἀντίπερα ἀκτῖν* V *ἀντιπέρας ἀκτὶν* L corr. vulg. || 32 *ἴεσαν* L || 33 *εἰς μέσους* VL corr. vulg. || 35 Σκλαβίναι L || 36 Ἄβαροι L *ἄρβαροι* V^2 eraso *β* || 37 *αὐτῶν* V corr. vulg. *προσεδρείας . . . ἑαυτῶν ἀνεζ. γῆν* L || 39 *προσέφερεν* L || 40 *δὲ* om. V || 41 *δομησάμενοι* L

14: 3 Ῥιζάτην V || *γενναιὄντα* V corr. V^2 || 5 *πρὸς μόνῳ* V || 7 *ἐξίει* L || 8 *ὀϊστὸν . . . χειλῶν* L || 9 *πάλιν* post *εἶτα* add. L || *τὸ* L *τὸν* V || 10 *σφῦρον* ex *σφυρὸν* V^2 || 12 Ῥιζάτου V || 12–13 *κατηκόντησε* V || 13 *ἐπεὶ* V || 16 *κράτως* L

also drew up some biremes near the opposite shore and immediately directed them to light fires. The Slavs, upon seeing this, put out from the river called Barbysses and advanced upon the City; but ⟨the Roman ships⟩ moved out against them and, catching them in the middle, slaughtered them forthwith so that the sea was dyed with much blood. Among the dead bodies one could observe even those of Slav women. When the barbarians beheld this, they gave up the siege and returned home. As for the archpriest of the City and Emperor Constantine, they proceeded to the church of the Mother of God at Blachernai to offer unto God their prayers of thanksgiving; and straightaway they erected a wall to protect that sacred church. So much, then, for the Avars.

14. When Chosroes had been informed that Herakleios was close to the Persian royal residence, he sent out against him a brave and experienced general named Razates. This man drew up ⟨his forces⟩ against the emperor and, coming forward in front of his lines, delivered a challenge to a duel. When Herakleios realized that none of his men would volunteer, he went forth himself against the barbarian. Being an expert archer, ⟨Razates⟩ discharged an arrow which grazed the emperor's lips. He then shot a second arrow which scraped his ankle. Now Herakleios urged on his horse, and one of his bodyguard, who was ahead of him, sliced off with his sword the shoulder of Razates; and when the latter had fallen down, the emperor speared him and straightaway cut off his head. At the sight of this victory the Roman army was filled with ardor. Perceiving the emperor's boldness, they moved energetically against the Persians, whom they utterly defeated and pursued, killing a great number of them.

15. Οἱ δὲ Περσῶν ἄρχοντες ἐπεὶ διεγνώκεσαν ὡς ὁ τῶν
Ῥωμαίων βασιλεὺς ὑπὲρ τῆς ἑαυτοῦ πολιτείας τῆς οἰκείας
ζωῆς κατεφρόνησε, μετὰ Σειρόου τοῦ υἱοῦ Χοσρόου βουλεύ-
ονται Χοσρόην ἀνελεῖν, μέγα περὶ τῆς οἰκείας πολιτείας
καταφρονήσαντα. τοῦτον οὖν ἐφ' ἑνὶ τῶν βασιλικῶν οἴκων
κατέκλεισαν, καὶ τροφὴν μὲν οὐκ ἐδίδοσαν, προύθηκαν δὲ
χρυσὸν καὶ | ἄργυρον καὶ λίθον πλεῖστον λέγοντες "τούτων $L34^r$
ἀπόλαυε οἷς κατεμάνης καὶ ἅπερ ἠγάπησας καὶ συνήγα-
γες". καὶ οὕτω λιμώττοντα ἐπελθόντες ἀνεῖλον, Σειρόην δὲ
τὸν τούτου υἱὸν βασιλέα Περσῶν ἀνηγόρευσαν· ὃς εὐθὺς πρὸς dB20
Ἡράκλειον διαπρεσβεύεται δῶρά τε ἐξέπεμψεν ὡς σπείσε-
σθαι αὐτῷ. γράφει δὲ πρὸς αὐτὸν ἑνοῦσθαί τε ἀλλήλαις τὰς
ὑπ' αὐτοὺς πολιτείας καὶ εἰρήνην παρὰ θεοῦ ἀσπάζεσθαι, ὡς
ἑκάστην καθ' ἑαυτὴν ἐφησυχάζειν. ᾧ ἀντέγραφε καὶ Ἡρά-
κλειος, τέκνον τὸν Σειρόην καλῶν, καὶ ὡς οὐκ ἦν αὐτῷ ποτε
κατὰ γνώμην βασιλέα τῆς ἑαυτοῦ δόξης ἐκπεπτωκέναι· διὸ
οὐδὲ Χοσρόην. "ἀλλ' εἰ καὶ πλεῖστα καὶ κάκιστα Ῥωμαίοις
καὶ Πέρσαις ἐπέδειξεν, ἔσπευσα ἄν", ἔφασκε, "περισω-
θέντα, εἰ καὶ τὰ μάλιστα ἐπικρατέστερος ἐγενόμην, εἰς τὴν
ἑαυτοῦ ἀποκαθιστᾶν βασιλείαν. θεὸς δὲ τὴν ἐκείνου πρό-
θεσιν ἐγνωκὼς μετῆλθεν αὐτῷ ἀξίαν τὴν δίκην, ὡς μὴ τῶν
πολλῶν γενέσθαι κατάλυσιν, ἡμῖν νῦν τὴν ἕ|νωσιν παρα- $V191^r$
σχόμενος". περί τε τῶν ζῳοποιῶν ξύλων ὧν εἷλε Σάρβαρος ἐξ
Ἱεροσολύμων λιπαρῶς ἐπέκειτο ἐπιζητῶν· ὁ δὲ ὑπέσχετο δώ-
σειν, εἴπερ αὐτῷ κατάφωρα γένοιτο· περί τε τῶν πρεσβευτῶν
οὓς Σάϊτος πρὸς Χοσρόην ἀπήγαγε δόλῳ, ⟨ἔφασκεν⟩ ὡς Λεόν-
τιος μὲν κοινῷ θανάτῳ ἐτελεύτα, τοὺς δὲ ἄλλους Χοσρόης | $L34^v$
ξύλοις ἔκτεινεν, αἰσθόμενος τὸν Ἡράκλειον εἰς τὴν Περ-
σικὴν εἰσβαλόντα.

16. Εὐθὺς οὖν Σειρόης ἐτελεύτα, κρατεῖ δὲ τῆς βασι-
λείας Περσῶν Καβόης, ὅστις οὐ μετὰ πολὺ τέθνηκε. μεθ' ὃν

15: 1 *ἐπειδὴ ἐγνώκησαν* L ‖ 3 Σειρόου ex *σείρου* L^2 ‖ 4 *περὶ ἑαυτοῦ φρονήσαντα καὶ τῆς οἰκείας* incerta manus in mg. V ‖ 6 *τροφὴν* V^2 ex *τροφῆς* ‖ *μὲν* om. V ‖ *ἐδίδωσαν* L ‖ 7 *λίθον* ex *πον* V^1 ‖ 9 *λιμόττοντα* L ‖ 11–12 *πείσεσθαι* L ‖ 13 *ὑπ' αὐτοὺς* V^2 ex *ὑπ' αὐτοῦ* ‖ 14 *ἡσυχάζειν* V^1 *ἐφ'* V^2 superscr. ‖ 18 *ἔφασκε* om. L ‖ 19 *ἐγενάμην* L ‖ 20 *αὐτοῦ* V ‖ 21 *μετῆλθεν αὐτὸν ἀξίᾳ τῇ δίκῃ* coni. dB cf. **1**.26 ‖ 24 *λειπαρῶς* L ‖ 24–25 *δωσιν ἅπερ αὐτ. κατάφορα γένοιντο* L *κατάφορα* etiam V ‖ 26 δόλῳ] litt. ό in ras. scripta L^2, altera rasura post ω ‖ *ἔφασκεν* addidi: v. comment. ‖ *ὡς*] *ὧν* coni. dB ‖ 28 *τὸν* scripsi *αὐτὸν* VL *αὖ τὸν* N. Oikonomides, *Byzantion* 41 (1971) 278 n. 1 ‖ 29 *εἰσβάλλοντα* L

16: 2 *ὅστις* V^2 ex *εἴτις* ‖ *οὐ μετὰ πολὺ* L *οὐ μετ' οὐ πολὺ* V *μετ' οὐ πολὺ* vulg. ‖ *ὃν* V^2 ex *ὧν*

15. When the Persian noblemen became aware that the Roman emperor had made light of his own life for the sake of his state, they plotted with Chosroes' son Seiroes to slay Chosroes, inasmuch as he had shown great neglect of his country. So they imprisoned him in one of the royal palaces and gave him no food, but set before him a heap of gold and silver and precious stones, saying: "Do enjoy these things which you have loved insanely and amassed." In this way they starved him to death and proclaimed his son Seiroes king of Persia. The latter immediately sent an embassy and gifts to Herakleios with a view to coming to terms. And he wrote to him that their respective states should be reconciled and embrace peace at God's hands so that each might live in tranquillity. Herakleios wrote back, calling Seiroes his son and ⟨saying⟩ that it had never been his wish that a king—not even Chosroes—should lose his glory. "Even though he had inflicted innumerable woes upon Romans and Persians, I would have hastened," he said, "were he to have survived, to restore him to his own kingship, complete though my victory over him might have been. But God, knowing his purpose, has wreaked upon him a just punishment so as to prevent universal destruction, and has now bestown concord upon us." He also made a fervent plea concerning the Holy Cross, which Sarbaros had removed from Jerusalem. ⟨Seiroes⟩ promised to deliver it if he was able to find it; and concerning the ambassadors whom Saitos had conducted to Chosroes by deceit, ⟨he said⟩ that Leontios had died a natural death, while the others Chosroes had killed by flogging when he heard that Herakleios had invaded Persia.

16. Soon thereafter Seiroes died and the Persian kingdom passed to Kaboes, who ⟨also⟩ died after a short time. After him Hormisdas became king

βασιλεύει Περσῶν Ὁρμίσδας, ὃς καὶ αὐτὸς διαπρεσβεύεται πρὸς Ἡράκλειον, τόν τε ἴδιον υἱὸν σὺν χρήμασι καὶ δώροις πολυτιμήτοις πρὸς αὐτὸν ἀπέστειλεν. ἐσήμαινε δὲ διὰ γραμμάτων τάδε "ὃν τρόπον λέγετε τὸν θεὸν ὑμῶν δοθῆναι γηραιῷ τινι ἀνθρώπῳ Συμεὼν εἰς τὰς ἀγκάλας, οὕτως καὶ τὸν δοῦλόν σου τὸν υἱόν μου δίδωμι εἰς τὰς χεῖράς σου. γνοίη δὲ θεὸς ὃν dB21 σέβῃ, ὡς ποιήσεις αὐτῷ". ὁ δὲ δεξάμενος μεγάλως ἐτίμησε, καὶ εἶτα τελευτήσαντος Ὁρμίσδου βασιλέα Περσῶν ἐτίμησε.

17. Σάρβαρος δὲ ἀκούσας ὅτι Χοσρόης καὶ Σειρόης, Καβόης καὶ Ὁρμίσδας ἐτελεύτησαν, ἐκ τῆς Ῥωμαίων ὑπενόστει χώρας, γράφει τε ἀπολογίαν πρὸς Ἡράκλειον, ὡς οὐχ ἑκὼν ἀλλὰ γνώμῃ τοῦ ἀποστείλαντος ἔπραττεν ἅπερ εἰς Ῥωμαίους πεποίηκε, καὶ παραγενέσθαι ὡς αὐτὸν ἐξῄτησε καὶ ὡς δοῦλον παρίστασθαι. λόγοις τε πίστεως παρὰ βασιλέως βεβαιωθεὶς ἧκεν πρὸς αὐτὸν καὶ χρήματα ἐκ Περσίδος διδόναι ὑπισχνεῖτο, δι' ὧν πάλιν καινίζοιντο ὅσα ἂν αὐτὸς ἐν χώρᾳ τῇ Ῥωμαίων κατεστρέψατο. ἐν τούτοις | ἐπιβουλεύεται L35r καὶ ἀναιρεῖται ὁ υἱὸς Ὁρμίσδου, καὶ Σάρβαρος παρὰ βασιλεῖ τὴν Περσῶν ἀρχὴν ἐξαιτεῖ. ὁ δὲ ἐδίδου, καὶ ἀλλήλοις συνετίθεντο πάντα τὰ ἐκ Ῥωμαίων ὑπὸ Πέρσαις γενόμενα Ῥωμαίοις ἀνασώζεσθαι. εἰρήνης τε βραβευθείσης εὐθὺς τήν τε Αἴγυπτον καὶ πᾶσαν τὴν ἀνατολικὴν γῆν Ῥωμαίοις ἀποδίδωσι Σάρβαρος, τοὺς ἐκεῖσε Πέρσας ἐξελών, τά τε ζῳοποιὰ ξύλα πρὸς βασιλέα στέλλει. Ἡράκλειος δὲ Νικήταν υἱὸν Σαρβάρου πατρικίου ἀξίᾳ ἐτίμησε, Νίκην τε τὴν θυγατέρα αὐτοῦ Θεοδοσίῳ τῷ ἐκ Μαρτίνης υἱῷ αὐτοῦ γαμετὴν πεποίηκε. Γρηγορίαν τε τὴν θυγατέρα Νικήτα ἐκ Πενταπόλεως ἐνέγκας Κωνσταντίνῳ τῷ βασιλεῖ Ῥωμαίων ζεύγνυσιν· ἣν δὴ καὶ προμνηστευσάμενος ἦν περιόντος ἔτι τοῦ αὐτῆς πατρός.

18. Ὑπὸ δὲ τὸν αὐτὸν καιρὸν ἐκ τοῦ Αἰθρίβου λεγομένου

---

5 *ἀπέστελλεν καὶ ἐσήμαινεν* L || 7 Συμεῶν V Συμεῶνι L || *οὕτως* ex *οὗτος* V^2 || 8 *σου* V *σον* L || 9 *σέβης . . . ποιήσης* L *σέβεις* ex *σέβῃ* V^2 || 10 *καὶ* om. L

17: 2 *καὶ* ante Καβόης add. L || Ὁρμήσδας ἐτελεύτησεν L || 3 *τὲ* accentu a V^2 addito || 5 *καὶ* superscr. L om. V || *ὡς* L] *δὲ* V signo % addito a V^2 || 6 *τὲ* V || 7 *βεβαιωθεὶς* V^2 ex *βεβαιωθὲν* ut vid. || *ἥκειν* V || 8 *ὑπισχεῖτο* V || 8–9 *καινοίζοιντο . . . τῆς* Ῥωμαίων L || 10 Ὁρμίσδου ex Ὁρμίδου V^1 || 11–12 *ἐζήτει . . . συνετήθοντο* L || 14–15 *ἀποδίδοσι* L || 18 *αὐτοῦ*]–*τοῦ* in lit. V^2 || Θεοδωσίω L || 19 *θυγατέραν* L || Πενταπόλεως V^2 ex Πεντάπολιν ut vid. || 21 *ἦν* om. L || *αὐτῆς* V *αὐτοῦ* L

of the Persians. He, too, treated with Herakleios and sent to him his own son along with a sum of money and precious gifts. He stated the following in his letter: "Just as you claim that your God was delivered into the arms of an old man ⟨called⟩ Symeon, so I am delivering into your hands my son who is your slave. May the God whom you worship watch how you treat him." Upon receiving him, ⟨Herakleios⟩ honored him greatly, and when Hormisdas had died, he recognized him as king of Persia.

17. Now Sarbaros, when he had heard that Chosroes and Seiroes, Kaboes and Hormisdas had ⟨all⟩ died, returned from the Roman country and wrote an apology to Herakleios, namely, that what he had done to the Romans was committed not of his own free will, but by order of his sovereign, and he begged permission to be received and to present himself like a slave. Upon receiving from the emperor a sworn assurance, he promised to appear before him and bring money from Persia so as to repair whatever he had destroyed in the Roman country. At this juncture the son of Hormisdas fell victim to a plot and was slain; and Sarbaros requested from the emperor the Persian crown. The latter gave it to him, and they agreed among themselves that all the Roman territory occupied by the Persians should be restored to the Romans. When peace had been concluded, Sarbaros immediately returned to the Romans both Egypt and all the eastern lands after withdrawing the Persians that were there; and he sent to the emperor the life-giving Cross. Now Herakleios conferred the dignity of patrician upon Niketas, son of Sarbaros, and gave the latter's daughter Nike in marriage to his own son Theodosios, born of Martina. He also brought from Pentapolis Gregoria, daughter of Niketas,[11] and wed her (whom he had already betrothed in her father's lifetime) to Constantine, emperor of the Romans.

18. At about this time the Saracens began to appear from Aithribos, as

[11] Herakleios' cousin.

Σαρακηνοὶ διεφαίνοντο (χώρα δὲ τοῦτο τῆς εὐδαίμονος Ἀραβίας) καὶ τὰ ἐκεῖσε χωρία προσπελάζοντα ληΐζεσθαι ἐπεχείρουν. Ἡράκλειος δὲ τὴν θυγατέρα Εὐδοκίαν τοῦ Βυζαντίου ἐξιέναι ἐπέτρεψεν ὡς τῷ Τούρκῳ ταύτην κατεγγυήσας· καὶ ἐπειδὴ ἔγνωστο ὅτι σφαγῇ ὁ Τοῦρκος ἀνῄρητο, ταύτην dB22 ὑπο|στρέφειν ἐκέλευεν. ὑπάρχοντι δὲ Ἡρακλείῳ ἐν τῇ Περσικῇ V191v ἐτελεύτησαν αὐτῷ δύο υἱοὶ καὶ θυγατέρες δύο. | αὐτὸς L35v δὲ λαβὼν τὰ ζῳοποιὰ ξύλα ἐσφραγισμένα, καθάπερ ἐλήφθησαν διαμείναντα, πρὸς τὰ Ἱεροσόλυμα ἀφίκετο, καὶ Μωδέστῳ τῷ ἀρχιερεῖ καὶ τῷ αὐτοῦ κλήρῳ ταῦτα ὑπέδειξεν. οἱ δὲ τὴν σφραγῖδα σώαν ἐπεγίνωσκον· καὶ ὡς ἀνέπαφα καὶ ἀθέατα βεβήλοις καὶ μιαιφόνοις χερσὶ τῶν βαρβάρων διετηρήθησαν, εὐχαριστήριον ᾠδὴν τῷ θεῷ ἀνέθεσαν. τήν τε κλεῖδα τὴν ἐπ' αὐτοῖς ὁ ἱεράρχης μείνασαν παρ' αὐτῷ ἤγαγε, καὶ ἀνοιγνὺς προσκυνοῦσιν ἅπαντες. ὑψωθέντων δὲ αὐτῶν ἐκεῖσε εὐθὺς εἰς τὸ Βυζάντιον ὁ βασιλεὺς ἐξέπεμψεν. ἃ δὴ Σέργιος ὁ τοῦ Βυζαντίου ἱεράρχης ἐκ Βλαχερνῶν (ἱερὸν δὲ αἱ Βλαχέρναι τῆς θεομήτορος) λιτανεύων ὑπεδέξατο καὶ πρὸς τὴν μεγίστην ἐκκλησίαν ἀγαγὼν ταῦτα ἀνύψωσε. δευτέρα δὲ ἦν ἰνδικτιὼν ἡνίκα ταῦτα ἐπράττοντο.

19. Μετ' οὐ πολὺ δὲ καὶ Ἡράκλειος πρὸς τὸ Βυζάντιον ἐχώρει, ὑπὸ πολλῆς εὐφημίας καὶ δόξης ὑπερβαλλούσης παρὰ τῶν ἐκεῖσε δεχθείς. τέσσαρας δὲ ἦγεν ἐλέφαντας, οὓς δὴ καὶ εἰς τοὺς ἱππικοὺς ἀγῶνας ἐθριάμβευεν ἐπὶ τῇ τῆς πόλεως τέρψει, ἡμέρας τε ἐπινικίους ἐπ' εὐφροσύνῃ πᾶσι δωρεαῖς φιλοτιμούμενος ἐπετέλει. ἐπειδὴ δὲ ἦν ἑλὼν τῆς οὐσίας τῆς μεγάλης ἐκκλησίας, ἐκέλευσεν ἐκ τοῦ βασιλικοῦ ταμιείου | αὐτῇ τε καὶ τῷ κατ' αὐτὴν κλήρῳ ἐτήσια χρήματα L36r

---

18: 2–3 Ἀραβείας L ‖ 5 κατεγγυῆσαι VL corr. vulg. ‖ 6 ἐπεὶ διέγνωστο L ‖ ἀναιρεῖτο VL corr. B ‖ 7 ἐκέλευσεν L ‖ ὑπάρχοντι usque ad **19.**11 cf. Sudam s.v. Ἡράκλειος βασιλεύς ‖ 9–10 ἐλείφθησαν V +ὑπὸ Σαρβάρου Sab ‖ 10 πρὸς] εἰς Suda ‖ 10–11 Μοδέστῳ Suda, Sab ‖ 11 αὐτοῦ κλήρῳ ταῦτα] –ου –ρω V^2 in ras.; –ρω τα– L^2 in ras.; αὐτῷ κλήρῳ Sab ‖ 12 τήν τε Sab ‖ σῶαν ἐπέγνωσαν L ἐπιγινώσκουσι Sab ‖ 13 καὶ μιαιφόνοις om. Sab ‖ 15 παρ' αὐτοῖς Sab ‖ 16 ἀνοιγνὺς scripsi ἀναγνὺς L ἀνοιγέντα ex ἀναγνόντας V (incerta manus) ἀνοιγνύντος Sab ‖ 17 εὐθὺς om. Sab ‖ ἐς Suda ‖ 18–19 ἱερὸν . . . θεομήτορος om. Sab ‖ 19 ὑπεδέχετο Sab

---

19: 1 πρὸς τὸ] ἐς Suda ‖ 2 ὑπὸ] μετὰ Suda ‖ 3 ἤγαγεν V^2 ‖ 4 ἐθριάμβευσεν Suda ‖ 5 πάσῃ ex πᾶσι V^2 πάσαις Suda ‖ 6 ἑλῶν L ‖ ἐκ τῆς οὐσίας Suda ‖ 7 βασιλικοῦ ex βασιλεικοῦ L ‖ 8 αὐτῇ] αὐτὴν L

it is called (this being a country of Arabia the Blessed) and attempted to lay waste neighboring villages. As for Herakleios, he directed that his daughter Eudokia should depart from Byzantium inasmuch as he had betrothed her to ⟨the lord of⟩ the Turks; but when it became known that the Turk had been slain, he ordered her to return. While Herakleios was in Persia, two of his sons and two of his daughters died. Taking the life-giving Cross (which had remained under seal as it was when it was removed), he came to Jerusalem and exhibited it to the archpriest Modestos and his clergy, who acknowledged the seal to be intact. Seeing that ⟨the Cross⟩ had been preserved untouched by the profane and murderous hands of the barbarians and unseen by them, they offered to God a hymn of thanksgiving. The bishop produced the appropriate key which had remained in his possession and, when the Cross was opened, everyone worshiped it. And after it had been elevated there, the emperor immediately sent it to Byzantium. Sergios, the archpriest of Byzantium, received it in procession at Blachernai (which is a church of the Mother of God) and, after bringing it to the Great Church, he elevated it. This happened in the 2nd indiction.

19. A short time thereafter Herakleios, too, came to Byzantium and was received by its inhabitants with great acclamation and exceeding honor. He brought four elephants, which he paraded at the hippodrome contests to the delight of the citizens, and celebrated ⟨several⟩ days of triumph and distributed largesse to everyone. And since he had alienated some of the property of the Great Church, he commanded that an annual subsidy should be paid to

παρέχεσθαι. καὶ μετὰ τοῦτο παρασκευάζει Κωνσταντῖνον τὸν υἱὸν ὑπατεῦσαι, Ἡράκλειον δὲ τὸν ἀπὸ Μαρτίνης Καίσαρα dB23 *προχειρίζεται.*

20. *Οὐ πολὺς δὲ χρόνος ἐν μέσῳ, καὶ Σαρακηνοὶ τὰ περὶ τὴν Ἀντιόχειαν κατέτρεχον. εὐθέως δὲ Ἡράκλειος σὺν Μαρτίνῃ τῇ γυναικὶ καὶ Ἡρακλείῳ τῷ παιδὶ πρὸς τοῖς τῆς ἀνατολῆς χωρίοις ἐπεξῄει. αὐτόθι δὲ γενόμενος Θεοδώρῳ τῷ ἀδελφῷ ὀργίζεται· ὑπεψιθυρίζετο δέ τισι λοιδορεῖσθαι αὐτὸν τῷ βασιλεῖ Μαρτίνης ἕνεκεν, λέγοντα ὅτι "ἡ ἁμαρτία αὐτοῦ ἐνώπιον αὐτοῦ διὰ παντός". καὶ αὐτὸν εἰς Βυζάντιον ἀποστέλλει, γράψας τῷ υἱῷ Κωνσταντίνῳ τοῦτον ἐπ' ἀθροίσματος λαοῦ ἀτιμώσαντα ὡς ἐν φρουρᾷ κατέχειν. στρατηγόν τε ἀνατολῆς ἐκπέμπει Θεόδωρον, τῶν βασιλικῶν χρημάτων ταμίαν, τὸ ἐπίκλην Τριθύριον. Σέργιος γὰρ ὁ κατὰ Νικήταν τελευτᾷ τρόπῳ τοιῷδε. κάμηλον οἱ Σαρακηνοὶ ἀποδείραντες τοῦτον ἐγκατακλείουσι τῇ δορᾷ καὶ ἀπέρραπτον. τῆς βύρσης οὖν κατεσκληκυίας συναπεξηραίνετο καὶ ὁ ἐντὸς ἀπειλημένος ἄνθρωπος, καὶ οὕτως ἀπομαρανθεὶς πικρῶς διώλετο. αἰτίαν δὲ αὐτῷ ἐπῆγον ὡς αὐτὸς πα|ρεσκεύ|ασεν Ἡράκλειον μὴ συγχωρεῖν* V192r *Σαρακηνοῖς ἐκ τῆς Ῥωμαίων γῆς ἐμπορεύεσθαι τάς* L36v *⟨τε⟩ συνήθως παρεχομένας αὐτοῖς τριάκοντα χρυσίου λίτρας δι' ἐμπορικῆς ἀμοιβῆς ἐκ τῆς Ῥωμαϊκῆς πολιτείας ἐκπέμπειν· ἐντεῦθέν τε αὐτοὺς ἄρξαι τῇ Ῥωμαίων λυμαίνεσθαι χώρᾳ. ἐκ τούτου παρήγγειλε Θεόδωρος μὴ συμβάλλειν πρὸς μάχην Σαρακηνοῖς. ὁ δὲ ὑπ' αὐτὸν στρατηγὸς τὰ κατὰ γνώμην τῷ βασιλεῖ οὐκ ἔπραττεν, ἐπεὶ νεώτερα αὐτῷ βουλευσάμενος ἦν, καὶ ἐπεὶ παρήγοντο πολεμεῖν ὡς ἀνελπίστων περιέσεσθαι τῶν πολεμίων, καὶ συνεργὸν ὑπελάμβανον τὴν νίκην τῆς κατὰ τοῦ βασιλέως ἐπαναστάσεως. ἔτι τοίνυν ἐν τόπῳ καλουμένῳ Γαβιθὰ συγκαταμίγνυσι Σαρακηνοῖς. οἱ δὲ*

---

10 δὲ] *τε* L Suda

20: 2 *εὐθέως* LV² *εὐθὺς* V ‖ 4 *ἐπεξείη . . . γενάμενος* L ‖ 5 *ὑπεψηθυρίζετο . . . λοιδορεῖσθαι αὐτῶ* L ‖ 6 *Μαρτιν* sine accentu V –*ης* suppl. V² ‖ Psalm. 50.5 ‖ 10 *τῶν*] *τὸν* superscr. V² ‖ 10–11 *ταμείαν τὸ* fort. ex *τὸν* ultima litt. erasa L ‖ 11 *ἐπίκλιν* V ‖ *Τρίθυρον* L ‖ 13 *ἐπέρραπτον* V ‖ 14–15 *ἀπειλειμμένος ἄνθρ.* L om. V *ἀπειλημμένος* Or ‖ 15 *καὶ* om. V add. V² ‖ *οὕτως* om. V ‖ *ἀπομαρανθεὶς* LV² *ἀπομαρανθὲν* V ‖ 16 *ἐπεῖγον* V ‖ 17 *ἐκ τῆς . . . ἐκπορεύεσθσι* (sic) secl. dB ‖ *ἐμπορεύεσθαι* L item ex *ἐκπορεύεσθαι* V² ‖ 18 *τε* addidi ‖ *λίτρας* V² in lacuna ‖ 21 *Θεοδώρω* V² ex *Θεοδωρο* vel *Θεοδωρος* sine accentu *Θεόδωρος* Ševčenko v. comment. ‖ 22–27 *ὁ δὲ . . . Σαρακηνοῖς* om. V ‖ 23 *νεώτερος αὐτῶ* L corr. Ševčenko ‖ 24 *ἀνελπίστων* scripsi *ἀνελπίστους* L

it and to its clergy. After this he made arrangements for his son Constantine to assume the consulship and appointed Herakleios, the son of Martina, Caesar.

20. After a short lapse of time the Saracens overran the region round Antioch. Straightaway Herakleios, together with his wife Martina and his son Herakleios, went forth to the eastern parts. When he arrived there, he became incensed at his brother Theodore, for it was rumored in some quarters that the latter was railing at the emperor on account of Martina and saying that "His sin is continually before him." So he dispatched him to Byzantium and instructed his son Constantine to have him dishonored in front of a public assembly and to hold him in prison. And he appointed commander of the eastern ⟨forces⟩ Theodore surnamed Trithyrios, the imperial treasurer. Now Sergios *kata Niketan*[12] died in the following manner. The Saracens, having flayed a camel, enclosed him in the hide and sewed it up. As the skin hardened, the man who was left inside also withered and so perished in a painful manner. The charge against him was that he had persuaded Herakleios not to allow the Saracens to trade from the Roman country and send out of the Roman State the 30 lbs. of gold which they normally received by way of commercial gain; and for this reason they began to lay waste the Roman land. On this account ⟨Herakleios⟩ ordered Theodore not to join battle with the Saracens; but his subordinate commander did not act according to the emperor's wishes because he had rebellion in mind and ⟨the men⟩ were induced to fight so as to overcome the enemy unexpectedly: they believed that victory would be on the side of the insurgents against the emperor. And so he joined battle with the Saracens at a place called Gabitha. But they, having set ambuscades beforehand and

[12] See Commentary.

προλοχήσαντες καὶ ὀλίγοις τισὶν ἀκροβολισάμενοι Ῥωμαίοις ὑπήγοντο. εἰσπίπτουσι δὲ αὐτοῖς οἱ ἐκ τῶν ἐνεδρῶν ἐξαπιναίως, καὶ μέσον ἀπολαβόντες πολλοὺς ἔκτειναν στρατιώτας dB24
τε καὶ ἄρχοντας.

21. Κατὰ δὲ τὸν καιρὸν ἐκεῖνον Μαρία ἡ ἀδελφὴ Ἡρακλείου χρήματα πρὸς τὸν χαγάνον Ἀβάρων ἔπεμψε καὶ τὸν υἱὸν Στέφανον ἀπέλαβε. τοῖς δὲ τοιούτοις δώροις ἡσθεὶς ὁ Ἄβαρος ἠρέθισεν Ἀνιανὸν τὸν μάγιστρον, ὡς καὶ αὐτὸς πέμψας δῶρα ἀπολήψεται καὶ τοὺς ἄλλους | οὕσπερ κατεῖχεν L37r
ὁμήρους. καὶ δὴ καὶ ἐγένετο οὕτως.

22. Ὑπὸ δὲ τὸν αὐτὸν καιρὸν ἐπανέστη Κούβρατος ὁ ἀνεψιὸς Ὀργανᾶ ὁ τῶν Οὐνογουνδούρων κύριος τῷ τῶν Ἀβάρων χαγάνῳ, καὶ ὃν εἶχε παρ' αὐτοῦ λαὸν περιυβρίσας ἐξεδίωξε τῆς οἰκείας γῆς. διαπρεσβεύεται δὲ πρὸς Ἡράκλειον καὶ σπένδεται εἰρήνην μετ' αὐτοῦ, ἥνπερ ἐφύλαξαν μέχρι τέλους τῆς ἑαυτῶν ζωῆς· δῶρά τε γὰρ αὐτῷ ἔπεμψε καὶ τῇ τοῦ πατρικίου ἀξίᾳ ἐτίμησεν.

23. Ἐν ᾧ δὲ ἐν τοῖς ἀνατολικοῖς μέρεσι διέτριβεν Ἡράκλειος, Ἰωάννην τὸν Βαρκαίνης στρατηγὸν προχειρίζεται καὶ πέμπει κατὰ Σαρακηνῶν τῶν ἐν Αἰγύπτῳ· οἷς συμβαλὼν πίπτει καὶ αὐτός. ἔτι καὶ Μαρῖνος ὁ τῶν Θρᾳκικῶν ἐκστρατευμάτων ἡγεμὼν συμμίξας αὐτοῖς ἡττήθη, πολύν τε στρατὸν ἀποβαλὼν καὶ αὐτὸς μόλις διασώζεται. μετ' ἐκεῖνον προβάλλεται στρατηγὸν Μαριανὸν κουβικουλάριον παρὰ Ῥωμαίων τὴν ἀξίαν καὶ πέμπει ἐκεῖσε, παραγγείλας ὡς ἀνακοινοῦσθαι Κύρῳ τῷ Ἀλεξανδρείας ἱεράρχῃ, καὶ ὡς ἂν κοινῇ βουλεύσοιντο ⟨καὶ⟩ τὰ πρὸς τοὺς Σαρακηνοὺς διάθοιντο. Κῦρος δὲ ἦν δεδηλωκὼς βασιλεῖ σπείσεσθαι ἐπὶ τελέσμασιν Ἄμβρῳ τῷ τῶν Σαρακηνῶν φυλάρχῳ, ἃ δὴ καὶ ὑπέχειν δι' ἐμπολαίου συνεισφορᾶς ἐσήμαινε, τὰ δὲ τῷ βασιλεῖ παρεχό-

---

28 ἀκροβολησάμενοι L ‖ 29 ὑπήγοντο LV² ὑπείγοντο V ‖ δὲ V γε L ‖ 29–30 ἐξαπηναίως VL

21: 2 χαγᾶνον V ‖ 6 ὁμείρους. καὶ δὴ οὕτως ἐγένετο L

22: 1 Κούβαρος L ‖ 2 Ἀργανᾶ . . . Οὐννογουνδούρων L ‖ 3 περιυβρήσας L ‖ 5 μεθ' εαυτοῦ . . . φυλάξει L ‖ 6 ἑαυτῶν V αὐτοῦ L ‖ γὰρ om. L

23: 5 τε L δὲ V ‖ 10 κοινὴ L ‖ βουλεύσοιντο secl. dB ‖ καὶ addidi ‖ 11 Κύρος V ‖ 13 ἐμπολέου . . . ἐσήμανεν. τάδε L ‖ τῶ βασιλει ex τῶν βασιλειῶν V¹

skirmished with a few men, advanced on the Romans. The ambushed men fell suddenly on the latter and, having surrounded them, slew many soldiers and officers.

21. At the same time Maria, the sister of Herakleios, sent money to the Chagan of the Avars and ransomed her son Stephen. Pleased with such gifts, the Avar ⟨chief⟩ urged Anianos the magister that he, too, should send gifts and ransom the other hostages he was holding; which, indeed, was done.

22. At about the same time Koubratos, the nephew of Organas and lord of the Onogundurs, rose up against the Chagan of the Avars and, after abusing the army he had from the latter, drove them out of his land. He sent an embassy to Herakleios and concluded a peace treaty which they observed until the end of their lives. ⟨Herakleios⟩ sent him gifts and honored him with the title of patrician.

23. While Herakleios was dwelling in the eastern parts, he appointed John of Barkaina general of the army and sent him against the Saracens in Egypt. He joined battle with them and was himself killed. Likewise Marinos, commander of the Thracian contingents, engaged them in battle and was defeated: he lost many soldiers and himself barely escaped. In succession to him ⟨Herakleios⟩ conferred the army command on Marianos, who held the Roman rank of *cubicularius*, and dispatched him with instructions to consult with Kyros, archpriest of Alexandria, that they might take joint action with regard to the Saracens. Now Kyros had informed the emperor that he was going to conclude an agreement with Ambros, phylarch of the Saracens, and ⟨pay him⟩ tribute which, he stated, he would raise by a commercial levy, while the impe-

μενα | ἀδιάπτωτα μένειν· κατεγγυηθῆναι δὲ αὐτῷ Εὐδοκίαν (L37v) τὴν Αὐγούσταν, [ἣ] μίαν τῶν θυγατέρων τοῦ βασιλέως, ὡς (dB25) ἐντεῦθεν καὶ τῷ θείῳ λουτρῷ βαπτισθησομένῳ καὶ Χριστιανῷ χρηματίσοντι. ἐπείθετο γὰρ Ἄμβρος τῷ Κύρῳ καὶ ὁ τούτου στρατός· καὶ γὰρ ἠγάπων αὐτὸν λίαν. καὶ τούτων Ἡράκλειος οὐδενὸς ἠνείχετο. ἐπειδὴ δὲ καὶ Μαριανὸς ταῦτα ἐξηπίστατο, διίστατο τῆς τοῦ Κύρου γνώμης, καὶ συμβαλὼν Σαρακηνοῖς πίπτει τε αὐτὸς καὶ σὺν αὐτῷ στρατὸς ἱκανός.

24. Τούτῳ τῷ χρόνῳ ἀνέζευξε πρὸς τὰ | οἰκεῖα Ἡράκλειος (V192v) καὶ ηὐλίζετο ἐν τῷ παλατίῳ τῷ καλουμένῳ τῆς Ἱερίας· ἐδεδίει γὰρ ἐπιβῆναι θαλάσσης, πολλά τε ἀξιοῦντες οἵ τε ἄρχοντες καὶ οἱ τῆς πόλεως ἐν τῇ πόλει εἰσελθεῖν ἔπειθον οὐδαμῶς. ἐν δὲ ταῖς ἑορταῖς μόνους τοὺς υἱοὺς ἐξέπεμπε, καὶ οὗτοι ἐπιτελοῦντες ἐν τῷ ἱερῷ τὴν θείαν λειτουργίαν εὐθὺς πρὸς αὐτὸν ἐξῄεσαν. ὡσαύτως καὶ τοὺς ἱππικοὺς ἀγῶνας ἡνίκα ἐθεῶντο, πάλιν πρὸς τὸν πατέρα ἀπεχώρουν. ἐν ᾧ δὲ διέτριβεν ἐκεῖσε, ἀγγέλλεται αὐτῷ ὡς ὁ υἱὸς αὐτοῦ Ἀταλάριχος καὶ Θεόδωρος ὁ τὴν ἀξίαν μάγιστρος, Θεοδώρου δὲ τοῦ βασιλέως ἀδελφοῦ υἱός, σὺν ἄλλοις τισὶν ἐπιβουλεύειν αὐτῷ ἤμελλον· καὶ τοῖς μηνύσασι πεισθεὶς | τούτων τὰς ῥῖνας καὶ (L38r) τὰς χεῖρας ἐξέτεμε, καὶ Ἀταλάριχον μὲν εἰς τὴν νῆσον τὴν λεγομένην Πρίγκιπον ἐξόριστον ἔπεμψε, Θεόδωρον δὲ πρὸς τὴν νῆσον Γαυδομελέτην προσαγορευομένην, ἐπιτρέψας τῷ ἐκεῖσε δουκί, ἡνίκα πρὸς αὐτὸν καταλάβοι, καὶ τὸν ἕτερον τῶν ποδῶν ἀφελέσθαι. κατὰ ταῦτα δὲ καὶ τοὺς συγγνόντας αὐτοῖς τὰ τῆς ἐπιβουλῆς ἐτιμωρήσατο.

25. Χρόνου δὲ ἱκανοῦ διελθόντος παρασκευάζουσιν οἱ τοῦ βασιλέως ἄρχοντες τὸν ἔπαρχον ὡς συναγαγεῖν πλεῖστα πλοῖα καὶ ἐχόμενα ἀλλήλοις ἐξάψας ὥσπερ γεφυρώσει τὸν (dB26)

---

15 ἣ secl. Ševčenko ἣ *μία* L || 16 *τῷ* om. L || 17 Κῦρω L accentu a corr. add. || 19 *δὲ* V *γὰρ* L || 20 *τοῦ Κύρου* V[1] ex *τούτου*

24: 2 Ἱερείας. *ἐδεδείη* L *τὰ* Ἡρία Suda s.v. Ἡράκλειος || 3 *θαλάσσῃ* V || 5 *τοὺς υἱοὺς ἐν τῇ πολει ἐξέπεμπε* L || 6 *οὗτοι* L *αὐτοὶ* V || 7 *ἐξίεσαν. ὡσαύτως δὲ καὶ* L || 8 *ἐθέοντο* VL corr. vulg. || 10 *μαγίστρος* VL || 11 *ἀδελφοῦ υἱός* om. L || 12 *ἔμελλον . . . πισθεὶς* L || 14 Πρίγγιπον VL corr. vulg. || 16 *τὸ ἕτερον* L || 17 *ταὐτὰ* coni. dB || *συγγνῶντας* L

25: 2–10 Cf. Sudam s.v. Ἡράκλειος || 2 *ἔπαρχον τῆς πόλεως* L *ὕπαρχον* Suda || 2–3 *συναγαγὼν . . . γεφυρώσειε* coni. dB

rial taxes would not be affected. ⟨He also recommended⟩ that the Augusta Eudokia or another of the emperor's daughters should be offered in marriage ⟨to Ambros⟩ with a view to his being consequently baptized in the holy bath and becoming a Christian; for Ambros and his army had confidence in Kyros and regarded him with great affection. But Herakleios would not brook any of this. Since Marianos, too, was aware of these matters, he rejected the policy of Kyros and, having attacked the Saracens, fell in battle as did many of his soldiers.

24. At this time Herakleios returned home and resided in the palace called Hieria; for he was afraid of embarking on the sea and remained unmoved by the noblemen and citizens who repeatedly begged him to enter the City. On feast days he would dispatch only his sons who, after attending holy liturgy in the church, immediately returned to him. And likewise, when they watched the hippodrome games, they went back to their father. While he was dwelling there he was informed that his son Atalarichos and Theodore, who had the rank of magister (the son of Theodore, the emperor's brother), together with some others, were about to plot against him. He was persuaded by the informants and cut off the noses and hands ⟨of the conspirators⟩. He exiled Atalarichos to the island called Prinkipos and Theodore to the island called Gaudomelete, with instructions to the local commander to amputate also one of ⟨Theodore's⟩ legs upon his arrival. He punished in the same manner those who were privy to the conspiracy.

25. After a considerable lapse of time the noblemen of the court caused the prefect to collect a great many ships and tie them one next to the other so

πορθμὸν τοῦ καλουμένου Στενοῦ, κλώνοις τε δένδρων καὶ φυλλάσιν ἑκατέρωθεν διατειχίσειεν, ὡς μηδὲ ὁρᾶσθαι παριόντι τὴν θάλασσαν. καὶ δὴ τὸ ἔργον εἰς τάχος προυχώρει, καὶ ὁ βασιλεὺς ἱππεὺς διὰ θαλάττης ὥσπερ διά τῆς ἠπείρου κατὰ τὰς ἀκτὰς τοῦ λεγομένου κόλπου Φιδαλείας ἐπεραιοῦτο, οὗ τε τὸν παράκτιον χῶρον παραμείψας διὰ τῆς γεφύρας τοῦ Βαρβύσσου ποταμοῦ πρὸς τὸ Βυζάντιον εἰσῄει. καὶ μετὰ ταῦτα Ἡράκλειον τὸν Καίσαρα στέφει βασιλέα.

26. Κατὰ δὲ τὴν δωδεκάτην ἰνδικτιόνα ἐτελεύτα Σέργιος ὁ τοῦ Βυζαντίου πρόεδρος. καὶ ἐπειδήπερ προσέκειτο Ἡράκλειος Πύρρῳ, ἀδελφόν τε | L38v ἐκάλει, ὡς ἡνίκα τῷ θείῳ λουτρῷ ἐφωτίζετο ἡ τοῦ βασιλέως ἀδελφὴ χερσὶν ἐδέξατο, καὶ ἅμα ᾠκειωμένον Σεργίῳ καὶ συνδιαιτώμενον ἐγίνωσκε, τοῦτον ἀρχιερέα τοῦ Βυζαντίου ἀνηγόρευσεν. ἤδη χρόνοις τισὶ πρότερον Κῦρον τὸν Ἀλεξανδρείας πρόεδρον μετάκλητον εἰς Βυζάντιον ἦν πεποιηκώς, καὶ ἐν αἰτίᾳ μεγάλῃ εἶχεν ὡς τὰ τῆς Αἰγύπτου πάσης Σαρακηνοῖς καταπροέμενον πράγματα. τηνικαῦτα δὲ περὶ τῶν αἰτιαθέντων ἐπὶ | V193r πλείστου ἀθροισθέντος τοῦ τῆς πόλεως ἐπεξῄει δήμου. ὁ δὲ ἀπελογεῖτο ὡς οὐδαμῶς τούτων ἔνοχος καθειστήκει, ὡς εἰ ἡ βουλὴ αὐτοῦ προυχώρει καὶ τοῖς Σαρακηνοῖς δι' ἐμπολῆς τὰ τῆς φορολογίας παρεῖχε καὶ ἐφ' ἑαυτοῖς ἡσύχαζον, καὶ τὰ τῷ βασιλεῖ παρεχόμενα οὐ καθυστερίζοιτο. ἄλλους τε ταῦτα ἐπῃτιᾶτο πράξαντας, καὶ αὑτὸν μάτην ὑπὲρ τούτων ἐγκαλούμενον ἰσχυρίζετο. ὁ δὲ ἕλληνα τὸν Κῦρον ἀπεκάλει ὡς ἕλληνι καὶ θεομάχῳ καὶ κατὰ Χριστιανῶν φρονοῦντι τῷ Ἄμβρῳ τῷ τῶν Σαρακηνῶν φυλάρχῃ συμβουλεύσαντα τὴν τοῦ βασιλέως κατεγγυηθῆναι dB27 θυγατέρα. ἐν τούτοις οὖν ἀγανακτήσας κατ' αὐτοῦ καὶ ἀναι-

---

4 *πόρθμον* VL || *κλόνοις* VL corr. B || 5 *φύλασιν* L || 8 *Φιδαλείας* scripsi cf. Hesych. Preger 8.7; 14.14: *Φαιδαλίας* V *Φειδαλίας* Suda om. L || 9 *οὗ τε* Ševčenko *οὔτε* V *οὔτε* L || 10 *Βαρυβύσσου* Suda || *εἰσείη* L

26: 1 *ινδικτίονα* L || 2 *καὶ* om. L || 2–3 *ἐπειδὴ δὲ Πύρρω προσέκειτο Ἡράκλειος* L loco *Πύρρῳ, Σεργίω* V || 5 *οἰκειωμένον* ex *ὠικειωμένον* V[2] *οἰκειωμένον* L || 6 *τοῦ Βυζαντίου* om. L || *ἤδη δὲ χρ. τισὶν* L || 7 *Κύρον* VL || 8 *τὸ* ante *Βυζ.* add L || *μεγάλῃ* om L || 9 *καταπρο[εμενον]* V in lac. *καταπροϊέμενον* L || 11 *ἐπεξείη* L || 12 *καθιστήκειν* L || *ὡς εἰ . . .* 15 *καθυστερίζοιτο* om. L || 13 *φωρολογίας* ex *φορολογίας* V[1] vel V[2] || 14 *παρείχετο* sugg. dB || *ἡσύχαζον* vulg. *ἡσυχάζων* V *ἡσυχάζοιεν* coni. dB || 15 *ἀλλ' ἄλλους ταῦτα ἐπαιτιᾶτο* L *ταὐτὰ* dB *ἐπαιτιᾶτο* ex *ἐπῃτιᾶτο* V[2] || 16 *αὐτὸν* VL corr. vulg. || *ὑπὲρ* V *περὶ* L || 17 *Κύρον* V

as to bridge the straits called Stenon,[13] and to make on either side a hedge of branches and foliage so that ⟨the emperor⟩, as he went by, would not even catch sight of the sea. Indeed, this work went ahead speedily, and the emperor crossed the sea on horseback, as if it were dry land, to the shore of the bay of Phidaleia (as it is called).[14] Avoiding the coastal area, he reached Byzantium by the bridge of the river Barbysses. After this he crowned emperor the Caesar Herakleios.

26. In the 12th indiction Sergios, bishop of Byzantium, died. Since Herakleios was devoted to Pyrrhos, whom he called his brother (because when he was being baptized in the holy bath the emperor's sister had received him in her arms) and knew him, furthermore, to have been on friendly terms with Sergios (whose quarters he had shared), he appointed this man archpriest of Byzantium. Some years previously he had recalled to Byzantium Kyros, the bishop of Alexandria, and held him under severe accusation of having surrendered to the Saracens the affairs of all of Egypt. He pursued these charges at the time in front of a large gathering of citizens. But ⟨Kyros⟩ defended himself by saying that he was in no way guilty of these matters, and that if his plan had gone forward and he had raised taxes for the Saracens by means of trade profit, the latter would have remained in peace and the imperial dues would not have been in arrears. And he accused others of having committed the misdeeds in question and alleged that he himself had made charges against them to no avail. But ⟨Herakleios⟩ called Kyros a pagan for having advised that the emperor's daughter should be betrothed to Ambros, phylarch of the Saracens, a pagan, an enemy of God and an opponent of the Christians. Waxing in-

[13] The Bosporos.

[14] The Golden Horn, so named after the wife of the mythical Byzas.

ρήσειν ἀπειλῶν, τῷ τῆς πόλεως αὐτὸν ὑπάρχῳ ὡς αἰκισομένῳ παραδίδωσι.

27. Μετὰ τοῦτο ἐδικαίου τὸν υἱὸν Ἡράκλειον ὑπατεῦσαι, Δαβίδ τε καὶ Μαρτῖνον τοὺς υἱοὺς αὐτοῦ Καίσαρας ἀνηγόρευσεν, Αὐγουστῖναν δὲ καὶ Μαρτῖναν τὰς θυγατέρας Αὐγούστας. χρόνου δὲ | διελθόντος νόσῳ ὑδερικῇ περιπίπτει, [L39r] καὶ ὁρῶν τὸ πάθος δυσίατον — ἐπὶ τοσοῦτο γὰρ ἐπετείνετο ὡς καὶ ἡνίκα ἀπουρεῖν ἤμελλε σανίδα κατὰ τοῦ ἤτρου ἐπετίθει· ἐστρέφετο γὰρ αὐτοῦ τὸ αἰδοῖον καὶ κατὰ τοῦ προσώπου αὐτοῦ τὰ οὖρα ἔπεμπεν. ἔλεγχος δὲ ἦν τοῦτο τῆς παρανομίας τῆς ἑαυτοῦ, ὑπὲρ ἧς ταύτην δίκην ὑστάτην ἐξέτισε τοῦ εἰς τὴν ἀνεψιὰν τὴν οἰκείαν γάμου. διαθήκας οὖν ἐξετίθει, ὥστε Κωνσταντῖνον καὶ Ἡράκλειον τοὺς υἱοὺς αὐτοῦ βασιλεῖς ἰσοτίμους εἶναι, καὶ Μαρτῖναν τὴν αὐτοῦ γυναῖκα τιμᾶσθαι παρ' αὐτῶν ὡς μητέρα καὶ βασίλισσαν. ἐκ τούτου λοιπὸν ἐτελεύτα ζήσας ἔτη ἓξ καὶ ἑξήκοντα, ἐν δὲ τῇ βασιλείᾳ διανύσας ἔτη τριάκοντα μῆνας τέσσαρας ἡμέρας ἕξ. θάπτεται δὲ ἐν τῷ ἱερῷ τῶν πανευφήμων ἀποστόλων, καὶ τρισὶν ἡμέραις ἀσκεπές, ὥσπερ ἦν διατάξας ἔτι περιών, τὸ ὑποδεξάμενον αὐτοῦ σῶμα διετέλει μνῆμα, περικαθημένων αὐτὸ εὐνούχων ὑπηρετῶν.

28. Μετὰ τοῦτο Μαρτῖνα ἡ Αὐγούστα προσκαλεῖται Πύρρον τὸν ἀρχιερέα καὶ τοὺς βασιλικοὺς ἄρχοντας, ἐκκλησιάσασα καὶ τὸν περὶ τὸ Βυζάντιον λαόν, τάς τε διαθήκας Ἡρακλείου ὑπεδείκνυ, ὡς περὶ αὐτῆς καὶ τῶν τέκνων διέθετο. ὁ δὲ παρὼν ἅπας δῆμος Κωνσταντῖνον καὶ Ἡράκλειον | τοὺς [L39v] βασιλεῖς ἐπεζήτει· ἡ δὲ ἦγεν αὐτούς, καὶ ἅμα διελέγετο νομίζουσα ἅτε βασίλισσα τὰ πρῶτα εἰς τὴν βασιλείαν φέρεσθαι. [dB28] τινὲς δὲ τοῦ συνεστῶτος λαοῦ ἀνεφώνουν πρὸς αὐτὴν ὅτι "σὺ

21–22 ἐπάρχῳ . . . παραδίδοσι L

27: 2 δᾶδ . . . Μαρῖνον V Δαυῖδ δὲ καὶ Μαρτίνον L ‖ 5 ἐπεκτείνετο vulg. dB cf. ἐπεκτάθη Georg. Mon. 673.14 ‖ 6 ἤμελλεν L cf. **24.**12 ἔμελλε V ‖ ἴτρου V Georg. Mon. 673.15 ‖ ἐπετίθη L ‖ 8 ἀναπέμπειν Georg. Mon. 673.16 ‖ 9 ἐξέτισε V[2] in lit. ex ἐξῄτησε ut vid.: ἐξαίτησεν ἕνεκεν τοῦ L ‖ 18 τὸ ante σῶμα add. V ‖ αὐτω L ‖ 19 ὑπηρετῶν om. L

28: 2 Πύρρον] Κύρον V ‖ 6 πρὸς αὐτοὺς L ‖ διελέγετο ex διελογίζετο V[2] ‖ 7 ante βασιλείαν litt. φ(?) a V[2] deleta ‖ 8 συνεστῶτος litteris συ superscr. V[1]

censed with him and threatening him with death, ⟨Herakleios⟩ handed him over to the prefect of the City for punishment.

27. After this he thought fit that his son Herakleios should assume the consulship. He proclaimed Caesars his sons David and Martinos, and his daughters Augustina and Martina Augustas. Sometime later he fell ill with the dropsy and realized that his disease was difficult to cure, for it grew to such an extent that when he was about to urinate, he would place a board against his abdomen: ⟨otherwise⟩ his private parts turned round and discharged the urine in his face. This was in reproof of his transgression (namely, his marriage to his own niece) on account of which he suffered this ultimate punishment. He set forth a testament whereby his sons Constantine and Herakleios were to be emperors of equal rank and his wife Martina was to be honored by them as mother and empress. So he died of this ⟨disease⟩ at the age of sixty-six after a reign of thirty years, four months, and six days. He was buried in the church of the all-praised Apostles and for three days, as he had ordained while he was still alive, the tomb containing his body remained uncovered and attended by ministering eunuchs.

28. After this the Augusta Martina summoned the archpriest Pyrrhos and the dignitaries of the court, and having gathered the people of Byzantium in an assembly, showed the testament of Herakleios and the provisions he had made concerning herself and her children. All the people who were present clamored for Emperors Constantine and Herakleios; so she brought them out while expressing her claim that she, as empress, would have the first place in the empire. But some of the people present cried to her: "You have the honor

μὲν τιμὴν ἔχεις ὡς μήτηρ βασιλέων, οὗτοι δὲ ὡς βασιλεῖς καὶ δεσπόται". ἐξαίρετον δὲ ἐδίδουν γέρας Κωνσταντίνῳ ὡς πρώτῳ εἰς τὴν βασιλείαν κατὰ τὴν | ἡλικίαν ἐκ παιδὸς (V193v) προχειρισθέντι. "οὐδὲ γὰρ βαρβάρων ἢ ἀλλοφύλων πρὸς τὰ βασίλεια εἰσερχομένων, ὦ δέσποινα," ἔφασκον, "δύνασαι ὑποδέχεσθαι ἢ λόγοις ἀμείβεσθαι· μηδὲ δοίη θεὸς ἐν τούτῳ τάξεως τὴν Ῥωμαϊκὴν ἐλθεῖν πολιτείαν". καὶ κατήρχοντο ἀνευφημοῦντες τοὺς βασιλεῖς. ταῦτα ἀκούσασα πρὸς τὸ ἑαυτῆς ὑπεχώρει παλάτιον.

29. Ἐξ οὗ καὶ Κωνσταντῖνος τῆς βασιλείας ἦρχε. προσαγγέλλει δὲ αὐτῷ Φιλάγριος, ὃς ἦν τῶν βασιλικῶν χρημάτων ταμίας, ὡς ἀσθενοῦντος τοῦ πατρὸς Ἡρακλείου χρήματα Πύρρῳ τῷ ἀρχιερεῖ παρατίθεσθαι Μαρτίνης τῆς βασιλίσσης ἕνεκεν, ὡς μή ποτε αὐτὴ ὑπὸ Κωνσταντίνου τοῦ βασιλέως καὶ προγόνου ἐκ τῶν βασιλείων διωθουμένη χρημάτων καθυστερίζοιτο. ὁ δὲ Πύρρον μεταστειλάμενος διεπυνθά|νετο (L40r) εἰ οὕτω ταῦτα ἔχοι. Πύρρος δὲ ὑπὸ Φιλαγρίου διελεγχόμενος προεδίδου καὶ οὐκ ἐθέλων τὰ χρήματα. ἐπεὶ δὲ νόσῳ χρονίᾳ Κωνσταντῖνος συνείχετο καὶ εὐκρασίας ἀέρων ἕνεκεν ἐν Χαλκηδόνι διέτριβεν ἐν τῷ ὑπ' αὐτοῦ κτισθέντι παλατίῳ, ἰδὼν Φιλάγριος ἀρρώστως αὐτὸν διακείμενον, καὶ ἐλπίσας τάχιον ἀποβιῶσαι, ἐδεδίει Ἡράκλειον καὶ Μαρτῖναν ὡς αὐτὸν κακώσοντας. ἐκ τούτου Κωνσταντίνῳ συνεβούλευε γράφειν τοῖς στρατευομένοις ὡς τελευτῆς συμβαινούσης αὐτῷ ἀντιλαβέσθαι τῶν τέκνων αὐτοῦ, καὶ μὴ συγχωρεῖν ἀδικεῖσθαι μηδὲ τῆς βασιλείας διωθεῖσθαι. ἐφ' οἷς ἡσθεὶς Κωνσταντῖνος Οὐαλεντῖνον τὸν Φιλαγρίου ὑπασπιστὴν τά τε γράμματα καὶ τὴν λοιπὴν τοῦ πράγματος ἐργασίαν ἐγχειρίσας πρὸς τὸ στράτευμα ἐξέπεμψε, δεδωκὼς αὐτῷ χρήματα συντελοῦντα εἰς (dB29) ποσότητα ἀριθμοῦ μυριάδων [πέντε] διακοσίων καὶ ἔτι μύρια καὶ ἑξακισχίλια νομίσματα, ὑποθέμενος πείθειν τοὺς τοῦ στρατιωτικοῦ καταλόγου μετὰ τελευτὴν Κωνσταντίνου ἀντι-

---

9 +τοὺς βασιλης επεζ⟨η⟩τη⟨σα⟩ν vel sim. in mg. L ‖ 10 ἐδίδου L ‖ 11 πρῶτον καὶ τὴν βασ. L ‖ κατὰ P: καὶ VL

29: 1–2 προσαγγέλει L ‖ 3 ταμείας L ‖ 6 διωθουμένην VL corr. vulg. ‖ 7 οὕτω in mg. V ‖ 12–13 τάχειον ἀποβιῶναι ἐδεδείη L ‖ 14 τούτω L ‖ 15–16 ἀντιλαμβάνεσθαι L ‖ 17–18 Οὐαλέντιον ex Οὐαλεντίου ut vid. L ‖ 21 πεντε punctis superpositis secl. V^2 om. L ‖ 22 ἑξάκισχηλια L

due to the mother of the emperors, but they that of our emperors and lords!" They paid particular respect to Constantine because, by reason of his seniority, he was first to have been appointed emperor when he was still a child. "Nor can you, O Lady," they said, "receive barbarian or ⟨other⟩ foreign ⟨emissaries⟩ who come to the palace or hold converse with them. May God forbid that the Roman State should come to such a pass." And they came down ⟨from their seats⟩[15] acclaiming the emperors. When ⟨Martina⟩ had heard these things, she withdrew to her palace.

29. From this time Constantine ruled the empire. Now Philagrios, who was imperial treasurer, informed him that his father Herakleios, when he was ill, had provided money to the archpriest Pyrrhos on behalf of Empress Martina so she would not be lacking in funds if she were driven out of the palace by her stepson, Emperor Constantine. The latter summoned Pyrrhos and inquired if that was so. Exposed by Philagrios, Pyrrhos surrendered the money even against his will. Since Constantine was afflicted by a chronic illness, he dwelt for reasons of climate at Chalcedon where he had built a palace. On seeing him in poor health and expecting him to die soon, Philagrios was afraid that Herakleios and Martina would do him harm. For this reason he advised Constantine to write to the army that his death was approaching and that they should assist his children and not suffer them to be wronged or ousted from the imperial office. Pleased by this ⟨advice⟩, Constantine entrusted the letters and the conduct of this business to Valentinos, an adjutant of Philagrios, whom he dispatched to the army with a sum of money amounting to 2,000,000 plus 16,000 solidi, and instructed him to persuade the enrolled soldiers that after Constantine's death they should oppose Martina and her

[15] In the Hippodrome.

καθίστασθαι Μαρτίνῃ *καὶ τοῖς τέκνοις αὐτῆς. συμβασιλεύσας δὲ τῷ πατρὶ ἔτη ὀκτὼ καὶ εἴκοσι, καὶ ἐπιβιοὺς εἰς τὴν*
βασι|λείαν ἔτι ἡμέρας ἑκατὸν τρεῖς, ἐτελεύτησε. L40^{v}

30. Μεθ' *ὃν αὐτοκράτωρ τῆς βασιλείας ἀναγορεύεται* Ἡράκλειος, *ᾧ συνελάμβανεν εἰς τὰ τῆς βασιλείας πράγματα καὶ ἡ μήτηρ* Μαρτῖνα. *εὐθὺς οὖν τὸν τοῦ πατρὸς στέφανον, ὃν καὶ συνέθαψαν αὐτῷ καὶ ὁ υἱὸς* Κωνσταντῖνος *τοῦ ναοῦ ἐξήνεγκε τιμηθέντα μέχρι χρυσίου λιτρῶν ἑβδομήκοντα, τῷ θεῷ προσφέρει ἐν τῷ ἱερῷ,* Κῦρον *δὲ τὸν πρόεδρον* Ἀλεξανδρείας *τῷ οἰκείῳ θρόνῳ ἀποκαθίστησι.* Φιλάγριον *δὲ ἀποκείρας ἐξόριστον εἰς τὸ* Σέπται *λεγόμενον φρούριον πρὸς*
ἥλιον δύ|νοντα κατὰ [*τὰ*] *θάτερα τῶν* Ἡρακλέος *στηλῶν πρὸς* V194^{r}
τῇ Λιβύῃ *κείμενον παρέπεμψεν. ἑτέρους τε πλείστους, οὓς εὗρε φίλους καὶ ὑπηρέτας αὐτοῦ, πληγαῖς καὶ ἑτέραις αἰκίαις ἠμύνατο.* Οὐαλεντῖνος *δὲ ὁ* Φιλαγρίου *ὑπασπιστὴς ταῦτα αἰσθόμενος τὸ στρατιωτικὸν κατὰ* Μαρτίνης *καὶ τῶν τέκνων αὐτῆς ἐτάραττε· μεθ' ὧν τὴν* Χαλκηδόνα *καταλαμβάνει ὡς τοῖς τέκνοις* Κωνσταντίνου *ἐπικουρήσων, καὶ αὐτοῦ διέτριβεν.* Ἡράκλειος *δὲ τήν τε πόλιν ἐν τῷ ἀσφαλεῖ εἶχε, καὶ πᾶσιν ἀπελογεῖτο ὡς* Ἡράκλειος *ὁ υἱὸς* Κωνσταντίνου *ἀπήμαντος διαμένει, καὶ πᾶσιν ὑγιᾶ καὶ σῶον ὑπεδείκνυ, καὶ*
ἅμα | ὡς τέκνου γνησίου περιείχετο. καὶ τοῦτο ἐπιστοῦτο τῷ L41^{r}
ἐκ τοῦ σωτηριώδους βαπτίσματος ἀγκάλαις δέξασθαι. καὶ dB30
συμπαρόντος Πύρρου *τοῦ τῆς πόλεως ἱεράρχου τῶν ζῳοποιῶν ξύλων ἥπτετο καὶ διώμνυτο ὡς οὔτε δι' αὐτοῦ οὔτε δι' ἑτέρου τὰ τοῦ* Κωνσταντίνου *τέκνα βλαβήσεται.* Οὐαλεντῖνον *δὲ ἀπισχυρίζετο δεικνύειν ὡς ἐπιβουλεύσαντα αὐτοῖς καὶ τῆς βασιλείας ἐπορεγόμενον. ὡς δὲ εἰς πλεῖον ἅπαντας βεβαιώσηται, συλλαβὼν μεθ' ἑαυτοῦ* Ἡράκλειον *πρὸς* Οὐαλεντῖνον *περαιοῦται, καὶ πάλιν ἐβουλεύετο διόμνυσθαι καὶ πείθειν αὐτοὺς ὡς φιλοστόργως διάκειται πρὸς* Ἡράκλειον. Οὐαλεν-

---

26 *ἔτη ἡμ.* $\overline{ρ γ}$ L

30: 2 *καὶ* Ἡρ. L ‖ *ᾧ* V *ὡς* L ‖ 5 *ἐξένεγκεν τιμιθέντα* L ‖ *λιτρῶν* in lacuna V^2 ‖ 6 *προσφέρειν* V ‖ 8 *ἐξώριστον* L ‖ *Σεπται* sine acc. V *Σέπτε* L *Σέπτας* vulg. ‖ 9 *τὰ* secl. vulg. *τὰ θέατρα τῶν Ἡρακλείων στηλῶν* L ‖ 14 *μεθ' ὃν* V ‖ Καλχηδόνα L Χαλκηδόνος V ‖ 18 *πᾶσιν ὑγειᾶ* L *πᾶσι ὑγιᾶ* ex *πάσῃ ὑγιεία* V^2 *πᾶσι ὑγιέα* dB ‖ *ἀπεδείκνυ* L ‖ 19 *τῷ*] *τὸ* V corr. vulg. om. L ‖ 24 *ἐπιβουλεύσοντα* L ‖ 25 *εἰς πλείονα πάντα* V *εἰς πλεῖον ἅπαντα* dB ‖ 27 *διομνῦσθαι* L *διωμνῦσθαι* V corr. vulg.

children. After reigning twenty-eight years together with his father and surviving another hundred and three days in the imperial office, ⟨Constantine⟩ died.

30. After him Herakleios was proclaimed emperor and shared the administration of the empire with his mother Martina. Straightaway he dedicated to God in the sanctuary the crown of his father—this had been buried with him, but his son Constantine removed it from the church because it was valued at 70 lbs. of gold. He also reinstated Kyros, bishop of Alexandria, in his own see. As for Philagrios, he had him tonsured and exiled him to a fortress called Septai[16] which lies toward the setting sun, opposite the Pillars of Hercules, on the side of Libya. And many others who happened to be friends and servants ⟨of Philagrios⟩ he punished by scourging and other torments. Now Valentinos, the adjutant of Philagrios, when he heard these things, roused the soldiery against Martina and her children. He came with the army to Chalcedon and remained there with a view to assisting Constantine's children. Herakleios held the City securely and offered to all and sundry the justification that Constantine's son Herakleios remained unharmed. He showed him hale and sound to everybody and protected him like his own child, which was confirmed by the fact that he had received him in his arms after the salutary baptism. In the presence of Pyrrhos, the archpriest of the City, he laid his hand on the life-giving cross and swore that Constantine's children would not be harmed either by him or anyone else. He also affirmed he would prove that Valentinos was plotting against them and reaching for the imperial office. In order to convince everyone even further, he took Herakleios along and crossed over to Valentinos, and was intending once again to swear and persuade ⟨the soldiers⟩ of his affection for Herakleios. Valentinos, however, did not receive

[16]Septem fratres (Ceuta). Called Septon by Procopius, *Bell. Vand.*, I.1.6; II.5.6; *De aed.*, VI.7.14 (fort rebuilt by Justinian). Septai in Theoph., 426.4.

τῖνος δὲ οὐκ ἐδέχετο ἀλλ' ἀπέπεμπε, καὶ δὴ ὑπενόστει καὶ διηγεῖτο πάντα τοῖς τῆς πόλεως. οἱ δὲ ἐπείθοντο καὶ Οὐαλεντῖνον ἐδυσφήμουν.

31. Τῆς τρύγης δὲ ἐπιλαβούσης, οἱ τῆς πόλεως αἰσθόμενοι ὡς ὁ μετὰ Οὐαλεντίνου στρατὸς τούς τε ἀμπελῶνας αὐτῶν διαφθείρει κἀκείνους οὐ συγχωρεῖ ἐκεῖσε περαιοῦσθαι, συνίστανται Πύρρῳ βοῶντες στέφειν Ἡράκλειον τὸν Κωνσταντίνου υἱόν. Πύρρος δὲ τὴν ταραχὴν καὶ τὴν στάσιν τοῦ λαοῦ περιαθρήσας ἀπελογεῖτο ὡς οὐ διὰ τοῦτο αὐτοὶ στασιάζουσιν, ἀλλ' Οὐαλεντίνῳ | τὴν βασιλείαν περιποιοῦνται. L41v ἔτι οὖν ἐπικειμένου τοῦ ὄχλου δῆλα ποιεῖ βασιλεῖ ἅπαντα. ὁ δὲ συλλαβόμενος τὸν ἀνεψιὸν Ἡράκλειον εὐθέως ἐπὶ τὸ ἱερὸν ἐχώρει καὶ ἀνέρχεται ἅμα Πύρρῳ ἐν τῷ ἄμβωνι καὶ προτρέπεται στέφειν Ἡράκλειον. οἱ δὲ ὄχλοι τὸν βασιλέα ἐβιάζοντο τὸ ἔργον ἐπιτελεῖν. ὁ δὲ λαβὼν ἐκ τῆς ἐκκλησίας τὸν τοῦ πατρὸς Ἡρακλείου στέφανον τὸ ἔργον ἐπλήρου. εὐθὺς οὖν τὸν στεφθέντα Κωνσταντῖνον οἱ ὄχλοι μετονομάζουσι. τὸ οὖν ἀχυρῶδες καὶ ἀγροικωδέστερον τοῦ λαοῦ κατὰ Πύρρου τὰς χεῖρας ὥπλιζον, καὶ πρὸς τὸ ἱερὸν γενόμενοι αὐτὸν μὲν οὐχ εὗρον, κατὰ δὲ τὸν καιρὸν τῆς τοῦ λυχνικοῦ συνάξεως εἰσέρχονται ἐπαγόμενοι Ἑβραίων καὶ ἄλλων κακοδόξων ὅμιλον ἐν τῷ θυσιαστηρίῳ. καὶ τὴν μὲν ἐνδυτὴν διαρρηγνῦσι, καὶ τὸν dB31 ἱερὸν χῶρον | αἰσχρῶς κατερρύπαινον, τάς τε κλεῖς τῶν πυλῶν V194v λαβόντες ἐπὶ κοντοῦ ἀνήρτων, καὶ οὕτω τὴν πόλιν ἀθέσμως περιῄεσαν. Πύρρος δὲ ταῦτα μαθὼν τῇ ἐπιούσῃ νυκτὶ ἐν τῷ ἱερῷ παραγίνεται καὶ πάντα τὰ ἱερὰ ἀσπάζεται καὶ τὸ περικείμενον αὐτῷ ὠμόφορον περιελὼν τῇ ἱερᾷ | ἀποτίθεται L42r τραπέζῃ, φήσας "τῆς ἱερωσύνης μὴ ἀφιστάμενος ἀποτάσσομαι λαῷ ἀπειθεῖ". ἐκεῖθεν ἡσυχῇ ἐξελθὼν παρὰ μιᾷ θεοσεβεστάτῃ γυναικὶ κρυφῇ κατήγετο καὶ καιροῦ εὐθέτου λαβόμενος πρὸς τὴν Χαλκηδόνα ἀπέπλει. οὗ τὴν ἔλευσίν τινες τῶν μοναζόντων ἐκεῖσε ἀκηκοότες περὶ τῶν ἐκτεθέντων παρὰ

---

29 δὴ V δι' L

31: 6 *περιαθροίσας* VL corr. vulg. ‖ 8 *τῷ βασ.* L ‖ 10 *ἄμβονι* L ‖ 14–15 *ἀχυρῶδες*] *ἀγυρτῶδες* coni. dB ‖ 18 *καὶ ἄλλων* om. L ‖ 19 *διαρήγνυσι* L ‖ 21–22 *κόντου . . . περίεσαν* L ‖ 24 *ὠμοφόριον* L ‖ 25–26 *ἱεροσύνης . . . ἀποτάσσωμαι* L ‖ 26 *ἐκεῖθεν οὖν* L ‖ 27 *κρυφεῖ* L ‖ 28 *Χαλκηδόνος* V

him and sent him away; so he returned and told the story to the inhabitants of the City who believed him and cursed Valentinos.

31. When vintage time had come, the citizens saw that the army accompanying Valentinos was destroying their vineyards and not allowing them to cross thither, and so they urged Pyrrhos by their clamors that he should crown Constantine's son Herakleios. On beholding the disturbance and uprising of the people, Pyrrhos excused himself on the grounds that the insurrection had a different purpose, namely, to gain the imperial office for Valentinos; but as the mob was insisting, he laid the whole matter before the emperor. The latter, taking along his nephew Herakleios, proceeded to the church and mounted the ambo together with Pyrrhos, whom he invited to crown Herakleios; and as the crowd was pressing him to accomplish the deed, he took from the church the crown of his father Herakleios and performed the ceremony. And straightaway the mob renamed the ⟨newly⟩ crowned one Constantine. Now the more ruffianly and boorish part of the people armed themselves against Pyrrhos and came to the church, but did not find him; so at the time of vespers they entered the sanctuary, accompanied by a group of Jews and other unbelievers. They tore the altar cloth, shamefully defiled the holy spot and, having seized the keys to the doors, affixed them to a pole and so went round the City in lawless fashion. When Pyrrhos had been informed of this, he came to the church the following night and, after embracing the sacred objects, took off his pallium and placed it on the altar table, saying, "Without renouncing the priesthood I abjure a disobedient people." So he went out quietly and found a secret refuge with a pious woman; then, seizing a favorable occasion, he sailed away to Carthage.[17] When some of the monks there heard of his arrival (their leaders

[17] Chalcedon in the text, but the confusion between the two names is frequent in Byzantine texts.

τοῦ πάλαι Ἡρακλείου τοῦ βασιλέως καὶ Σεργίου τοῦ τῆς πόλεως ἱεράρχου, ἕνεκεν τῶν δύο ἐπὶ τοῦ σωτῆρος Χριστοῦ θελημάτων καὶ ἐνεργειῶν ἀνηρεύνων, ὧν προασπισταὶ ἐτύγχανον Μάξιμος καὶ Θεοδόσιος ὄντες ἐν Ἀφρικῇ. καὶ τὰ μὲν κατὰ Πύρρον οὕτω πως ἔσχεν.

32. Ἐπεὶ οὖν τοὺς περὶ Οὐαλεντῖνον ἡ Χαλκηδὼν εἶχεν, ἀναγκαιοτέρως ⟨ἔσχον⟩ Ἡράκλειος καὶ Μαρτῖνα, ὡς μὴ ἐπὶ πλεῖον τὰ ἐκεῖσε προάστεια βλάπτοιτο, ἑνωθῆναί τε αὐτῷ καὶ ὅρκοις τὰ πρὸς ἀλλήλους θέσθαι· καὶ ἀξίᾳ αὐτὸν ἐτίμησαν ἣν Ῥωμαῖοι καλοῦσι κόμητα ἐξσκουβιτόρων, καὶ μηδ' ὅλως ἐγκαλεῖσθαι περὶ ὧν παρὰ Κωνσταντίνου ἐδέξατο χρημάτων, φιλοτιμηθῆναι δὲ χρήμασι τοῖς συνελθοῦσιν αὐτῷ στρατιώταις, στεφθῆναί τε καὶ Δαβὶδ τὸν Καίσαρα καὶ μετονομασθῆναι Τιβέριον. | καὶ τούτων οὕτω τελεσθέντων προ- L42v χειρίζεται Παῦλος, οἰκονόμος γεγονὼς τῆς μεγάλης ἐκκλησίας, ἀρχιερεὺς Κωνσταντινουπόλεως, κατὰ τὸν Ὀκτώβριον μῆνα τῆς πεντεκαιδεκάτης ἰνδικτιόνος.

33. Κωνσταντῖνος οὖν ἐν Σικελίᾳ ὑπὸ τῶν ἰδίων ὑπηρετῶν δόλῳ φονευθεὶς ἐν τῷ λουτρῷ, ἤδη ἐν τῇ βασιλείᾳ εἰκο- dB32 στὸν ἕβδομον ἀνύσας ἔτος, ἐτελεύτα.

34. Μεθ' ὃν Κωνσταντῖνος ὁ υἱὸς τὰ τῆς βασιλείας ἐγχειρίζεται σκῆπτρα. καὶ τούτου ἀρξαμένου εὐθὺς ὁ τῶν Σαρακηνῶν ἡγούμενος ναῦς πλείστας κατασκευάσας κατὰ τοῦ Βυζαντίου ἐκπέμπει, ἡγεμόνα τούτων ἐπιστήσας, ἅτε πιστότατον καὶ τὰ πολέμια ἔμπειρον, κατὰ τὴν ἑαυτῶν διάλεκτον Χαλὲβ ὀνομαζόμενον· ὃς ἀναχθεὶς προσωρμίζετο ἐν προαστείοις τοῦ Βυζαντίου, κατὰ τὸν παραθαλάσσιον τόπον τὸν καλούμενον Ἕβδομον. τοῦτον αἰσθόμενος Κωνσταντῖνος ἀντιπαρατάττεται καὶ αὐτὸς στόλῳ μεγάλῳ. ὑφ' ὧν πλεῖσται ναυμαχίαι ἑκάστης ἡμέρας ἐγίνοντο, τοῦ πολέμου συγκροτουμέ-

---

33 Θεοδόσιος ex Θεοδόσιον L

32: 1 Οὐαλεντίνου V corr. P || τῆς περὶ Οὐαλεντίνου ἡ Χαλκηδόνα L || 2 ἀναγκαιωτέρως L || ἔσχον add. dB || 3 βλάπτοι . . . αὐτὸν L || 5 κώμητα ἐκκουβητόρων L || 7 φιλοτιμιθῆναι L

33: 2–3 εἰκοστοέβδομον L

34: 1 μεθ' ὧν L || 4 ἡγεμώνα L || τοῦτον V || 5 πολέμεια V || αὐτῶν L || 6 Χαλὲφ . . . προσορμίζεται L || 8–9 ἀντιπαρατάσσεται L || 9–10 ναυμαχεῖαι L

were Maximos and Theodosios, who dwelt in Africa), they interrogated him concerning the Exposition made by the former emperor Herakleios and by Sergios, archpriest of the City, regarding the two wills and energies of Christ our Savior. So much for Pyrrhos.

32. Now since the followers of Valentinos were still at Chalcedon, Herakleios and Martina deemed it imperative, lest the estates in those parts suffered further damage, to come to an agreement with him and compose their differences under oath; so they honored him with the rank which the Romans call *comes excubitorum* and ⟨promised⟩ that he would not be called to account for the monies he had received from Constantine; that the soldiers who had joined him would be rewarded with gold; and that the Caesar David would be crowned and renamed Tiberios. When these things had been done, Paul, the former *oikonomos* of the Great Church, was appointed archpriest of Constantinople in October of the 15th indiction.

33. Then, after a reign of twenty-seven years, Constantine was treacherously killed by his own servants in his bath in Sicily and so ended his life.

34. After him, his son Constantine was invested with the imperial office. Immediately after his accession the leader of the Saracens built many ships and sent them against Byzantium under the command of Chaleb[18] (as he was called in their language), a man most loyal and experienced in war. On his arrival, he put in at a seaside suburb of Byzantium called Hebdomon. When he became aware of his ⟨presence⟩, Constantine, too, deployed a great fleet against him. Many naval battles were fought every day between the two sides,

[18] Χαλέφ in L, Χαλέ or Χάλε in Theoph. Not recorded in the Arabic sources.

νου ἀπὸ τοῦ ἐαρινοῦ μέχρι φθινοπωρινοῦ καιροῦ. | χειμῶνος V195r *δὲ ἐπιγινομένου ὁ τῶν Σαρακηνῶν στόλος διαπεραιωθεὶς ἐν* Κυζίκῳ *διεχείμαζε, | καὶ πάλιν ἔαρος ἀρχομένου ἐκεῖθεν ἀντ-* L43r *αναχθεὶς ὡσαύτως τοῦ διὰ θαλάσσης πολέμου εἴχετο. ἑπτὰ οὖν ἔτεσι τοῦ πολέμου διαρκέσαντος τέλος οὐδὲν πλέον ὁ τῶν* Σαρακηνῶν *ἤνυσε στόλος, ἀλλὰ πολλούς τε ἄνδρας μαχίμους ἀποβαλόντες καὶ δεινῶς τραυματισθέντες καὶ χαλεπῶς ἡττημένοι ὑπενόστουν πρὸς τὰ οἰκεῖα καταίροντες. πρὸς δὲ τοῖς πελάζουσι τοῦ* Συλλαίου *γενόμενοι ὑπὸ σκληρῶν πνευμάτων καὶ θαλασσίου κλύδωνος καταληφθέντες πανστρατιᾷ διώλοντο. ὁ δὲ τῶν* Σαρακηνῶν *βασιλεὺς τὸ τοῦ στόλου ἀκούσας δυστύχημα πρέσβεις ἀποστέλλει πρὸς* Κωνσταντῖνον *ὡς σπεισόμενος πρὸς αὐτὸν ἐπὶ τελέσμασιν ἐνιαυσίοις. ὁ δὲ τούτους δεξάμενος καὶ τὰ δηλωθέντα ἀκηκοὼς συνεκπέμπει αὐτοῖς* Ἰωάννην *τὸν πατρίκιον, τὸ ἐπίκλην* Πιτζιγαύδιον, *πολυπειρίᾳ καὶ φρονήσει διαφέροντα, ὡς τὰ ἐπὶ τῇ εἰρήνῃ* dB33 *διαλεχθησόμενον· ὃς πρὸς τὰ τῶν* Σαρακηνῶν *γενόμενος ἤθη συμβαίνει τε αὐτοῖς ὅρκοις τὴν εἰρήνην βεβαιωσάμενος ἐπὶ τριάκοντα ἔτεσιν, ὥστε παρέχεσθαι* Ῥωμαίοις *ὑπὸ τῶν* Σαρακηνῶν *ἀνὰ ἔτος ποσότητα χρυσίου τρεῖς χιλιάδας ἄνδρας τε αἰχμαλώτους | πεντήκοντα καὶ ἵππους πεντήκοντα. ταῦτα* L43v *ἀκηκοότες καὶ οἱ πρὸς τὰ ἑσπέρια οἰκοῦντες μέρη, τουτέστιν ὁ τῶν* Ἀβάρων *ἡγεμὼν καὶ οἱ ἐπέκεινα ἄρχοντες τῶν πρὸς δύσιν παρακειμένων ἐθνῶν διὰ πρέσβεων δῶρα τῷ βασιλεῖ στείλαντες εἰρήνην ἐζήτησαν· ἐφ' οἷς εἴξαντος τοῦ βασιλέως εἰρήνη τὸ λοιπὸν καὶ γαλήνη ἔν τε τοῖς ἑῴοις ἔν τε τοῖς ἑσπερίοις ἐβραβεύετο. καὶ ταῦτα μὲν οὕτως ἔσχε.*

35. Λεκτέον *δὲ ἤδη περὶ τῆς τῶν λεγομένων* Οὔννων *καὶ* Βουλγάρων *ἀρχῆς καὶ καταστάσεως αὐτῶν. περὶ τὴν* Μαιῶτιν *λίμνην κατὰ τὸν* Κώφινα *ποταμὸν καθίσταται ἡ πάλαι καλουμένη μεγάλη* Βουλγαρία *καὶ οἱ λεγόμενοι* Κότραγοι,

---

11 *φθεινοπορινοῦ* L || 12 *διαπεραιωθεὶς* ex *διαπεραιωθὲν* V^2 || 13 *ἐρχομένου* V || 17 *ἀποβάλλοντες* L || *καὶ*[2] om. L || *χαλεπῶς* V *δεινῶς* L || 19 Συλλέου L || 19–20 *γενόμενοι . . . καταληφθέντες* V^2 ex *γενομένου . . . καταληφθέντων* || 23 *πεισόμενος* L || 25 *ἐπίκλιν* VL corr. vulg. || Πιτζιγαύδιον ex Πιτζιγαύα*ον V^2 || 27 *τὰ Σαρ. ἤθη γενόμενος* L || 30 *ἀνέτους* L || 34 *πρεσβείων* L || 35 *ἐξήτησαν . . . ἤξαντος* L || 37 *οὕτω πῶς ἔσχεν* L

35: 1–2 Οὐνογουνδούρων Βουλγάρων propos. V. Beševliev, *REB* 28 (1970) 156 || 2 *ἀρχῆς* V *ἄρχοντας* L || 2–3 Μαιῶτιν ex Μαρσοτιν L^1 || 4 *καλουμένη* V *λεγομένη* L || Κώτραγοι L

the engagements starting in the spring and continuing until autumn. When the bad weather came, the fleet of the Saracens crossed over to Kyzikos and wintered there, and in the beginning of spring it returned thence and continued in the same fashion the war on sea. So the war lasted seven years, and finally the Saracen fleet met with no success; on the contrary, they lost many fighting men. Badly injured and grievously defeated, they set out on their homeward journey. And when they came to the region of Syllaion,[19] they were overtaken by violent winds and a tempest at sea which destroyed their entire armament. On hearing of the disaster of his fleet, the king of the Saracens sent ambassadors to Constantine with a view to concluding a treaty on payment of an annual tribute. The latter received them and, after hearing their message, sent out in their company the patrician John surnamed Pitzigaudios, a man of outstanding experience and wisdom, that he might negotiate the peace. On his arrival in the country of the Saracens, he reached an agreement with them and confirmed by oath a peace treaty for thirty years ⟨which stipulated⟩ that every year the Saracens would deliver to the Romans the sum of 3,000 ⟨pieces⟩ of gold, fifty captives, and fifty horses. When this news had reached the peoples that live in the West, namely, the chief of the Avars and the princes of neighboring nations further west, they ⟨too⟩ sent ambassadors to the emperor bearing gifts and asked for peace. The emperor consented to this, and so peace and tranquillity prevailed in both East and West. So much for this.

35. It is now time to speak of the dominion of the Huns (as they are called) and the Bulgarians and their affairs. In the area of the Maeotic lake,[20] by the river Kophis,[21] lies Great Bulgaria (as it was called in olden times) and

---

[19] In Pamphylia. The name is also spelled Sillyon or Syllion. For a description of the site see G. E. Bean, *Turkey's Southern Shore* (London, 1968), 59ff.

[20] The Sea of Azov.

[21] Presumably the Kuban: Κοῦφις in Theoph., 356.27, 357.9, 434.11 (who, however, appears to have the Bug in mind) and *DAI*, 42.59 (see also Commentary of *DAI*).

ὁμόφυλοι αὐτῶν καὶ οὗτοι τυγχάνοντες. ἐν δὲ τοῖς Κωνσταντίνου χρόνοις ὃς κατὰ τὴν δύσιν ἐτελεύτα, Κοβρᾶτός τις ὄνομα κύριος γενόμενος τῶν φύλων τούτων τὸν βίον μεταλλάξας πέντε καταλιμπάνει υἱούς, ἐφ' οἷς διατίθεται μηδαμῶς τῆς ἀλλήλων ἀποχωρισθῆναι διαίτης, ὡς ἂν διὰ τῆς πρὸς ἀλλήλους εὐνοίας τὰ τῆς ἀρχῆς αὐτῶν διασώζοιτο. οὗτοι μικρὰ τῆς πατρικῆς φροντίσαντες παραινέσεως ὀλίγου παρῳχηκότος χρόνου διέστησαν | ἀλλήλων, ἕκαστος αὐτῶν τοῦ λαοῦ L44r *ἴδιον μέρος ἀποτεμνόμενος. ὧν ὁ μὲν πρῶτος υἱὸς λεγό|μενος* V195v *Βαϊανὸς κατὰ τὰ ἐνταλθέντα αὐτῷ παρὰ τοῦ πατρὸς ἐν τῇ προγονικῇ γῇ διέμεινε μέχρι τοῦ δεῦρο, ὁ δὲ δεύτερος λεγόμενος Κότραγος τὸν Τάναϊν περαιωθεὶς ποταμὸν ᾤκησε τού-* dB34 *του ἀντικρύ, ὁ δὲ τέταρτος τὸν Ἴστρον ποταμὸν διαβὰς ἐν Παννωνίᾳ τῇ νῦν ὑπὸ Ἀβάροις κειμένῃ αὐλίζεται ὑπόσπονδος τῷ ἐγχωρίῳ ἔθνει γενόμενος, ὁ δὲ πέμπτος κατὰ τὴν Ῥαβεννησίαν Πεντάπολιν ἱδρυσάμενος ὑπόφορος Ῥωμαίοις ἐγένετο. τούτων ὁ λοιπὸς τρίτος ἀδελφὸς ὄνομα Ἀσπαροὺχ τὸν Δάναπριν καὶ τὸν Δάναστριν ποταμὸν περαιωθεὶς περὶ τὸν Ἴστρον οἰκίζεται, τόπον πρὸς οἴκησιν ἐπιτήδειον, Ὄγγλον τῇ σφῶν καλούμενον φωνῇ, καταλαβόμενος, δυσχερῆ τε καὶ ἀνάλωτον πολεμίοις ὑπάρχοντα· ἀσφαλής τέ ἐστι τὰ μὲν ἔμπροσθεν τῇ τε δυσχωρίᾳ καὶ τῷ τελματώδης εἶναι τυγχάνων· τὰ δ' οὖν ὄπισθεν κρημνοῖς ἀβάτοις τετειχισμένα. οὕτω τοίνυν τοῦ ἔθνους διαιρεθέντος καὶ σκεδασθέντος, τὸ τῶν Χαζάρων φῦλον ἀπὸ τοῦ ἐνδοτέρου τῆς Βερσιλίας λεγομένης χώρας ὡς πλησίον | τῶν Σαρματῶν ᾠκημένον πλείστης ἀδείας ἐντεῦθεν* L44v *† ἐπέτρεχον. τὰ τοιαῦτα πάντα κατέδραμον χωρία τῆς ὑπὲρ Πόντου τὸν Εὔξεινον γῆς καὶ θαλάττης ἐπέρασε· † μεθ' ὧν καὶ Βαϊανὸν ὑπεξούσιον ποιησάμενον εἰς ὑπαγωγὴν φόρων κατέστησε.*

36. *Κωνσταντῖνος δὲ ἐπειδὴ ἔγνω ὡς τὸ σκηνῶσαν*

---

6 Κοβράτος L ‖ *ὀνόματι* V^2 ex *ὄνομα* ‖ 7 *φυλῶν* VL corr. vulg. ‖ 8 *τῆς* ex *τοὺς* V^1 ‖ 13–14 Βαιανὸς (ex Βασιανὸς) *υἱὸς λεγόμενος* V ‖ 15 *γῇ* om. L ‖ 16 Κώτραγος *τὸν* Τανάϊν L ‖ *περαιωθεὶς* ex *περαιωθὲν* V^2 ‖ 16–17 *τούτου* scripsi *τούτων* V *τοῦτον* L ‖ 18 *τῆς* . . . *κειμένης* ex *τῆς* . . . *κοιμένοις* V^2 Πανωνία *τῆς νὺν ὑπὸ* Ἀβάρους *κειμένης* L corr. vulg. ‖ 19 *ἔθει* V ‖ 19–20 Ῥαβεννησίων L ‖ 21 *ὀνόματι* V^2 ex *ὄνομα* ‖ 22 Δάνιστριν L ‖ 23 Ὄγλον V ‖ 26 *τῷ τελματώδεις* V *τὸ τελματώδεις* L corr. vulg. ‖ 29 *ἀπὸ*] *ὑπὸ* VL corr. vulg. ‖ Βερυλίας V ‖ *λεγόμενον* VL corr. B ‖ 30 Σαρμάτων V ‖ *ὠκημένων* L ‖ 31–32 *ὑπὲρ πόν* (*πόν* a V^2 deletum) *πόντου* V vide comment. ‖ 32 *μεθ' ὂν* L ‖ 33 *ποιησάμενον* scripsi *ποιησάμενος* VL

⟨here lived⟩ the so-called Kotragoi, who are also of the same stock ⟨as the Bulgarians⟩. In the days of Constantine who died in the West, a certain man by the name of Kobratos became master of these tribes. On his death he left five sons, upon whom he enjoined not to part company under any circumstances, so that their dominion might be preserved thanks to their mutual friendship. But they took little account of the paternal injunction and a short time thereafter they divided, each one of them taking his own share of their people. The eldest son, called Baianos, in accordance with his father's command, has remained until this day in his ancestral land. The second, called Kotragos, crossed the river Tanais[22] and dwelt opposite the first; the fourth went over the river Istros[23] and settled in Pannonia, which is now under the Avars, becoming an ally of the local nation. The fifth established himself in the Pentapolis of Ravenna[24] and became tributary to the Romans. The remaining third brother, called Asparuch, crossed the rivers Danapris and Danastris[25] and settled near the Istros, where he found a suitable place for habitation (called Onglos in their language), which happened to be difficult ⟨of access⟩ and impregnable by the foe: for it is secure in front because it is impassable and marshy, while at the back it is fenced by inaccessible cliffs. When this nation had thus divided and scattered, the tribe of the Chazars, ⟨issuing⟩ from the interior of the country called Bersilia, where they had lived next to the Sarmatians, invaded with complete impunity all the places that are beyond the Euxine Sea. Among others, they subjected Baianos to paying tribute to them.

36. When Constantine became aware that the nation which had settled

[22] The Don.
[23] The Danube.
[24] Between Ravenna and Ancona.
[25] The Dnieper and Dniester.

⟨παρὰ⟩ τὸν Ἴστρον ἔθνος τὰ πλησιάζοντα τῆς ὑπὸ Ῥωμαίων ἀρχῆς χωρία καταθέον διαφθείρειν ἐπεχείρει, στρατὸν ὁπλίτην ἐπὶ τὴν Θρᾳκῴαν διαβιβάσας χώραν, ἔτι τε καὶ στόλον ὁπλίσας κατὰ τοῦ ἔθνους ὡς ἀμυνόμενος ᾤχετο. οἱ δὲ Βούλγαροι dB35 τῶν τε ἱππικῶν καὶ πλοΐμων τὰ πλήθη θεασάμενοι καὶ τῷ αἰφνιδίῳ καὶ ἀνελπίστῳ καταπλαγέντες πρὸς τὰ ἑαυτῶν ὀχυρώματα ἔφυγον, τέτρασιν ἡμέραις ἐκεῖσε ὑπομείναντες· καὶ τῶν Ῥωμαίων μὴ δυνηθέντων αὐτοῖς πολέμῳ συμμῖξαι διὰ τὴν δυσχωρίαν τοῦ τόπου, ἀνελάμβανόν τε αὐτοὺς καὶ προθυμότεροι ἐγίνοντο. ὁ δὲ βασιλεὺς νόσῳ ποδαλγικῇ συσχεθεὶς καὶ ὀξυπαθήσας ἐπὶ Μεσήμβρειαν τὴν πόλιν ἀπέπλει θεραπείας ἕνεκεν, προστάξας τοῖς ἄρχουσι καὶ τοῖς λαοῖς προσεδρεύειν τῷ ὀχυρώματι καὶ ὅσα πρὸς ἄμυναν τοῦ ἔθνους κατεργάσασθαι. φήμη δέ τις ἐδέδοτο | L45ʳ τὸν βασιλέα φεύγειν μηνύουσα, δι' ἣν θορυβηθέντες οὐδενὸς διώκοντος συντόνως ἔφευγον. οἱ δὲ Βούλγαροι ἐπιδόντες ἐπεδίωκον καρτερῶς, | V196ʳ καὶ ὅσους μὲν τοῦ λαοῦ κατελάμβανον ἀνῄρουν, πλείστους δὲ καὶ ἐτραυμάτιζον. περαιωθέντες δὲ τὸν Ἴστρον ἐπὶ τὴν λεγομένην Βάρναν πλησίον Ὀδύσσου καὶ τοῦ ὑπερκειμένου μεσογαίου, τὸ ὀχυρὸν καὶ ἀσφαλὲς τοῦ τόπου πάντοθεν ἔκ τε τοῦ ποταμοῦ καὶ τῆς ἄγαν δυσχωρίας θεασάμενοι ἐνταῦθα σκηνοῦσι. κρατοῦσι δὲ καὶ τῶν [ἐγγιζόντων] παρῳκημένων Σκλαβηνῶν ἐθνῶν, καὶ οὓς μὲν τὰ πρὸς Ἀβάρους πλησιάζοντα φρουρεῖν, οὓς δὲ τὰ πρὸς Ῥωμαίους ἐγγίζοντα τηρεῖν ἐπιτάττουσιν. ἐν τούτοις ὀχυρωθέντων καὶ αὐξηθέντων τὰ ἐπὶ Θρᾴκης χωρία τε καὶ πολίσματα καταδῃοῦν ἐπεχείρουν. τῷ βασιλεῖ δὲ ἀνάγκη ἦν ταῦτα ὁρῶντι ἐπὶ τελέσμασι πρὸς αὐτοὺς σπένδεσθαι.

37. Οὕτως τοιγαροῦν εἰρηνευούσης πάντοθεν τῆς Ῥωμαίων βασιλείας ἡ τῶν Μονοθελητῶν δυσσεβὴς αἵρεσις ἐκρα-

---

36: 2 *παρὰ* add. dB || *ἔθνος* om. L || 7 *αἰφνηδίω . . . κατὰ πλαγέντες* L || 10 *ἀνελάμβανόν* (ex *ἐνελάμβανόν*) *τε ἑαυτοὺς* L *αὐτοὺς* V || 11 *κατασχεθεὶς* L || 12 *Μεσεμβρίαν* L || 16 *θορυβηθέντες* ex *θορυβέντες* V || *οὐδενὸς διώκοντος*: cf. Le 26.36; Pr 28.1; Mi 2.11 || *συντόμως* VL corr. vulg. || 17 *ἐπειδόντες* L || 18 *ἀνήρουν* ex *ἀρήρουν* ut vid. L || 19 *περαιωθέντ[ων] δὲ τ[οῦ] Ἴστρ[ου]* V *περαιωθέντων τὸν Ἴστρον* L corr. dB || 20 *Βαρνᾶν* V *Βαρύαν* L corr. B || *Ὀδύσσου* L || 23 *ἐγγιζόντων* secl. B || *πανωκημένων* VL *παρακειμένων* Theoph. 359.13 || 24 *Σκλαβηνῶν ἐθνῶν* om. L || 27 *κατὰ δηοῦν* L || 29 *σπένδεται* L

37: 1 *οὕτω* L || 1–2 *τῶν Ῥωμαίων* L || 2 *δυσεβὴς* L

by the Istros was attempting to devastate by its incursions the neighboring places that were under Roman rule, he conveyed an army to Thrace and, furthermore, fitted out a fleet and set out to ward off that nation. On seeing the multitude of cavalry and ships and amazed as they were by the unexpected suddenness ⟨of the attack⟩, the Bulgarians fled to their fortifications and remained four days there. Since, however, the Romans were unable to engage them in battle because of the difficulty of the terrain, they regained strength and eagerness. Now the emperor was seized by an attack of gout and being in much pain, sailed off to the city of Mesembria for treatment after giving orders to the officers and soldiers to keep on investing the fort and do whatever was necessary to oppose the nation. But a rumor spread about that the emperor had fled and, being on this account thrown into confusion, they fled headlong although no one was on their heels. Seeing this, the Bulgarians pursued them in strength, killing those they caught and wounding many others. After crossing the Istros in the direction of Varna, which is near Odyssos, and perceiving how strong and secure was the inland area thanks to the river and the great difficulty of the terrain, they settled there. Furthermore, they subjugated the neighboring Slavonic tribes, some of which they directed to guard the area in the vicinity of the Avars and others to watch the Roman border. So, fortifying themselves and gaining in strength, they attempted to lay waste the villages and towns of Thrace. Seeing this, the emperor was obliged to treat with them and pay them tribute.

37. The Roman Empire being thus at peace on all sides, the impious heresy of the Monotheletes (which had begun in the days of Emperor

τύνετο, ἤδη τῶν ἀφ' Ἡρακλείου τοῦ βασιλέως χρόνων λαβοῦσα τὴν ἀρχήν· καὶ σχίσμα ἦν περὶ τὴν καθολικὴν ἐκκλησίαν. dB36 *ταῦτα διαγνοὺς Κωνσταντῖνος σύνοδον οἰκουμενικὴν συγκροτεῖ, ἣ τὰς μὲν προλαβούσας | πέντε ἁγίας οἰκουμενικὰς συν-* L45v *όδους ἐκύρωσε καὶ τὰ δύο ἐπὶ τοῦ σωτῆρος Χριστοῦ θελήματα καὶ δύο φυσικὰς ἐνεργείας, τέλειον αὐτὸν ἐν θεότητι καὶ τέλειον ἐν ἀνθρωπότητι διατρανώσασα καὶ τῷ ἀναθέματι τοὺς τῆς αἱρέσεως ἄρξαντας παραπέμψασα. οὕτως ἐν γαλήνῃ καὶ εἰρηνικῇ καταστάσει τὸ λοιπὸν τῆς ζωῆς διατελέσας τῷ ἑπτακαιδεκάτῳ ἔτει τῆς βασιλείας αὐτοῦ ἐτελεύτα. καὶ κατατίθεται αὐτοῦ τὸ λείψανον ἐν τοῖς βασιλείοις τῶν ἁγίων ἀποστόλων μνήμασι.*

38. Καταλιμπάνει δὲ εἰς τὴν βασιλείαν τὸν υἱὸν Ἰουστινιανὸν ἑκκαιδέκατον ἔτος τῆς ἡλικίας ἄγοντα, ὃς τῆς βασιλείας ἐπιλαβόμενος τὰ ὑπὸ τοῦ πατρὸς τῆς εἰρήνης ἕνεκεν καὶ τῆς ἄλλης πολιτικῆς εὐταξίας βραβευθέντα διέστρεφε. μεθ' ὧν λύει καὶ τὴν πρὸς τοὺς Βουλγάρους γενομένην εἰρήνην. ἱππικὰ δὲ στρατεύματα πρὸς τοῖς Θρᾳκῴοις διαγαγὼν χωρίοις κατὰ τῶν Σκλαβηνῶν εὐθέως ὥρμησε. μέχρι δὲ Θεσσαλονίκης ἐκδραμὼν πόλεως, πολλὰ τῶν ἐκεῖσε Σκλαβηνῶν γένη τὰ μὲν πολέμῳ τὰ δὲ ὁμολογίᾳ παραλαβών, εἰς τὴν τοῦ Ὀψικίου λεγομένην χώραν διὰ τῆς Ἀβύδου διαβιβάσας κατέστησεν. ἐξ ὧν στρατεύει ἄχρι καὶ εἰς τριά|κοντα χιλιάδας L46r λαόν, οὓς ἐξοπλίσας λαὸν ἐκάλεσε περιούσιον, ἄρχοντα αὐτοῖς ἐκ τῶν εὐγενεστέρων ἐπιστήσας Νέβουλον τοὔνομα. εἰς οὓς θαρρήσας λύει τὴν πρὸς τοὺς Σαρακηνοὺς παρὰ τοῦ πατρὸς γενομένην εἰρήνην, μεθίστησι δὲ καὶ τοὺς ἐν τῷ ὄρει τοῦ Λιβάνου λοχοῦντας ἐκ παλαιοῦ χρόνου ὁπλίτας. ἐκστρατεύει δὲ κατ' αὐτῶν, καὶ κατὰ τὴν Σεβαστόπολιν γίνεται. καὶ αὐτοὶ δὲ ἐπιστρατεύσαντες πρὸς αὐτοὺς παραγίνονται· καὶ τὰ μὲν τῆς εἰρήνης φυλάτ|τεσθαι βέβαια παρ' αὐτῶν ἔφασκον, εἰ δὲ V196r βούλοιντο διαστρέφειν Ῥωμαῖοι, θεὸν κριτὴν τῶν αἰτίων γίνε- dB37

7 *καὶ τὰ* om. L ‖ 13 *ἀποτίθεται* L

38: 1–2 Ἰουστινιανὸν ex Ἰουστιανὸν V[2] ‖ 2 *ἐξκαιδέκατον* L ‖ 4 *διέστρεψε* L ‖ 5 *γεναμένην* L ‖ 7 *Σκλαβίνων ἐθνῶν ὥρμησεν* L *εὐθ[έως]* V ‖ 7–8 Θεσσαλονικῆς V ‖ 8–9 *Σκλαβίνων γένει* L *γένει* etiam V ‖ 11 *εἰς* B *ἕως* VL ‖ 11–12 *χηλιάδας . . . ἐξοπλήσας* L ‖ 13 Νεβοῦλον V ‖ 15 *μεθήστησι* L ‖ 16 *ἐκστρατεύσας* L ‖ 17 *καὶ*[1] om. L ‖ 20 *δια[στρέ]φειν* V ‖ *θεὸν κατ' αυτῶν τὸν αἴτιον* L

Herakleios) was gaining in strength and a schism prevailed in the Catholic Church. On perceiving this, Constantine convened an ecumenical council which confirmed the five preceding ecumenical synods as well as ⟨the dogma of⟩ the two wills and two natural energies of Our Lord Christ, whom it proclaimed perfect in His divinity and in His manhood, while condemning to anathema the leaders of the heresy. After thus spending the rest of his life in tranquillity and peace, he died in the seventeenth year of his reign. His body was laid down in the imperial sepulchers at ⟨the church of⟩ the Holy Apostles.

38. He left the empire to his son Justinian, who was then in his sixteenth year and who, on assuming power, undid the measures which his father had taken for the sake of peace and the good order of the state. In addition to other things, he broke the peace that had been concluded with the Bulgarians. He conveyed a force of cavalry to the Thracian region and straightaway advanced against the Slavonians. Having pushed on as far as the city of Thessalonica, he captured many of the Slavonic tribes that were there—some by war, others by treaty—and after conveying them by way of Abydos to the land of Opsikion (as it is called), he established them there. Among them he raised an army of thirty thousand, whom he equipped and named "the Peculiar People," and placed under the command of one of their noblemen called Neboulos. Putting his trust in them, he broke the peace that his father had concluded with the Saracens and also dislodged the armed men who from olden times had been lurking in the mountains of Lebanon. He made an expedition against them ⟨the Saracens⟩ and came to Sebastopolis. They, too, raised an army and came to meet him; and they declared that they had in their possession the pledges of the peace treaty, but if the Romans wished to break them,

σθαι. Ἰουστινιανοῦ δὲ μᾶλλον τῆς μάχης αἱρουμένου, οὗτοι τὸν τῆς εἰρήνης ἔγγραφον λόγον ἐφ' ὑψηλοῦ ἀναρτήσαντες σημείου προάγειν ἐκέλευον, καὶ δὴ κατὰ Ῥωμαίων ἐχώρουν. οἱ δὲ εἰς φυγὴν ἐτράποντο. καὶ ὁ κληθεὶς περιούσιος τῶν Σκλάβων λαὸς τοῖς Σαρακηνοῖς προστίθεται, καὶ σὺν αὐτοῖς Ῥωμαίους ἀνῄρουν. ἐξ οὗ πλεῖον προσκτησάμενοι θάρσος πλειόνως τὴν Ῥωμαίων ἀρχὴν ἐλυμαίνοντο. καὶ τὰ μὲν πρὸς τὸ ἔθνος οὕτω πως ἔσχεν.

39. Εἰς δὲ τὰς πολιτικὰς ἀρχὰς καθίστα ἄνδρας ἀπηνεῖς καὶ ὠμοτάτους, ὧν ἦν Στέφανος | εὐνοῦχος Πέρσης, ταμίας L46v τῶν βασιλικῶν χρημάτων· καὶ πολλὰ τοὺς ὑπὸ χεῖρα αἰκιζόμενος ἄχρι καὶ εἰς τὴν μητέρα Ἰουστινιανοῦ τὴν τόλμαν ἐξήνεγκε, μάστιγας αὐτῇ [ἐν σχήματι] ὥσπερ τοὺς παῖδας οἱ γραμματισταὶ ἐπιθέμενος. Θεόδοτον δέ τινα μοναχόν, ἔγκλειστον τὸ πρότερον κατὰ τὰ Θρᾳκῷα τοῦ Στενοῦ λεγομένου πόρου γεγονότα, τῶν δημοσίων λογιστήν, ὃν τὸ δημῶδες γενικὸν λογοθέτην καλοῦσι, κατέστησεν, ὃς ὑπερβολῇ ὠμότητος οὐ τοὺς ὑπ' αὐτὸν μόνον χρήματα ἔπραττε, μετεώροις σχοινίοις ἀναρτῶν καὶ ἀχύροις περικαπνίζων, ἀλλ' ἤδη καὶ ἑτέρους περιφανεστέρους ἄνδρας δημεύων καὶ ἀφορήτους ποινὰς ἐπιφέρων ἀπέκτεννε.

40. Λεόντιον δέ τινα πατρίκιον ἐκ τῆς τῶν Ἰσαύρων ὁρμώμενον χώρας καὶ στρατηγὸν γενόμενον τοῦ ἀνατολικοῦ καλουμένου στρατεύματος, εὐδόκιμόν τε ἐν τοῖς πολέμοις πολλάκις γενόμενον, καὶ αὐτὸν ὑποφρούριον τρισὶ χρόνοις Ἰουστινιανὸς ἐποίησεν· εἶτα τῆς φρουρᾶς λύσας στρατηγὸν dB38 τῆς Ἑλλάδος προβάλλεται, αὐθημερὸν ἀναγκάσας τοῦ Βυζαντίου ἀπαίρειν. πρὸς ὃν γίνονται φίλοι τυγχάνοντες ἀωρὶ

---

21 ἐρωμένου L || 23 ἐκέλευεν καὶ ἤδη L || 24 ἐτρέποντο L || 26 Ῥωμαίοις L || 27 τῶν Ῥωμαίων . . . ἐλοιμαίνοντο L || 28 ἔθνος V πάθος L

39: 1 usque ad **40**.12 cf. Sudam s.v. Ἰουστινιανὸς ὁ Ῥινότμητος || 1 ἐς Suda || καθίστει L καθίστη Suda || ἀπεινῆς L || 2 ὁ εὐνοῦχος Suda || ταμείας L || 5 μάστιγος L || αὐτῇ V² ex αὐτῆς || ἐν σχήματι seclusi om. L || 6 γραμματεῖς L || 6–7 ἔγκλειστον Suda || 8–9 γενηκὸν L om. V || 10 οὐ om. L || τοῖς VL corr. vulg. || 11 περικαπνήζων L || 12 περηφανεστέρους L περιφανεστάτους Suda || 13 ἀπέκτεινεν Suda

---

40: 1 Ἠσαύρων L || 3 ἐν πολλοῖς V || 5–6 στρατ. Ἑλλάδος Suda || 7 ἀωρὶ B ἄωροι L ἄωρ[ον] V accentu sec. m. add.

God would judge the guilty. Since Justinian indicated his preference for battle, they affixed the written peace treaty to a tall standard and ordered it to be carried forward; and so they advanced against the Romans who turned to flight. The "Peculiar People" of the Slavonians (as they had been called) joined the Saracens, along with whom they massacred the Romans. Gaining as a result added courage, they ⟨the Saracens⟩ caused greater damage to the Roman State. Thus it was with the ⟨Slavonian⟩ nation.

39. As for civil magistracies, he appointed to them men of a cruel and exceedingly harsh character, among them the eunuch Stephen the Persian, treasurer of the imperial monies,[26] who inflicted many punishments not only on those under his authority, but went so far in his insolence as to inflict lashes on Justinian's mother as teachers do to children.[27] And a certain monk Theodotos, who had formerly been a recluse on the Thracian side of the Bosporos, he appointed treasurer of public funds (or, as ordinary folk say, general logothete). This man not only exacted money with exceeding cruelty from those placed under his power, whom he suspended by ropes and suffocated with smoking straw, but even confiscated ⟨the property⟩ of persons of high position and put them to death by inflicting unbearable torments on them.

40. Justinian also imprisoned for three years a certain patrician Leontios, a native of Isauria, who had been commander of the Anatolic army (as it is called) and had often achieved success in war. Then he freed him from prison and appointed him *strategos* of Hellas, forcing him to depart from Byzantium that very day. At a late hour of the night his friends—a certain monk Paul

---

[26] I.e., *sacellarius*. Cf. Theoph., 367.15.

[27] We have omitted from the translation the words ἐν σχήματι which do not appear to yield any satisfactory sense.

τῆς νυκτὸς Παῦλός τις μοναχὸς τῶν Καλλιστράτου μονῆς | L47[r] ὑπάρχων, ἀστρονόμος τὴν ἐπιστήμην, καὶ Γρηγόριος μοναχὸς καὶ ἡγούμενος ἐν τῇ Φλώρου μονῇ, Καππαδόκης τὸ γένος, ὡς προπέμψοντες. αὐτὸς δὲ ἰδὼν ἐνεκάλει λέγων ὡς "μάτην μοι τὰ τῆς βασιλείας προεμαντεύσασθε· νῦν γὰρ ἐνθένδε ἀποχωροῦντα τὸ τέλος με τῆς ζωῆς πικρὸν καταλήψεται". οἱ δὲ τῆς ὁδοῦ εἶργον, βέβαια παρεχόμενοι ⟨ὡς⟩ εἰ μὴ ὀκνήσειεν τῆς ἐξουσίας κρατήσειεν. τούτοις πεισθεὶς εὐθὺς ἐπικομίζων τινὰς τῶν ὑπηρετῶν ἔτι τῆς νυκτὸς ἐνισταμένης καὶ ὅπλα ἀνελόμενος εἰς τὸ πραιτώριον ἄνεισιν ἡσυχῇ. καὶ σημηνάντων ὡς τὸν βασιλέα παρεῖναι ἐν τοῖς ἐκεῖσε πρᾶξαι τὰ κατὰ γνώμην, ὁ τοῦ πραιτωρίου ὕπαρχος ὑπήντα διανοιγνὺς τὰς πύλας· ὃν αὐτίκα χεῖρας καὶ πόδας ἐπέδησεν. ἐντὸς δὲ γενόμενος Λεόντιος πάντας τοὺς καθειργμένους ἔλυσε καὶ ὁπλίσας ἐπὶ τὸν καλούμενον Φόρον ἐξώρμησε· | V197[r] κἀκεῖθεν σκεδαννυμένους ἀνὰ πάντα μέρη τῆς πόλεως βοῇ κράζειν ἐκέλευσε πάντας Χριστιανοὺς εἰς τὸ ἱερὸν τῆς Σοφίας παραγενέσθαι. ἐξ ὧν πᾶν τὸ πλῆθος θορυβηθὲν σπουδῇ πρὸς τὸν λουτῆρα τῆς ἐκκλησίας ἠθροίζετο. ὁ δὲ σὺν τοῖς μοναχοῖς καὶ ἑτέροις τῶν φίλων πρὸς Καλλίνικον τὸν | L47[v] τηνικαῦτα ἱεράρχην τῆς πόλεως ἔρχεται, καὶ βιάζεται κατελθεῖν καὶ φωνῆσαι πρὸς τὸν λαόν "αὕτη ἡ ἡμέρα ἣν ἐποίησεν ὁ κύριος". τὸ δὲ πλῆθος Ἰουστινιανὸν ἐδυσφήμει. καὶ οὕτως ἅπαντες ἐπὶ τὸν χῶρον τῆς ἱπποδρομίας ᾤχοντο. ἡμέρας δὲ ἐπιγενομένης ἐκφέρουσιν Ἰουστινιανὸν πρὸς αὐτούς. καὶ τῆς πληθύος βοώσης βασιλέα ξίφος διαδέχεσθαι, Λεόντιος τοῦ αἵματος αὐτοῦ φει- dB39 σάμενος διὰ τὴν πρὸς Κωνσταντῖνον τὸν πατέρα αὐτοῦ ἀγάπην, τεμὼν τὴν γλῶτταν καὶ τὴν ῥῖνα ἐν Χερσῶνι τῇ πόλει ἐξώρισε, δέκατον ἤδη ἔτος ἐν τῇ βασιλείᾳ διανύσαντα. Λεόντιος δὲ ὑπὸ τοῦ πλήθους βασιλεὺς ἀναγορεύεται. Στέφανον δὲ τὸν εὐνοῦχον καὶ Θεόδοτον τὸν μοναχόν, δι' ἣν ὑπέμειναν παρ' αὐτῶν κάκωσιν, καὶ ἄκοντος τοῦ βασιλέως συλλαβόμενοι καὶ τῶν ποδῶν ἐξαναρτήσαντες διὰ σχοίνων συρέντας

---

8 τῶν L τῆς V Suda || 10 ἐν Φλόρου μονῆς L τῆς τοῦ Φλ. Suda || 12 προυμαντεύσασθαι L || 14 ὡς add. vulg. om. VL || 15 κρατήσειν L fort. recte omisso ὡς || 16 ἐπισταμένης V || 18 σημαίνων L || 19 πραιτωρίου P πραίτωρος VL v. comment. || 19–20 διαναγνὺς L || 20 ἐπέδισαν L || 23 σκεδαννύμενοι VL corr. B || 24 ἐκέλευσε ex ἐκέλυσε V[1] || 26 ἠθρύζετο L || 27 Καλλήνικον L || 28 βία κατελθεῖν L || 29 Ps. 117 (118).24 || 31 ἐπιγεναμένης L || 33 διαδέχεται· Λεόντιος δὲ L || 34 τὴν ex τῆς V[2] || 35 ῥιναν L || 38 Θεόδοτον B Θεοδόσιον VL || ὑπέμεινε V || 40 σχοινίων L

of the monastery of Kallistratos, who was an expert astronomer, and the monk Gregory, a Cappadocian by origin, who was abbot of the monastery of Florus—came to see him off. On seeing them, he rebuked them, saying: "In vain have you predicted that I would become emperor; for now, as I depart hence, I shall be overtaken by a cruel death." But they dissuaded him from the journey by assuring him that he would attain power if he showed determination. Convinced by them, he assembled some of his servants and taking up arms (it was still night) he went quietly up to the Praetorium. On their announcing that the emperor had arrived to carry out his wishes there, the prefect of the Praetorium[28] met them and opened the gates; immediately they bound him hand and foot. Getting inside, Leontios released all the prisoners, whom he armed and then rushed to the Forum (as it is called); and from there he ordered them to scatter throughout the City and to call loudly to all Christians to assemble at the church of Sophia. Being thus roused, the entire multitude gathered in haste at the fountain[29] of the church. Together with the monks and other friends of his, ⟨Leontios⟩ presented himself to Kallinikos, who was then archpriest of the City, and forced him to come down and cry to the people: "This is the day that the Lord hath made!" The multitude, for its part, insulted Justinian. Thus they all proceeded to the Hippodrome; and when it became day, Justinian was brought out to them. While the crowd was shouting that the emperor should be put to the sword, Leontios spared his life because of his affection for ⟨Justinian's⟩ father Constantine and, after cutting off his tongue and his nose, exiled him to the city of Cherson; by then he had reigned ten years. And so Leontios was proclaimed emperor by the crowd. As for the eunuch Stephen and the monk Theodotos, even against the emperor's wish, they arrested them for the mistreatment they had suffered at their hands and, tying them up by their feet with ropes, dragged them to the so-called market

[28]Not the praetorian prefect, an office that no longer existed at the time, but the prefect of Constantinople, whose seat was at the Praetorium.

[29]I.e., the atrium.

πρὸς τὴν καλουμένην τοῦ Βοὸς ἀγορὰν πυρὶ παραδεδώκεσαν. καὶ τὰ μὲν ἐν Κωνσταντινουπόλει οὕτω διέκειτο.

41. Ἡ δὲ ὑπὸ Ἀφρικὴν Καρχηδὼν πρῴην ὑπὸ Ῥωμαίοις τελοῦσα τότε ὑπὸ χεῖρα τῶν Σαρακηνῶν γίνεται, πολέμῳ παρ' αὐτοῖς ληφθεῖσα. τοῦτο διαγνοὺς Λεόντιος ἅπαντα τὰ Ῥω|μαϊκὰ ἐξώπλισε πλόϊμα, στρατηγόν τε ἐπ' αὐτοῖς Ἰωάννην [L48r] τὸν πατρίκιον ὡς ἔμπειρον τῶν πολεμίων προχειρισάμενος πρὸς Καρχηδόνα κατὰ τῶν Σαρακηνῶν ἐξέπεμψεν· ὃς ἐκεῖσε παραγενόμενος τοὺς μὲν ἐν αὐτῇ τῶν Σαρακηνῶν πολέμῳ ἐτροπώσατο, τὴν δὲ πόλιν Ῥωμαίοις ἀνεσώσατο, καὶ τἆλλα πάντα τὰ ἐκεῖσε πολίσματα τῆς τοῦ ἔθνους ἀπαλλάξας ἐξουσίας καὶ στρατὸν ὁπλίτην πρὸς φυλακὴν ἐν αὐτοῖς ἐγκαταλείψας αὐτοῦ διεχείμαζεν. ὁ δὲ τῶν Σαρακηνῶν βασιλεὺς ταῦτα μεμαθηκὼς πλείονα κατ' αὐτοῦ ἐκίνησε πόλεμον, δι' οὗ καὶ τὸν μὲν Ἰωάννην σὺν τῷ περιόντι αὐτῷ Ῥωμαϊκῷ στόλῳ ἐξώθησε, καὶ τὴν Καρχηδόνα παραλαμβάνει πάλιν καὶ τὰ περὶ αὐτὴν πολίσματα πάντα. ὁ δὲ Ἰωάννης ἀφορμήσας πρὸς βασιλέα ἀνήγετο, ἐν δὲ τῇ νήσῳ Κρήτῃ γενόμενος ὑπό τε τῶν ἀρχόντων καὶ τοῦ στρατιωτικοῦ πλήθους ἐστασιάζετο, ὡς οὐδαμῶς βουληθεὶς αἰσχύνῃ καὶ δέει κατεχόμενος πρὸς βασιλέα παραγενέσθαι. διὰ τοῦτο Λεόντιον μὲν δυσφημοῦντες [dB40] ἀθετοῦσι, ψηφίζονται δὲ Ἀψίμαρον ὄνομα, στρατοῦ ἄρχοντα τῶν Κουρικιωτῶν τυγχάνοντα τῆς ὑπὸ Κιβυραιωτῶν χώρας, ὃν δρουγγάριον Ῥωμαίοις καλεῖν ἔθος, Τιβέριον αὐτὸν ἐπονομάσαντες. ἐν δὲ τῷ μεταξὺ | νόσος λοιμικὴ | τῇ πόλει [V197v] ἐπέσκηψε καὶ πλῆθος λαοῦ ἐν μησὶ τέτρασι διέφθειρεν. Ἀψίμαρος [L48v] δὲ σὺν τῷ συνόντι αὐτῷ στόλῳ εἰς Βυζάντιον ἀναχθεὶς ἀντικρὺ τῆς πόλεως ἐν Συκαῖς λεγομένῳ παραθαλασσίῳ χωρίῳ προσορμίζεται. ἐπὶ χρόνον δέ τινα πόλεμον συμβαλὼν τοῖς ἐν τῇ πόλει, τέλος τοὺς ὑπὸ τοῦ τείχους Βλαχερνῶν φρουροὺς καὶ τοὺς τούτων ἄρχοντας ὑποφθείρας δόλῳ ὑπ' αὐτῶν παραλαμβάνει τὴν πόλιν. καὶ ὁ σὺν αὐτῷ στρατὸς εἰσελθὼν

---

41 παραδέδωκε L

41: 1 Καλχηδὼν V ‖ 4 ἐξώπλησεν L ‖ 7 τοῖς L ‖ 8 τὴν . . . ἀνεσώσατο om. L ‖ 11 ἐνκαταλέξας L ‖ 12 ἐκήνησε L ‖ 15 πάντα om. V ‖ 17 στρατιωτηκοῦ L ‖ 18–20 ὡς . . . ἀθετοῦσι om. L ‖ 20 ψιφήζονται L ‖ Ἁψίμαρον V ubique Ἀψήμαρον L ‖ 21 τῆς om. L ‖ 22 τῆς χώρας L ‖ 23 τῶ V τὸ L ‖ 23–24 λοιμικὴ ex λοιμικῇ V[1] λυμικὴ . . . ἐπέσκηψεν . . . τέσαρσι L ‖ 24–25 Ἀψήμαρος . . . συνῶντι L ‖ 30 ὁ om. L

of the Bull, where they burned them. Such were the events at Constantinople.

41. At that time Carthage in Africa (which had previously been subject to the Romans) passed under the dominion of the Saracens who took it by war. On becoming aware of this, Leontios fitted out the entire Roman fleet, to whose command he appointed the patrician John because of his experience in military matters and sent him against the Saracens at Carthage. Arriving there, he routed in battle the Saracens who were in Carthage and regained the city for the Romans. He also delivered from the dominion of that nation all the other towns that are there, left soldiers to guard them, and wintered in those parts. When the king of the Saracens had heard of this, he mounted a stronger campaign against him, by which means he drove out John together with the Roman fleet and reoccupied Carthage and all the towns round about. Setting sail, John was making his way back to the emperor, but when he reached the island of Crete, a rebellion broke out among his officers and the mass of his soldiers, being as he was [30] quite unwilling to return to the emperor in the grip of shame and fear. For this reason they insulted and repudiated Leontios and elected a man called Apsimaros, whom they renamed Tiberios, the commander of the Korykiote contingent of the Kibyraiot region—an office which the Romans are wont to call *drungarios*. In the meantime a plague fell upon the City and destroyed a multitude of men within four months. Having sailed up to Byzantium with the fleet that accompanied him, Apsimaros put in at Sykai (as it is called), a seaside spot opposite the City. For some time he joined battle with the inhabitants of the City, which he finally took by deceit after bribing the guards of the Blachernai walls and their officers. The army

[30] Nikephoros has here confused the meaning of his source: it was, of course, the army, not John, that was reluctant to return to Constantinople, as Theoph., 370.20 makes clear.

τὰ χρήματα τῶν πολιτῶν διήρπαζε. Λεόντιον δὲ χειρωσάμενος τρίτον ἔτος ἐν τῇ βασιλείᾳ διάγοντα τὴν ῥῖνα αὐτοῦ ἐξέτεμε, καὶ ἐν τῷ καλουμένῳ τῆς Δελμάτου μοναστηρίῳ ἡσυχάζειν προσέταξε.

42. *Καὶ οὕτως μὲν ταῦτα ἐπ' αὐτοῖς συνέβαινεν· Ἰουστινιανὸς δὲ ἐπεὶ πρὸς τῇ Χερσῶνι διέτριβε, συχνότερον δημηγορῶν ὡς πάλιν κρατήσειν τῆς βασιλείας ἐπαρρησιάζετο. οἱ δὲ ὧδε πολῖται κίνδυνον ἑαυτοῖς ὑπονοούμενοι ἐβουλεύσαντο αὐτὸν ἀνελεῖν ἢ δεσμώτην πρὸς Ἀψίμαρον ἀναπέμπειν. αὐτὸς δὲ τοῦτο αἰσθόμενος ἐκεῖθεν διέφυγε καὶ εἰς τὸ φρούριον τὸ λεγόμενον Δόρος πρὸς τῇ Γοτθικῇ κειμένον χώρᾳ ἀπέδρασεν. | [L49r] αἰτεῖ δὲ τὸν τῶν Χαζάρων ἡγεμόνα (χαγάνους δὲ τούτους αὐτοὶ καλοῦσιν) ὡς αὐτὸν παραγενέσθαι. ὁ δὲ τῇ αἰτήσει εἶξε καὶ αὐτὸν μετὰ τιμῆς ἐδέξατο, καὶ φιλιωθεὶς αὐτῷ τὴν ἑαυτοῦ ἀδελφὴν Θεοδώραν καλουμένην εἰς γυναῖκα ἐξέδοτο. ὁ δὲ τῇ αὐτοῦ συναινέσει ἐν Φαναγώρῃ ἐλθὼν σὺν αὐτῇ διέτριβε. ταῦτα διαγνοὺς Ἀψίμαρος ἐνέκειτο συχνῶς [dB41] τὸν τῶν Χαζάρων ἄρχοντα ἐκλιπαρῶν, πλεῖστα δὲ χρήματα καὶ δῶρα ὑπισχνεῖτο, εἰ ζῶντα Ἰουστινιανὸν ἢ τὴν κεφαλὴν αὐτῷ ἐκπέμψαι. ὁ δὲ ταῖς πολλαῖς εἴξας παρακλήσεσιν ὑπέσχετο τοῦτο πληροῦν. πέμπει οὖν ἄνδρας εἰς φυλακὴν αὐτοῦ καθεστάναι, τῷ μὲν προσχήματι ὡς μὴ ὑπὸ τῶν ὁμοφύλων ἐπιβουλευθείη, τῷ ὄντι δὲ φυλάσσειν, ὡς μὴ ἀποδράσαι ποτὲ προασφαλιζόμενος. κελεύει δὲ τῷ ἄρχοντι τῶν ὁμοεθνῶν, ᾠκειωμένῳ δὲ Ἰουστινιανῷ ὄντι, ἔτι δὲ καὶ τῷ ἄρχοντι τῷ τοῦ Βοσπόρου τοῦ Σκυθικοῦ ἐπιτηρεῖν ἡνίκα αὐτοῖς ἐπιτρέψει ἀνελεῖν αὐτὸν ὡς τάχιστα. ταῦτα δὲ μηνύεται Θεοδώρᾳ παρά τινος τῶν τοῦ πατρὸς οἰκετῶν· ἡ δὲ τὰ τῆς ἐπιβουλῆς τῷ ἀνδρὶ ἀνετίθει. καὶ αὐτὸς τὸν οἰκεῖον ἐκεῖνον τὸν Χάζαρον | [L49v] καλέσας καὶ ἀπιδιάσας μετ' αὐτοῦ ἀγχόνῃ παρέδωκε, τῷ αὐτῷ τε τρόπῳ ἀναιρεῖ καὶ τὸν Βοσπόρου ἄρχοντα. εὐθὺς δὲ Θεο-*

31–32 *χειρισάμενος* L ‖ 32 *ῥῖνα* om. L ‖ 33 *τῆς Δ.*: fort. *τοῦ* vel *τῶν Δ.* legendum

---

42: 1 *οὕτως μετὰ ταῦτα . . . συνέβενεν* L ‖ 5 *Ἀψήμαρον* L ‖ 6 *αἰσθώμενος* L ‖ 6–7 *φρούρειον τὸ λεγόμεν Δώρος* L ‖ 8 *τὸν τὸν* V ‖ 8–9 *ἡγεμῶνα χαγάνοις δὲ τούτοις* L ‖ 10 *ἦξεν* L ‖ 12 *ἐξέδωτο . . . συνε*[ras. 1 litt.]*ν*[ras. 2 litt.]*έσει* L ‖ *Φαναγῶρι* L ‖ 13 *αὐτῇ* om. L ‖ 14 *ἐκληπαρῶν* L ‖ 15 *ὑπισχνίτο* L ‖ *εἰ* vulg. *ἢ* VL ‖ 16 *πολλαῖς* (ex *πολλαῖσι*) *εἴξας* V[1] *ἤξας* L ‖ 18 *ὑπὸ* V *ἐπὶ* L ‖ 19 *φυλάσσειν* secl. dB ‖ 20 *ὁμοέθνων* V ‖ 21 *δὲ*[1] om. L ‖ 22 *αὐτοὺς* VL corr. vulg. ‖ 23 *ὡς* om. L ‖ *μηνοίεται* L ‖ 26–27 *ἀγχῶνι . . . δὲ τρόπῳ* L

that was with him entered and seized the monies of the citizens. He arrested Leontios (who was then in the third year of his reign) and, after cutting off his nose, directed that he should live quietly in the monastery of Delmatos (as it is called).

42. So much for them. As for Justinian, he was making, while he dwelt at Cherson, frequent declarations in public that he would regain the empire. Suspecting themselves to be in danger, the inhabitants of that city planned to kill him or to deliver him prisoner to Apsimaros. On becoming aware of this, he escaped from that place and fled to the fortress called Doros, which lies in the country of the Goths.[31] He requested from the chieftain of the Chazars (whom they call Chagan) leave to pay him a visit. The latter consented and received him with honor; and after becoming friendly with him, gave him his own sister Theodora in marriage. With ⟨the Chagan's⟩ consent he came to Phanagoria and dwelt there with her. When Apsimaros had been informed of these matters, he pressed the chieftain of the Chazars with repeated requests, promising him great sums of money and gifts if the latter delivered Justinian alive to him or, ⟨if not,⟩ his head. ⟨The Chagan⟩ yielded to the numerous requests and promised to do so. He accordingly sent a band of men to guard ⟨Justinian⟩ on the pretext that he should not fall vicitim to a plot by his fellow countrymen, but in reality to make sure that he would not escape. He also gave orders to the chief of his tribesmen, who was on friendly terms with Justinian, and to the commander of the Scythian Bosporos to be in readiness for his order to kill him at the earliest opportunity. These matters were announced to Theodora by one of her father's servants and she confided to her husband the details of the plot. So he invited his Chazar friend and, taking him aside, had him strangled; and in the same manner he killed the com-

[31] Usually placed in the area of medieval Mangup in the SW part of the Crimean peninsula. Δόρυ in Procopius, *De aed.*, III.7.13; Δαρᾶς or Δαράς in Theoph., 372.30; Δόρος in *Notit.* III. 42, 611, ed. J. Darrouzès, *Notitiae episcopatuum*, 231, 241. See A. A. Vasiliev, *The Goths in the Crimea* (Cambridge, Mass., 1936), 52ff.; L. V. Firsov, *VizVrem* 40 (1979), 104–13.

δώραν τὴν γαμετὴν πρὸς τὸν πατέρα ἐκπέμπει, αὐτὸς δὲ ἀπάρας εἰς Τόμιν καλούμενον παραθαλάσσιον χωρίον κατῆλθε. κἀκεῖσε νηΐ ἐπιβὰς σὺν ἑτέροις τισὶν ἀνδράσι καὶ ταύτην παραπλεύσας ἦλθε μέχρι | [V198^r] Συμβόλου τῇ πόλει πλησιάσας Χερσῶνι. καὶ προσορμίσας τῷ ἐκεῖσε λιμένι πέμπει ἕνα τῶν ἑταίρων ἐπὶ τῇ πόλει, κἀκεῖθεν ἄγει πρὸς αὐτὸν τὸν Βαρασβακούριον καὶ τὸν τούτου ἀδελφὸν τόν τε Σαλιβᾶν καὶ ἑτέρους τινὰς ἄνδρας. καὶ σὺν αὐτοῖς ἐκπλεύσας, τὰ λεγόμενα Νεκρόπηλα παρελθὼν πρὸς τὸν Ἴστρον ποταμὸν παραγίνεται. ἐκεῖθεν ἐκπέμπει τῶν συνόντων τινὰ Στέφανον πρὸς Τέρβελιν κύριον ὄντα τηνικαῦτα τῶν ἐκεῖσε Βουλγάρων, παρακαλῶν συλλαβέσθαι αὐτῷ ὥστε τὸν τῆς βασιλείας ἀπολήψεσθαι θρόνον, ἄλλα τε πλεῖστα δῶρα ὑποσχόμενος καὶ [dB42] τὴν ἑαυτοῦ θυγατέρα εἰς γυναῖκα αὐτῷ δώσειν ἐπαγγειλάμενος. ὁ δὲ προθύμως ἐν πᾶσιν ὑπεῖκε, καὶ Ἰουστινιανὸν σὺν τιμῇ μεγάλῃ ἐδέξατο, καὶ ἅπαντα τὸν ὑπ᾽ αὐτῷ λαὸν ὁπλίσας σὺν αὐτῷ ἐπὶ τὴν βασιλεύουσαν ᾤχετο. | [L50^r] προσεδρεύει δὲ τῷ τείχει Βλαχερνῶν ἐπὶ τρισὶν ἡμέραις, ἀξιῶν τοὺς τῆς πόλεως εἰσδεχθῆναι αὐτὸν βασιλέα. οἱ δὲ αἰσχρῶς ὑβρίζοντες ἀπέπεμπον. ὁ δὲ νυκτὸς εἰσδύεται σὺν ὀλίγοις τισὶ κατὰ τὸν τῆς πόλεως ἀγωγὸν κἀντεῦθεν παραλαμβάνει τὴν πόλιν καὶ πρὸς βραχὺ σκηνοῦται ἐν τῷ παλατίῳ Βλαχερνῶν. Ἡράκλειον δὲ τὸν ἀδελφὸν Ἀψιμάρου στρατηγὸν τοῦ ἀνατολικοῦ στρατοῦ γενόμενον καὶ τοὺς ἄλλους ἄρχοντας καὶ ὑπασπιστὰς αὐτοῦ πρὸς τῷ τείχει ἐπὶ ξύλου ἀνήρτησεν. Ἀψίμαρον δὲ συλλαβὼν ἕβδομον ἔτος ἐν τῇ βασιλείᾳ διανύσαντα, ἔτι δὲ καὶ Λεόντιον σιδήροις πεδήσας κατέσχεν ἐν εἱρκτῇ· μετὰ δὲ ταῦτα ἱππικὸν ἐπιτελέσας ἀγῶνα, θάτερον μὲν ἐκ δεξιῶν θάτερον δὲ ἐξ ἀριστερῶν πρὸς τοῖς ποσὶν αὐτοῦ πατεῖσθαι ῥίψας ἐπὶ ὥρας βραχείας, μετὰ ταῦτα ἐκπέμπει ἐν τῷ καλουμένῳ Κυνηγίῳ τμηθῆναι τὰς κεφαλάς. τὸν δὲ Βουλγάρων ἄρχοντα Τέρβελιν ἔξω τείχους Βλαχερνῶν σκηνούμενον πολλὰ φιλοφρονησάμενος, τέλος παραγενόμενον πρὸς αὐτὸν χλανίδα τε περιβάλλει βασιλικὴν | [L50^v] καὶ Καίσαρα ἀναγορεύει, καὶ συμ-

29 Τομῖν L || χωρίον om. L || 30 νιῇ L || τισὶν ex τρσὶν V^1 || 31 ταύτην V αὐτὴν L || 32 προσορμήσας V || 33 ἑτέρων L || 34 Σαλίβαν L || 38 τηνικαῦτα om. L || 39–40 ἀπολήψασθαι L || 41–42 ἐπαγγηλάμενος L || 42 ἐν πᾶσιν om. L || ὑπῆκεν L || 43 αὐτοῦ L || 44 τῷ V τὰ L || 51 γενάμενον L || 52 ξύλων L || 53 διανοίσαντα L || 55 τούτων θάττερον L || θάττερον^2 L || 58 τὸν V τῶν L

mander of the Bosporos. Straightaway he dispatched his wife Theodora to her father and he himself departed to a coastal spot called Tomis.[32] There he boarded a boat together with several men and, sailing by, came as far as Symbolon,[33] close to the city of Cherson. Putting in at the harbor which is there, he sent one of his companions to the city to fetch Barasbakourios, the latter's brother, Salibas, and a number of other men. Setting sail with them, he went past the so-called Nekropela[34] and came to the river Istros. From there he sent his companion Stephen to Terbelis, who at the time was lord of the local Bulgarians, begging him for assistance that he might regain the imperial throne and promising him, in addition to many gifts, his own daughter in marriage. ⟨Terbelis⟩ readily complied in all respects and received Justinian with great honor. He then armed his whole people and proceeded to the Imperial City along with ⟨Justinian⟩. For three days ⟨Justinian⟩ encamped by the walls of Blachernai and demanded the inhabitants of the City to receive him as emperor; but they dismissed him with foul insults. However, he crept with a few men at night into the aqueduct of the City and in this way captured Constantinople. For a short time he established himself in the palace of Blachernai. He hanged on gibbets upon the walls Herakleios, the brother of Apsimaros, who was *strategos* of the Anatolic army, and other officers who were in the latter's retinue. He also apprehended Apsimaros (who had reigned seven years) as well as Leontios, bound them with fetters, and kept them in prison. Thereafter he celebrated horse races and had them thrown down at his feet, one on the right, the other on the left, and after treading on them for a short time, sent them to be beheaded at the so-called Kynegion. He showed many favors to the Bulgarian chief Terbelis, who was encamped outside the Blachernai wall, and finally sent for him, invested him with an imperial mantle and proclaimed him Caesar. He had him sit by his side and ordered the

---

[32] All the MSS of Theoph. at 373.15 give *Τόμην* (acc.). This cannot be Tomi/Costanţa, but must refer to a harbor near Phanagoria. H. Grégoire, "Le nom de la ville de Tmutarakan," *Nouv. Clio* 4 (1952), 288–92, argues that Τομή (cutting) became transformed to Taman and produced the name Τομή(ν) *τάριχα* = Tmutarakan.

[33] Modern Balaklava. Cf. *DAI*, 53.296, 302, 309.

[34] The Karkinitic Gulf. Spelled Νεκρόπυλα by the editors of *DAI*, 42.5, 69, 79 (but Νεκρόπηλα in cod. P, the best MS).

πάρεδρον ποιησάμενος προσκυνεῖσθαι σὺν αὐτῷ ὑπὸ τοῦ λαοῦ ἐκέλευε, καὶ πλεῖστα παρασχόμενος δῶρα πρὸς τὰ ἑαυτοῦ ἐξέπεμπε. Καλλίνικον *δὲ τὸν τῆς πόλεως ἱεράρχην, ὡς δυσφημήσαντα αὐτὸν ἐπὶ τῇ τοῦ* Λεοντίου *ἀναγορεύσει, τυφλώσας ἐν τῇ* Ῥώμῃ *ἐξέπεμψε,* Κῦρον *ἀντ' αὐτοῦ εἰς τὴν ἱερωσύνην προχειρισάμενος τὸν ἐν* Ἀμάστριδι *ἐγκλειστὸν γενόμενον, προσημάναντα αὐτῷ ἐκεῖσε παριόντι τὴν τῆς δευτέρας βασιλείας κατάστασιν. πολύν τε φόνον καὶ κάκωσιν* dB43 *ἐν τοῖς ὑπηκόοις ἐποιεῖτο· τοὺς μὲν γὰρ εἰς ἄρχοντας προβαλλόμενος αὐτίκα ἑτέρους ὄπισθεν ἐκπέμπων ἀνῄρει, οὓς δὲ ἐν δείπνῳ συγκαλῶν δόλῳ ἀπέκτεινεν, ἄλλους ἐν τῷ βυθῷ σάκκοις ἐμβαλὼν ἀπέρριπτε, καὶ συνελόντα εἰπεῖν, ὠμότητι πολλῇ καὶ θηριώδει γνώ|μῃ πρὸς τὸ ὑπήκοον διακείμενος.* V198v *ἐν τούτοις δὲ μεταστέλλεται ἀπὸ* Χαζαρίας Θεοδώραν *τὴν ἑαυτοῦ γαμετὴν καὶ* Τιβέριον *τὸν ἐξ αὐτῆς τεχθέντα αὐτῷ υἱόν, καὶ στέφει αὐτοὺς εἰς βασιλέας.*

43. *Μετὰ τοῦτο λύει τὴν πρὸς τοὺς* Βουλγάρους *εἰρήνην, καὶ στρατεύματα πλεῖστα διά τε γῆς καὶ θαλάσσης πρὸς τοῖς* Θρᾳκῴοις *μέρεσι διαγαγὼν πρὸς τῇ* | Ἀγχιάλῳ *πόλει ὡς πολεμήσων* L51r *αὐτοὺς παραγίνεται. ἀφυλάκτως δὲ τοῦ λαοῦ πρὸς τὰ ἐκεῖσε πεδία ἐπὶ κομιδῇ χόρτου σκεδαννυμένου ἐπιπίπτουσιν ἀθρόως οἱ* Βούλγαροι *καὶ πολλοὺς αὐτῶν διαφθείρουσι, πολλοὺς δὲ καὶ αἰχμαλώτους εἷλον. καὶ* Ἰουστινιανῷ *ἐν τῇ πόλει* Ἀγχιάλῳ *ἀπολειφθέντι ἐπὶ τρισὶν ἡμέραις προσεδρεύουσιν. ὁ δὲ νυκτὸς ναυσὶν ἐπιβὰς φυγῇ ἐκεῖθεν ἀπέπλευσε καὶ εἰς* Βυζάντιον *ἐπανάγεται.*

44. Ἐν *τούτοις ὄντων τῶν πραγμάτων ὁ τῶν* Σαρακηνῶν *βασιλεὺς λαὸν πλεῖστον ὁπλίτην ἐκπέμπει, ἡγεμόνας αὐτοῖς ἐπιστήσας* Μασαλμᾶν *καὶ* Σολυμᾶν *κατὰ τὴν αὐτῶν διάλεκτον καλουμένους, ὡς τὰ* Τύανα *τὴν πόλιν πολιορκήσοντας. οἱ δὲ ἐκεῖσε παραγενόμενοι, πολέμους πλείστους συνάψαντες,*

---

63 *παρασχώμενος* L ‖ 64 *ἐξέπεμψεν* L ‖ 67 *ἔγκλειστον* V ‖ 68 *γενάμενον* (ex *γενάμενος*) *προσημήναντι* L ‖ 72 *ἀπέκτενεν* L ‖ 73 *σάκοις ἐμβάλλων* L ‖ 73–74 *συντελοῦντα . . . ὠμωτητι . . . θηριώδη* L ‖ 74 *ὑπείκοον* V ‖ 75 Χαζαρίαν VL corr. vulg. ‖ 76 *αὐτοῦ* L ‖ 77 *βασιλέα* L

43: 3–4 *πολεμίσων αὐτοῖς* L ‖ 5 *κομηδεὶ* L ‖ 6 *πολλοῖς* L ‖ *αὐτοὺς* V ‖ 8 *πόλει* ex *πόλω* L

44: 3 Μάσαλμαν *καὶ* Σολιμὰν L ‖ 4 Τοίανα ubique V hic solum L ‖ *πολιορκήσοντας* ex *πολιορκήσαντας* L ut vid. ‖ 5 *παραγενάμενοι* L

people to pay homage to them jointly, and after showering him with many gifts, sent him home. As for Kallinikos, the archpriest of the City, who had cursed him at the proclamation of Leontios, he blinded him and exiled him to Rome, and elevated to the priesthood in his stead one Kyros, who had been a hermit at Amastris and had foretold him the circumstances of his second reign when he was passing through those parts. He inflicted many deaths and injuries on his subjects: some men he promoted to magistracies and immediately sent emissaries after them to have them killed; others he invited to dinner and slew by deceit; others he placed in sacks and cast in the sea. In brief, he treated his subjects with great cruelty and a savage disposition. At this juncture he fetched from Chazaria his wife Theodora and his son Tiberios, who was born of her, and invested them with the imperial crown.

43. Thereafter he broke the peace with the Bulgarians and, after conveying a great army to Thrace by land and by sea, proceeded to the city of Anchialos with a view to fighting them. While his men scattered heedlessly to gather hay, the Bulgarians fell suddenly upon them, killing many of them and taking many prisoners. Then for three days they besieged Justinian, who had remained in the city of Anchialos. Embarking on a ship at night, he fled from there and returned to Byzantium.

44. At this juncture the king of the Saracens sent a large army under the command of Masalmas and Solymas (as they are called in their language) to besiege the city of Tyana. When they arrived there, they fought many encoun-

μέρος δὲ καὶ τοῦ τείχους ἐκ τῶν πρὸς τειχομαχίαν ὀργάνων καταβαλόντες καὶ πλέον οὐδὲν ἀνύσαι ἰσχύσαντες, ἀποχωρεῖν πρὸς τὰ οἰκεῖα ἐβούλοντο. ἐν ᾧ ἐκπέμπει Ἰουστινιανὸς πρὸς τῇ μεσογείᾳ, καὶ πλεῖστον λαὸν ἄγροικόν τε καὶ γεωργικὸν ἀθροίσας πρὸς τὰ Τύανα ἀφικνεῖσθαι ἐκέλευσεν ὡς τοὺς πολιορκουμένους ἐπαμυνόμενος. τούτους ἀόπλους οἱ Σαρακηνοὶ θεασάμενοι ὁρμῶσι κατ' αὐτῶν, καὶ τοὺς μὲν | dB44 ξίφει ἀνεῖλον τοὺς δὲ αἰχμαλώτους συνέλαβον. ἐντεῦθεν θαρ- L51v ραλεώτερον διατεθέντες τῆς προσεδρίας Τυάνων εἴχοντο. οἱ δὲ ἀπορίᾳ δαπανημάτων τῶν πρὸς μάχην ἀπειπόντες τῆς τε παρὰ βασιλέως βοηθείας οὐκ εὐπορήσαντες, ὁμολογίᾳ ἑαυτοὺς τοῖς ἐχθροῖς παρέδοσαν καὶ πρὸς τὰ τῶν Σαρακηνῶν ἤθη ἀπῴχοντο. ἐξ ἐκείνου λοιπὸν πλείστη τοῖς ἐχθροῖς παρρησία ἐδέδοτο ἀδεῶς τὰς Ῥωμαίων καταληΐζεσθαι χώρας, οὐδενὸς τούτοις ἰσχύοντος ἀντιτάττεσθαι, καί τινα τούτων ἀποδασμὸν εἰς τριάκοντα ἄνδρας περιιστάμενον ἄχρι Χρυσοπόλεως κατελθεῖν (παραθαλάσσιον χωρίον ἀντικρὺ Βυζαντίου πρὸς ἥλιον ἀνίσχοντα ἱδρυμένον), καὶ τοὺς μὲν αὐτόσε οἰκήτορας ἀποσφάξαι, τὰς δὲ πορθμίδας ἐμπρῆσαι ναῦς.

45. Ἰουστινιανὸς δὲ ἐν μνήμῃ ἔχων περὶ τῆς γενομένης αὐτῷ πρὸς Ἀψίμαρον παρὰ τῶν ἐν Χερσῶνι διαβολῆς, ναῦς πολὺ πλείστας καὶ διαφόρους συναγείρας, ἐμβιβάσας | παρ' V199r αὐτοῦ ἄχρι εἰς ἑκατὸν χιλιάδας ἀριθμὸν ἀνδρῶν, [εἰδότας] ἔκ τε τῶν στρατιωτικῶν καταλόγων, | ἔτι δὲ καὶ τοῦ γεωργικοῦ L52r καὶ τῶν βαναυσικῶν τεχνῶν τῶν τε ἐκ τῆς συγκλήτου βουλῆς καὶ τοῦ τῆς πόλεως δήμου, Στέφανον δέ τινα πατρίκιον τὸ ἐπίκλην Ἄσμικτον τοῦ τοιούτου στόλου ἡγεμόνα προβαλόμενος ἐξέπεμψε, προστάξας πάντας τοὺς ἐν Χερσῶνι καὶ Βοσφόρῳ καὶ τοὺς τῶν ἄλλων ἀρχοντιῶν λαοὺς ξίφεσιν ἀνηλωκέναι, Ἡλίαν δὲ τὸν αὐτοῦ δορυφόρον σὺν αὐτῷ ἀπιόντα ἄρχοντα

---

6 *τειχομαχείαν* L ‖ 7 *ἀνοίσαι* L ‖ 9 *τὴν μεσογίαν* L ‖ 10 *ἐκέλευεν* L ‖ 11 *τούτοις ἀόπλοις* L ‖ 13 *συλλαβόντες* L ‖ 13–14 *θαρραλεώτεροι* V *θαρσαλαιώτεροι* L corr. vulg. ‖ 14 *προσεδρείας* L ‖ 15 *ἀπορεῖα* L ‖ *τῶν* om. L ‖ *μάχην* V *βραχὺ* L ‖ 17 *παρέδωσαν* L ‖ *ἴθη* L ‖ 20 *τούτους* L ‖ *ἀπόδασμον* L *ἀποδρασμὸν* V ‖ 23 *ἀνήσχον τὸ* L ‖ 23–24 *αὐτώσε . . . πορθμήδας* L

45: 1 *ἔχων* V *ὢν* i.e. *ὢν* L fort. recte ‖ *γεναμένης* L ‖ 2 *αὐτῶν* L ‖ 3 *ἐνβιβάσας* L ‖ 3–4 *παραυτὰ* coni. dB fort. recte ‖ 4 *χηλιάδας* L ‖ *εἰδότας* seclusi *ἰδιώτας* coni. dB ‖ 6 *τόν τε* L ‖ 7 *Στέφανον τὸν πατρ.* L ‖ 7–8 *ἐπίκλιν* VL corr. vulg. ‖ 8 *ἡγεμῶνα* L ‖ *προβαλλόμενος* VL corr. B ‖ 10 *ἀρχοντι[ῶν]* V ‖ 11 *δωρυφόρον* L ‖ post *ἄρχοντα* ras. unius litt. V

ters and threw down part of the walls by means of their siege engines, but were unable to achieve any further success and were intending to return home. Thereupon Justinian sent emissaries into the interior and, after collecting a numerous body of peasants and farmers, ordered them to proceed to Tyana and relieve the besieged. On seeing them unarmed, the Saracens rushed against them, and some of them they put to the sword, while others they captured. Thus emboldened, they pursued the siege of Tyana. Renouncing to do battle because of the lack of necessities and deprived of the emperor's help, ⟨the inhabitants⟩ surrendered to the enemy under treaty and departed to the country of the Saracens. On this account the enemy gained complete freedom to devastate the Roman lands without fear, since no one was able to oppose them, so that a contingent of them consisting of thirty men advanced as far as Chrysopolis (this is a seaside settlement standing opposite Byzantium in the direction of the rising sun), massacred the local inhabitants, and set fire to the ferry boats.

45. Still remembering the denunciation made against him by the people of Cherson to Apsimaros, Justinian collected a large fleet of different ships and embarked in them as many as a hundred thousand men recruited from the army registers as well as among farmers and artisans and from the senate and the population of the City. He appointed a certain patrician Stephen surnamed Asmiktos to command this fleet and sent him out with orders to put to the sword all the people of Cherson and Bosporos and the other principalities; to install as governor of Cherson his bodyguard Helias, who embarked along with

Χερσῶνος ἐγκαταστῆσαι, ἔτι δὲ καὶ Βαρδάνην Ἀρμένιον
τῷ γένει ἐξόριστον ἐκεῖσε καταλιπεῖν. Στέφανος δὲ διὰ τῆς
Ποντικῆς θαλάσσης πρὸς τὰ ἐκεῖσε περαιωθεὶς τὰ προσ- dB45
τεταγμένα ἐπλήρου, μειράκιά τινα ὀλίγα τῷ συνόντι αὐτῷ
λαῷ ὡς δῆθεν αἰχμάλωτα περιποιήσας. Τουδοῦνον δὲ τὸν
Χερσῶνος ἄρχοντα καὶ Ζωΐλον πρωτοπολίτην λεγόμενον καὶ
ἑτέρους ἄνδρας τεσσαράκοντα τῶν ἐμφανεστέρων δεσμώτας
σὺν γυναιξὶ καὶ παισὶ πρὸς Ἰουστινιανὸν ἔπεμψεν, ἄλλους τε
τῶν πρωτευόντων Χερσῶνος ἄνδρας ἑπτὰ ξυλίνοις ὀβελοῖς
προσαρτήσας ἐπὶ πυρὸς διώπτησε. τοὺς δὲ τῶν ἑτέρων προ-
στατεύοντας πολισμάτων ἄνδρας ἄχρι καὶ εἰς εἴκοσι ἀκατίῳ
ἐμβαλὼν καὶ προσδήσας λίθους τε τούτῳ πλείστους * τῷ
βυθῷ παραδέδωκεν. Ἰουστινιανὸς δὲ φιλανθρω|πότερον τὸν L52ᵛ
Στέφανον διατεθέντα παρὰ τὰ διατεταγμένα αὐτῷ νομίσας
διὰ τὴν τῶν μειρακίων περιποίησιν, σπουδαιότερον ἐπαν-
ήκειν πρὸς αὐτὸν ἐκέλευσεν. αὐτὸς δὲ κατὰ τὰ προσταχθέντα
ἐκεῖθεν ἀπάρας μηνὸς Ὀκτωβρίου ἐνισταμένου χειμῶνι με-
γάλῳ καὶ ναυαγίῳ περιπίπτει, εἰς τρεῖς καὶ ἑβδομήκοντα χι-
λιάδας τῶν καταποντισθέντων ἀριθμηθέντων, ὧν τὰ πτώματα
ἐξ Ἀμάστριδος πόλεως μέχρις Ἡρακλείας ὑπὸ τῆς θαλάσσης
ἀπερρίπτετο. ἐφ᾽ οἷς οὐ λυπηθεὶς ἀλλὰ καὶ λίαν περιχαρὴς
γενόμενος Ἰουστινιανὸς πάλιν βουλεύεται ἕτερον ἐκεῖσε ἐκ-
πέμπειν στόλον. οἱ δὲ τῶν χωρῶν τούτων ἄρχοντες τῆς φήμης
αἰσθόμενοι ἑαυτοὺς ὅση δύναμις ἠσφαλίζοντο, πρὸς δὲ τοὺς
Χαζάρους διαπρεσβεύονται ὥστε ἐπὶ φυλακὴν τούτων λαὸν
ἀποστέλλειν καὶ περισώζειν τοὺς ἐν αὐταῖς περιλειφθέντας.
ταῦτα Ἰουστινιανὸς μεμαθηκὼς Γεώργιον τὸν πατρίκιον ἀπο-
στέλλει καὶ Ἰωάννην τὸν τῆς πόλεως ὕπαρχον σὺν ἑτέροις
ἄρχουσι καὶ στρατῷ ἄχρι τριακοσίων ἀνδρῶν, παραδοὺς αὐ-
τοῖς Τουδοῦνον καὶ Ζωΐλον, ὥστε ἀποκαταστῆσαι αὐτοὺς
ταῖς οἰκείαις ἀρχαῖς, Ἡλίαν δὲ ἀγαγεῖν ὡς αὐτόν. τούτων ἐν dB46
Χερσῶνι παραγενομένων οἱ τῆς πόλεως μόνους Γεώργιον καὶ
τοὺς σὺν αὐτῷ ἄρχοντας ἀξιοῦσιν ἐντὸς γενέσθαι τῆς πόλεως·

---

12 ἐγκαταστῆσαι V[2] ex ἐγκαταστήσει ‖ Βαρδάνιν V ‖ 13 ἐξώριστον . . . καταλειπεῖν L ‖ 16 τὸν δοῦνος V ‖ 19–20 ἀνέπεμψε . . . προτευόντων L ‖ 23 τοῦτο L ‖ post πλείστους verbum 'iniciens' sonans excidisse vid. λίθοις τοῦτο γεμίσαντες Theoph. 378.10 ‖ 26 σπουδαιώτερον L ‖ 26–27 ἐπανήκειν vulg. ἐπανήσειν V ἐπανισιν L ‖ 29 ναυαγείω L ‖ 29–30 χηλιάδας L ‖ 31 Ἀμαστρίδος L ‖ 32 ἀπερρήπτετο L ‖ 35 ἠσφαλίζοντο ex ἠσφαλήζοντο L ‖ 36 Χαζαρεις sine acc. V ‖ διαπρεσβεύεται . . . φυλακῆ L ‖ 37 αὐταῖς scripsi αὐτοῖς VL ‖ 37–40 περιλειφθέντας . . . ἄχρι om. L ‖ 41 τὸν δοῦνον V ‖ 43 παραγεναμένων L ‖ σμόνης V, η deleto et ου sec. m. superscr.

him, and to leave there in banishment the Armenian Bardanes. After crossing to those parts by way of the Pontic sea, Stephen set about carrying out his orders, but spared a small group of children, allegedly as being captives. He made prisoner Toudounos, governor of Cherson, Zoilos, who was styled first citizen, and another forty distinguished men, whom he sent to Justinian with their wives and children; and another seven prominent men of Cherson he affixed to wooden spits and roasted in the fire. He also placed in a boat and tied up as many as twenty men who administered the other towns and, after ⟨filling the boat with⟩ a mass of stones, sank it in the sea. Now Justinian deemed, because of the consideration shown to the children, that Stephen had behaved more mercifully than he had been ordered and directed him to return with all speed. Embarking from there in accordance with the command in the month of October, Stephen was overtaken by a violent storm ⟨and suffered⟩ shipwreck, so that as many as seventy-three thousand were drowned and their bodies were cast up by the sea from the town of Amastris to Herakleia. Far from being distressed by these events, Justinian was overjoyed and decided to send another fleet there. On hearing this rumor, the dignitaries of those parts made themselves secure to the best of their ability and sent ambassadors to the Chazars ⟨asking them⟩ to send an army for their protection to save those among them who had survived. When he had been informed of this, Justinian dispatched the patrician George and John the prefect of the City together with other dignitaries and three hundred soldiers, to whom he handed Toudounos and Zoilos so as to restore them to their former commands and bring Helias back to him. When these men had arrived at Cherson, the citizens allowed only George and the dignitaries accompanying him to enter the city; and when

οὗ γεγονότος τὰς μὲν πύλας | ἐπ' αὐτοῖς ἔκλεισαν, Γε|ώργιον L53r *δὲ καὶ Ἰωάννην ξίφει ἀναιροῦσι. τοὺς δὲ ἔξω τοῦ τείχους* V199v *ἀπολειφθέντας στρατιώτας, ἔτι δὲ καὶ* Τουδοῦνον *καὶ* Ζωΐλον *τοῖς ἐκεῖσε προσεδρεύουσι* Χαζάροις *παραδόντες τῷ χαγάνῳ παρέπεμψαν, οὓς παραλαβόντες οἱ* Χάζαροι *κατὰ τὴν ὁδὸν ἔκτειναν. οἱ δὲ τῆς πόλεως* Χερσῶνος Ἰουστινιανὸν *μὲν αἰσχρῶς δυσφημήσαντες καθύβριζον,* Βαρδάνην *δὲ τὸν ἐκεῖσε ὄντα ἐξόριστον ὡς βασιλέα εὐφήμουν. τούτων αἰσθόμενος* Ἰουστινιανὸς *καὶ μείζονι θυμῷ ἐξαπτόμενος τὰ μὲν* Ἡλία *τέκνα τῷ μητρῴῳ κόλπῳ φερόμενα ἀνήλισκεν, τὴν δὲ αὐτοῦ γυναῖκα τῷ ἰδίῳ μαγείρῳ ζευχθῆναι ἠνάγκασεν,* Ἰνδῷ *τῷ γένει καὶ ὅλῳ δυσειδεῖ τυγχάνοντι. ἕτερον δὲ πάλιν μέγαν στόλον ἀποστέλλει, ἡγεῖσθαι τούτου προχειρισάμενος* Μαῦρον *τὸν πατρίκιον, προστάξας τὴν μὲν πόλιν* Χερσῶνος *καταστρέψασθαι καὶ ἅπαντας τοὺς ἐν αὐτῇ ἀφειδῶς κατακτεῖναι. ὁ δὲ πρὸς* Χερσῶνα *περαιωθεὶς τοῦ ἔργου εἴχετο. λαοῦ δὲ* Χαζάρων *ἐξαπιναίως ἐπιπεσόντος ἡ μὲν πόλις περιεσώζετο,* Βαρδάνης *δὲ ὡς τὸν κύριον τῶν* Χαζάρων *φυγὰς ᾤχετο.* Μαῦρος *δὲ ὁ πατρίκιος πρὸς μὲν τὴν πολιορκίαν | ἀμηχανή-* L53v *σας, παλινοστεῖν δὲ πρὸς* Ἰουστινιανὸν *δεδιώς, συμφρονεῖ τῇ πόλει* Χερσωνιτῶν. *καὶ* Ἰουστινιανὸν *μὲν ἀπηναίνοντο,* Βαρδάνην *δὲ ὡς βασιλέα εὐφήμουν,* Φιλιππικὸν *αὐτὸν μετονομάσαντες. καὶ πρὸς τὸν* Χάζαρον *διαπρεσβεύονται τοῦτον ὡς αὐτοὺς ἀπεσταλκέναι. ὁ δὲ ὅρκοις ἐμπεδοῖ τὸ* Ῥωμαϊκὸν *πλῆθος περὶ τῆς* Βαρδάνου *σωτηρίας χρήματα αὐτοὺς πραξάμενος, κατ' ἄνδρα ἕκαστον νόμισμα εἰληφώς.* Ἰουστινια- dB47 *νὸς δὲ χρόνου παρερχομένου ὑπώπτευεν ὡς καὶ παρ' αὐτῶν ἠθετημένος εἴη. διὰ τοῦτο αἱρεῖται* Τέρβελιν *τὸν ἄρχοντα τῶν* Βουλγάρων *καὶ τηνικαῦτα συμμαχεῖν αὐτῷ. ὁ δὲ πέμπει πρὸς αὐτὸν ἄνδρας ὡς τρισχιλίους, οὓς δεξάμενος συμπεραιοῦται αὐτοῖς, καὶ ἅμα τῷ τοῦ* Ὀψικίου *λεγομένῳ στρατῷ εἰς τὸ καλούμενον πεδίον τοῦ* Δαματρῦ *ἱδρύσασθαι παρεκέλευεν. αὐτὸς δὲ τούς τε ἄρχοντας ἑαυτοῦ καὶ στρατὸν ὁπλίτην ἕτερον παραλαβὼν πρὸς τοῖς* Ποντικοῖς *ἐξέδραμε χωρίοις, ἄχρι*

---

47 *τὸν δοῦνον* V ‖ 50 *Ἰουστινιανῷ* L ‖ 52 *ἐξώριστον* L ‖ 53 *μείζωνι* L ‖ 53–54 Ἡλία etc.] *ἐν ἡλικίᾳ τέκνα τῶν μητρῴων κόλπων* L ‖ 54 *ἀνηλίσκει* V ‖ 56 *ὅλως* L ‖ 56–57 *ἕτ. δὲ μέγα στόλον πάλιν* L ‖ 61 *ἐξαπηναίως* VL ‖ *ἐπιπεσόντος* vulg. *ἐπιπεσόντων* V *ἐπεισπεσόντων* L ‖ 64 *δεδειὼς* L ‖ 65 *ἀπένοντο* gloss. Barocc. f. 293v ‖ 66 *ἀνευφήμουν* L ‖ 67 *διεπρεσβεύετο* L ‖ 68 *ὡς αὐτοὺς* V *πρὸς αὐτὸν* V2 ‖ *ἀποσταλκέναι* L ‖ 69 *αὐτοῖς* VL corr. vulg. ‖ 70 *ἑκατὸν νομίσματα* V ‖ 71 *ὑπόπτευεν* L ‖ 76 Δαματρὺ L ‖ 77 *αὐτὸς* vulg. *αὐτοὺς* VL

this had happened, they shut the gates on them and put George and John to the sword. As for the soldiers who had remained outside the walls, along with Toudounos and Zoilos, they delivered them to the Chazars who were encamped there and sent them off to the Chagan. Taking them along, the Chazars killed them on the way. Now the inhabitants of Cherson cursed Justinian with foul insults and proclaimed as emperor Bardanes who was in banishment there. When he had been informed of this, Justinian was all the more inflamed with anger: he killed the children of Helias while their mother was holding them in her lap and forced his wife to marry his own cook, who was an Indian and extremely ugly. Once again he sent out another great fleet under the command of the patrician Mauros, whom he ordered to destroy the city of Cherson and to massacre without pity all its inhabitants. Crossing to Cherson, he took his task in hand, but the city was saved by the sudden sortie of a Chazar army, and Bardanes escaped to the lord of the Chazars. Having failed in the siege and being afraid of returning to Justinian, Mauros made an accord with the city of Cherson. They abjured Justinian and acclaimed Bardanes emperor, whom they renamed Philippikos. They then sent an embassy to the Chazar ⟨lord⟩ asking ⟨Philippikos⟩ to be dispatched to them. ⟨The Chagan⟩ imposed an oath on the Roman army concerning the safety of Bardanes and exacted one *nomisma* from each man. As time went by, Justinian began to suspect that he had been rejected by them, too. For this reason he asked once again help from Terbelis, chief of the Bulgarians, who sent him three thousand men. After receiving them and crossing ⟨the Bosporos⟩ with them, he ordered them to encamp in the plain of Damatrys (as it is called)[35] together with the army of Opsikion. He himself, taking along his dignitaries and another armed contingent, proceeded to the Pontic region as far as a seaside village called Gingilissos with

[35]Probably modern Samandra: Janin, *Grands centres*, 50–51 and map on p. 62.

παραθαλασσίου κώμης Γιγγιλίσσου ὀνομαζομένης, ὥστε ἀναμανθάνειν οἷα τὰ ἐν Χερσῶνι αὐτῷ πεπραγμάτευτο. ἐπὶ χρόνον δέ τινα ἐκεῖσε διατρίψας καὶ θεασάμενος τὸν τοιοῦτον στόλον σὺν τῷ | Φιλιππικῷ βασιλεύοντι πρὸς Βυζάντιον καταί- L54r ροντα, πρὸς τὸν καταλειφθέντα αὐτῷ λαὸν κατὰ τὸν Δαματρὺν παλινοστεῖ. Φιλιππικὸς δὲ πολέμου ἐκτὸς εἰς τὴν πόλιν εἰσῄει, καὶ αὐτίκα Ἡλίαν σὺν ὁπλίτῃ λαῷ κατὰ Ἰουστινιανοῦ ἀποστέλλει. καὶ αὐτὸς τῷ μὲν συνόντι Ἰουστινιανῷ πλήθει ὅρκοις τὰ τῆς σωτηρίας ἐ|βεβαίωσε καὶ τὸν τῶν Βουλγάρων V200r λαὸν σώους ἐπανήκειν ὑπέσχετο, αὐτοῦ δὲ Ἰουστινιανοῦ τὴν κεφαλὴν ἐκτέμνει, ἤδη ἔτος ἕκτον ἀνύσαντος ἐν τῇ δευτέρᾳ αὐτοῦ βασιλείᾳ, καὶ πρὸς Φιλιππικὸν ἐκπέμπει. ὁ δὲ ταύτην δεξάμενος πρὸς τοῖς ἑσπερίοις τόποις ἄχρι Ῥώμης ἀπέστελλε. Μαῦρον δὲ τὸν πατρίκιον καὶ Ἰωάννην τὸν βασιλικὸν δορυφόρον, ἐπίκλην Στροῦθον, κατὰ Τιβερίου τοῦ υἱοῦ Ἰουστινιανοῦ ἐξέπεμψεν, ὃν καταλαμβάνουσιν ἐν τῷ θυσιαστηρίῳ καταφυγόντα τοῦ ἱεροῦ τῆς πανάγνου θεομήτορος τοῦ ἐν Βλαχέρναις ὄντος, ἐν ᾧ εἰσπηδήσας Ἰωάννης ἀφέλκεται τῆς ἱερᾶς ἐξημμένον τραπέζης, μήτε τὰ ἐκ τοῦ θυσιαστηρίου εὐλαβηθεὶς μήτε τοῖς πολλοῖς δάκρυσιν Ἀναστασίας τῆς αὐτοῦ μάμμης εἴξας· παρῆν γὰρ καὶ αὐτὴ τῷ ἐγγόνῳ συγ- dB48 κινδυνεύουσα. καὶ τοῦτον εἰς τὴν τοῦ ὑπερκειμένου τείχους πυλίδα | τὴν καλουμένην τῶν Καλλινίκων ζῴου ἀλόγου δίκην L54v μαχαίρᾳ ἀποσφάττουσιν, ἐν τῷ ἱερῷ τῶν θείων Ἀναργύρων τῶν καλουμένων τῶν Παυλίνης ταφῆναι προστάξαντες. μεθ' ὃν συλλαμβάνονται καὶ Βαρασβακούριον καὶ τοὺς λοιποὺς Ἰουστινιανοῦ ἄρχοντας, καὶ πάντας ξίφει ἀναιροῦσι.

46. Φιλιππικὸς δὲ ἀσέμνως καὶ ῥαθύμως τὰ βασίλεια διέπων ἐφαίνετο, τοὺς δὲ ἐν τῇ ἕκτῃ οἰκουμενικῇ συνόδῳ πατέρας ἀναθέματι καθυπέβαλε, τὰ παρ' αὐτῶν ἐνθέως δογματισθέντα δύο τοῦ σωτῆρος θελήματα καὶ ἐνεργείας μὴ ἀποδεχόμενος, συλλήπτορας εὑρηκὼς Ἰωάννην τὸν τηνικαῦτα τῆς πόλεως ἀρχιερέα καὶ Γερμανὸν τὸν Κυζίκου μητροπολίτην καὶ ἑτέρους ἱερεῖς καὶ συγκλητικοὺς πλείστους.

---

79 *παραθαλάσσιον* L ‖ *Γιγγιλισσου* sine acc. V ‖ 83 *καταληφθέντα* L ‖ 84 *Φιλιππικὸς* ex *Φιλιππικοῦ* V[2] ‖ 85 *εἰσείη* L ‖ 89 *ἀνοίσαντος* L ‖ 91–92 *ἀπέστειλεν* L ‖ 93 *ἐπίκλιν* VL corr. vulg. *Στροῦθον* ex *Στροῦθρο* V[1] ‖ 99 *ἦξας* L ‖ *ἐκγόνω* L ‖ 101 *πυλίδα* om. V

46: Cf. Sudam s.v. *Φιλιππικός* ‖ 2 *δὲ*] *τε* Suda ‖ 5 *εὑρηκὼς* L Suda *εὑρίσκων* V ‖ 7 *καὶ ἑτέρους ἱερεῖς* om. L

a view to finding out how things were going for him at Cherson. After spending some time there, he saw the fleet sailing down to Byzantium with Emperor Philippikos, and so returned to the army he had left at Damatrys. Now Philippikos entered the City without a struggle and immediately sent Helias with a band of soldiers against Justinian. This man gave a sworn pledge of safety to the army that accompanied Justinian and promised a safe return to the Bulgarian host. He then cut off Justinian's head (the latter having completed six years in his second reign) and sent it to Philippikos, who received it and dispatched it to the West as far as Rome. He sent out the patrician Mauros and the imperial bodyguard[36] John, surnamed Strouthos, against Justinian's son Tiberios, whom they apprehended in the church of the most-pure Mother of God at Blachernai, where he had taken refuge in the sanctuary. John rushed inside and dragged him away as he was clutching the holy table, without respect either for the sanctuary or the tears of his grandmother Anastasia, who was present to share her grandchild's danger. They killed him with a knife, like a senseless animal, at the so-called postern of the Kallinikoi of the wall that rises above, and ordered him to be buried in the church of the holy Anargyroi in the quarter named after Paulina. Next day they arrested Barasbakourios and Justinian's remaining dignitaries and put them all to the sword.

46. As for Philippikos, he appeared to administer the empire in an indecorous and negligent manner. ⟨In particular⟩ he subjected to anathema the Fathers of the Sixth Ecumenical Synod because he did not accept the two wills and energies of Our Savior that had been piously defined by them. In this he was supported by John, who was at the time archpriest of the City, Germanos, metropolitan of Kyzikos, as well as other priests and many senators.

[36] I.e., *spatharios* as in Theoph., 377.22.

47. Ἐν τούτοις τῶν Βουλγάρων ὁπλίτης ὅμιλος ἀθρόως ⟨κατὰ⟩ τοὺς ἐν τῷ Θρᾳκικῷ Βοσπόρῳ οἰκοῦντας ἐπεισπίπτει· καὶ λαὸν πλεῖστον τῶν ἐγχωρίων καὶ τῶν ἐκ Βυζαντίου διαπερώντων τέρψεως καὶ ἡδυπαθείας ἕνεκεν ἀναιροῦσιν, ἄλλους τε ᾐχμαλώτευσαν καὶ ἄργυρον ὡς πλεῖστον καὶ σκεύη οὐκ ὀλίγα παρ' αὐτῶν προσκτησάμενοι· ἀδείας δὲ αὐτοῖς προσγενομένης καὶ πρὸς τῷ χερσαίῳ τείχει τῆς πόλεως σκεδάννυνται, ἄχρι καὶ τῆς Χρυσῆς καλουμένης πύλης προεκδραμόντες. ἐκεῖθεν ὑπονοστήσαντες πολλὰ τὰ ἐπὶ Θρᾴκης χωρία καταληΐζονται. | μετὰ δὲ ταῦτα καὶ τὸ τῶν Σαρακηνῶν L55r ἔθνος τὴν Ῥωμαίων κατέθεον χώραν, καὶ τὰ πλεῖστα μέρη διεκτρέχοντες πλείστην ὅσην βλάβην ἀνθρώπων τε καὶ κτηνῶν ἐποιοῦντο, τήν τε Μισθίαν καὶ ἕτερα πολίσματα συμπαρα- dB49 λαμβάνουσι.

48. Φιλιππικὸς δὲ γενέθλιον τῆς πόλεως ἡμέραν ἐπιτελέσας καὶ ἁμιλλητήριον τῶν ἵππων ἀγῶνα ἐπιδειξάμενος, εἶτα τοῖς φίλοις συμποσιάσας εἰς ὕπνον κατὰ τὸν μεσημβρινὸν τῆς ἡμέρας καιρὸν ἐτράπετο. συμβαίνει δέ γε αὐτῷ τὰ τῆς ἐπιβουλῆς ἐντεῦθεν. Γεώργιός τις ὄνομα, τὸ ἐπίκλην Βούραφος, πατρίκιος τυγχάνων καὶ τοῦ Ὀψικίου | στρατοῦ ἡγού- V200v μενος, πρὸς τῇ Θρᾴκῃ τηνικαῦτα ἐπιδημῶν φυλακῆς ἕνεκα τῆς χώρας διά τὴν τῶν Βουλγάρων καταδρομήν, γνώμῃ Θεοδώρου τοῦ πατρικίου τὸ ἐπίκλην Μυακίου πέμπει τῶν ὑπηρετῶν τινά, Ῥοῦφον ὄνομα, σὺν ὀλίγοις στρατιώταις πρὸς τὸ Βυζάντιον τὰ πρὸς τὴν Φιλιππικοῦ ἐπιβουλὴν ἐπιτελέσοντας· ὃς ἀθρόως κατὰ τὰ βασίλεια ἐπεισπίπτει, καὶ τὸν βασιλέα καθεύδοντα καταλαβὼν ἐξανίστησί τε τοῦ ὕπνου καὶ πρὸς τὸν τοῦ ἱπποδρομίου ἐξάγει χῶρον κἀκεῖσε αὐτοῦ τὰς ὄψεις ἀπετύφλωσε, δεύτερον ἔτος ἐν τῇ βασιλείᾳ διάγοντα. τῇ ἐπαύριον (ἡμέρα ἦν τῆς πεντηκοστῆς ἑορτάσιμος) ἀθροισθεὶς ὁ τῆς πόλεως ἅπας δῆμος πρὸς τὸ ἱερὸν τοῦ θείου λόγου τέμενος

47: 1 ἀθρώως L ‖ 2 κατὰ add. esse coni. dB ‖ ἐπεισπίπτει οἰκοῦντας L ‖ 3–4 διαπερόντων L ‖ 4 ἀπαίρουσιν L ‖ 5 αἰχμαλώτευσαν . . . σκεύει L ‖ 6 προσκτισάμενοι L ‖ αὐτοῖς vulg. αὐτῶν VL ‖ 7 προσγινομένης L ‖ 8 πύλης καλουμένης L ‖ 10 χωρεια L ‖ 11 καὶ τὰ V κατὰ L ‖ μέρει L ‖ 13 Μισθίαν ex Μίσθιαν L Μήδειαν V ‖ 13–14 παραλαμβάνουσιν L

48: 2 ὁμιλλιτήριον L ‖ 3 συμποτιάσας L ‖ 5 ἐπίκλιν VL corr. vulg. ‖ 5–6 Βούραμφος L ‖ 7 τὴν Θράκην L ‖ 9 τοῦ om. L ‖ ἐπίκλιν VL corr. vulg. ‖ Μυακίνου ut vid. L ‖ 12 ἀθρώως L ‖ 14 ἱπποδρόμου L ‖ 15 post διάγοντα des. L

47. At this juncture an armed Bulgarian band suddenly fell upon the inhabitants of the Thracian Bosporos. They killed a great many people both among the local population and among those who had crossed over from Byzantium for the sake of pleasure and recreation; others they took captive and robbed of much silver and a considerable number of utensils. Taking advantage of this opportunity, they fanned out toward the land walls of the City and advanced as far as the so-called Golden Gate. On their return from there they devastated many villages in Thrace. After this, the Saracen nation, too, raided the Roman country and, as they overran many regions, inflicted much damage on men and animals and took Misthia[37] as well as other townships.

48. Now Philippikos, after celebrating the birthday of the City[38] and putting on an equestrian contest, banqueted with his friends and lay to sleep at midday. At this juncture a plot was hatched against him. A certain George surnamed Bouraphos, who was a patrician and commander of the Opsikian army and happened at the time to be stationed in Thrace in order to guard the country because of the Bulgarian raid, sent at the instigation of the patrician Theodore surnamed Myakios one of his subordinates called Rouphos to Byzantium together with a few soldiers so as to carry out the plot against Philippikos. This man broke suddenly into the palace and, finding the emperor asleep, woke him up and brought him into the area of the Hippodrome, where he blinded him, ⟨this being⟩ in the second year of his reign. The next day, which was the feast of Pentecost, all the people of the City gathered in the church of

---

[37] Modern Beyşehir in Lycaonia: K. Belke and M. Restle, *Galatien und Lykaonien*, Tabula Imperii Byzantini 4 (Vienna, 1984), 205–6.

[38] The anniversary of the dedication of Constantinople on 11 May.

ἀναγορεύουσιν εἰς βασιλέα Ἀρτέμιον Φιλιππικοῦ γραμματέα τυγχάνοντα, οὓς τῇ Ἰταλῶν φωνῇ καλοῦσιν ἀσηκρῆτις, ἐπονομάσαντες αὐτὸν Ἀναστάσιον. ὀλίγων δὲ ἡμερῶν διελθουσῶν τυφλοῦσι Θεόδωρον τὸν πατρίκιον, ὡσαύτως καὶ Γεώργιον, καὶ τοῦτον ἐξόριστον ἐν Θεσσαλονίκῃ πέμπουσιν.

49. *Ἀναστάσιος δὲ δι' ἐπιμελείας τὰ πολεμικὰ πράγματα εἶχε καὶ ἄρχοντας ἱκανοὺς πρὸς τὰς τούτων διοικήσεις καθίστη. αἰσθόμενος δὲ ⟨ὅτι⟩ ὁ τῶν Σαρακηνῶν βασιλεὺς βουλὰς ἐκίνει ὡς κατὰ τῆς Ῥωμαίων χώρας στρατευσόμενος, ἀποστέλλει [δὲ] πρὸς αὐτὸν Δανιὴλ τὸν πατρίκιον ⟨ἐκ⟩ τῆς Σινωπιτῶν ὁρμώμενον πόλεως, ὕπαρχον τηνικαῦτα τῆς βασιλίδος* dB50 *ὑπάρχοντα, ὡς δῆθεν τὰ τῆς εἰρήνης ἐπικηρυκευσόμενον, τῷ ὄντι δὲ διοπτευσόμενον οἷα αὐτοῖς τὰ κατὰ Ῥωμαίων ἐξηρτύετο· ὃς ἐπανήκων ἐπήγγειλε μεγίστην ἔσεσθαι τοῦ ἔθνους διά τε ἱππικῶν καὶ πλοΐμων στρατευμάτων τῆς Ῥωμαϊκῆς πολιτείας καταδρομήν. ὁ δὲ ἀκούσας ἑκάστῳ τῶν ἐν τῇ πόλει * ὡς εἴ τις τῶν ἀναγκαίων εὐπορήσοι ἐπὶ τριετῆ χρόνον διαρκούντων αὐτῷ, μένειν, ὁ δὲ τούτων ὑστερῶν οὗ ἂν βούλοιτο ἀποτρέχειν. τὰ δὲ τείχη τῆς πόλεως ἐπιμελέστερον καινίζει καὶ τὰ πολεμητήρια ὄργανα διασκευάζει, πλεῖστα δαπανήματα τῇ πόλει ἀποθέμενος καὶ ἑτέροις οἷς ἀνῆκε πρὸς πολεμίων ἔφοδον ταύτην κατοχυρώσας.*

50. *Φήμης δὲ γενομένης ὡς ὁ τῶν Σαρακηνῶν στόλος ἀπὸ Ἀλεξάνδρου πόλεως ἐπὶ τὸν Φοίνικα παρεγένετο ναυπηγησίμης ξυλῆς κυπαρισσίνης ἕνεκεν, ἐκλέγεται σκάφη ταχυπλόϊμα, στρατόν τε ἐν αὐτοῖς ἐγκαταλέγει ἐκ τῶν τῆς χώρας τοῦ καλουμένου Ὀψικίου καὶ πρὸς τῇ νήσῳ τῇ Ῥόδῳ ἀποστέλλει. κἀκεῖσε ἀθροισθῆναι καὶ ἄλλα Ῥωμαϊκὰ πλόϊμα συνέταξε. τούτοις ἡγεμόνα ἐφίστησιν Ἰωάννην διάκονον τῆς μεγάλης ἐκκλησίας καὶ τῶν δημοσίων φόρων λογιστήν, ὃν λογοθέτην γενικὸν οἶδε καλεῖν | ἡ συνήθεια, ὑπάρχοντα ἔμφρονά* V201r *τε καὶ ἔμπειρον καθιστάμενον, ὅστις τὸν ἅπαντα παρέλαβε στόλον. ὃς πρὸς τῇ Ῥόδῳ γενόμενος καὶ τὰ ἐντεταλμένα*

49: 3 *καθίστει* V corr. dB ‖ *ὅτι* addidi v. comment. ‖ 5 *δὲ* seclusi ‖ *ἐκ* add. dB ‖ 7–8 *ἐπικηρυκευσάμενον . . . διοπτευσάμενον* V corr. vulg. ‖ 12 lacunam verbo *διέταττεν* suppl. P, verbo *ἐπιτρέπει* B: v. comment. ‖ 15 *καινίζοι* V corr. vulg. ‖ *πλεῖστα δὲ* V *δὲ* del. vulg.

50: Cf. Sudam s.v. *Ἀρτέμιος* ‖ 2 *τῆς Ἀλεξάνδρου* coni. dB ‖ 2–3 *ναυπηγησίμοις ξύλοις κυπαρισσίνοις* V corr. B ‖ 9 *ὑπάρχοντα* fort. delendum

the Divine Logos and proclaimed emperor Artemios, who was a secretary of Philippikos (such men are called *a secretis* in the Italian tongue) and renamed him Anastasios. A few days later they blinded the patrician Theodore as well as George; the latter they exiled to Thessalonica.

49. Anastasios bestowed care on military affairs and appointed capable commanders to take charge of them. Having been informed that the king of the Saracens was intending to invade the Roman country, he sent to him the patrician Daniel, a native of the town of Sinope, who was at the time prefect of the Imperial City, on the pretext of negotiating peace, but in reality to observe their preparations against the Romans. When this man had returned, he announced that the foreigners were about to launch a major attack on the Roman State with both horse and sea-borne armies. On hearing this, ⟨the emperor commanded that⟩ each inhabitant of the City could remain if he had provisions for a period of three years, but anyone who was not so provided should depart wherever he wished. He restored carefully the walls of the City and refurbished the military engines. He also stored a great quantity of provisions in the City and fortified it by such other means as befitted a hostile attack.

50. When a rumor had spread that the Saracen fleet had come from Alexandria to Phoenix[39] for the sake of cypress wood ⟨suitable⟩ for shipbuilding, he selected some fast vessels on which he embarked an army from the region called Opsikion and sent them to the island of Rhodes. He also arranged for other Roman ships to gather there. The command over them was given to John, a deacon of the Great Church and inspector of public taxes (commonly called general logothete), a prudent and experienced man who took charge of the whole fleet. When he had reached Rhodes and announced the orders that

[39] Presumably the Phoenix in the Rhodian Peraea, on which see *RE*, Phoenix 14 (W. Ruge) rather than the Phoenix in Lycia (modern Finike).

ἀπαγγέλλων καταπειθεῖς εὕρισκε καὶ προθύμους πρὸς τὸν διάπλουν ὑπάρχοντας τοὺς συνειλεγμένους ἅπαντας. μόνοι δὲ οἱ παραγενόμενοι τοῦ Ὀψικίου στρατοῦ τὴν τοιαύτην ὁδοιπορίαν δεδοίκεσαν. στασιάζουσιν οὖν ἐξ αὐτοῦ, καὶ τὸν μὲν dB51 βασιλέα Ἀναστάσιον ἐδυσφήμουν, Ἰωάννην δὲ τὸν διάκονον ῥομφαίᾳ ἀναλίσκουσιν. ἐντεῦθεν λοιπὸν οἱ στόλοι σκεδάννυνται, καὶ πρὸς τὰ οἰκεῖα ἀπέπλευσαν ἕκαστοι. αὐτοὶ δὲ ἐπὶ τὴν ἑαυτῶν ἀνιόντες καὶ πρὸς τὸ Ἀδραμύντιον γενόμενοι ἐκεῖσε εὑρίσκουσι Θεοδόσιόν τινα ὄνομα, τῶν δημοσίων φόρων πράκτορα, ἀπράγμονά τινα καὶ ἰδιώτην τυγχάνοντα, καὶ πρὸς τὴν τῆς βασιλείας ἀξίαν προτρέπουσιν. ὁ δὲ φυγὰς ᾤχετο καὶ εἰς ὄρος κατεκρύπτετο. αὐτοὶ δὲ ἐπιδραμόντες καὶ βιασάμενοι βασιλέα τε ἀναγορεύουσι καὶ μεθ' ἑαυτῶν ἄγουσι.

51. Ταῦτα Ἀναστάσιος μεμαθηκὼς τὸ μὲν Βυζάντιον ἤδη προκατοχυρώσας ἐν τῇ πόλει Νικαίας τῆς κατὰ Βιθυνίαν ἐξέρχεται, κἀκεῖσε ἑαυτὸν κατασφαλίζεται. ὁ δὲ μετὰ Θεοδοσίου στρατὸς συλλαβὼν ἅπαντα τὸν τοῦ Ὀψικίου στρατὸν καὶ πλεῖστα σκάφη ἐμπορικά, [καὶ] κατὰ τὸ ἤδη καὶ πρόσθεν εἰρημένον παραθαλάσσιον χωρίον Χρυσοπόλεως παραγίνεται. ἐκεῖθέν τε ἐφ' ἑκάστου τοῖς ἐκ τῆς πόλεως πόλεμον προσέβαλεν, ἐπὶ μησί τε ἓξ τὰ τῆς μάχης διήρκεσε. καὶ ὁ τοῦ Ἀναστασίου στόλος πρὸς τῷ Νεωρίῳ τῆς πόλεως καλουμένῳ λιμένι κατῆρε, ὁ δὲ τοῦ Θεοδοσίου στόλος ἀδείας ἐπιλαβόμενος διαπορθμεύεται πρὸς τὰ Θρᾳκῷα καὶ τούτων ἐκράτησεν. ἐπὶ προδοσίᾳ δέ τινας ὑποφθείραντες διὰ τῆς πύλης τῆς καλουμένης Βλαχερνῶν τὴν πόλιν εἷλον, καὶ νυκτὸς ἐπιγενομένης εἰς τοὺς οἴκους τῶν πολιτῶν εἰσδραμόντες μεγίστην αὐτοῖς βλάβην εἰργάζοντο. τοὺς δὲ ἐν αὐτῇ ἄρχοντας ἅμα Γερμανῷ τῷ τηνικαῦτα ἱεράρχῃ τῆς πόλεως ἀποστέλλει ὡς τὰ πεπραγμένα αὐτῷ πιστωσόμενος Ἀναστασίῳ. ὁ δὲ τούτους ἰδὼν λόγον ᾔτησεν ὡς μή τι κακὸν πάθῃ, καὶ τὸ μοναχικὸν περιβαλόμενος σχῆμα πρὸς Θεοδόσιον ᾤχετο· ὁ δὲ ἕτερον dB52 μηδὲν βλάψας κατὰ τὴν Θεσσαλονίκην ἐξόριστον ἔπεμψεν.

---

12 *καταπειθ*[*εῖς*] V ‖ *προθύμους* V² *προθύμως* V ‖ 19 *ἀδραμύντ*[*ειον*] V ‖ 20 *ὀνόματι* ex *ὄνομα* V²

51: 5 *καὶ* secl. dB ‖ 6 *παραθαλασσίω χωρίω Χρυσοπό*[*λεως*] V dubit. corr. dB ‖ 10 *κατήρει* V corr. P ‖ 18 *ἰδὼν* scripsi *ἤδη* V: cf. Theoph. 386.11 *θεασάμενος* ‖ 18–19 *πάθει . . . περιβαλλόμενος* V corr. vulg.

had been given to him, he found that all present were obedient and ready for the crossing, save only for those who had come from the Opsikian army, who were afraid of such a journey. The latter consequently revolted, cursed the emperor Anastasios, and killed the deacon John with a sword. Thereupon the fleet dispersed, each ⟨contingent⟩ returning home. Now ⟨the Opsikians⟩, when they had come on their homeward journey to Adramytion, found there a certain Theodosios, a collector of public taxes, an ordinary man uninvolved in politics, whom they urged ⟨to assume⟩ the imperial office. He ran away and hid on a mountain; but they pursued him, proclaimed him emperor under pressure, and took him along.

51. When Anastasios had been informed of these things, ⟨he left⟩ Byzantium, which he had previously fortified, and went to the city of Nicaea in Bithynia, where he made himself secure. As for the army accompanying Theodosios, they rounded up all the forces of Opsikion and many trading vessels and came to the aforementioned coastal village of Chrysopolis. From there they launched every day an attack on the inhabitants of the City, and for six months this battle continued. When the fleet of Anastasios moved to the city harbor of Neorion (as it is called), the armada of Theodosios seized this opportunity to cross over to the Thracian side, which it occupied. After treasonably subverting certain persons, they took the City through the gate of Blachernai (as it is called) and, while it was night, broke into the houses of the citizens and inflicted heavy losses on them. ⟨Theodosios⟩ sent forth the dignitaries who were in the City along with Germanos, who was then archpriest of Constantinople, to give evidence of his deeds to Anastasios. On seeing them, the latter requested a promise that he would suffer no harm and, after donning the habit of a monk, presented himself to Theodosios, who exiled him to Thessalonica without any further injury.

52. Ἐπεὶ οὖν πυκναὶ τῶν βασιλέων ἐπαναστάσεις ἐγένοντο καὶ ἡ τυραννὶς ἐκράτει τά τε τῆς βασιλείας καὶ τῆς πόλεως κατημελεῖτο καὶ διέπιπτε πράγματα, ἔτι μὴν καὶ ἡ τῶν λόγων ἠφανίζετο παίδευσις καὶ τὰ τακτικὰ διελύετο. ἐξ ὧν συνέβαινε καὶ τοὺς πολεμίους τῆς τῶν Ῥωμαίων κατατρέχειν ἀδεῶς πολιτείας, φόνοι τε πολλοὶ καὶ ἀπαγωγαὶ καὶ πόλεων ἁλώσεις. ἐντεῦθεν καὶ οἱ Σαρακηνοὶ ὁρμῶσι κατ' αὐτῆς τῆς βασιλευούσης, διὰ τῆς ἠπείρου στέλλοντες ἐκ διαφόρων ἐθνῶν τῶν ὑπὸ χεῖρα ἱππικά τε | καὶ πεζικὰ στρα- V201ᵛ τεύματα ἀριθμοῦ κρείττονα. ὡσαύτως καὶ στόλον πολὺν ἀπέστειλαν ἄχρι καὶ εἰς χιλίας ὀκτακοσίας ναῦς, ἡγεμόνα τούτοις τινὰ καταστήσαντες Μασαλμᾶν τῇ σφῶν διαλέκτῳ καλούμενον. ταῦτα μαθόντες οἵ τε στρατιωτικοὶ καὶ πολιτικοὶ ἄρχοντες καὶ τὴν τοῦ Θεοδοσίου ἀπειρίαν, καὶ ὡς οὐχ ἱκανῶς ἔχει τὰ πρὸς τοὺς πολεμίους ἀντικαθίστασθαι, ἐφίστανται αὐτῷ παραινοῦντες τὴν βασιλείαν παραιτήσασθαι καὶ ἀβλαβῶς ἰδιωτεῦσαι. καὶ αὐτὸς ὑπεχώρει, ἐνιαυτὸν ἕνα ἐν τῇ βασιλείᾳ διαρκέσας. εἶτα εἰς ψῆφον ἐληλυθότων τοῦ βασιλεύσοντος ἡρέθη Λέων ὁ πατρίκιος, τηνικαῦτα στρατηγὸς ὢν τοῦ τῶν Ἀνατολικῶν λεγομένου στρατοῦ. καὶ ὡς ἦν ἔθος βασιλεῦσι, διὰ προπομπίου δοχῆς διὰ τῆς Χρυσῆς καλουμένης πύλης εἰς τὸ Βυζάντιον εἰσελαύνει, καὶ ἐν τῇ μεγάλῃ ἐκκλησίᾳ γενόμενος ἐκεῖσε τὸν τῆς βασιλείας ἀνεδήσατο στέφανον.

53. Ὁ δὲ τῶν Σαρακηνῶν λαὸς πλεῖστα τῶν Ῥωμαίων καθελὼν πολίσματα καταλαμβάνει τὴν Πέργαμον καλουμένην πόλιν, καὶ ἤδη τῆς πρὸς αὐτὴν πολιορκίας εἴχοντο. καὶ ταύτην αἱροῦσιν ἐξ αἰτίας τοιᾶσδε. ἔκ τινος δαιμονικῆς ἐπι- dB53 νοίας οἱ τῆς πόλεως ἔνδον πρωτοτόκον κόρην λαβόντες ἐγκυμονοῦσαν καὶ ἤδη πρὸς τὸ τεκεῖν ἐγγίζουσαν, καὶ ταύτην τε ἀνέτεμον καὶ τὸ ἐν αὐτῇ βρέφος ἄραντες ἐπὶ λέβητος ὕδατι ἕψουσιν, ἐφ' οὗ οἱ πρὸς τὸ πολεμεῖν τοῖς ἐχθροῖς παρασκευαζόμενοι τὰς χειρίδας τῶν δεξιῶν χειρῶν κατεβάπτισαν. ἐκεῖθέν τε τὰ ἐξ ὀργῆς τοῦ θεοῦ κατελάμβανεν· αἱ γὰρ χεῖρες

52: 1 *πυκναὶ κατὰ τῶν* B ‖ 5 *πολέμους* V corr. vulg. ‖ *τῆς* ex *τοὺς* V² ‖ 6 *πολλοὶ* V² *πολλαὶ* V ‖ 14 *Θεοδοσίου θεασάμενοι ἀπειρίαν* coni. dB ‖ 19 *εὑρέθη* V corr. B

53: 4 *αἴρουσιν* V corr. vulg. ‖ 5 *πρωτότοκον* V

52. On account of the frequent assumptions of imperial power and the prevalence of usurpation, the affairs of the empire and of the City were being neglected and declined; furthermore, education was being destroyed and military organization crumbled. As a result, the enemy were able to overrun the Roman State with impunity ⟨and to cause⟩ much slaughter, abduction, and the capture of cities. For this reason also the Saracens advanced on the Imperial City itself, sending forth by land an innumerable host of horse and foot ⟨recruited⟩ from the various peoples subject to them, as well as a great fleet numbering as many as eighteen hundred ships under the command of a certain Masalmas (as he was called in their tongue). When the military and civil dignitaries became aware of these matters, ⟨taking account⟩ of Theodosios' lack of experience and his incapacity of offering resistance to the enemy, they pressed him with exhortations to abdicate the imperial office and assume without harm a private station. He accordingly withdrew after a reign of one year. Thereupon they held a ballot of who was to become emperor and elected the patrician Leo, who was at the time *strategos* of the so-called Anatolic army. According to imperial custom, he was received in procession as he entered Byzantium through the Golden Gate and, having come to the Great Church, was invested with the imperial crown.

53. The Saracen army, after destroying numerous Roman towns, reached the city called Pergamon and set about besieging it. They captured it for the following reason. By some devilish intention the inhabitants of the city took a pregnant girl who was about to give birth to her first child, cut her open and, having removed the infant from inside her, boiled it in a pot of water, in which the men who were preparing to fight the enemy dipped the sleeves of their right arms. For this reason they were overtaken by divine wrath: their hands

αὐτῶν ἐφάπτεσθαι ὅπλου διείργοντο, καὶ ἀπρακτούντων οἱ πολέμιοι τὴν πόλιν εἶλον ἀμαχητί.

54. Ἐκεῖθεν ἄραντες οἱ Σαρακηνοὶ πρὸς τῷ στενῷ τῆς Ἀβύδου καταλαμβάνουσι καὶ εἰς τὰ ἐπὶ Θρᾴκης ἀντιπεραιοῦνται. καὶ πλεῖστα ταύτης ἑλόντες πολίσματα ἐπὶ τὴν βασιλεύουσαν ἀφίκοντο καὶ χάρακα ταύτῃ περιβάλλουσι καὶ τῆς πολιορκίας εἴχοντο, τρισκαιδεκαμηνιαῖον χρόνον ἐν τῇ προσεδρίᾳ διανύσαντες, ἰδέας μηχανημάτων ὡς πλείστας προσενεγκόντες. ἐν τούτῳ καταλαμβάνει καὶ ὁ τῶν Σαρακηνῶν στόλος, οὗ ἡγεῖτο Σολιμᾶν ὀνόματι Ἀράβων φωνῇ καλούμενος. ἐν ᾧ δὲ τῶν ὑπὸ τὸ Βυζάντιον πόρων ἀνήγοντο, αἱ κατόπιν ἰοῦσαι ναῦς, οἷάπερ νωτοφυλακοῦσαι καὶ φόρτῳ πολλῷ βεβαρημέναι ἔκ τε στρατιωτῶν πλήθους καὶ ὅπλων, καὶ ἅμα μικροῦ πνεύματος ἀντιπνεύσαντος καὶ τοῦ ῥείθρου εἰς τοὐπίσω ἄγεσθαι βιαζομένου, σχολαιότερον ὑπέπλεον. ταύτας ὁ βασιλεὺς θεασάμενος διήρεσιν ἐπιβὰς καὶ διέκπλους ποιησάμενος πυρὶ κατέφλεξεν, οὔσας τὸν ἀριθμὸν εἴκοσι. | ὁ δὲ V202r λοιπὸς ἅπας στόλος τῷ Θρᾳκικῷ προσπλεύσας Βοσπόρῳ τῷ λιμένι τῷ καλουμένῳ Σωσθενίῳ προσορμίζεται καὶ αὐτοῦ διεχείμαζεν. ἐν ᾧ συμβέβηκε χειμῶνα μέγιστον γενέσθαι, ὥστε μηδαμῶς γῆν ὀφθῆναι ἐκ πληθύος τῆς κατενεχθείσης χιόνος ἄχρι εἰς τὰς ἑκατὸν ἡμέρας· ἐξ οὗ πλῆθος οὐκ ὀλίγον ἀνδρῶν τε καὶ ἵππων καὶ καμήλων καὶ λοιπῶν ζῴων ἀπ- dB54 έβαλον. ἔαρος δὲ ἐπιγενομένου ἐπικαταλαμβάνει καὶ ἕτερος τῶν Σαρακηνῶν στόλος πλεῖστος ἐξ Αἰγύπτου, οὗ ἡγεῖτο Σοφιὰμ ὄνομα ἄρχων, φόρτον ἄγων ἐν ταυτῷ σίτου τε πλείστου καὶ ὅπλων. ὀλίγου δὲ διελθόντος χρόνου καὶ ἕτερος ἐφίσταται στόλος ἐκ τῶν περὶ Ἀφρικὴν ἀναχθείς, ὅπλων τε πολλῶν καὶ δαπανημάτων καταγέμων, οὗ ὑπῆρχεν ἡγεμὼν Ἰέζιδος Σαρακηνῶν ὄνομα. οὗτοι, ὥς φασι, τὴν ἐκ τοῦ ἐσκευασμένου παρὰ Ῥωμαίοις πυρὸς ὑφορώμενοι βλάβην, τὸν [οὖν] Βυζάντιον πόρον ἀπογνόντες τοῖς πρὸς Βιθυνίαν μέρεσι προσέσχον, ὁ μὲν πρὸς τὸν καλούμενον λιμένα Καλοῦ ἀγροῦ, ὁ δὲ πρὸς ταῖς ἀκταῖς τοῦ λεγομένου Σατύρου. οἱ δὲ ἐν αὐτοῖς εἰσπλέοντες Αἰγύπτιοι νυκτὸς τοὺς ἐνεστηκότας λέμβους τῶν νηῶν εἰσβάντες πρὸς τὸ Βυζάντιον ἧκον καὶ τὸν βασιλέα

54: 9 ⟨διὰ⟩ *τῶν* coni. dB ‖ 12 *αὐτιπνεύσαντος* V corr. vulg. ‖ 17 *αὐτοῦ* vulg. *αὐτῷ* V ⟨*ἐν*⟩ *αὐτῷ* coni. dB ‖ 20 *ὀλίγον* B *ὀλίγων* V ‖ 24 *ὄνομα* V –*τι* superscr. V^2 item **54**.28 ‖ 28 *Σαρακηνῶν* ⟨*φωνῇ*⟩ coni. dB ‖ 29 *οὖν* punctis supra et infra positis secl. V^2

became incapable of taking up weapons and, in the face of their inactivity, the enemy captured the city without resistance.

54. Setting out from there, the Saracens proceeded to the straits of Abydos and crossed over to Thrace. After taking many towns there, they reached the Imperial City. They threw a palisade around it and began the siege, which they pursued for thirteen months ⟨with the help of⟩ many kinds of engines they had brought along. At this point there arrived a Saracen fleet under the command of Soliman (as he was called in the Arab tongue). As they were sailing up the straits next to Byzantium, the ships that were guarding the rear, being heavily laden with a great number of soldiers and arms, met with a light contrary wind and were forced back by the current, thus falling behind. On seeing them, the emperor embarked on biremes and, after breaking the enemy's line, burned twenty of their ships. The remainder of the ⟨Arab⟩ fleet, after sailing up the Thracian Bosporos, put in at the harbor of Sosthenion[40] and wintered there. That winter happened to be very severe and so much snow fell that the ground was made invisible for a hundred days. Consequently, ⟨the Arabs⟩ lost no small number of men, horses, camels, and other animals. When spring had come, another great Saracen fleet arrived from Egypt under the command of a general called Sophiam and brought a large cargo of corn and weapons. A short time thereafter yet another fleet came up from Africa, laden with a mass of arms and provisions: its leader was a Saracen named Iezidos. These fleets, it is said, for fear of being injured by the artificial fire of the Romans, avoided the straits of Byzantium and landed on the Bithynian side, the first at the harbor called Kalos Agros,[41] the second at the shore called Satyros.[42] Now the Egyptian sailors entered at night the skiffs that were on their ships, came to Byzantium, and acclaimed the emperor. Taking courage

[40] Modern Istinye, halfway up the European side of the Bosporos: Janin, *CP*, 479.

[41] Exact situation unknown; presumably near the mouth of the gulf of Nicomedia (north side). Cf. *Synax.CP*, 777.10 and Janin, *Grands centres*, 94 note 1.

[42] Near modern Bostanci: Janin, *Grands centres*, 42–43.

εὐφήμουν. ἐφ' οἷς ἀναθαρσήσας ὁ βασιλεὺς πυρφόρους ναῦς κατὰ τῶν τοιούτων στόλων ἐξέπεμψε καὶ πάσας αὐτῶν τὰς ναῦς ἐνέπρησεν. ἐκεῖθεν λαφυραγωγήσαντες καὶ ἐκ τῶν ὑπαρχόντων αὐτοῖς ὅπλων καὶ δαπανημάτων καταφορτισθέντες πρὸς βασιλέα ὑπέστρεφον.

55. Τούτῳ τῷ χρόνῳ Σέργιος ὁ πατρίκιος ὁ τῆς Σικελίας στρατηγὸς καὶ οἱ τὰ ἑσπέρια οἰκοῦντες, τὰ περὶ τὸ Βυζάντιον καὶ τὸν βασιλέα αὐτὸν ἀπογνόντες τῆς γενομένης τῶν πολεμίων χάριν κατ' αὐτῶν ἐφόδου, ἴδιον στέφουσι βασιλέα τῶν ὑπηρετῶν τινα Σεργίου, Βασίλειον τοὔνομα, υἱὸν γεγονότα Γρηγορίου τὸ ἐπίκλην Ὀνομαγούλου, Τιβέριον αὐτὸν ὀνομάσαντες. τοῦτο ἀκηκοὼς ὁ βασιλεὺς Παῦλον τὸν πατρίκιον στρατηγὸν Σικελίας προβάλλεται ἅτε πιστὸν καὶ οἰκεῖον ὑπάρχοντα καὶ τακτικῶν ἔμπειρον, καὶ πρὸς Σικελίαν ἐκπέμπει. οὗτινος ἐκεῖσε καταλαβόντος Σέργιος φυγὰς ἐκεῖθεν dB55 οἴχεται καὶ πρὸς Λογγουβάρδους γίνεται, Παῦλος δὲ ἐν τῇ νήσῳ λαὸν περιαθροίσας τὰ βασιλέως ὑπαναγινώσκει γράμματα, δι' ὧν εἰς πίστωσιν ἐλθόντες τόν τε βασιλέα εὐφήμησαν καὶ Βασίλειον καὶ τοὺς ὑπ' αὐτοῦ προχειρισθέντας ἄρχοντας δεσμίους αὐτῷ παραδεδώκασιν. ὁ δὲ τούτους παραλαβὼν Γεώργιόν τινα καὶ ἑτέρους ἀνεῖλε καὶ τούτων τὰς κεφαλὰς πρὸς τὸν βασιλέα ἀνέπεμψε, τοὺς δὲ ἄλλους σὺν πληγαῖς καὶ αἰκίαις πολλαῖς, ὧν δὲ καὶ τὰς ῥῖνας ἐκτεμών, ὑπερορίαις παρέπεμψε. Σέργιος δὲ τῆς ἑαυτοῦ σωτηρίας λόγον αἰτήσας πρὸς τὸν Παῦλον ἐκομίσθη. ἐντεῦθεν τὰ τῆς ἑσπέρας πράγματα ἐν εἰρήνῃ | καὶ ἡσυχίᾳ κατέστη. V202v

56. Μετὰ τοῦτο τίκτεται υἱὸς τῷ βασιλεῖ, ὃν ἐπωνόμασε Κωνσταντῖνον. πεντεκαιδεκάτῃ δὲ τοῦ ἐπεισιόντος μηνὸς Αὐγούστου πάντα τά τε ἱππικὰ καὶ πλόϊμα τῶν Σαρακηνῶν ἐκστρατεύματα τῆς βασιλευούσης ἀπεχώρουν, πλείστας ναῦς ἀποβαλόντες ὑπό τε ζάλης καὶ ἀνέμων ἀγρίων καταληφθείσας, καὶ πολλῶν μὲν εἰς τὰς νήσους ἄχρι καὶ εἰς τὴν Κύπρον

35 πυρφόρους ex πυρφόρος V²

55: 6 ἐπίκλιν V corr. vulg. ‖ 10 Σεργίου V corr. vulg. ‖ 13 εὐφημήσας V corr. vulg. εὐφημήσαντες, Βασίλειον coni. dB ‖

56: 5 ἀποβαλόντες ex καταβαλόντες V² ‖ 5–6 καταλειφθείσας V corr. vulg.

at this, the emperor sent out fire-bearing ships against those fleets and burned all of their vessels. They made much booty and, after loading the weapons and provisions that were in them, came back to the emperor.

55. At this time the patrician Sergios, who was *strategos* of Sicily, along with the inhabitants of the West, gave up hope for Byzantium and the emperor himself on account of the enemy attack against them, and crowned their own emperor, one of the adjutants of Sergios, called Basil, the son of Gregory surnamed Onomagoulos, and renamed him Tiberios. On being informed of this, the emperor appointed the patrician Paul *strategos* of Sicily, inasmuch as he was a faithful friend and experienced in military matters, and dispatched him to Sicily. When he had arrived there, Sergios fled to the Lombards. As for Paul, he gathered together the inhabitants of the island and read to them the imperial letters. Being reassured by them, they acclaimed the emperor and surrendered both Basil and the magistrates who had been appointed by him as prisoners to ⟨Paul⟩. Taking hold of them, he executed a certain George and others, and sent their heads to the emperor, while the rest ⟨he punished⟩ with blows and torments, cut off the noses of some, and sent them into exile. After requesting an assurance of his safety, Sergios, too, was brought to Paul. As a consequence, the affairs of the West returned to peace and tranquillity.

56. After this a son was born to the emperor, whom he named Constantine. And on the 15th of the following month of August the entire Saracen armament, both cavalry and fleet, withdrew from the Imperial City. They lost many ships, which were overtaken by storm and violent winds, and many were dispersed among the islands as far as Cyprus, while others sank with

σκεδασθεισῶν, ἑτέρων δὲ καὶ αὐτάνδρων τῷ βυθῷ παραδοθεισῶν.

57. *Ἀρτέμιος δὲ ἐν Θεσσαλονίκῃ ἐξόριστος ὢν πάλιν πειρᾶται τῆς βασιλείας ἐπικρατήσειν, καὶ ἐπεχείρει τοιάδε πράττειν. γράφει πρὸς Σισίννιον πατρίκιον τὸ ἐπίκλην Ῥενδάκιον, πρὸς τῇ τῶν Βουλγάρων διατρίβοντα χώρᾳ παρὰ βασιλέως τηνικαῦτα ἀποσταλέντα ὡς ἂν συμμαχίαν παρ' αὐτῶν κατὰ τῶν Σαρακηνῶν λήψοιτο, ὅπως αὐτῷ τοῖς κατὰ γνώμην συμπράξειεν, ἀναπείσῃ δὲ καὶ Βουλγάρους συνεργήσειν αὐτῷ. ὁ δὲ τοῦτο ὑπέσχετο. γράφει δὲ καὶ πρὸς Νικήταν τὸν μάγιστρον τὸ ἐπίκλην Ξυλινίτην, ἐν Κωνσταντινουπόλει* dB56 *ὑπάρχοντα, ἔτι δὲ καὶ πρὸς Ἰσώην πατρίκιον καὶ τοῦ λεγομένου βασιλικοῦ Ὀψικίου ἡγεμόνα, καὶ Θεόκτιστον τὸν πρώτιστον τῶν βασιλικῶν γραμματέων καθ' οὓς ἐβασίλευε χρόνους γενόμενον, καὶ Νικήταν ἐπίκλην Ἄνθρακα ἄρχοντα τειχῶν, παλαιᾶς φιλίας ἀναμιμνήσκεσθαι, καὶ ἑτοίμους εἶναι συντρέχειν αὐτῷ καὶ τὴν πόλιν ἀνοιγνύναι καὶ ὡς βασιλέα ὑποδέχεσθαι. τὰ γραφέντα οὖν εὐθὺς τῷ βασιλεῖ διαγινώσκεται, καὶ τοὺς τὰ γράμματα δεξαμένους χειροῦται καὶ πληγαῖς αἰκίζεται, καὶ αὐτοὶ ὁμολογοῦσι. καὶ Νικήτα μὲν τοῦ τὴν ἀξίαν μαγίστρου καὶ Θεοκτίστου τὰς κεφαλὰς ἐξέτεμε, τοὺς δ' ἄλλους οὐ μικρῶς αἰκισάμενος καὶ δημεύσας ἐξορίαις ἀπέπεμψεν. Ἀρτέμιος δὲ ἅμα Σισιννίῳ τῷ πατρικίῳ καὶ τοῖς Βουλγάροις μέχρις Ἡρακλείας καταλαμβάνει, σὺν αὐτοῖς δὲ καὶ ἅπερ ἦγον ἐκ Θεσσαλονίκης ἀκάτια· μονόξυλα δὲ αὐτοὶ προσαγορεύουσι. γράφει δὲ Βουλγάροις ὁ βασιλεὺς ὡς τὴν εἰρήνην μᾶλλον ἀσπάσοιντο καὶ τοὺς ἐχθροὺς προδοῖεν. οἱ δὲ εἰς ἀπολογίαν κατέστησαν συγγνώμην αἰτήσαντες καὶ τὰ πρὸς εἰρήνην ὑπισχνούμενοι. καὶ τὸν μὲν Ἀρτέμιον σὺν τῷ ἀρχιερεῖ Θεσσαλονίκης καὶ ἄλλους πλείστους δεσμώτας πρὸς βασιλέα πέμπουσι, καὶ Σισιννίου τοῦ πατρικίου τὴν κεφαλὴν ἐκτεμόντες ὡσαύτως στέλλουσιν, οὕτω τε πρὸς τὴν ἑαυτῶν ἀπεχώρουν. Ἀρτέμιον δὲ σὺν τῷ ἀρχιεπισκόπῳ παραλαβὼν ἐν τῷ λεγομένῳ Κυνηγίῳ ἀπέτεμεν. ἱππικὴν δὲ ἅμιλλαν ἐπιτελέσας τῶν ἀποτμηθέντων τὰς κεφαλὰς διὰ τοῦ ἱπποδρομίου ἐπὶ κοντοῦ ἀνηρτημένας*

57: 3 *ἐπίκλιν* V ‖ 9 *μαγιστρον* sine acc. *τὸ ἐπίκλιν* V ‖ 11 *Θεόκτιστον* P (cf. **57.19**) *Θεοδόσιον* V ‖ 13 *ἐπίκλιν* V ‖ 18 *Νικήταν* V corr. vulg. ‖ 25 *ἀσπάσαιντο* coni. dB ‖ 32 *κυνηγείω* V corr. vulg. ‖ 34 *ἐπὶ κοντῶ* V corr. dB

their crews.

57. Now Artemios, who had been banished to Thessalonica, attempted once again to win the empire by means of the following actions. He wrote to the patrician Sisinnios surnamed Rhendakios, who was then dwelling in the land of the Bulgarians (whither he had been sent by the emperor with a view to concluding an alliance with them against the Saracens), ⟨asking him⟩ to assist him in his designs and persuade the Bulgarians to cooperate with him. ⟨Sisinnios⟩ promised to do so. ⟨Artemios⟩ also wrote to the magister Niketas surnamed Xylinites, who was resident at Constantinople, as well as to the patrician Isoes, who was commander of the imperial Opsikion (as it is called), to Theoktistos, who had been first imperial secretary at the time when he was emperor, and to Niketas surnamed Anthrax, commander of the Walls, reminding them of their old friendship and ⟨urging them⟩ to assist him, open the city to him, and receive him as emperor. These letters were immediately revealed to the emperor, who arrested their recipients and punished them with blows, and they confessed. He cut off the heads of Niketas, who had the dignity of magister, and of Theoktistos, while the others he chastised severely, confiscated their possessions, and sent them into exile. As for Artemios, he advanced as far as Herakleia with the patrician Sisinnios and the Bulgarians; and ⟨they had⟩ with them the boats they had brought from Thessalonica, which they call *monoxyla*.[43] The emperor, however, wrote to the Bulgarians that they should embrace peace and surrender his enemies. They apologized and asked his forgiveness, promising to bring about peace. Accordingly, they sent Artemios along with the archpriest of Thessalonica and many others as captives to the emperor. They also cut off the head of the patrician Sisinnios and sent it likewise, and so departed to their own country. Having gained possession of Artemios and the archpriest, ⟨the emperor⟩ beheaded them in the so-called Kynegion. He then performed an equestrian race and paraded their heads, af-

[43] Canoes hollowed out of single tree trunks. See *DAI*, Commentary, 23–25.

ἐξεπόμπευε. τοὺς δὲ ἄλλους πάντας αἰκισάμενος καὶ τὰς ῥῖνας αὐτῶν ἐκτεμὼν καὶ δημεύσας ὑπερορίαις κατεδίκασε.

58. Ταῦτα οὖν καταπραξάμενος προσκα|λεῖται Γερμα- V203^r νὸν τὸν τηνικαῦτα ἀρχιερέα πέμπτῃ καὶ εἰκάδι τοῦ Μαρτίου dB57 μηνὸς τῆς τρίτης ἰνδικτιόνος, τῇ σωτηρίῳ τοῦ Χριστοῦ ἀναστάσει, ἔν ⟨τε⟩ τῷ Τριβουναλίῳ λεγομένῳ δεκαεννέα ἀκουβίτων στέφει τὸν υἱὸν Κωνσταντῖνον εἰς βασιλέα.

59. Οἷον δὲ κατὰ τοὺς χρόνους ἐκείνους περὶ τὰς νήσους τῆς τε Θήρας καὶ Θηρασίας καλουμένας συμβέβηκεν, αἳ πρὸς τῷ Κρητικῷ πελάγει κεῖνται, παραδραμεῖν οὐκ ἄξιον. θέρους ὥρας ἐνεστηκυίας συνηνέχθη τὸν θαλάττιον βυθὸν πλεῖστον ὅτι καπνώδη ἀτμὸν ἐξερεύγεσθαι, ἐξ οὗ ἐπὶ πολὺ πυκνουμένου τοῦ ἀέρος πῦρ ἐξαφθῆναι, καὶ μετὰ τὸ πῦρ λίθους κισηρώδεις διεκβρασθῆναι εἰς πλῆθος μέγιστον, ὥστε εἰς εἶδος νήσου τοὺς λίθους συστῆναι, ἑνωθῆναί τε τὴν γῆν τῇ Ἱερᾷ καλουμένῃ νήσῳ, ἣν δὴ καὶ αὐτήν φασι τῷ ὁμοίῳ τρόπῳ τοῦ βυθίου ἀναδοθῆναι χώρου, καθάπερ καὶ τὰς ῥηθείσας λόγος Θήραν καὶ Θηρασίαν νήσους. τῷ ἀπείρῳ δὲ πλήθει τῶν ἀναδιδομένων λίθων ἀνὰ πᾶσαν κατεστορέσθαι τὴν ἐκείνῃ θάλασσαν, ἐνθένδε τε ἀφικέσθαι ἄχρις Ἀβύδου καὶ τῆς Ἀσιάτιδος παραθαλασσίου, ὑπεκκαίεσθαι δὲ τὸ προσπελάζον ῥεῖθρον ὡς μηδὲ θιγγάνειν αὐτοῦ τινὰ ἱκανῶς ἔχειν.

60. Ταῦτά φασιν ἀκούσαντα τὸν βασιλέα ὑπολαμβάνειν θείας ὀργῆς εἶναι μηνύματα, καὶ ἥτις αἰτία ταῦτα κεκίνηκε διασκέπτεσθαι. ἐντεῦθεν λοιπὸν κατὰ τῆς εὐσεβείας ἵσταται καὶ τῶν ἱερῶν εἰκονισμάτων μελετᾷ τὴν καθαίρεσιν ὡς ἐκ τῆς τούτων ἱδρύσεώς τε καὶ προσκυνήσεως γεγονέναι οἰόμενος τὸ τεράστιον, κακῶς εἰδώς. ἐκδιδάσκειν δὲ τὸν λαὸν τὸ οἰκεῖον ἐπεχείρει δόγμα. πολλοὶ γοῦν τὴν ὕβριν τῆς ἐκκλησίας ἀπωλοφύροντο. διὸ δὴ καὶ οἱ τὴν Ἑλλάδα καὶ τὰς Κυκλάδας νήσους οἰκοῦντες οὐ προσιέμενοι τὸ δυσσέβημα dB58

58: 4 *τε* addidi || 5 *στέφει τε* B *στέφειν τὸν* coni. dB

59: 7 *κισσιρώδεις* V || 8 *τῇ γῇ* V corr. B || 9 *ὁμοιοτρόπω* V corr. vulg. || 11 *τὰ ἄπειρα δὲ πλήθη* coni. dB || 12 *καταστορέσθαι* V corr. vulg. || *ἐκείνην* V corr. B

60: 5 *τῆς τούτων* ex *τῆς των* V^1 || 9 *προϊέμενοι* V corr. vulg.

fixed to poles, through the Hippodrome. All the other ⟨conspirators⟩ he chastised, cut off their noses, confiscated their possessions, and condemned them to banishment.

58. After accomplishing these things, he invited the then archpriest Germanos on the 25th of March of the 3rd indiction (which was the day of Christ's salutary resurrection) to the so-called Tribunal of the Nineteen Couches[44] and crowned his son Constantine emperor.

59. It is not proper to pass over in silence what occurred in those days near the islands called Thera and Therasia, which lie in the Cretan sea. During the summer season the watery deep happened to belch forth a quantity of smoky steam, out of which, as the air became thicker, a fire burst and, after the fire, an enormous mass of pumice-like stones was cast out, so that they formed a kind of island and the land was joined to the so-called Sacred Island which, they say, had also emerged from the deep in a similar manner, as is also reported of the aforementioned islands Thera and Therasia. The sea in those parts was everywhere covered by the immense quantity of stones that were thrown up, and they spread from there as far as Abydos and the coast of Asia. The adjacent water was so hot that one could not even touch it.

60. The emperor, it is said, when he had heard of these things, considered them to be signs of divine wrath and was pondering what cause might have brought them about. On this account he took up a position contrary to the true faith and planned the removal of the holy icons, mistakenly believing that the portent had occurred because they were set up and adored. He tried to expound his own doctrine to the people, while many men lamented the insult done to the Church. For this reason the inhabitants of Hellas and the Cyclades, disapproving as they did of this impiety, rebelled against the emperor and,

[44] A court of honor in front of the ceremonial dining room of the imperial palace. See J. Ebersolt, *Le Grand Palais de Constantinople* (Paris, 1910), 58 ff.

πρὸς τὸν βασιλέα διαστασιάζουσι, καὶ πλεῖστον στόλον ἀθροίσαντες Κοσμᾶν τοὔνομα ἐφ' ἑαυτοῖς βασιλεύουσι. καὶ πρὸς τὴν βασιλεύουσαν ἧκον· οἷς συμμίσγουσι πολέμῳ οἱ τῆς πόλεως καὶ πολλὰς τῶν περὶ αὐτὸν νηῶν ἐνέπρησαν. οἱ δὲ τὴν ἧτταν θεασάμενοι τῷ βασιλεῖ προσφεύγουσι. τῶν δὲ περὶ αὐτὸν ἀρχόντων τις Ἀγαλλιανὸς ὄνομα, ταῦτα θεασάμενος καὶ τῆς σωτηρίας ἑαυτοῦ ἀπογνούς, σὺν τῇ πανοπλίᾳ ἑαυτὸν τῷ βυθῷ παραδέδωκε. Κοσμᾶς δὲ καὶ ἕτερός τις Στέφανος συλληφθέντες τὰς κεφαλὰς ἀπετμήθησαν.

61. Τῷ δὲ ἐπιγενομένῳ θέρει πάλιν ἱππικὰ στρατεύματα τῶν Σαρακηνῶν πλεῖστα τῆς Ῥωμαίων ἀρχῆς κατέθεον, ὧν ἡγοῦντο Ἄμερος καὶ Μανίας ὀνομαζόμενοι Σαρακηνοί· καὶ καταλαμβάνουσι πρὸς τὴν προκαθεζομένην τῆς Βιθυνίας πόλιν Νίκαιαν καλουμένην· ἐπί ⟨τε⟩ τινα χρόνον τῆς πολιορκίας ἐχόμενοι τέλος ἄπρακτοι ἀπεπέμποντο.

62. Μετὰ δὴ ταῦτα ὁ βασιλεὺς ἀθροίζει πλεῖστον λαὸν τῆς πόλεως περὶ τὰ βασίλεια, καὶ συγκαλεῖ τὸν τότε | τῆς V203v πόλεως ἀρχιερέα Γερμανόν, καὶ συγγράφειν κατὰ [τῆς καθαιρέσεως] τῶν εἰκόνων τῶν ἁγίων ἠνάγκαζεν. ὁ δὲ παρῃτεῖτο καὶ τὴν ἱερωσύνην ἀπέβαλε, λέγων ὡς "ἄνευ οἰκουμενικῆς συνόδου ἔγγραφον πίστιν οὐκ ἐκτίθεμαι". ἐκεῖθεν ἐπὶ τὸν πατρικὸν οἶκον γενόμενος αὐτοῦ τὸν τῆς ζωῆς βιοτεύων διετέλεσε χρόνον. μετ' αὐτὸν δὲ προχειρίζονται ἀρχιερέα Ἀναστάσιον κληρικὸν τῆς μεγάλης ἐκκλησίας τυγχάνοντα. ἐξ ἐκείνου τοίνυν πολλοὶ τῶν εὐσεβούντων, ὅσοι τῷ βασιλείῳ οὐ συνετίθεντο δόγματι, τιμωρίας πλείστας καὶ αἰκισμοὺς ὑπέμενον.

63. Ἐν ᾧ δὲ οὕτω ταῦτα ἐπράττετο, ἐκπέμπει ὁ βασιλεὺς πρὸς τὸν τοῦ ἔθνους τῶν Χαζάρων ἡγούμενον, καὶ τὴν αὐτοῦ θυγατέρα μεταπέμπεται καὶ τῷ υἱῷ Κωνσταντίνῳ εἰς dB59 γυναῖκα κατηγγύησε. χρόνου δὲ μεταξὺ παρελθόντος σεισμὸς ἐνσκήπτει κατὰ τὸ Βυζάντιον, μεθ' οὗ καὶ πόλεσιν ἑτέραις καὶ χώραις ἰσχυρῶς ἐπιφύεται. καὶ ἤδη ἄλλους τε πολλοὺς οἴκους

---

13 *περὶ αὐτῶν* V corr. dB ‖ 15 *περὶ αὐτῶν* V corr. vulg. ‖ *ὄνομα* V –*τι* superscr. V[2]

61: 4 *καθεζομένην* V *προ*– in mg. add. V[2] ‖ 5 *τε* addendum esse coni. dB

62: 3–4 *τῆς καθαιρέσεως* seclusi *τῆς καθιερώσεως* perperam coni. dB ‖ 7 *βιωτεύων* V

after collecting a great fleet, made a certain Kosmas their emperor. And so they came to the Imperial City. The men of Constantinople joined battle with them and set fire to many of their ships. Beholding their defeat, they went over to the emperor. One of their commanders, called Agallianos, when he had seen these things, despaired of his salvation and cast himself in the deep in the armor ⟨he was wearing⟩. Kosmas and another man called Stephen were arrested and beheaded.

61. The following summer a numerous force of Saracen cavalry again overran the Roman State. Led by Saracens called Ameros and Mauias, they came to the chief city of Bithynia, namely, Nicaea. After besieging it for some time, they finally departed without having accomplished anything.

62. After this the emperor convened to the palace a great throng of people from the City and summoned Germanos, who was then archpriest of Constantinople, whom he pressed to subscribe to the suppression of the holy icons. The latter declined to do so and laid aside his priesthood, saying, "Without an ecumenical synod I cannot make a written declaration of faith." Retiring thence to his ancestral house, he spent in it the remainder of his life. In succession to him Anastasios, who was a cleric of the Great Church, was appointed archpriest. From that time onward[45] many pious men who would not accept the imperial doctrine suffered many punishments and tortures.

63. While these things were being done, the emperor sent ⟨an embassy⟩ to the chief of the Chazar nation and fetched the latter's daughter, whom he betrothed in marriage to his son Constantine. After a lapse of time an earthquake occurred at Byzantium and likewise shook violently other towns and regions. In addition to many other buildings, holy churches, and porticoes

[45] Or perhaps "at his hands," i.e., those of Anastasios.

καὶ ἱεροὺς ναοὺς καὶ στοὰς ἀθρόον ἐπικαταβάλλει, ἐκ πρώτων βάθρων αὐτῶν ἔστιν οὓς τούτων ἀνατρέψας, καὶ τὸν θεῖον νεὼν ὃν τῆς ἁγίας Εἰρήνης ἐπώνυμον καλοῦσι κατέσεισεν, ὃς πλησιαίτατα τῆς μεγάλης ἐκκλησίας ἵδρυται. μεθ᾽ ὃν καὶ ὁ Ἀρκαδίου τοῦ πάλαι Ῥωμαίων τὰ σκῆπτρα ἰθύνοντος ἀνδριάς, ὃς κατὰ τὸν λεγόμενον λόφον Ξηρόλοφον καθύπερθε τοῦ γλυφαίου ἵδρυται κίονος, κατὰ γῆς ἄνωθεν ἔρριπτο. διέμεινε δὲ τὰ τοῦ σάλου ἄχρι καὶ εἰς ἐνιαυτὸν ὅλον· διὸ πλεῖστοι τῆς πόλεως προϊόντες καὶ ἔξω τειχῶν αὐλιζόμενοι ἐν καλύβαις κατέμενον.

64. Λέων δὲ ⟨μετὰ⟩ τέσσαρα καὶ εἴκοσι ἔτη τῆς βασιλείας μεταλλάττει τὸν βίον ὑδέρῳ χαλεπῷ περιπεσών, διάδοχον δὲ τῆς ἀρχῆς τὸν υἱὸν Κωνσταντῖνον καταλιμπάνει. Ἀρτάβαζος δέ, ὃς γαμβρὸς Κωνσταντίνου ἐπ᾽ ἀδελφῇ ὑπῆρχεν, ἅμα τῷ περιόντι λαῷ (στρατηγὸς δὲ τοῦ Ὀψικίου λαοῦ ἐτύγχανε) καὶ τοῖς δυσὶν υἱέσιν, ὧν ὁ μὲν ἕτερος Νικήτας θάτερος δὲ Νικηφόρος ἐκέκλητο, κατὰ τὸ λεγόμενον τοῦ Δορυλαίου πεδίον ηὐλίζετο. καὶ δὴ τυραννίδα εὐθὺς κατ᾽ αὐτοῦ μελετᾷ, τὸν τοῦ πενθεροῦ θάνατον πυθόμενος· καὶ ὅρκοις τὸν ὑπὸ χεῖρα κατεδέσμει λαὸν αὐτῷ μὲν εὔνουν ἔσεσθαι, ἕτερον δὲ εἰς βασιλέα μὴ δέχεσθαι. Κωνσταντῖνος δὲ τῆς βασιλείας κρατήσας ἀπόμοιράν τινα στρατοῦ ἐπιλεξάμενος τῆς πόλεως ἔξεισι καὶ τὸ πεδίον ὃ Κρασὸς προσαγορεύεται καταλαμβάνει καὶ Ἀρταβάζῳ ἐσήμαινεν ἥκειν πρὸς αὐτόν, ὡς ἂν ἅμα V204r dB60 | τῶν πολεμίων χάριν βουλεύσοιντο. ὁ δὲ ἤδη ὥρμα, οὐ βουλῆς ἕνεκεν, ἀλλὰ τῆς βασιλείας αὐτὸν καθαιρήσων. Κωνσταντῖνος δὲ τὰ τῆς τυραννίδος πυθόμενος, καὶ Βίσηρον τὴν ἀξίαν πατρίκιον προϋπαντήσαντα καὶ τῷ ξίφει τῶν ἀντιπάλων πεσόντα αἰσθόμενος, καὶ ὡς τὸ βασιλικὸν ἐσκευαγώγουν στρατόπεδον εἰσιδών, αὐτὸς πρὸς τῇ χώρᾳ τῶν Ἀνατολικῶν καλουμένῃ φυγὰς ἐνθένδε ἀπιὼν τὴν σωτηρίαν τὴν ἑαυτοῦ περιεποιήσατο. καὶ αὐτοὶ εὐνοϊκῶς ὑποδεξάμενοι ἐνωμότους αὐτῷ συνθήκας δεδώκεσαν ὡς μέχρις αἵματος ὑπὲρ αὐτοῦ ἀνελέσθαι τὸν κίνδυνον, καὶ Ἀρτάβαζον αἰσχρῶς δυσ-

---

63: 12–13 *γλυφάνου* V corr. vulg.

64: 1 *μετὰ* add. P || *ἔτι* V || 6 *ὧν* V corr. vulg. || 14 *πρὸς* signo ∼ superscr. *ἀντὶ τοῦ πρὸς* (sic) in mg. V[1], *ὡς* ut vid. loco *πρὸς* in textu scribere animo habens || 18 *προσυπαντήσαντα* V corr. P

which it caused to fall down at once, some of them being overturned from their very foundations, it also threw down the sacred church which bears the name of St. Eirene and stands very close to the Great Church. Furthermore, the statue of Arkadios, the former Roman emperor, which stood on the hill called Xerolophos above the sculpted column, was cast from its height to the ground. The quakes continued for a whole year; for which reason many people went out of the City and dwelt in huts outside the walls.

64. After a reign of twenty-four years Leo contracted a violent case of dropsy and departed from this life, leaving his son Constantine heir to the empire. Now Artabazos,[46] who was Constantine's brother-in-law (he was his sister's husband), together with his army (for he was commander of the Opsikian host) and his two sons, of whom one was called Niketas and the other Nikephoros, was encamped in the plain of Dorylaion (as it is called). Immediately on being informed of the death of his father-in-law, he planned a usurpation against ⟨Constantine⟩; and he imposed an oath on the army under his command that they would remain loyal to him and not accept another emperor. As for Constantine, after he had acceded to the throne, he selected a contingent of soldiers and went out of the City to the plain called Krasos, from where he sent a message to Artabazos that he was coming to ⟨join⟩ him that they might confer regarding the enemy. The latter had already set out, not with a view to taking counsel, but in order to depose ⟨Constantine⟩ from the throne. When Constantine had been informed of the rebellion and became aware that the patrician Biser, who had gone forward to meet ⟨Artabazos⟩ had fallen by the sword of his opponents; when he saw that the imperial camp was being looted, he fled to the country of the Anatolics (as it is called) and made himself safe. They received him favorably and gave him a sworn undertaking that they would risk their lives on his behalf, while cursing Artabazos with

[46]The normal spelling is Artabasdos.

φημοῦντες καθύβριζον. μεταστέλλονται γοῦν καὶ Σισίννιον τὸν πατρίκιον καὶ σύμφωνα καθίστων ἅμα τῷ ὑπ' αὐτὸν στρατηγουμένῳ τῶν Θρᾳκησίων λεγομένῳ λαῷ, καὶ ἅπαντες κατὰ Ἀρταβάζου ὁμῶς ἐχώρουν. Θεοφάνης δέ, ὃν Μονώτιον ἐκάλουν, τὴν τοῦ μαγίστρου ἀξίαν διέπων καὶ τὴν βασιλέως χρείαν εἰς Βυζάντιον ἀποπληρῶν, Ἀρταβάζῳ προσέθετο καὶ βασιλέα ἀνεκήρυττε, καὶ Βυζαντίους ἀνέπειθεν ὡς Κωνσταντῖνος τεθνήκει. τὸν δὲ υἱὸν Νικηφόρον τοὔνομα κατὰ τὴν Θρᾴκην τότε στρατηγοῦντα μεταπέμπεται καὶ σὺν τῷ περὶ αὐτὸν στρατῷ πρὸς φυλακὴν τῆς πόλεως ἐγκαθίστησι. τῶν βασιλικῶν δὲ ὑπηρετῶν οὓς μὲν ἀπετύφλου οὓς δὲ καὶ ἑτέρως κατῄκιζε. καὶ Ἀρτάβαζος εὐθὺς τῷ συνόντι ἅμα λαῷ τῇ πόλει ἐφίσταται καὶ αὐτίκα τῶν ἁγίων ἀνίστη τὰ ἱερὰ ἀπεικονίσματα. τούτου δὲ κατόπιν ἰὼν Κωνσταντῖνος τὴν Χρυσόπολιν καλουμένην καταλαμβάνει· ἐπίνειον δὲ τοῦτο ἀντικρὺ Βυζαντίου πρὸς τῇ Ἀσιάτιδι γῇ διακείμενον. κἀνταῦθα βραχὺν διατρίψας χρόνον ὑπενόστει καὶ πρὸς τὴν πόλιν ἣν Ἀμόριον καλοῦσι διεχείμαζε.

65. Τῷ δὲ ἑξῆς ἐπιγενομένῳ ἐνιαυτῷ τὸν ἕτερον τῶν dB61
υἱῶν Νικήταν στρατηγὸν τοῦ καλουμένου τῶν Ἀρμενιάκων στρατοῦ Ἀρτάβαζος ἀποστέλλει, τὸν δ' αὖ ἕτερον Νικηφόρον εἰς βασιλέα στέφει. ἐπιστρατεύει δὲ κατὰ τῆς τῶν Ἀσιανῶν χώρας, καὶ τὰ ἐκείνῃ χωρία ἐσιαίνετο πικρῶς. καθ' ὃ ἐπιτίθεται Κωνσταντῖνος καὶ πρὸς τὰς Σάρδεις ὑπαντιάζει, πολέμῳ τε αὐτῷ συμμίξας κραταιῶς ἐτροπώσατο, τόν τε ὑπόντα λαὸν δουλωσάμενος τήν τε ὑποῦσαν αὐτοῖς ἀποσκευὴν εἰσποιησάμενος. Ἀρτάβαζος δὲ φυγὰς [πρὸς] τὴν πόλιν Κύζικον καταλαβὼν κἀκεῖθεν ἀποπλεύσας ἐπὶ τὸ Βυζάντιον ᾤχετο. Νικήτας δὲ ὁ αὐτοῦ υἱὸς κατὰ Κωνσταντίνου τὴν ὁρμὴν ἐποιεῖτο. ὁ δὲ πρός τι χωρίον αὐτῷ μάχῃ προσβαλών, Μωδρινὴ τῇ ἐπιχωρίῳ φωνῇ προσαγορευόμενον, | αὐτὸν μὲν Νικήταν V204v
ἐτρέψατο, τοῦ δὲ συνόντος λαοῦ πλείστους ἀναιρεῖ. ἐντεῦθεν ἐν μεγίσταις συμφοραῖς τὰ Ῥωμαίων διέκειτο, ὁπηνίκα ἡ παρ' ἐκείνοις περὶ τῆς ἀρχῆς ἅμιλλα τὸν ἐμφύλιον Χριστια-

26 *σύμφωνα* in *σύμφρονα* mut. V[2] ‖ 28 *ὠμῶς* V dB corr. vulg. ‖ 36 λαῷ ex *τῷ* V[1] ‖ 40 *βραχὺ* V corr. vulg.

65: 5 *καθὸ* V *καθ' οὗ* coni. dB ‖ 9 *πρὸς* seclusi ‖ 12 Μωδρινὴν edd. ‖ 15–16 *εἰ παρ' ἐκείνοις περὶ τὴν τῆς ἀρχῆς ἅμιλλαν* V corr. P

foul insults. They also brought over the patrician Sisinnios and made an agreement with the army of the so-called Thrakesians which he commanded; and so, all together, they set out against Artabazos. Now Theophanes, surnamed Monotios, who held the rank of magister and was administering the emperor's affairs in Byzantium, gave his support to Artabazos, whom he proclaimed emperor, while informing the people of Byzantium that Constantine had died. He summoned his son Nikephoros, who was *strategos* in Thrace, and set him to guard the City with his army. As for the imperial servants, some of them he blinded, while others he maltreated in different ways. Straightaway Artabazos arrived in the City with the army that accompanied him and speedily restored the holy images of the saints. Marching in pursuit, Constantine reached Chrysopolis, as it is called (this is a port lying opposite Byzantium on the Asiatic shore). After remaining there for a short time, he returned and wintered in the town called Amorion.

65. The following year Artabazos appointed one of his sons, Niketas, commander of the so-called army of the Armeniacs, while he crowned emperor his other son Nikephoros. He also mounted an expedition against the country of the Asians[47] and cruelly devastated the villages that are there. Whereupon Constantine attacked him and met him at Sardis; and, having joined battle, routed him mightily, captured his army and took possession of their baggage. Artabazos fled to the city of Kyzikos and thence sailed off to Byzantium, while his son Niketas advanced on Constantine. The latter met him in battle near a place called Modrine[48] in the native dialect, routed Niketas, and killed many of his men. Under these circumstances the Roman State was in extreme distress, inasmuch as the struggle for power among those men aroused an internecine war among Christians. What terrible things are

[47] I.e., the ancient province of Asia.

[48] In Bithynia, east of Nicaea, probably modern Mudurnu. See *RE*, Modra (W. Ruge).

νοῖς ἀνερρίπισε πόλεμον. οἷα γὰρ καὶ ὅσα συμβαίνειν τοῖς τοιούτοις εἴωθε τὰ δεινότατα, ὡς καὶ τὴν φύσιν ἑαυτὴν ἐπιλανθάνεσθαι καὶ καθ' ἑαυτῆς ἵστασθαι (καὶ τί γὰρ δεῖ τἆλλα λέγειν;), πολλοὺς ἂν ἐν πείρᾳ καθεστηκέναι.

66. Ἐν τούτοις καθυπέρτερος Κωνσταντῖνος γενόμενος πρὸς τὰ Θρᾳκικὰ περαιοῦται χωρία καὶ τῷ τείχει προσεδρεύει τῆς πόλεως διεκώλυέ τε τὴν τῶν ἀναγκαίων εἰσφοράν· καὶ ἐκ τούτου ἐν μεγάλῃ ἦν ἡ πόλις ἀνάγκῃ, ὥστε [τοῦ] μεγίστου λιμοῦ τοὺς Βυζαντίους κατατείνοντος πολλοὺς μὲν συνέβαινε διαφθείρεσθαι, ἄλλους ὑπὲρ τειχῶν ἑαυτοὺς ἔξω ῥίπτειν βιαζομένους. οἳ δὲ καὶ δώροις ἔπειθον τοὺς ἐπὶ τῶν πυλῶν φύλακας κρύβδην ἐξιέναι τῆς πόλεως. Κωνσταντῖνος dB62 δὲ ἅπαντας εὐμενῶς ἐδέχετο καὶ περιεποιεῖτο μάλιστα. αὖθις οὖν Νικήτας ἐπιστρατεύει καὶ μέχρι Χρυσοπόλεως παραγίνεται. Κωνσταντῖνος δὲ πάλιν αὐτῷ ἐπιτίθεται καὶ κατὰ τὴν Νικομηδέων καταλαμβάνει πόλιν, καὶ αὐτὸν μὲν χειρωσάμενος σιδήροις ἐδέσμει, Μαρκελλίνου δὲ τοῦ συνόντος αὐτῷ ἀρχιερέως τῆς Γαγγρηνῶν μητροπόλεως τὴν κεφαλὴν ἐξέτεμε. κἀκεῖθεν ἐπανελθὼν παραλαμβάνει τὸ Βυζάντιον. Ἀρτάβαζος δὲ ἀποδρὰς πρὸς τὴν ἐν Βιθυνίᾳ Νίκαιαν πόλιν διασώζεται, καὶ τοὺς ἐν αὐτῇ ἀνέπειθεν ὡς ἥκοι στρατολογήσων καὶ δύναμίν τινα ἐκεῖ περιβαλλόμενος * ἐξ ὧν ὀλίγους στρατιώτας προσλαβὼν ἐπὶ τὸ φρούριον τὸ λεγόμενον Πουζάνης ἀπιὼν ἐγκατακλείεται. Κωνσταντῖνος δὲ ἀπόμοιραν εἰς δίωξιν αὐτοῦ ἐκπέμψας αὐτόν τε χειροῦται, καὶ σὺν τοῖς υἱέσιν αὐτοῦ δεσμώτας ἐπὶ ἀγῶνος ἱππικοῦ ἕλκων θριαμβεύει ἐκεῖθέν τε ἐν εἱρκτῇ τηρεῖσθαι ἀσφαλῶς παραδέδωκεν. οὐ πολὺ δὲ τὸ ἐν μέσῳ, καὶ Σισίννιος ὁ πατρίκιος τυραννίδα ἐφωράθη κατὰ Κωνσταντίνου μελετήσας, ἐφ' ᾗ διαγνωσθεὶς τοὺς ὀφθαλμοὺς ἐκκόπτεται. μετὰ ταῦτα δὲ καὶ Ἀρτάβαζος

---

19 *ἑαυτ[ῆς]* V ‖ *δεῖ* dB *δὴ* V ‖ 20 *ἂν*] *οἶμαι* coni. B fort. *πολλοῖς . . . καθέστηκεν* legendum seu *καθεστηκέναι πέπεισμαι* vel sim.

66: 2 *περατοῦται* V corr. B ‖ 4 *τοῦ* seclusi ‖ 5 *τοῖς βυζαντίοις* V corr. vulg. ‖ *κατατείνων, τοὺς πολλοὺς* V *κατατείνοντος τοὺς πολλοὺς* vulg. *τοὺς* del. dB ‖ 7 *οἳ* scripsi *οἵ* V ‖ 8 *πυλῶν* in mg. V ‖ 9 *καίπερ ἐποίει τὸ* (sive *τὰ*) V^1 *καὶ περιεποιεῖτο* V^2 ‖ 14 *γαγγρινῶν* V corr. vulg. ‖ 17 *τοῖς* V corr. dB ‖ *ἥκοι*] *οἴκοι* V corr. P sed v. comment. ‖ 18 post *περιβαλλόμενος* lacunam statuit P. Speck, *Artabasdos*, 306 n.68

wont to happen in such conditions—so much so that ⟨human⟩ nature is neglected and made to oppose herself (not to say any more)—is, indeed, known to many from experience.

66. At this juncture Constantine gained the upper hand, crossed over to Thrace, and laid siege to the City walls, while preventing the introduction of necessary supplies. For this reason the City was reduced to great distress and a severe famine racked the inhabitants of Byzantium, so that many of them died, while others were forced to throw themselves over the walls. Some, indeed, bribed the guards of the gates ⟨to be allowed⟩ to leave the City in secret. Constantine received them all with favor and treated them very well. Once again Niketas undertook an expedition and came as far as Chrysopolis. And again Constantine attacked him; overtaking him at the city of Nicomedia, he captured him and put him in fetters, while he cut off the head of Markellinos, archpriest of the metropolis of Gangra, who accompanied ⟨Niketas⟩. Returning from there, he took Byzantium. Artabazos fled to the city of Nicaea in Bithynia, to whose inhabitants he alleged that he was going to recruit an army and deploy a force round about. Taking a few soldiers from among them, he went off to the fort called Pouzane[49] and shut himself up. But Constantine sent a detachment to pursue him and apprehended him. Having brought him captive together with his sons, he paraded them at the hippodrome games and then confined them to a well-guarded prison. A short time thereafter the patrician Sisinnios was also detected to have planned a rebellion against Constantine and, after being convicted, was blinded. Later on, Artabazos and

[49] Situation unknown. Ramsay, *Hist. Geogr.*, 190, places it south of Nicaea. Cf. the village of Pouza or Pazoukome near the source of the Sangarios: Belke and Restle, TIB 4, 221, 238.

καὶ οἱ αὐτοῦ υἱοὶ τῇ αὐτῇ τιμωρίᾳ ᾐκίσθησαν, πλείσταις δὲ πληγαῖς καὶ τιμωρίαις καὶ οἱ συγγνῶντες αὐτοῖς τὰ τῆς ἐπιβουλῆς ὑποβληθέντες ὑπερωρίαις κατεδικάσθησαν.

67. Ταῦτα οὕτω τὰ τῆς ἰδίας ἀρχῆς διαθεὶς Κωνσταντῖνος μετὰ χρόνον οὐ πολὺν κατὰ τὴν χώραν τῶν Σαρακηνῶν ἐκστρατεύει, ὧν εἷλε πόλιν Γερμανίκειαν τῆς Εὐφρατησίας χώρας. εἰσπίπτει δὲ κατὰ τὴν βασιλεύουσαν καὶ τὰς κύκλῳ χώρας * καὶ καθ' οὓς τόπους τὸ φθοροποιὸν ἐπεφύετο πάθος, ἅπαν ἀνθρώπων γένος ἐπινεμόμενον διώλλυ|έ τε καὶ ἄρδην V205r ἐξηφάνιζε. διεσώθη δ' ἄν τις θείᾳ πάντως βουλήσει, ὅστις ὡς dB63 πορρωτάτω τούτων τῶν χωρῶν ἀπέδρα. ἐπετείνετο δὲ τὰ τῆς φθορᾶς μάλιστα περὶ τὸ Βυζάντιον. τεράστια δ' οὖν καὶ δείματα ἐξαπίνης ἐφαίνετο· (τύποι σταυροειδεῖς ἔν τε ταῖς τῶν ἀνθρώπων στολαῖς καὶ τῶν ἱερῶν ἐσθημάτων ἐπανατέλλοντες, θύραις τε ὡσαύτως καὶ τοῖς τῶν θυρῶν σταθμοῖς,) ἃ δὴ φαινόμενα φρίκην μεγάλην καὶ ἀπορίαν πᾶσιν ἐνέτικτεν ὡς παραχρῆμα τὸν ὄλεθρον μηνύοντα ἔσεσθαι. ὥσπερ δὲ ἐξεστηκότες τῷ δέει οἱ ἄνθρωποι καὶ φαντασιούμενοι ἐδόκουν αὐτοῖς ὡς ξένοις τισὶ συνοδεύειν καὶ εἰδεχθέσιν ἀνθρώποις, καὶ εἶτα ὡς γνωρίμοις δῆθεν τοῖς ἐντυγχάνουσι προσαγορεύοντες, καὶ τὰ πρὸς τὴν ὁδὸν ὡμιλημένα ἑτέροις ἔπειτα ἀφηγούμενοι· καὶ ἄλλοι φάσμασί τισιν ἐκδειματούμενοι ἑώρων ξίφεσιν ἀλλήλους τινὰς βάλλοντας. καὶ δὴ οὕτω τὰ πλεῖστα ἐξέβαινεν. οὐδὲ οἷοί τε ἦσαν οἱ περισωζόμενοι τῶν ἀποιχομένων ταφῇ παραδιδόναι τὰ σώματα καὶ τὴν ὁσίαν ἐπ' αὐτοῖς ποιεῖσθαι, ὀλιγοστοὶ μάλα πλείστους ἄγαν ἐκκομίζοντες. διὸ μηχανὰς ἔκ τινος περινοίας κατεσκεύαζον, σεσαγμένοις τοῖς ἀχθοφόροις ζῴοις σανίδας ἐπιστρωννύντες καὶ ἐπὶ μέγα τι χωρίον ἀπευρύνοντες τὸ μηχάνημα, οὕτω τε τὰ πλεῖστα τῶν πτωμάτων ἀκόσμως καὶ ὡς ἂν ἔτυχεν ἐπετίθεσαν. ἤδη δὲ καὶ ἅμαξαι πρὸς τὴν ἐκφορὰν τοῦ πλήθους τῶν νεκρῶν φορούμεναι ὑπηρέτουν, τῶν ὑποζυγίων αὐτοῖς μὴ

27–29 *πλείσταις . . . κατεδικάσθησαν* in mg. add. V²

67: 3 *Γερμανικίαν* V corr. B ‖ 5 post *χώρας* verba *λοιμὸς μέγιστος* vel sim. excidisse videntur ‖ 8 *τούτω* V corr. vulg. ‖ *δὲ οἱ τὰ* V *οἱ* om. B ‖ 11 *καὶ ἐπὶ τῶν* coni. dB ‖ 11–12 *ἐπανατέλλων ταῖς θ.* V corr. dB ‖ 16 *αὐτοῖς* V corr. B ‖ *ἠδεχθέσιν* V corr. vulg. ‖ 19 *ἄλλους* ex *ἄλλοι* V² ‖ 20 *ἀλλήλοις* V corr. vulg. ‖ 21 *οὐδὲ* dB *ἐνουδε οἷοί τε* V¹ *ἐνουδεν οἰοι* (accentibus deletis) *τε* V² *ἐνουδενὶ δ'* vulg. *οὐδαμοῦ* B ‖ 23 *ὀλιγωστοὶ* V ‖ *πλείστοις* V corr. B

his sons underwent the same penalty, while their accomplices in the plot were subjected to flogging and various ⟨other⟩ punishments and condemned to exile.

67. After making such disposition concerning his own rule, Constantine undertook a little later an expedition against the country of the Saracens, from whom he captured the city of Germanikeia in the region of Euphratesia. ⟨Now a great plague⟩ fell upon the Imperial City and the surrounding lands, and wherever this destructive disease prevailed it consumed and entirely annihilated all human beings. Only those who fled as far away as possible from those parts were able to be saved, surely by God's will. The pestilence was particularly intense at Byzantium. Frightful portents were suddenly to be seen: cruciform markings appeared on men's garments and holy cloths, upon doors and door posts, and these phenomena aroused in everyone great fear and consternation as if they were foreshadowing an instant doom. Being out of their wits through terror and subject to hallucinations, men imagined that they were being accompanied by certain hideous strangers, whom they addressed as if these were known to them and later recounted to others the words that had been spoken on the way. Others, terrified by phantasms, saw certain people striking one another with swords. And, indeed, most of ⟨these visions⟩ were fulfilled. Nor were the survivors able to inter the bodies of the deceased and conduct their funerals, so few were they in carrying out so many to burial. For which reason they invented a device, namely, to lay planks upon harnessed beasts of burden and, after making this construction very wide, they heaped upon it the corpses without decorum and in whichever way. And as the

ἐπαρκεῖν ἔτι δυναμένων. ἐπιλελοίπασι δὲ εἰς ἅπαξ καὶ οἱ τάφοι, ὥστε καὶ τὰς ἀνύδρους τῶν δεξαμενῶν νεκρῶν ἐμπλησθῆναι σωμάτων. ἄρουραι δὲ ἀνετέμνοντο καὶ ἀμπελῶνες διωρύσσοντο καὶ κῆποι διεσκάπτοντο πρὸς τὴν τῶν ἀπείρων σωμάτων ταφὴν καινοτομούμενοι. ἐξ ὧν συνέβαινε dB64 τοὺς πλείονας τῶν οἴκων κατακλείστους πάμπαν γίνεσθαι. παρέτεινε δὲ τὰ τῆς θραύσεως μέχρις ἐνιαυτοῦ, καὶ ἐξ ἐκείνου ἐνεδίδου τὰ πλεῖστα, καὶ κατὰ μικρόν, ὥσπερ τὴν ἀρχὴν ηὔξανεν, οὕτω δὴ καὶ ἐλώφησεν ἡ φθορά. ταῦτα ἐκρίνετο τοῖς ὀρθὰ φρονεῖν εἰδόσιν ἐκ θείας ἐπισκήπτειν ὀργῆς, ἡνίκα ὁ τότε ἀθέως καὶ δυσσεβῶς κρατῶν, καὶ ὅσοι αὐτῷ συνῄνουν τῷ ἀθέσμῳ φρονήματι, τὰς χεῖρας ἐπαφεῖναι κατὰ τῶν ἁγίων ἀπεικονισμάτων εἰς ὕβριν τῆς τοῦ Χριστοῦ ἐκκλησίας τετολμήκασιν.

68. Ἐντεῦθεν τοίνυν ἀοίκητον σχεδὸν ἤδη γεγονυῖαν τὴν πόλιν ταύτην κατοικίζει ἐκ τῶν χωρῶν καὶ τῶν νήσων τῆς ὑπὸ Ῥωμαίοις ἐξουσίας λαῶν πλήθη μετάγων. ὑπὸ δὲ τοῦτον τὸν χρόνον στόλον ἐκπέμπει κατὰ τῆς τῶν Σαρακηνῶν χώρας, οὗ ἡγεῖτο ὁ τηνικαῦτα στρατηγῶν τῶν Κιβυραιωτῶν καλουμένου | στρατοῦ. καθορμίζεται δὲ ὁ στόλος κατὰ τὴν Κύπρον V205v νῆσον. ἔνθα αὐτίκα μάλα κατῆρεν ἐκ τῆς Ἀλεξάνδρου πόλεως καὶ τῶν Σαρακηνῶν πλόϊμον. ὅπερ ὁ στρατηγὸς προαισθόμενος ἐξαπιναίως εἰσπίπτει κατ᾽ αὐτοῦ πυρί τε διαφλέξας τὰς ναῦς τὰ αὐτῶν σφετερίζεται ἅπαντα, καὶ κατὰ κράτος ἑλὼν τοὺς πολεμίους πρὸς Κωνσταντῖνον ὑπενόστει.

69. Μετὰ ταῦτα τίκτεται τῷ βασιλεῖ υἱός, ὃν Λέοντα ἐπωνόμασε. τηνικαῦτα καὶ ἐν Συρίᾳ σεισμὸς μέγας γίνεται καὶ ὄλεθρος ἐκεῖθεν ἐφίσταται μέγιστος. αἱ μὲν γὰρ τῶν ἐκεῖ πόλεων * ἐπὶ μέγα ἡ γῆ περὶ αὐταῖς ἔχανεν, αἱ δὲ παρὰ μέρος τοῦτο πεπόνθεισαν. ἄλλαι τῶν ὑψηλῶν ἀποκινηθεῖσαι χώρων πρὸς τὰ ὑποκείμενα πεδία σὺν τείχεσιν αὐτοῖς καὶ οἰκήμασι σῶοι κατεσύρησαν, μέχρι σημείων ἓξ [καὶ] τῆς

---

32 *σώματων* V^2 *σώματα* V^1 || 34 *κενοτομούμεναι* V corr. vulg. || 42–43 *τετολμηκόσιν* V corr. vulg.

68: 2 *κατοικίζοι* V corr. vulg. || 5 *κιβυριωτῶν* V corr. dB || 7 *κατήρει* V corr. dB || 9 *ἐξαπηναίως* V || 10–11 *κατακράτως* V corr. B

69: 4 post *πόλεων* lacunam statui *ὅλαι κατεπόθησαν καὶ* suppl. B || 7 *καὶ* del. dB

beasts did not suffice, they used hand-borne wagons to carry out the multitude of the dead. The tombs gave out altogether, so that empty cisterns were filled with dead bodies. Fields were plowed up, vineyards and orchards dug up to serve the novel purpose of burying the immense number of bodies. As a result, most of the houses were completely shut up. The pestilence lasted for a year, after which time it gave way for the most part and, as in the beginning it had increased, so now it gradually abated. Those who were able to think aright judged that these ⟨misfortunes⟩ were inflicted by God's wrath inasmuch as the godless and impious ruler of the day and those who concurred with his lawless purpose dared to lay their hands on the holy images to the disgrace of Christ's Church.

68. The City having consequently become almost deserted, ⟨Constantine⟩ populated it by transferring to it a multitude of people from the lands and the islands subject to the Romans. At the same time he sent a fleet against the Saracen country, at whose head was the commander of the Kibyraiot army (as it is called). The fleet put in at the island of Cyprus. Straightaway a Saracen armada from Alexandria arrived there too. Forewarned of this, the commander made a sudden attack, burned the enemy ships with fire, gained possession of all their ⟨equipment⟩ and, after defeating them soundly, returned to Constantine.

69. Thereafter a son was born to the emperor, whom he named Leo. At the same time a severe earthquake occurred in Syria, causing enormous damage. For some cities that were there ⟨were completely destroyed and⟩ the ground round about opened up to a great extent, while others suffered this fate but partially. Others were shifted from their high positions and slipped down entire, with their walls and houses, to the plains below, moving a distance of

οἰκείας μεταστᾶσαι ἱδρύσεως, ἢ μικρῷ πρός. ἤδη δέ τινες ἔφασαν τὴν γῆν θεάσασθαι τὴν κατὰ τὴν Συρίαν Μεσοπο- dB65 ταμίας ῥαγεῖσαν ἐπὶ σημείοις δύο βύθιον ἑτέραν ἀναβράσαι κάτωθεν γῆν ὥσπερ ἀμμώδη καὶ λευκοτάτην, συναναδοθῆναι δὲ ταύτῃ ἡμίονον θήλειαν ἀνθρωπείᾳ φωνῇ τὴν τῶν Ἀράβων κατάλυσιν προαναφωνοῦσαν. οὐ πολὺ γὰρ τὸ μεταξύ, καὶ τῆς ὑπερέκεινα ἐρήμου ἔθνος ἐπιφυὲν πλήθη τούτων πολλὰ ἀμαχὶ διεχειρίσατο.

70. Μετὰ δὴ ταῦτα στέφει Κωνσταντῖνος τὸν υἱὸν Λέοντα εἰς βασιλέα καὶ εὐθὺς κατὰ Σαρακηνῶν ἐκστρατεύει. καὶ γενόμενος κατὰ τὴν Μελιτηναίων πόλιν ταύτην πολιορκίᾳ εἷλε, λαὸν πολὺν δοριάλωτον καὶ πλεῖστα σκῦλα ἐκεῖθεν ἀπενεγκάμενος. ἐν τούτῳ δὲ ἐτελεύτα καὶ Μαρία ἡ Αὐγούστα ἡ αὐτοῦ γαμετή.

71. Ὅπερ δὲ μετ' ὀλίγον συνέβαινε μνήμης ἄξιον, οὐ παραδραμεῖν δίκαιον. συνηνέχθη γὰρ τηνικαῦτα θέαμα φοβερὸν καὶ τεράστιον ξένον ἐξ ἀερίου γενέσθαι συμπτώματος, ὅπερ περὶ λύχνων ἁφὰς κατάρξαν διὰ πάσης ἐφαίνετο νυκτός, ἔκπληξιν καὶ δέος μέγα τοῖς θεωμένοις ἐμποιοῦν ἅπασιν. ἐδόκει γὰρ αὐτοῖς ὡς οἱ ἀστέρες ἅπαντες τοῦ τεταγμένου αὐτοῖς οὐρανίου χώρου παρακινούμενοι κατὰ γῆς ἐφέροντο. οἱ δὲ περίγειοι γενόμενοι ἀθρόον διελύοντο, ἥκιστα τὴν οἱανοῦν βλάβην ποιησάμενοι πώποτε. φασὶ δὲ πολλοὶ ὡς διὰ πάσης τῆς οἰκουμένης τὸ τοιοῦτον ἐξαίσιον διεδείκνυτο θέαμα.

72. Καὶ τὰ μὲν τῶν ἀστέρων ἐν τούτοις ὤφθη· χρόνου δέ τινος διῳχηκότος Ἀναστάσιος ὁ τοῦ Βυζαντίου ἐτελεύτα ἱεράρχης. Κωνσταντῖνος δὲ καθ' ἅπαξ πρὸς τὴν ὕβριν τῆς ἐκκλησίας ἰδὼν καὶ πρὸς τὴν εὐσέβειαν ἤδη ἀπομαχόμενος, ὡς ὑπὸ τοῦ ἄγοντος αὐτὸν ἐναντίου πνεύματος κινούμενος, σύνοδον | ἱερέων ἀθροίζει ὀκτὼ καὶ τριάκοντα καὶ τριακοσίους V206r τὸν ἀριθμὸν τυγχάνουσαν, (ταύτης ἐξῆρχε Θεοδόσιος ὁ τῆς Ἐφεσίων πόλεως ἀρχιεπίσκοπος) ἀρχιερέα τε τῆς πόλεως dB66 ἀνακηρύσσει Κωνσταντῖνόν τινα τὸ τῶν μοναχῶν σχῆμα

12 *ταύτην* V corr. vulg. || *απια* V corr. dB

71: 3 *συμπτώματα* V corr. vulg.

72: 1 *ἀστέρων* V[2] in lacuna || 6 *ἱερέων*] litt. *ν* V[2] in ras. || 8 *τε* ex *τω* V[1]

as much as six miles, more or less, from their original situation. Some affirmed they had seen the ground in Mesopotamia (which is near Syria) crack deeply along ⟨a distance⟩ of two miles, and another ground, sandy and very white, thrown up from below; and that along with the latter was cast up a female mule, which proclaimed in a human voice the destruction of the Arabs. A short time thereafter a tribe appeared from the desert beyond and slew many multitudes ⟨of Arabs⟩ without resistance.

70. After these events Constantine crowned his son Leo emperor and straightaway marched against the Saracens. He came to the town of Melitene, which he took by siege and carried off from there a great number of captives and much booty. At this time the Augusta Maria, his wife, died.

71. We ought not to pass over in silence a memorable event that happened a little later. Indeed, a terrible sight and a strange prodigy occurred at that time through some aerial circumstance. It began at twilight and was visible all through the night, causing amazement and great fright to all spectators. For it appeared to them that all the stars moved from their appointed celestial stations and were borne down toward the earth. When they came near the earth they vanished at once without ever causing the slightest damage. Many men affirmed that this extraordinary sight was visible throughout the whole world.

72. So much for the spectacle of the stars. After some time Anastasios, the archpriest of Byzantium, died. Now Constantine, who was completely determined to insult the Church and was, by now, making war on piety (driven as he was by the evil spirit that directed him) convened a council of 338 priests under the presidency of Theodosios, archbishop of Ephesos, and appointed to be archpriest of the City a certain Constantine, who wore the monastic habit

περιβεβλημένον, ἐπίσκοπον δὲ τῆς τοῦ Συλλαίου πόλεως γεγονότα. ὅρον δὲ πίστεως ἐκτίθενται, ἐν ᾧ ὑπεσημήναντο ἅπαντες κακῶς καὶ δυσσεβῶς συμφρονήσαντες, τὴν τῶν ἱερῶν εἰκονισμάτων καθαίρεσιν ἐκφωνήσαντες· καὶ ὥσπερ νηπιώδεις ἐπ' ἀγορᾶς ταῦτα ἀνεθεμάτιζον. μεθ' ὧν καὶ Γερμανὸν τὸν ἀρχιερέα τοῦ Βυζαντίου γεγονότα Γεώργιόν τε τὸν ἐκ Κύπρου τῆς νήσου ὁρμώμενον καὶ Ἰωάννην τὸν ἀπὸ Δαμασκοῦ τῆς Συρίας τὸ ἐπίκλην Μανσούρ.

73. Ταῦτα ἐπιτελῆ ποιήσας Κωνσταντῖνος ἦρξε δομεῖσθαι τὰ ἐπὶ Θρᾴκης πολίσματα, ἐν οἷς οἰκίζει Σύρους καὶ Ἀρμενίους, οὓς ἔκ τε Μελιτηναίων πόλεως καὶ Θεοδοσιουπόλεως μετανάστας πεποίηκε, τὰ εἰς τὴν χρείαν αὐτοῖς ἀνήκοντα φιλοτίμως δωρησάμενος. ταῦτα τοίνυν οἱ Βούλγαροι ὡς ἐπολίζοντο θεασάμενοι, φόρους ᾔτουν παρὰ βασιλεῖ δέξασθαι. τοῦ δὲ μὴ δεξαμένου οἵ γε στρατευσάμενοι τὰ ἐπὶ Θρᾴκης χωρία κατέτρεχον καὶ μικροῦ τοῦ Μακροῦ καλουμένου Τείχους ἐπεξέθεον. ὁ δὲ ἀντεπεξῄει καὶ συμβαλὼν πολέμῳ εἰς φυγὴν ἐτρέψατο καὶ ἐδίωκεν ἀνὰ κράτος καὶ πλείστους Βουλγάρους ἀνεῖλε. μετ' οὐ πολὺ πλοΐ καὶ πεζῇ κατ' αὐτῶν ἐστράτευεν. οἱ γοῦν τὰς ναῦς ἔχοντες ἄχρι καὶ εἰς πεντακοσίους τὸν ἀριθμὸν συντελούσας, διὰ τοῦ Εὐξείνου ἐκπλεύσαντες καὶ πρὸς τῷ Ἴστρῳ γενόμενοι ποταμῷ χώρας τε Βουλγάρων ἐπίμπρασαν καὶ δοριαλώτους οὐκ ὀλίγους εἷλον· αὐτὸς δὲ μάχῃ συμμίξας αὐτοῖς κατὰ τὰς λεγομένας Μαρκέλλας (φρούριον δὲ τοῦτο πλησιαίτατα Βουλγάρων κείμενον) εἰς φυγὴν ἐτρέψατο καὶ πολλοὺς αὐτῶν ἔκτεινεν. ἐντεῦθεν dB67 ἐκεῖνοι τὸ ἧττον ἀπενεγκάμενοι περὶ εἰρήνης διεπρεσβεύοντο ἐκ τῶν οἰκείων τέκνων ὁμήρους προϊέμενοι.

74. Ἔτι πρὸς τούτοις οὐδὲ ἐκεῖνο νῦν παραδραμεῖν ἄξιον. ὥρα ἐνέστηκε φθινοπώρου, καὶ ἐν αὐτῇ χειμέριον γίνεται τὸ κατάστημα καὶ τῷ ὄντι κρυερὸν καὶ δριμύτατον, ὡς ξένην τινὰ καὶ ἐξαίσιον τοῖς τηνικαῦτα ὁρῶσιν ἀποτελέσαι τῆς

---

14 νηπιώδεις scripsi νηπιωδ[ῶς] V νηπιωδεῖς dB || μεθ' ὂν V corr. B || 17 ἐπίκλιν ex ἐπίκλιο V^1 corr. vulg.

73: 1 ἐπὶ τέλει V corr. P || 8 μικροῦ δεῖν μέχρι coni. dB || 10 πόλεμον coni. dB || φυγὴν ex φρυγὴν V^1 || ἀνακράτως V corr. B || 11 πεζὶ V corr. vulg. || 13 συντελούσας V^2 συνελθούσας V^1 || 14 ἴστρω V corr. vulg. || 20 ὁμείρους V

and had been bishop of Syllaion. They drew up a definition of the faith in which all of them, by an evil and impious agreement, set down a proclamation of the destruction of the holy icons. These they childishly anathematized in public and, along with them, Germanos, who had been archpriest of Byzantium, George, a native of the island of Cyprus, and John of Damascus in Syria, surnamed Mansour.

73. Having accomplished these matters, Constantine started building towns in Thrace in which he settled Syrians and Armenians, whom he had transferred from Melitene and Theodosioupolis and bountifully endowed with all necessities. When the Bulgarians saw these towns being founded, they demanded taxes from the emperor. On meeting with his refusal, they took up arms and overran the Thracian region nearly as far as the Long Wall. ⟨The emperor⟩ marched out against them and, having joined battle with them, put them to flight. He pursued them mightily and killed many Bulgarians. A short time thereafter he made an expedition against them by sea and land. Those who were embarked on the ships (which numbered five hundred) set sail by way of the Euxine and, upon reaching the river Istros, burned the Bulgarian lands and made many captives; while ⟨the emperor⟩ himself joined battle with them at the so-called Markellai (this is a fort lying very near to the Bulgarians),[50] put them to flight, and killed many of them. Being thus worsted, they petitioned for peace and delivered hostages from among their children.

74. The following ⟨incident⟩ should also not be passed over in silence. In the autumn season the weather became wintry—indeed cold and extremely harsh—to the extent of congealing the liquid element (a strange and extraordinary sight to those who beheld it then), and this not only in the case of fresh

[50] Believed to have been at Karnobadski Hisarlŭk, SW of Karnobad.

ὑγρᾶς οὐσίας ἐκ τῆς περὶ αὐτὴν συμβάσης πήξεως τὴν θέαν, οὐκ ἐν τοῖς γλυκέσιν ὕδασι μόνον, ἀλλά, τὸ δὴ παραδοξότερον, καὶ κατὰ τῆς ἁλμυρᾶς ἰσχῦσαν ποιότητος, καὶ ἐν ἄλλοις μὲν πλείστοις τοῖς ἀνὰ τὴν οἰκουμένην τόποις, οὐχ ἥκιστα δὲ τά τε ὑπερβόρεια καὶ προσάρκτια καταπῆξαν δεινότατα. ἐπὶ τοσοῦτο δὲ κατεπυκνοῦτο καὶ διεπήγνυεν ὥστε τὴν ὑπερπόντιὸν τοῦ Εὐξείνου | V206ᵛ *θάλασσαν ἐπὶ σημείοις ἑκατόν που ἀποκρυσταλλωθῆναι κατὰ τὸ πέλαγος, εἶτα καὶ τοὺς ὑπερκειμένους μεγίστους ὅτι μάλιστα καὶ πλείστους ποταμῶν, καὶ ἔτι τὸν ἐπὶ* Μεσήμβρειαν *καὶ* Μήδειαν *πόλιν ἐρχόμενον παράκτιον χῶρον τῷ πάγει συναποπετρωθῆναι, διὰ βάθους χωρησάσης τῆς τοιαύτης πήξεως ἄχρι καὶ εἰς τριάκοντα πήχεις· ἐπὶ τούτοις ἀφάτου καταρραγείσης χιόνος εἰς ὕψος διαρθῆναι τὸ κρύος ὑπερανεστηκὸς τῆς ἐπιφανείας μέχρι πηχῶν που ἄλλων εἴκοσι, καί πως συμφυῆναι τῇ ἠπείρῳ τὴν θάλασσαν ὡς μηδὲ διακρῖναι ῥᾳδίως ποτέρα ἑτέρας ἀποκέκριται. οὕτω τε ἅπαν τὸ πρὸς ἄρκτον ἠπειρωθὲν ὕδωρ πεζεύειν κατὰ νώτου συνεχώρει τοῖς βουλομένοις, βάσιμά τε ἦν τὰ ἐκείνῃ ἅπαντα, ὅσα τε ἐν τοῖς τῶν* Χαζάρων *γῆς μεθορίοις καὶ τοῖς πλησιοχώροις* Σκυθικοῖς *ἔθνεσι, καὶ οὐκ ἀνθρώποις μόνον ἀλλὰ καὶ* dB68 *κτήνεσι καὶ ζῴοις ἑτέροις γενόμενα· ἄπλωτον δὲ ἤδη ἐντεῦθεν γενέσθαι τὴν* Ποντικὴν *τότε θάλασσαν. ἡμέραις δέ τισι διιππευούσαις καὶ ὁ ἄπλετος ἐκεῖνος τοῦ παγέτου ὁλκὸς εἰς διάφορα συρρήγνυται τμήματα, ἅπερ εἰς τοσοῦτον ὕψος ἀνέσχεν ὡς ὄρη δοκεῖν εἶναι ὑπερύψηλα. τούτων ἀπορραγέντα μέρη τινὰ καὶ τῇ βίᾳ τῶν πνευμάτων συνωθούμενα πρός τε* Δαφνουσίαν, *φρούριον [ὄν] τι τῆς* Ποντικῆς *μοίρας ἐρυμνότατον τυγχάνον, ἐξοκέλλουσι καὶ ἄχρι τοῦ στομίου τοῦ* Εὐξείνου *κατέρρουσι· συστραφέντα δὲ πρὸς ἑαυτὰ κατὰ τὸν αὐτόθι στενὸν πόρον, τὸν μεταξὺ πορθμὸν πληρώσαντα τὰς ἑκατέρωθεν ἠπείρους, τήν τε* Θρᾴκην *καὶ τὴν* Ἀσιάτιδα, *ἀλλήλαις συνήνωσαν, ὡς ἐξ ἑκατέρας πρὸς θατέραν πεζῇ μᾶλλον ἢ πλοΐ διαπεραιοῦσθαι ἐξεῖναι τῷ βουλομένῳ. ἐκεῖθεν συνωθούμενα ἀνὰ τὴν* Προποντίδα *μέχρις* Ἀβύδου *ἐξεχύθησαν,*

74: 7 *ἴσχυσαν* V¹ *ἰσχύσασαν* V² corr. vulg. || *πιότης* V corr. vulg. || 9 *ὑπερβόρια* V corr. vulg. || 12–13 *το[ὺς] ὑπερκειμένους μεγίστο[υ]ς* V || 13 *πλείστους* ex *πλείστων* ut vid. V² || 14 *τὸν . . . ἐρχόμενον* B *τοῦ . . . ἀρχομένην* V || 19 *τῆς θαλάσσης* V¹ corr. V² || 21 *ἄρκτον* V² *ἄρκτους* V¹ || 22 *ἐκείνης* V¹ corr. V² || 31 *φρουρίων ὄντι* V *φρούριον ὄντι* V² *ὄν* secl. dB || 32 *ἐξωκέλλουσι* V || 34 *πόρθμον* V || 36 *πεζὶ* V corr. vulg.

water, but, even more amazingly, in overcoming the salty kind. The freezing ⟨occurred⟩ in many parts of the world, but was especially severe in the hyperborean and northerly ⟨regions⟩. So hard was the congealment that the Euxine sea beyond the Pontos was frozen for about a hundred miles from the shore, as well as the numerous great rivers that lie beyond. Furthermore, the coastal region that lies by Mesembria and the city of Medeia[51] was turned to rock by the cold, such coagulation extending to a depth of thirty cubits. In addition, an extraordinary amount of snow fell, so that the icy matter was piled up to a height of about another twenty cubits from the ground and the sea became somehow conjoined with the land, so much so that one could not easily distinguish their respective boundaries. Thus, all the water having turned solid in the direction of the north, anyone who so wished could walk on it, and all those parts became passable—those bordering on the lands of the Chazars and the neighboring Scythian nations—not only for men but also for cattle and other animals. For this reason, too, the Pontic sea ceased at the time to be navigable. After the passage of a few days that immense mass of ice was fractured into several portions, which rose to such a great height that they seemed to be tall mountains. Some parts that broke off, driven by the force of the winds, drifted to Daphnousia[52] (a very strong fort in the Pontic region) and moved down to the mouth of the Euxine. Compressed in the narrow passage that is there, they filled the intervening strait and joined the continents on either side, namely, Thrace and Asia, so that anyone who so wished was able to cross on foot rather than by ship from one to the other. Propelled from there, ⟨the ice⟩ spread as far as Abydos on the Propontis, which no longer looked

[51] Ancient Salmydessos, modern Midye.

[52] Ancient Thynias, modern Kefkenadasī, an island in the Black Sea on the Bithynian coast.

[147]

ἥπερ δὴ οὐδὲ θάλασσα εἶναι τὸ λοιπὸν ὑπωπτεύετο. τούτων ἓν ἀποσπασθὲν τῇ ἀκροπόλει τοῦ Βυζαντίου προσαράσσεται καὶ τὸ αὐτόθι τεῖχος περιέσεισεν ὡς καὶ τοὺς ἔνδον οἰκοῦντας συμμετασχεῖν τοῦ σάλου. καὶ τοῦτο τριχῇ διαιρεθὲν παρ' ἑκάτερα μέρη τῆς ἀκροπόλεως τὰς ἀκτὰς ἐμπίπλησι. τὸ δὲ ὕψος αὐτοῖς τῶν τῆς πόλεως τειχῶν ὑπερανέστηκε, δι' αὐτῶν τέ τινες ἐξ ἀκροπόλεως πρὸς τὸ ἀντικρύ, ἐν οἷς τῶν Γαλάτου λεγόμενον ἵδρυται φρούριον, πεζῇ διεπεραιοῦντο. ταῦτα ἔκπληξιν μεγίστην τοῖς τῆς πόλεως ἐνεποίει· τῷ παραδόξῳ γὰρ καὶ ἀδοκήτῳ τῆς θέας ἐν ἀπορίᾳ γενόμενοι θρήνοις καὶ δάκρυσι πλείστοις συνεχόμενοι ἐνθένδε ἀπηλλάσσοντο. |

75. Χρόνων δὲ οὐκ ὀλίγων διελθόντων, Σκλαβηνῶν γένη V207r τῆς ἑαυτῶν μεταναστάντα γῆς φυγάδες διαπερῶσι τὸν Εὔξεινον. συνετέλει δὲ αὐτῶν τὸ πλῆθος ἄχρι καὶ εἰς ἀριθμὸν ὀκτὼ καὶ διακοσίας χιλιάδας. καὶ πρὸς τὸν ποταμὸν ὃς Ἀρτά- dB69 νας καλεῖται αὐτοὶ κατοικίζονται.

76. Τὰ δὲ κατὰ τοὺς Οὔννους Βουλγάρους ἐπράττετο τῇδε. οὗτοι τὰ πρὸς ἀλλήλους συνθέμενοι τοὺς μὲν ἐκ σειρᾶς τὴν κυρείαν τὴν ἐπ' αὐτοὺς κεκτημένους κτείνουσιν, ἡγεμόνα δὲ ἐφ' ἑαυτοῖς καθιστᾶσιν Τελέσσιον ὄνομα, ἄνδρα σοβαρὸν καὶ τὸ ἐκ νεότητος θράσος ἅμα ἐπιδεικνύμενον. οὗτος λαὸν συναγείρας ὁπλίτην καὶ μάχιμον τὰ πλησιαίτερα τῶν Ῥωμαίων χωρία καὶ φρούρια κατέτρεχε καρτερῶς. οὗ τὸ θρασὺ καὶ αὔθαδες Κωνσταντῖνος θεασάμενος ναῦς ἱππαγωγοὺς ἄχρι καὶ εἰς τὰς ὀκτακοσίας κατεσκεύασε, καὶ ταύτας ἱππικῷ στρατῷ πληρώσας διὰ τοῦ Εὐξείνου πρὸς τὸν Ἴστρον ἐξέπεμψεν. αὐτὸς δὲ στρατὸν ἕτερον ἐπαγόμενος πρὸς Ἀγχίαλον πόλιν παραγίνεται. καθ' ὃν Τελέσσιος ἐξέρχεται ἔχων εἰς συμμαχίαν καὶ Σκλαβηνῶν οὐκ ὀλίγα πλήθη. καὶ ἡττηθεὶς μάχῃ εἰς φυγὴν ἐτράπετο. πλεῖστοι δὲ τῶν πολεμίων ἀφ' ἑκατέρου μέρους πίπτουσι, καὶ ἄλλοι οὐκ ὀλίγοι καὶ τῶν ἐπιφανεστέρων ἐζωγρήθησαν. οὕτω τε τοῦ πολέμου κρατήσας πρὸς τὸ Βυζάντιον Κωνσταντῖνος ᾤχετο, καὶ οὓς ἐπήγετο τῶν

39 *εἴπερ . . . θάλασσαν* V corr. vulg. || 46 *διεπεραιοῦτο* V corr. vulg.

76: 2 *σειρᾶς* ex Theoph. scr. dB *ξηρᾶς* V || 3 *αὐτ*[*οὺς*] *κεκτημέν*[*ους*] V *ἐπ' αὐτοῖς* coni. dB || 4 *τελέσσιον* V^2 *τελεσσιων* V^1 *ὀνόματι* ex *ὄνομα* V^2 || 10 *ἴστρον* V corr. vulg. || 12 *καθ' ὧν* coni. dB || *τελέσιος* V || 17 *ἐπείγετο* V signo super primum *ε* posito *ή* in mg. scr. pr. m. *ἠπείγετο* legendum esse monens; corr. vulg.

like a sea. One part that broke off struck against the Acropolis of Byzantium and gave such a jolt to the wall that is there that those dwelling inside felt the quake. Dividing into three, ⟨the ice⟩ covered the shore on either side of the Acropolis. In height it rose above the city walls. Over it some men were able to cross on foot from the Acropolis to the opposite shore, upon which stands the fort of Galata (as it is called). These things caused great astonishment to the inhabitants of the City: distressed by this strange and unexpected spectacle, they were seized by lamentation and weeping and so went home.

75. Several years later some Slavonian tribes left their own country and fled across the Euxine. Their number amounted to 208,000. They were settled by the river Artanas.[53]

76. As for the Bulgarian Huns, the following events took place. Coming to an agreement among themselves, they killed their hereditary lords and appointed as their ruler one called Telessios, a haughty man who yet exhibited the rashness of youth. This man gathered a band of armed fighters and overran vigorously the Roman villages and forts that were nearest to him. On seeing his insolent boldness, Constantine built as many as eight hundred horse-carrying ships and, after loading them with a force of cavalry, sent them by way of the Euxine to the Istros. He himself came to the city of Anchialos with another army. Telessios marched out against him with a great multitude of Slavonian allies, but was defeated in battle and fled. Many of the belligerents[54] fell on both sides, and a considerable number of prominent men were captured. Having thus won the war, Constantine returned to Byzantium and delivered to

[53] Or Artanes. In Bithynia, between the mouth of the Bosporos and Daphnousia, by modern Şile. See Arrian, *Periplus*, 17; anon. *Periplus*, 3. Both in A. Baschmakoff, *La synthèse des Périples pontiques* (Paris, 1948), 92, 108–10.

[54] Literally "of the enemy," which is probably what Nikephoros meant, without noticing the contradiction with the phrase "on both sides."

ἐζωγρημένων τοῖς τε πολίταις καὶ τοῖς ἐκ τῶν λεγομένων χρωμάτων δημόταις ὡς ἀναιρήσειν αὐτοχειρίᾳ παραδίδωσιν. οἱ δὲ λαβόντες ἔξω τείχους τοῦ πρὸς τῷ χερσαίῳ κειμένου ἀνεῖλον. καὶ τούτων τὰ λάφυρα τὸν ἱππικὸν ἀγῶνα θεώμενος ἐθριάμβευσε. μεθ' ὧν καὶ δύο χρυσοῖ λουτῆρες, οἳ ἐν τῇ νήσῳ κατεσκευάσθησαν Σικελίᾳ, δημοσιεύονται, ὁλκὴν χρυσοῦ ἄχρι καὶ εἰς ὀκτακοσίας λιτρῶν ἕκαστον ἄγοντα.

77. Οἱ δὲ Βούλγαροι τὸ δυστυχὲς Τελεσσίου θεασάμενοι dB70
τοῦτόν τε στασιάσαντες κτείνουσι, καὶ κύριον αὐτῶν καθιστῶσιν ἕνα τῶν ἐν αὐτοῖς ἀρχόντων τυγχάνοντα, ᾧ Σαβῖνος ὑπῆρχεν ὄνομα· ὃς εὐθὺς τὸ κῦρος δεξάμενος πρὸς βασιλέα διαπρεσβεύεται, εἰρήνην αὐτὸν αἰτούμενος βεβαιότατα. Βουλγάρους δὲ οὐκ ἤρεσκε τὸ πραττόμενον· ἀλύοντες γὰρ ἐν τούτῳ ἰσχυρῶς ἀντέλεγον, οἰόμενοι ὡς Ῥωμαίοις αὐτίκα δουλωθησόμενοι. τούτους δεδιὼς Σαβῖνος φυγὰς πρὸς βασιλέα ᾤχετο. εὐζώνων δὲ ἀποστείλας ἀνδρῶν τινὰς τὰς γυναῖκας αὐτῶν καὶ τοὺς συγγενεῖς κεκρυμμένους εὑρὼν πρὸς Σαβῖνον ἄγει. ἐν τούτοις μεταμεληθέντες οἱ Βούλγαροι καὶ αὐτοὶ πέμπουσι πρὸς βασιλέα τοὺς τὴν εἰρήνην αἰτήσοντας. ὁ δὲ οὐκ ἐδέχετο, ἀλλ' εὐθὺς κατ' αὐτῶν ἐξεστράτευσεν. οἱ δὲ τὰς δυσχωρίας τοῦ περὶ αὐτοὺς ὄρους ἀνέφραττον. καὶ τούτων ὁ κύριος
| τὰ πιστὰ παρὰ βασιλέως λαβὼν σὺν τοῖς ἄρχουσιν αὐτοῦ V207ᵛ
πρὸς βασιλέα παραγίνεται. αὐτὸς δὲ τούτους δεξάμενος ἅμα Σαβίνῳ συμπαρεδρεύοντι ὠνείδισε τὴν ἀταξίαν καὶ τὸ μῖσος ὃ κατὰ Σαβίνου ἐπεδείξαντο, καὶ εἰρηνεύειν αὐτοῖς συνετίθετο.

78. Ταῦτα διεπράττετο κατὰ τὴν πρώτην ἰνδικτιόνα. ἔτι καὶ υἱὸς τίκτεται τῷ βασιλεῖ, ὃν Νικήταν ὠνόμασεν. ὑπὸ δὲ τὸν αὐτὸν χρόνον στόλος τῶν Σαρακηνῶν ἐξ Ἀφρικῆς ἀπάρας κατὰ τῆς νήσου Σικελίας παραγίνεται· τὸ δὲ ἐν αὐτῇ στρατιωτικὸν γενναίως ἀντιταξάμενον τούτοις, μηδὲν τῆς ἐλπίδος ἠνυκότας ἀπέπεμψε.

79. Κατὰ δὲ τὴν τρίτην ἰνδικτιόνα εἰσέρχεται Κωνσταν-

---

20 τοῦ ex τῶ V[1] ‖ κειμένω V corr. B ‖ 22 χρυσοὶ V ‖ 23 ὀλκὴν V

77: 2 αὐτῶν vulg. αὐτὸν V ‖ 3 ᾧ vulg. ὃς V ‖ 4 ὀνόματι ex ὄνομα V[2] ‖ 5 αὐτὸν dB αὐτῷ V ‖ βεβαιώτατα V ‖ 14 τοῦ περὶ αὐτοὺς ὄρους vulg. το . . . περὶ αὐτ . . . ὅρους V[1] τοὺς περὶ αὔτους (ultima litt. postea deleta) τὸ ὅρος V[2] ‖ 17 ἀταξίαν P cf. Theoph. 436.13 ἀξίαν V

78: 1 δὴ ἐπράττετο coni. dB

the citizens and to the members of the so-called "colors" the captives he had brought along so that they would kill them with their own hands. Taking them outside the wall that lies on the landward side, they slew them. He exhibited their spoils while they were watching the equestrian games. At the same time were displayed two golden basins that had been made in the island of Sicily, each one weighing 800 lbs. of gold.

77. Now the Bulgarians, on seeing the bad fortune of Telessios, rose in revolt and killed him, and appointed as their lord one of their commanders named Sabinos. Immediately on being invested with his authority, he sent an embassy to the emperor asking for a secure peace. This action did not please the Bulgarians: for in their distress at this they objected strenuously, thinking that they would be straightaway enslaved by the Romans. Being in fear of them, Sabinos fled to the emperor. He[55] sent a number of well-equipped men and, having found their wives and kinsmen, who were in hiding, brought them to Sabinos. At this the Bulgarians changed their minds and they, too, made overtures of peace to the emperor. The latter did not accept ⟨their proposals⟩ and immediately took up arms against them. They, for their part, fortified the difficult ⟨passes⟩ of the mountain range that surrounds them. Upon receiving pledges from the emperor, their lord came before him together with his dignitaries. The emperor received them with Sabinos seated by his side, reproached them for their disorderly conduct and the hatred they had shown to Sabinos, and agreed to make peace with them.

78. These events took place in the 1st indiction. Furthermore, a son was born to the emperor, whom he called Niketas. At the same time a Saracen fleet set sail from Africa and came to the island of Sicily, but they failed in their purpose because the army that was there opposed them bravely and repelled them.

79. In the 3rd indiction Constantine entered Bulgaria in order to re-

[55] Meaning unclear; see Commentary.

τῖνος εἰς Βουλγαρίαν τῷ τὸν ἀρχηγὸν αὐτῶν κατασταθέντα ὑπὸ Σαβίνου Οὔμαρον ὄνομα τῆς ἀρχῆς μεταστῆσαι [Βουλγάρους], ἀνειπεῖν δ' ἐν αὐτῇ Τόκτον ἄνδρα Βούλγαρον τὸν Βαϊανοῦ ἀδελφόν. οἱ δὲ Βούλγαροι φυγάδες ἐν ταῖς ὕλαις τοῦ dB71 *ποταμοῦ τοῦ Ἴστρου ἀπῴχοντο, οὐκ ὀλίγοι δὲ αὐτῶν κατακτείνονται, μεθ' ὧν καὶ ὁ Τόκτος ἅμα τῷ ἀδελφῷ Βαϊανῷ ἀναιρεῖται καὶ ἕτεροι. ἄλλος δέ τις ἄρχων αὐτῶν, ὃν ὀνομάζουσι Καμπαγάνον, ἐν Βάρνῃ προσφυγεῖν * ὡς ἐδόκει προσρύεσθαι ὑπὸ τῶν ἰδίων δούλων ἀνῃρέθη. τότε δὴ καὶ Βουλγαρίας ὑπὸ Ῥωμαίων πυρίκαυτα ὡς πλεῖστα χωρία γέγονε καὶ διόλωλεν.*

80. *Ἤδη δὲ ἡ ἀσέβεια τοῦ κρατοῦντος ἐπαρρησιάζετο, καὶ πᾶσα εὐσεβείας ὁδὸς διεβάλλετο καὶ τῶν εὐσεβούντων καὶ θεῷ προσανακειμένων ὁ βίος ἐχλευάζετο καὶ διεσκώπτετο, μάλιστα δὲ τῶν μοναζόντων τὸ ἱερὸν ἐκθέσμως ἐδιώκετο τάγμα. τούτων γὰρ τοὺς τὴν ἑαυτῶν ὁμολογίαν φυλάξαντας καὶ ἐπὶ τοῦ οἰκείου διαμείναντας σχήματος καὶ τῷ ἀνοσίῳ αὐτῶν ἀνθεστηκότας δόγματι ποικίλαις βασάνοις καὶ διαφόροις αἰκίαις παρεδίδοσαν, καὶ ὧν μὲν τὴν γενειάδα ἀφειδῶς ἐνεπίμπρων, ὧν δὲ τῶν ταύτης τριχῶν βίᾳ ἀποσπῶντες ἀφῄρουν. κεφαλὰς δ' ἄλλων τοῖς ἱεροῖς πίναξιν, ἐν οἷς τῶν ἁγίων τὰ ἐκτυπώματα ἐκεχάρακτο, διέθραυον παίοντες. καὶ μέντοι καὶ ὀφθαλμοὺς τούτων διώρυττον ἢ τῶν μελῶν ἕτερα τοῦ σώματος ἐξέκοπτον ἀπανθρώπως οἱ δείλαιοι. καὶ ἅπαν ὡς εἰπεῖν τὸ εὐσεβὲς διωθεῖτο καὶ ἀπηλαύνετο, καὶ ὥσπερ ἑλληνισμοῦ δευτέρου Χριστιανοῖς ἐπιφυέντος πᾶσα μηχανὴ κακουργίας ἐπενοεῖτο, δι' ἧς τοὺς κατὰ θεὸν ζῆν αἱρουμένους ἐπηρεάζειν καὶ πημαίνειν ἐσπούδαζον. ἤδη δὲ τούτων ἐνίους πρὸς τὸ τῆς οἰκείας ἀπωλείας καθείλκυσαν βάραθρον * καὶ τῷ δυσσεβεῖ | αὐτῶν εἶξαν θεσπίσματι ἢ βίᾳ ἑλκόμενοι ἢ* V208r *ἀπάτῃ ὑποσυρόμενοι ἢ θωπείαις ὑποκλεπτόμενοι ἢ χρήμασι δελεαζόμενοι ἢ στρατείαις καὶ ἀξιωμάτων * φιλοτιμούμενοι,* dB72

79: 2 *τῷ τὸν* vulg. *τὸ τὸν* (ex *τῶν*) V[1] ‖ 3 *ὀνόματι* ex *ὄνομα* V[2] ‖ 3–4 *μεταστήσειν· βουλγάρους ἂν εἰπεῖν* V *μεταστῆσαι Βουλγάρους, ἀνειπεῖν* vulg. Βουλγάρους seclusi ‖ 5 *βουλγάρων* V[1] corr. V[2] cf. **65.9** ‖ 6 *ἴστρου* V corr. vulg. ‖ 7 *μεθ' ὧν* V[2] *μέων* V[1] ‖ 9 post *προσφυγεῖν* lacunam statui *προσφυγὼν* B *προσφυγεῖν* del. dB

80: 2 *διεβάλετο* V ‖ 17 *πημαίνειν* V[2] *ποιμαίνειν* V[1] ‖ 18 lacunam statui ‖ 19 *ἧξαν* V corr. vulg. ‖ 21 *ἀξιωμάτων ὑποσχέσεσι φιλ.* vel. *ἀξ. φιλοτιμίαις κινούμενοι* suppl. esse coni. dB

move from office their leader who had been appointed by Sabinos, a man called Oumaros, and proclaim in his stead the Bulgarian Toktos, brother of Baianos. The Bulgarians fled to the forests of the river Istros and many of them were slain, including Toktos together with his brother as well as others. Another one of their commanders, whom they call Kampaganos, was killed by his own slaves while he was attempting to escape to Varna and join ⟨the emperor⟩.[56] At that time a great many Bulgarian villages were burned and destroyed by the Romans.

80. The emperor's irreligion was by now freely expressed: every avenue leading to piety was brought into discredit; the manner of life of the pious and those devoted to God was ridiculed and mocked; and, in particular, the holy regiment of monks was lawlessly persecuted. Those of them who had kept their profession, had clung to their habit, and had opposed the unholy doctrine of those men were subjected to diverse tortures and different outrages: some had their beards burned without pity, others had the hairs of their beard plucked out by force. They also broke the heads of some ⟨monks⟩ by striking them with the holy boards upon which were represented the images of saints; indeed, they even gouged out their eyes and cruelly cut off other parts of the body, wretched men that they were. Every form of piety was, so to speak, rejected and driven away and, as though a second paganism had grown up among Christians, all kinds of wicked devices were invented whereby they sought to maltreat and injure those who had chosen to live according to God. Some of them they dragged down to the pit of their own perdition, ⟨those who⟩ yielded to the impious decree being driven by force or seduced by deceit or cheated by flattery or beguiled by money or honored by imperial[57] appoint-

[56] See Commentary.

[57] The term *strateia* denoted not only military, but every kind of imperial service.

ἢ ἑτέραις πολυτρόποις τοῦ πονηροῦ μεθοδείαις τὴν ἐξαπάτην εἰσδεχόμενοι τὸ ἐπάγγελμά τε ἠθέτουν καὶ τὸ σεμνὸν μεταμφιεννύμενοι στόλισμα κομῆται αὐτοὶ ἀντὶ κεκαρμένων διεδείκνυντο καὶ εἰς λαϊκῶν σχῆμα εὐθὺς μεθηρμόζοντο, γυναιξί τε ὁμιλεῖν κατεδέχοντο καὶ τὸ πρὸς αὐτὰς ἠσπάζοντο συνοικέσιον. ἐπράττετο γοῦν ταῦτα, ὡς ἂν διὰ πάντων αὐτός τε ὁ τῶν ὅλων θεὸς τό γε ἐπ' αὐτοῖς ἀτιμάζηται καὶ τὰ τῆς ἐκκλησίας καθυβρίζηται τίμια.

81. Ἐντεῦθεν συλλαμβάνονται Στέφανόν τινα, ἄνδρα ὅσιον καὶ θεοφιλῆ τυγχάνοντα, μοναστὴν δὲ τῷ σχήματι καὶ περιειργμένον ἐν οἰκιδίῳ στενωτάτῳ πάνυ ὑπάρχοντα, ὑπὸ τὴν τοῦ μεγίστου ὄρους ἱδρυμένον ἀκρώρειαν, ὃ καλοῦσι τοῦ ὁσίου Αὐξεντίου λόφον. ἔγκλημά τε εὐσεβείας ἐπάγουσιν αὐτῷ οἱ ἀνόσιοι, "ὡς πολλούς", φασίν, "ἐξαπατᾷ διδάσκων δόξης τῆς παρούσης καταφρονεῖν οἴκων τε καὶ συγγενείας ὑπερορᾶν καὶ τὰς βασιλείους αὐλὰς ἀποστρέφεσθαι καὶ πρὸς τὸν μονήρη βίον μεταρρυθμίζεσθαι". καὶ διὰ ταῦτα πληγαῖς τε πλείσταις αἰκισάμενοι καὶ δεσμωτήριον οἰκεῖν καταδικάσαντες, τέλος σχοινίοις αὐτὸν κατὰ τοὺς πόδας ἐξάψαντες καὶ τῶν βασιλικῶν ἀφορμήσαντες περιβόλων, μέχρι τῆς λεγομένης τοῦ Βοὸς ἀγορᾶς ἑλκύσαντες διέσπασαν, καὶ αὐτοῦ τὸ σῶμα ἐν τοῖς καλουμένοις τάφοις τῶν Πελαγίου ὡς κακούργου οἱ δυσσεβεῖς ἀπέρριψαν· αὐτόθι γὰρ τά τε τῶν ἐθνικῶν ἀμυήτων σώματα καὶ τῶν ἐπὶ θανάτῳ ἀπηγορευμένῳ τελευτώντων ἐξεπέμπετο. πλείστους τῶν τε ἐν τέλει καὶ τοῦ στρατιωτικοῦ ὑπευθύνους καθιστῶντες, προσκυνεῖν ἱεραῖς εἰκόσι dB73 καταιτιώμενοι, ὥσπερ ἐπὶ καθοσιώσει ἁλόντας διέφθειραν, οὓς μὲν διαφόροις θανάτοις παραδιδόντες, οὓς δὲ τιμωρίαις ξέναις καθυποβάλλοντες, πλήθη τε ἄπειρα ὑπερορίαις παραπέμποντες. ἐφ' οἷς ὅρκοις βεβαιοῦν ἐβουλεύσαντο ἅπαν αὐτοῖς τὸ ὑπήκοον ὡς τὸ λοιπὸν εἰκόνι μὴ προσκυνεῖν ἁγίων τινά. φασὶ δὲ ὡς καὶ τὸν τηνικαῦτα τῆς πόλεως ἀρχιερέα θεασάμενοι ὑψώσαντα τὰ ζῳοποιὰ ξύλα ὀμωμοκέναι μηδ' αὐτὸν εἶναι τῶν προσκυνούντων τὰς ἱερὰς εἰκόνας. τοιαῦτα τῶν ἀσεβούντων τὰ τολμήματα.

---

22 *μεθοδίαις* V ‖ 24 *κομῖται* V

81: 5 *ὁσίου* V[2] in ras. *ὀν'. . . . ς* (fort. *ὀνόματος*) V[1] ‖ 9 *μεταρυθμίζεσθαι* V ‖ *διὰ* vulg. *δὴ* V ‖ 10 [*οἰκ*]*εῖν ὡς* V *οἰκ*– sec. m. in ras. scripto *ὡς* deleto ‖ 14–15 *κακοῦργον* ultima litt. in *ν* ras. mutata V

ments and dignities or who, having once swallowed the deceit through some of the multifarious devices of the Devil, set their profession at nought, put off their decorous raiment, grew their hair instead of being tonsured, changed immediately into lay costume, and consented to have intercourse with women and embrace marriage with them. These things were done so that the God of the universe should in every way be dishonored (as far as this was possible to them) and the holy ⟨institutions⟩ of the Church insulted.

81. For this reason they apprehended a certain Stephen, a holy and God-loving man, who wore a monk's habit and was confined to a tiny cell situated below the summit of that great mountain which is called the hill of St. Auxentios.[58] Unholy as they were, they brought against him a charge relating to religion,[59] saying that "he deceived many men by teaching them to despise the glory of this world, to disregard family and relatives, to avoid the imperial court, and to adopt the monastic life." On this account they inflicted many blows on him and condemned him to prison; finally, tying a rope round his feet, they dragged him from the imperial palace to the so-called market of the Bull and broke him to pieces and, impious as they were, threw his body, as if he had been a criminal, in the so-called tombs of Pelagios;[60] for it was customary to convey thither the bodies of unbaptized pagans and of those who had died an illicit death. They brought under accusation many men invested with authority as well as members of the army, charging them with worshiping holy icons, and killed them as if they had been found guilty of sacrilege; some they subjected to different kinds of death, on others they inflicted unusual punishments, while a great multitude were exiled. Furthermore, they resolved that all the subjects ⟨of the state⟩ should affirm under oath that henceforth none of them would worship the icon of a saint. It is even said by eyewitnesses that the then archpriest of the City elevated the life-giving Cross and swore that he, too, was not a worshiper of the holy icons. Such were the daring deeds of the impious.

---

[58] Modern Kayişdağ, SE of Chalcedon: J. Pargoire, "Mont Saint-Auxence," *Revue de l'Orient chrétien* 8 (1903), 266–79 (for identification); Janin, *Grands centres*, 43ff.

[59] Or possibly "to loyalty," which would be more appropriate to the nature of the charges.

[60] In the west part of Constantinople; exact situation unknown. See Janin, *CP*, 405.

82. Τῷ δὲ αὐτῷ ἔτει ἐπιστρατεύει Κωνσταντῖνος κατὰ Βουλγάρων καὶ παραγίνεται σὺν τῷ περιόντι λαῷ ἐγγύτατα τῆς Βουλγάρων γῆς καὶ σκηνοῦται παρὰ τὴν λεγομένην ἐμβολὴν Βεριγάβων. πλόϊμον δὲ ἐξοπλίσας συντελοῦν περὶ τὰ δισχίλια καὶ ἑξακόσια σκάφη, ναυτικὸν δὲ πλῆθος καὶ στρατιωτικὸν | ἔκ τε τῶν πλοΐμων στρατηγίδων καὶ ἑτέρων χώρων V208v ἐμβαλὼν ἐν αὐτοῖς ἀπέστειλεν, ὥστε παραγενέσθαι περί τε Μεσήμβρειαν καὶ Ἀγχίαλον τὰ πολίσματα καὶ προσπελάζειν Βουλγάροις. ἐντεῦθεν οὖν περικτυπηθέντες οἱ Βούλγαροι τότε, τὸ ἱππικὸν καὶ πλόϊμον θεασάμενοι πλῆθος, εἰς συμβάσεις τῷ βασιλεῖ ἐτράποντο. ἐπεὶ δὲ τὸ πλόϊμον πρὸς ταῖς ἀκταῖς τῆς ἐκείνῃ θαλάσσης καθωρμίζετο (ἀλίμενος γὰρ ὁ τόπος καὶ τοῖς πλέουσι δυσφορώτατος), πνεῦμα βίαιον καὶ σκληρὸν κατ' αὐτῆς πνεῦσαν (βορέας δ' ἦν ἄνεμος) τάς τε ναῦς πρὸς ταῖς ἀκταῖς περιτρέψας συνέτριψε καὶ πλήθη τῶν εἰσπλεόντων οὐκ ὀλίγα τῷ ῥοθίῳ κατεπόντισεν. ἐν τούτοις ἄγαν θορυβηθέντα τὸν βασιλέα κελεῦσαι τοὺς ἄρχοντας δικτύοις περιβαλεῖν τὴν θάλασσαν, ὡς ἀνελέσθαι τῶν ἀποπνιγέντων τὰ σώματα καὶ τῇ γῇ παραδιδόναι, οὕτω τε πρὸς τὰ βασίλεια ὑποστρέψαι.

83. Ἔτι δὲ πνέων κατὰ τῆς εὐσεβείας τὸ ἱερὸν τῶν Ναζηραίων dB74 σχῆμα καθύβριζεν. εὐθὺς γὰρ ἀγῶνα ἱππικὸν ἐπετέλει, καί τινας τούτων ἐπιτρέπει ἐν μέσῳ τῷ θεάτρῳ διέλκεσθαι καὶ αὐτῶν ἕκαστον γυναῖκα μονάστριαν παρὰ χεῖρα φέρειν· πολλῶν τε παρὰ τοῦ πλήθους τῶν θεωμένων ὕβρεων αὐτοῖς καὶ ἐμπτυσμάτων, οἷα περὶ τὸ ὀχλῶδες καὶ ἀγελαῖον συμβαίνειν εἴωθε, καταχεθέντων οὕτω τὸν ἄθεσμον ἐκεῖνον καὶ αἴσχιστον διήνυσαν δίαυλον. μετὰ δὲ ταῦτα ἄνδρας τινὰς τῶν ἐν ὑπεροχαῖς καὶ ἀξιώμασιν ἐγκλήμασι βαρυτάτοις συκοφαντῶν ὑπάγει ὡς εἰς τὴν ἀρχὴν αὐτῷ ἐπιβουλεύειν πειρωμένους. τούτων δ' ἦν Ἀντίοχος μὲν ὁ τῶν δημοσίων πραγμάτων τὰς ὑπομνήσεις αὐτῷ διακομίζων (λογοθέτην δὲ τοῦ δρόμου τὴν ἀξίαν οἱ περὶ τὰ βασίλεια καλοῦσι), Θεοφύλακτος δὲ ἐν τοῖς πατρικίοις καὶ στρατηγοῖς διατελῶν, ἔτι μὴν

82: 7 *παραγενέσθαι* dB *γενέσθαι* praecedente lacuna V ‖ 10–11 *συμβάσ[εις]* V ‖ 16 *ῥωθίῳ* V ‖ 17 *θορυβηθέντα* B *θορυβηθέντες* V

83: 1 *ἀσεβείας* V corr. B ‖ 7 *κατασχεθέντων* V corr. dB *καταχυθέντων* vulg.

82. In the same year Constantine made an expedition against Bulgaria and came with his army very close to the Bulgarian land, where he encamped by the pass called Verigava.[61] He also fitted out a fleet of about 2,600 vessels, which he manned with a multitude of sailors and soldiers drawn both from the naval commands and from other regions, and sent them to the townships of Mesembria and Anchialos in order to draw near to the Bulgarians. Upon seeing the multitude of cavalry and ships, the Bulgarians were distraught and begged the emperor for terms. But as the fleet was anchored by the coast of the sea that is there (for that place is lacking in harbors and difficult for sailors), a violent and harsh blast blew against it (it was a north wind), overturned and broke the ships against the shore, and sank in the surf a great number of the crews. The emperor was greatly distressed by this and commanded the officers to cast nets in the sea in order to collect the drowned bodies and bury them; and thus he returned to the palace.

83. Still breathing hard against the pious faith, he insulted the sacred habit of the Nazarenes. For straightaway he conducted hippodrome games and directed that some of them should be dragged in the midst of the theater, each holding a nun by the hand. After the throng of the spectators had poured upon them a mass of insults and had spat upon them (as is the custom of the vulgar rabble), was this unlawful and most shameful procession completed. After this he falsely brought under grave accusation several men in high positions and dignities, ⟨alleging⟩ that they were attempting to plot against his authority. Among these were Antiochos, who conveyed to him memoranda of public affairs (⟨the holder of⟩ this post is called logothete of the course by those who belong to the court), Theophylaktos, who was patrician and *strategos*, in ad-

[61] Probably the pass of Riš.

καὶ ἄλλοι τῶν περὶ αὐτὸν ἀσπιδηφόρων καὶ δορυφόρων τυγχάνοντες, πρὸς δὲ καὶ τούτων ἐκτὸς ἕτεροι. μετ' οὐ πολὺ τὴν ὁμοίαν ἐπιτελῶν ἅμιλλαν δεσμώτας ἐνταῦθα περιελκύσας ἐθριάμβευε· καὶ τῇ ἑξῆς Κωνσταντῖνον μὲν καὶ Στρατήγιον ἀδελφοὺς ὑπάρχοντας θανάτῳ κατεδίκασε, καὶ ἤδη τούτων τὰς κεφαλὰς ἐν τῷ λεγομένῳ τῆς πόλεως Κυνηγίῳ ἀπέτεμεν, ἄλλων δ' αὖ τοὺς ὀφθαλμοὺς ἐξέκοψε. καὶ τῇ ὑστεραίᾳ παρασκευάζει τῶν οἰκείων τινὰς Κωνσταντίνου τοῦ τῆς πόλεως ἀρχιερέως ὅρκιον κατ' αὐτοῦ ἐξυφῆναι κατηγορίαν, διελέγχειν δὲ φανερῶς ὡς παρ' αὐτοῦ ἀκηκοέναι πάντα τὰ παρὰ τῶν περὶ Ἀντίοχον καὶ Θεοφύλακτον μελετώμενα. καὶ εὐθὺς ἐκεῖνον μὲν ἐξόριστον ἐν τῇ Ἱερίᾳ, οὕτω καλουμένου βασιλικοῦ παλατίου ἀντιπέρα πρὸς εὖρον ἄνεμον τοῦ Βυζαντίου dB75 κείμενον, παρέπεμψε, Νικήταν δὲ | πρεσβύτερον τῆς τῶν V209r ἁγίων ἀποστόλων ἐκκλησίας εὐνοῦχον προχειρίζεται ἀρχιερέα. ταῦτα δὲ πάντα ἐπράττετο κατὰ τὸν Αὔγουστον μῆνα τῆς τετάρτης ἰνδικτιόνος.

84. [Κατὰ δὲ τὸν Ὀκτώβριον μῆνα τῆς ἕκτης ἰνδικτιόνος] Μετ' οὐ πολὺ δὲ μεταπέμπεται Κωνσταντῖνον καὶ ἀποστέλλει πρὸς τὸ ἱερὸν φορείῳ ἐποχούμενον. συνεκπέμπει δέ τινα αὐτῷ τῶν βασιλικῶν γραμματέων κομίζοντα ἐν γραμματίῳ ὅσα κατ' αὐτοῦ· ἅπερ εἰς ἐπήκοον τοῦ ἀθροισθέντος ἐκεῖσε λαοῦ ἀνέγνω, παίων αὐτὸν κατὰ κόρρης ἐφ' ἑνὶ ἑκάστῳ τῶν κατηγορουμένων. καὶ οὕτως ἐπὶ τοῦ ἄμβωνος ἀνενέγκαντες καθαιροῦσι, τοῦ νέου πατριάρχου πρὸς τῷ θυσιαστηρίῳ τὰ τοιαῦτα αἰτιάματα ὑπαναγινώσκοντος. καὶ τῇ ἑξῆς τὴν συνήθη αὐτῷ ἱππικὴν ἀγωνίαν ἐπιτελῶν ἐπιτρέπει αὐτὸν ἐπ' ὄνου προσιζηκότα, τῆς καθέδρας αὐτῷ πρὸς τοῖς ὀπισθίοις τοῦ ζῴου περιτραπείσης, [καὶ] ἐκεῖσε διέλκεσθαι καὶ ὑπὸ τοῦ λαοῦ παντὸς δυσφημεῖσθαί τε καὶ καταπτύεσθαι. εἶτα μετ' οὐ πολὺ ἐν τῷ τῆς πόλεως Κυνηγίῳ τὴν κεφαλὴν αὐτοῦ ἀποτμηθῆναι προστέταχε, καὶ τὴν μὲν ἐν τῷ καλου-

---

15 *ἀσπιδιφόρων* V corr. B ‖ 16 *ἑτέρους μετ' οὐ πολὺ* coni. dB *οὓς μετ'* B ‖ 17 *ὁμοῖαν . . . ἄμιλλαν* V ‖ 23 *ὅρκιον* gloss. Barocc. f. 313ᵛ *ὅρκον* V *ἔνορκον* P ‖ 24–25 *παρὰ τὸν* V corr. vulg. ‖ 26 *ἐκείνων* V corr. vulg. ‖ 27 *αὐτιπέρα* V corr. vulg.

84: 1 v. comment. ‖ 3 *φορίῳ* V corr. B ‖ 5 *ἐπήκοον* B et Theoph. 441.12 *ὑπήκοον* V ‖ 6 *αὐτῶ* V corr. B ‖ 12 *καὶ* seclusi

dition to some members of ⟨the imperial⟩ bodyguard as well as a number of others. Shortly thereafter he performed a similar contest[62] and paraded them there as prisoners. The following day he condemned to death the brothers Constantine and Strategios and cut off their heads in the so-called Kynegion of the City, while others he blinded. And the next day he contrived that some friends of Constantine, archpriest of the City, should concoct a sworn accusation against him, proving clearly that they had heard from him all the designs of the companions of Antiochos and Theophylaktos. Straightaway he exiled Constantine to Hieria (this is the name of an imperial palace that lies across the water from Byzantium in an easterly direction) and appointed as archpriest the eunuch Niketas, who was a presbyter of the church of the Holy Apostles. All these events took place in the month of August of the 4th indiction.

84. Shortly thereafter he had Constantine fetched and sent him to the church riding in a cart. He had him accompanied by one of the imperial secretaries bearing the written charges against him; these ⟨the secretary⟩ read out before the gathered people, striking him on the face for every item of the accusation. In this way they brought him up to the ambo and deposed him, while the new patriarch read out these same charges in front of the sanctuary in a low voice. The next day ⟨the emperor⟩ conducted the customary hippodrome games and directed that ⟨Constantine⟩ should be pulled along, seated on a donkey, facing toward the rear of the animal, and should be cursed and spat upon by the whole people. Not long thereafter he commanded that his head should be cut off in the Kynegion of the City and exposed aloft at the so-called

---

[62] I.e., chariot races in the Hippodrome.

μένῳ Μιλίῳ *ἐξαρτηθεῖσαν μετέωρον φέρεσθαι, τὸ δ' αὐτοῦ σῶμα σχοινίοις διασύρουσιν ἀνὰ τὰς λεωφόρους τῆς πόλεως εἴς ⟨τε⟩ τοὺς τῶν* Πελαγίου *καλουμένους τάφους ἐξέρριπτον.*

85. Πέμπτῃ *δὲ ἰνδικτιόνι ἀβροχίας ἐπικρατούσης αὐχμῶδες καὶ ξηρὸν γέγονε τὸ κατάστημα, ὡς καὶ αὐτὴν ἐπιλελοιπέναι τὴν ἀέριον δρόσον, ἔτι καὶ τὰ πηγαῖα ὑποστέλλεσθαι νάματα, ἀργά τε μένειν ἐντεῦθεν καὶ τὰ λουτρὰ τῶν ἐκδοχείων κενῶν ὑπαρξάντων. ἐκ τούτου βουλεύεται* Κωνσταντῖνος *τὸν τοῦ ὕδατος ὁλκὸν ἀνακαινίζειν ὃν* Βαλεντινιανὸς *ὁ βασιλεὺς κατεσκεύασεν, ὑπὸ δὲ* Ἀβάρων *ἐπὶ τῶν* Ἡρακλείου *χρόνων τοῦ βασιλέως καταστραφέντα.* dB76 *καὶ πλείστους ἄνδρας τεχνίτας εἰς οἰκοδομὴν ἐμπείρους ἐκ τῆς ὑπὸ* Ῥωμαίων *ἀρχῆς συναθροίσας, πολλά τε δαπανήματα αὐτοῖς ἐκ τῶν δημοσίων χρημάτων προσαναλώσας, οὕτω τὸ τοιοῦτον ἔργον ἐτέλεσε. φιλόχρυσος δὲ ὢν ὁ μισόχριστος νέος* Μίδας Κωνσταντῖνος *ἀναδείκνυται καὶ τὸν χρυσὸν ἅπαντα ἀποθησαυρίζει. ἐν οἷς συνέβαινεν ἐν ταῖς τῶν φόρων πράξεσι τῶν φορολογουμένων βιαζομένων εὐώνως τὰ τῆς γῆς καρπήματα καὶ γεννήματα διαπιπράσκεσθαι, ὡς τῷ νομίσματι ἑξήκοντα μοδίους σίτου διαγοράζεσθαι, κριθῆς δὲ ἑβδομήκοντα, καὶ πλεῖστα ἄγαν βραχείᾳ πάνυ ἀπεμπολεῖσθαι ποσότητι. ὅπερ τοῖς μὲν ἀνοήτοις εὐφορία τε γῆς καὶ πραγμάτων εὐθηνία ἐνομίζετο, τοῖς δὲ εὖ φρονοῦσι τυραννίδος καὶ φιλοχρηματίας ἔργον καὶ ἀπανθρωπίας νό|σος ἐκρίνετο.* V209ᵛ

86. Κατὰ *δὲ τὴν ἑβδόμην ἰνδικτιόνα τίκτεται υἱὸς* Κωνσταντίνῳ, *ὃν ἐκάλεσεν* Ἄνθιμον. *ὑπὸ δὲ τὸν αὐτὸν καιρὸν* Νικήτας *ὁ τῆς πόλεως πρόεδρος τινὰ μὲν [τῶν] ἐκ χρόνου διαφθαρέντα τῆς καθολικῆς ἐκκλησίας ἀνακαινίζει κτίσματα, τὰς δὲ ἐν τοῖς ἐκεῖσε ἱδρυμένοις τῶν προόδων οἴκοις, οὓς* Ῥωμαῖοι *σέκρετα καλοῦσι, τό τε μικρὸν δόμημα καὶ τὸ μέγα, τοῦ σωτῆρος καὶ τῶν ἁγίων οὔσας διὰ ψηφίδων χρυσῶν καὶ*

---

18 *εἰς τῆς τῶν πελαγίων καλουμένης ταφῆς* V corr. dB, qui autem pravam lectionem *Πελαγίων* retinuit. Cf. **81.**14

85: 12 *ὁ νέος* V ὁ del. V² ‖ 16 *γενήματα* V corr. B

86: 3 *τῶν* del. esse coni. dB ‖ 5 *οὓς* dB *ἃς* V ‖ 6 *ῥωμαίοις* V corr. vulg. *σεκρετα* sine acc. V ‖ *δώμημα* V corr. vulg.

Milion,[63] while his body was dragged by a rope through the streets of the City and cast in the tombs known as those of Pelagios.

85. In the 5th indiction there was a drought. The weather became parched and dry, so that even the aerial dew disappeared and the flow of springs was interrupted. For this reason the baths remained idle, since the reservoirs were empty. Consequently Constantine decided to renew the aqueduct which had been built by Emperor Valentinian and had been destroyed by the Avars in the days of Emperor Herakleios.[64] He collected from the Roman dominions a great number of artisans skilled in construction, on whom he lavished many allowances from the public treasury and so completed this work. Avaricious as he was, Christ's enemy Constantine proved to be a new Midas, who stored away all the gold. As a result, the taxed people, hard pressed as they were by the exaction of imposts, sold cheaply the fruit and produce of the earth, so that 60 *modii* of wheat and 70 of barley could be bought for 1 *nomisma* and many ⟨other goods⟩ were sold for very small sums. This was considered by the senseless as a sign of the earth's fertility and the abundance of commodities, but by the wise as the result of oppression and avarice and as an inhuman sickness.

86. In the 7th indiction a son was born to Constantine, whom he called Anthimos. At the same time Niketas, the bishop of the City, restored certain structures of the cathedral church that had fallen into decay with ⟨the passage of⟩ time. He also scraped off the images of the Savior and of the saints done in golden mosaic and in encaustic that were in the ceremonial halls that stand there (these are called *secreta* by the Romans), both in the small one and in

[63] An arch placed at the starting point of the Mesē, the main street of Constantinople: C. Mango, *The Brazen House* (Copenhagen, 1959), 47–48; Müller-Wiener, *Bildlexikon*, 216–18.

[64] I.e., the siege of 626. The aqueduct is usually attributed to Emperor Valens.

κηροχύτου ὕλης εἰκονογραφίας ἀπέξυσε. Κωνσταντῖνος δὲ ⟨πρὸς⟩ τοὺς τῶν Σκλαβηνῶν ἀποστέλλει ἄρχοντας καὶ ἀνακαλεῖται τοὺς ἐκ πλείονος χρόνου παρ' αὐτοῖς αἰχμαλωτισθέντας Χριστιανοὺς ἀπό τε Ἴμβρου καὶ Τενέδου καὶ Σαμοθρᾴκης τῶν νήσων, σηρικοῖς ἱματίοις τούτους ἀμειψάμενος, τὸν ἀριθμὸν ὄντας ἄχρι δισχιλίων καὶ πεντακοσίων, καὶ πρὸς ἑαυτὸν ἀγαγὼν καὶ μικρὰ φιλοτιμησάμενος ἀπέπεμψε πορεύεσθαι οὗ ἂν βούλοιτο ἕκαστος.

87. Τῇ ἑβδόμῃ ἰνδικτιόνι, κατὰ τὸν Ἀπρίλιον μῆνα, τῷ dB77
ἁγίῳ σαββάτῳ στέφει Κωνσταντῖνος τὴν ἑαυτοῦ γυναῖκα Εὐδοκίαν Αὐγούσταν, καὶ τῇ ἐπαύριον τῶν υἱῶν αὐτοῦ τοὺς μὲν δύο Χριστοφόρον καὶ Νικηφόρον Καίσαρας, Νικήταν δὲ νοβελίσιμον. τῆς δὲ βασιλικῆς προόδου κατὰ τὸ εἰωθὸς ἐπὶ τὴν καθολικὴν ἐκκλησίαν γενομένης ὑπατείαν ἐποίησαν καὶ τοῖς παρελθοῦσι χρήματα διένειμαν, ἐκ τοῦ παλατίου ἀρξάμενοι μέχρι τῆς ἐκκλησίας τοῦτο ἐπιτελοῦντες.

88. Ὀγδόῃ δὲ ἰνδικτιόνι ἄγεται Κωνσταντῖνος εἰς υἱὸν Λέοντα γαμετὴν ἐκ τῆς Ἑλλάδος Εἰρήνην, καὶ τῷ Δεκεμβρίῳ μηνὶ στέφει τε αὐτὴν Αὐγούσταν καὶ τῷ υἱῷ ζεύξας τὸν γάμον ἐπιτελεῖ.

---

9 *πρὸς* add. esse coni. dB || 12 *σειρικοῖς* V corr. B

87: 1 *ἀπρήλιον* V corr. vulg. || 3 *ἐπ' αὔριον* V || *τῶν υἱῶν* om. V[1] *τὸν υἱὸν* in mg. V[2] || 5 *ὀβελίσιμον* V corr. vulg.

the big one. As for Constantine, he sent emissaries to the chieftains of the Slavonians and ransomed in exchange for silken vestments the Christian captives they had taken a long time previously on the islands of Imbros, Tenedos, and Samothrace, to the number of 2,500. After bringing them in his presence and giving them some small rewards, he let each man go wherever he wished.

87. In the month of April of the 7th indiction, on Holy Saturday, Constantine crowned his wife Eudokia as Augusta, and the next day ⟨he made⟩ two of his sons, namely, Christopher and Nikephoros, Caesars and ⟨the third⟩, Niketas, *nobilissimus*. In the course of the customary imperial procession to the cathedral church they gave largesse and distributed money to passers by, starting at the palace and continuing to do so as far as the church.

88. In the 8th indiction Constantine brought from Hellas a wife for his son Leo, namely, Eirene, and in the month of December he crowned her Augusta and, after uniting her with his son, celebrated their wedding.

ΧΡΟΝΟΓΡΑΦΙΚΟΝ ΝΙΚΗΦΟΡΟΥ ΤΟΥ ΑΓΙΩΤΑΤΟΥ ΚΑΙ ΟΙΚΟΥΜΕΝΙΚΟΥ ΠΑΤΡΙΑΡΧΟΥ

L24r

1. Μετὰ τὴν Μαυρικίου τοῦ βασιλέως ἀναίρεσιν Φωκᾶς, ἐπεὶ ταύτην κατειργάσατο, τῆς βασιλείας ἐπιλαμβάνεται· ὑφ' οὗ ἐπὶ τοσοῦτον κακώσεως Χριστιανοῖς ἤλασε τὰ πράγματα ὡς παρὰ πολλοῖς ᾄδεσθαι ὅτι Πέρσαι μὲν τὴν Ῥωμαίων ἀρχὴν ἐκτὸς κατεπόνουν, Φωκᾶς δὲ ἔνδον χείρω τούτων ἔπραττεν. διὸ οἱ περὶ τὴν Λιβύην στρατηγοῦντες τῷ μεγίστῳ διαστήματι τὸ θαρρεῖν ἔχοντες, ἅμα δὲ καὶ παρὰ Μαυρικίου τὰ τῆς στρατηγείας ἐγχειρισθέντες (δύο δὲ ἤστην ἀδελφώ, Ἡράκλειος καὶ Γρηγόριος), οὗτοι κοινῇ βουλευσάμενοι τοὺς ἑαυτῶν υἱεῖς πρὸς τὸ Βυζάντιον ἐκπέμπουσιν, ὡς τὸν προφθάσαντα τούτων τῆς βασιλείας, εἰ δυνατόν, ἐπιλήψεσθαι. καὶ Ἡράκλειον μὲν τὸν Ἡρακλείου παῖδα πλείστῳ καθοπλίσαντες στόλῳ ἔκ τε τῶν Ἄφρων καὶ Μαυρουσίων πληρώσαντες, πλοΐ ἐκπέμπουσιν, Νικήταν δὲ τὸν υἱὸν Γρηγορίου ἱππικῇ στρατιᾷ πολλῇ περιβαλόντες διὰ τῆς ἠπείρου ἀπέστελλον. δεξιᾷ δὲ τύχῃ χρησάμενος καὶ πνεύμασιν ἐπιφορωτάτοις ἀπαχθεὶς | L24v Ἡράκλειος προφθάζει Νικήταν εὐπλοΐσας εἰς Βυζάντιον, καὶ ἤδη τῇ πόλει προσεπέλαζεν. Κρίσπος δὲ ὁ τοῦ Φωκᾶ γαμβρός, ὃς ἦν τὴν ἀξίαν τῆς πόλεως ἔπαρχος, μεγάλα ἐν τοῖς βασιλείοις δυνάμενος, ἐπεὶ ἀπεχθάνετο Φωκᾷ, περιυβρισμένος παρ' αὐτοῦ διὰ τὴν τῆς οἰκείας εἰκόνος καθαίρεσιν, ἥν ποτε οἱ τῶν ἀντιθέτων χρωμάτων δημόται τῇ τοῦ Φωκᾶ συμπεριέγραψαν εἰκόνι, δόλῳ αὐτὸν μετήρχετο, καὶ πονεῖν ὑπὲρ αὐτοῦ ἔπειθεν, καὶ Ἡράκλειον ἐπ' ἀπωλείᾳ τῇ ἑαυτοῦ ἥκειν ἀπισχυρίζετο, συνήργει δὲ Ἡρακλείῳ καὶ τὰ ὑπὲρ

1: 3 *τοσοῦτον* corr. ex *τοσοῦτων* L[1] ut vid. || 5 *χείρο* L corr. Or || 11 *ἐπιλείψασθαι* L corr. Or ex V || 12–13 *καθοπλήσαντες* L corr. Or || 14–15 *ἱππικὴ στρατεια πολλὴ* L corr. Or || 16 *δεξιὰ* L corr. Or || *ἐπιφοροτάτοις* L corr. Or || 23 *σὺν περίεγραψαν* L corr. Or

αὐτοῦ εἰς τὰ μάλιστα ἔπραττεν. οἱ οὖν περὶ τὸν Φωκᾶν θεασάμενοι ὅτι καὶ οἱ τῆς πόλεως ἐστασίαζον — ἤδη γὰρ καὶ οἱ τοῦ πρασίνου χρώματος δημόται τὰ περὶ τὴν Καισαρείου τὸ πῦρ ὑφῆπτον καὶ τὸν ἔπηλυν βασιλέα ἀνευφήμουν — ἐπικειμένους δὲ αὐτοῖς κραταιῶς καὶ τοὺς ἐκ τῶν Ἡρακλείου στρατευμάτων, καταλιπόντες αὐτοὺς ἀνεχώρουν. Φώτιος δέ τις ὄνομα, ὅς παρ' αὐτοῦ εἰς τὴν σύζυγον ἐπεβουλεύθη ποτέ, ἐπελθὼν εἰς τὸ παλάτιον μετὰ πλήθους στρατιωτῶν, κατέσχεν τε αὐτόν, καὶ τὴν βασιλικὴν ἀπαμφιάσας ἐσθῆτα καὶ περίζωμα μέλαν αὐτὸν περιθέμενος, τάς τε χεῖρας περιηγμένας εἰς τοὐπίσω ἀποδήσας, πλοίῳ ἐμβαλὼν | πρὸς Ἡράκλειον L25r δεσμώτην ἀπήγαγεν. ὃν ἰδὼν ἔφη· "οὕτως, ἄθλιε, ἐδιοίκησας τὴν πολιτείαν;" ὁ δέ· "σὺ μᾶλλον" ἔφη "κάλλιον ἔχεις διοικῆσαι." εὐθὺς οὖν ἐπιτρέπει ἀποτμηθῆναι αὐτοῦ ἐν τῷ πλοίῳ τὴν κεφαλήν, τόν τε ὦμον τὸν δεξιὸν σὺν τῇ χειρὶ ἐκκοπῆναι καὶ τῶν αἰδοίων ἐκτμηθῆναι καὶ κοντοῖς ἀναρτηθῆναι, οὕτω τε αὐτὸν συρέντα σὺν Δομνητζιόλῳ τῷ αὐτοῦ ἀδελφῷ, Βουνούσῳ τε καὶ Λεοντίῳ, τῷ τῶν βασιλικῶν χρημάτων ταμίᾳ, κατὰ τὴν Βοὸς λεγομένην ἀγορὰν πυρίκαυτον γενέσθαι.

2. Μετὰ τοῦτο εὐγνωμόνως παρά τε Σεργίου τοῦ τῆς πόλεως ἱεράρχου καὶ τῆς λοιπῆς πληθύος εἰσδέχεται. καὶ εὐθὺς Κρίσπον, εἰς τὴν βασιλείαν προτρέπεται, φάσκων οὐ τῆς βασιλείας ἕνεκεν ἐληλυθέναι, τιμωρήσασθαι δὲ μᾶλλον τὸ Μαυρικίου αἷμα καὶ τῶν αὐτοῦ τέκνων. ὁ δὲ οὐκ ἐδέχετο. τέλος ὑπὸ τῆς συγκλήτου βουλῆς καὶ τοῦ δήμου Ἡράκλειος βασιλεὺς ἀνακηρύσσεται καὶ ὑπὸ τοῦ ἀρχιερέως στέφεται. Κρίσπον δὲ στρατηγὸν ἀποστέλλει τῶν ἐν Καππαδοκίᾳ στρατευμάτων. καὶ ἐπεὶ φήμη διέτρεχεν ὡς Πέρσαι κατὰ Ῥωμαίων ἐπιστρατεύουσιν, Ἡράκλειος τοῦ Βυζαντίου ἀπάρας πρὸς Κρίσπον ἐν Καισαρείᾳ παραγίνεται, | ὡς δὴ αὐτῷ τῶν πολεμίων L25v ἕνεκεν βουλευσόμενος. ὁ δὲ νοσεῖν προσεποιεῖτο, καὶ τὸν βασιλέα οὐκ ἐδόκει δέχεσθαι, καὶ πάλιν παραγενόμενον μόλις ἐδέχετο ἐν σχήματι ἀρρώστου ἀνακλινόμενος· εἶτα

---

27 ἤδει L corr. Or || 28 δημῶται L corr. Or || 29–30 ἐπικείμενος L corr. Or || 31 καταλειπόντες L corr. Or || 34 βασιλεικὴν L corr. Or || 36 τουπήσω L corr. Or || 41 ἐδύων L corr. Or || κόντοις L corr. Or || 43 βασιλεικῶν L corr. Or || ταμεία L corr. Or || 44 πυρίκαυτος L corr. Or

---

2: 1 τούτω L corr. Or || 4 τιμωρίσασθαι L corr. Or || 12 βουλενόμενος L corr. Or ex V

ἠκούετο ὡς καὶ διελοιδορεῖτο αὐτῷ. ὁ δὲ τὸ πρᾶγμα συνῆκε, καὶ τὴν ὕβριν τέως ἤνεγκε, καὶ ἤδη ἐκαιροφυλάκει. ἀλλ' ἔδοξέ πως γνησιώτερον διαλέγεσθαι ὑπὲρ τοῦ δεῖν πονεῖν ὑπὲρ ἀλλήλων τῆς πολιτείας χάριν. ὁ δὲ ὥσπερ ἐπιχλευάζων ὑπεκρίνετο, ὡς οὐκ ἐξὸν βασιλεῖ καταλιμπάνειν τὰ βασίλεια καὶ ἐν τοιαύταις ἐκστρατείαις παραγίνεσθαι. ἐν τούτοις τίκτεται παῖς τῷ βασιλεῖ Ἡράκλειος, ὃν καὶ Κωνσταντῖνον ὠνόμασε. τότε παραγίνεται καὶ Νικήτας ὁ πατρίκιος ἐν Κωνσταντινουπόλει. διὰ ταῦτα Ἡράκλειος ἐν τοῖς βασιλείοις ἐπεισέρχεται, καὶ Νικήταν μετὰ τιμῆς μεγάλης ὥσπερ ἀδελφὸν γνήσιον καὶ ὁμότιμον δέχεται, ὡς ἦν αὐτοῖς συντεταγμένον ἐκ Λιβύης ἀπαίρουσι. Κρίσπος δὲ εἰσέρχεται εἰς Βυζάντιον, ὡς τῇ εἰσόδῳ Νικήτα συγχαρισόμενος. σκήπτεται δὲ ὁ βασιλεὺς βαπτίζειν τῷ θείῳ λουτρῷ τὸν υἱόν, υἱοθετεῖσθαι δὲ αὐτὸν ὑπὸ Κρίσπου. ὁ δὲ ἐπὶ τούτοις εἰσέρχεται εἰς τὸ παλάτιον. Ἡράκλειος δὲ ἀθροίσας τὸν ἐκ τῆς συγκλήτου βουλῆς καὶ τὸν ἄλλον ὅμιλον | τὸν τῆς πόλεως ἅμα Σεργίῳ τῷ L26r ἱεράρχῃ λέγεται εἰπεῖν πρὸς αὐτούς· "ὁ ὑβρίζων βασιλέα τίνι προσκρούει;" τοὺς δὲ φάναι· "τῷ θεῷ τῷ ποιήσαντι αὐτὸν βασιλέα." καὶ πρὸς Κρίσπον εἶπεν. ὡσαύτως καὶ αὐτὸς ἀπεφήνατο τὸ δοκοῦν ὀρθῶς. τὸν δὲ οὐκ εἰδότα τὸ πρᾶγμα λέξαι, οὐδὲ φιλανθρωπίας τὸν τοιοῦτον ἀξιωθήσεσθαι. λέγει ὁ βασιλεύς· "τί σοι ἔπταισα ὅτι καὶ τὴν βασιλείαν ἐξευτέλισας;" ἀναμιμνήσκοντα ἤδη ἅπερ ἐν Καισαρείᾳ ἐπὶ τῇ νόσῳ ἐδραματουργεῖτο· "οὐχὶ καὶ βασιλεῦσαί σε πρότρεψα;" καὶ ἅμα λαβόντα τόμον, κατὰ τῆς κεφαλῆς τοῦτον παίων ἔλεγεν· "ὡς γαμβρὸν οὐκ ἐποίησας, φίλον πῶς ἂν ἐποίησας;" εὐθὺς δὲ ἐπέτρεψεν εἰς κληρικοῦ σχῆμα τὴν κεφαλὴν κείρασθαι καὶ τὸν ἀρχιερέα τὴν εὐλογίαν ἐπιθεῖναι. ἐξελθόντα δὲ αὐτὸν τοῖς μετὰ Κρίσπου στρατιώταις εἰπεῖν (βουκελλαρίους δὲ τούτους ἐπιχωρίῳ διαλέκτῳ ἐκάλουν)· "ὁ παπᾶς Κρίσπος ἕως τοῦ νῦν ὑπηρέτας αὐτοῦ εἶχεν ὑμᾶς, ἡμεῖς δὲ σήμερον οἰκιακοὺς τῆς βασιλείας ὑπηρέτας." προσθεῖναι δὲ αὐτοῖς καὶ τὸ σιτηρέσιον ἐκέλευσεν καὶ πρώτους καλεῖσθαι ἐν τοῖς ἐκστρατεύμασιν· αὐτούς τε ἀσμένως ταῦτα δεξαμένους τὸν βασιλέα

---

15 *διελυδορεῖτο* L corr. Or || 16 *ἐκαιροφυλάκη* L corr. Or || 19 *ἐξῶν* L corr. Or || *καταλειμπάνειν* L corr. Or || 25 *ὁμότημον* L corr. Or || 27 *συγχαρησόμενος* L corr. Or || 32 *ἱεράρχη* ex –*ει* L[1] || 40 *παίον* L corr. Or || 43 *ἐπιθῆναι* L corr. Or || 44 *στρατιώτα*[*ις*] in ras. L[2] || 46 *αὐτου* L corr. Or || 47 *προσθῆναι* L corr. Or

ἐπευφημῆσαι ἅμα τῇ ἄλλῃ πληθύϊ. | L26v μετὰ τοῦτο Κρίσπον περιορίζει εἰς τὸ λεγόμενον τῆς Χώρας μοναστήριον, ὃς ζήσας ἐνιαυτὸν ἐτελεύτησεν. Θεόδωρον δὲ τὸν ἑαυτοῦ ἀδελφόν, κοροπαλάτιον ὄντα τὴν ἀξίαν, ἔξαρχον ἀνατολῆς ἐξέπεμψεν, ὡσαύτως καὶ Φιλιππικὸν τηνικαῦτα κληρικὸν τυγχάνοντα, ὃς μικρὸν ἐπιβιοὺς ἐτελεύτα, καὶ ἐν Χρυσοπόλει τάφῳ παραδίδοται πρὸς τῇ παρ' αὐτοῦ δωμηθείσῃ ἐκκλησίᾳ.

3. Ὀλίγου δὲ χρόνου διιππεύσαντος νόσῳ ἐπιληψίας ἡ τοῦ βασιλέως γαμετὴ ἐτελεύτησεν. ἐν ᾧ δὲ τὸ ἑαυτῆς ἐκκομίζεται σῶμα, συνέβηκε τῶν παρακυπτόντων τινὰ ἐπὶ τῇ θέᾳ κόρην βάρβαρον ἀποπτύσαι, καὶ τὸ περίττωμα ἐνεχθῆναι κατὰ τῆς πολυτελοῦς ἐσθῆτος ἐκείνης, ἣ τὸ τῆς βασιλίδος σῶμα περιεκόσμει. ἄγουσιν οὖν οἱ περὶ τὴν ἐκφορὰν τὴν κόρην καὶ πυρίκαυστον κατὰ τὴν λεγομένην τοῦ Βοὸς ἀγορὰν ἐποίησαν. περιεζήτουν δὲ καὶ τὴν αὐτῆς κυρίαν, ὡς καὶ αὐτῇ ὁμοίως χρήσασθαι. ἡ δὲ αἰσθομένη διέφυγεν, τὸ λοιπὸν μὴ ὁραθεῖσα πώποτε.

4. Ἐν δὲ χώρᾳ τινὶ τῶν περιφανῶν τις ἦν καὶ εὔπορος, οὗ τὸ ἐπώνυμον Βιζουλῖνος, τὴν δὲ ἀξίαν ἦν κανδιδάτος Ῥωμαῖοι καλοῦσι. τούτῳ ἐγειτόνευε γυνή τις χήρα. καὶ μάχης | L27r αὐτοῖς περὶ μεθορίων γῆς συμβαινούσης, ἐπιτρέπει τοῖς δούλοις αὐτοῦ ἐπιέναι τοῖς γειτονεύουσιν· οἱ δὲ ξύλοις ἕνα τῶν ἐκείνης υἱῶν ἀναιροῦσιν. αὕτη λαβοῦσα τοῦ τεθνηκότος ἡμαγμένον τὸ ἱμάτιον εἰς Βυζάντιον ὡς Ἡράκλειον παραγίνεται, καὶ ἐπεὶ προϊόντα εἶδεν, εἰσδραμοῦσα τοῦ χαλινοῦ τοῦ ἵππου ἐπιλαμβάνεται, καὶ ἅμα τὸ τοῦ παιδὸς ἱμάτιον ἐπιδεικνῦσα φησὶ πρὸς αὐτόν· "οὕτω γένοιτο τοῖς τέκνοις σου, ἐὰν μὴ τὸ αἷμα τοῦτο ἐκδικήσῃς." τῶν δὲ περὶ τὸν βασιλέα ἐπιόντων αὐτῇ καὶ πλήττειν ἐπειγομένων αὐτὸς διεκώλυσε, φήσας τῇ γυναικὶ μηκέτι τολμᾶν προσιέναι, ἐπεξιέναι τε τὰ τῆς δίκης ἡνίκα ἂν αὐτῷ δεδογμένον εἴη. ἀπῆλθεν οὖν εὐθὺς μὴ δίκης τυχὸν ὀλολύζον τὸ γύναιον. χρόνος δὲ διήρχετο, καὶ ὁ τὸν

---

50 *τούτω* L corr. Or || 56 *δομηθεῖση* L corr. Or

3: 2 *ἑαυτῆς* L *ταύτης* Or ex V

4: 2 *ἐπώνοιμον* L corr. Or || *κανδιδάτον* Or ex V || 5 *αὑτοῦ* Or || *ἐπειέναι* L corr. Or || 11 *ἐκδικήσις* L corr. Or || 12 *αὐτῇ* scripsi *αὐτὴν* L || *διεκόλυσε* L corr. Or

φόνον ἐπιτρέψας ἐδεδίει, ὡς καὶ αὖθις τὴν γυναῖκα περὶ τοῦ φόνου τὸν βασιλέα διενοχλεῖν. διὰ τοῦτο εἰς τὸ δημοτικὸν μέρος ἑαυτὸν ἐγκαταμίγνυσι, καὶ ἱππικοῦ ἀγῶνος ἐπιτελουμένου τοῦτον ὁ βασιλεὺς ἐν μέσοις τοῖς δημόταις θεασάμενος τῷ ἐπάρχῳ ἐπιτρέπει φρουρᾷ παραδίδοσθαι. εἶτα τὴν μητέρα τοῦ φονευθέντος παιδὸς μεταπέμπεται, καὶ ἀσφαλῶς τὰ περὶ τοῦ φόνου ἐξετάσας κελεύει τὸν Βιζουλῖνον ὑπὸ | τῶν παίδων L27v αὐτοῦ ξύλοις ἀναιρεθήσεσθαι, ὡσαύτως καὶ τοὺς παῖδας αὐτοῦ ὑπ' ἀλλήλων κτείνεσθαι.

5. Ἡράκλειος δὲ τὸν υἱὸν Ἡράκλειον ὑπὸ Σεργίου τοῦ ἀρχιερέως βαπτισθέντα ἀγκάλαις ἐκ τῆς ἁγίας κολυμβήθρας ἐδέξατο, στέφει τε αὐτὸν εὐθὺς βασιλέα σὺν τῇ ἀδελφῇ, καὶ τὴν θυγατέρα Νικήτα τοῦ πατρικίου αὐτῷ κατηγγύησεν· οὗ καὶ στήλην κεχρυσωμένην καθύπερθε τοῦ τετρακιονίου λεγομένου ἔστησεν ἐν τῇ τοῦ Φόρου ἀγορᾷ. καὶ ὧδε μὲν ταῦτα ἔσχε.

6. Χοσρόης δὲ ὁ τῶν Περσῶν βασιλεὺς κατὰ Ῥωμαίων ἐπεστράτευσεν, ἡγεμόνα τῶν Περσικῶν στρατευμάτων Σάϊτον ἐπιστείλας, ὃς ἐλθὼν τήν τε Ἀλεξάνδρειαν παραλαμβάνει καὶ τὴν ὅλην Αἴγυπτον, καὶ πᾶσαν τὴν ἀνατολικὴν μοῖραν κατεδῄου τε καὶ αἰχμαλώτους πλείστους ἦγε καὶ ἄλλους ἀνῄρει. τὴν Χαλκηδόνα οὖν μετὰ ταῦτα καταλαμβάνει, καὶ περιεκάθητο ταύτῃ χρόνον ἱκανόν, ἠξίου τε τὸν βασιλέα εἰς ὁμιλίαν λόγου παραγενέσθαι. ὁ δὲ διεπεραιοῦτο πρὸς αὐτὸν σὺν ἄρχουσί τε καὶ στρατῷ καὶ τῇ βασιλικῇ δορυφορίᾳ. τοῦτον Σάϊτος ἰδὼν ἐξανέστη τῆς καθέδρας καὶ τῇ γῇ προσρίψας ἑαυτὸν προσκυνεῖ. ὁ δὲ ἐκ τοῦ ἀκατίου ἐν ᾧ ἐπέπλει προσε | φώνει αὐτῷ τὸ χαῖρε καὶ χαρίσμασιν ἠμείβετο. L28r Σάϊτος δὲ αὐτῷ ἔλεγεν· "ὦ δέσποτα, ἔδει τὸν βασιλέα Ῥωμαίων καὶ Περσῶν μήτε ἐν διαστάσει εἶναί ποτε, ἀλλ' ὡς ἀδελφοὺς γνησίους τὰς πολιτείας ἑαυτῶν διοικεῖσθαι ἕκαστον· οὐδὲ γάρ ἐστι βασιλεία ἑτέρα ταύταις ὁμοία." ὁ δὲ τῶν

---

16 ἐδεδείη L corr. Or || 18 ἐγκαταμήγνυσι L corr. Or || 19 δημῶταις L corr. Or

---

5: 5 κεχρυσομένην L corr. Or

6: 3 ἐπιστείλας] an ἐπιστήσας? || 9–10 συνάρχουσί τε . . . καὶ τῆς βασιλικῆς δωρυφορίας L || 11 προσκυνῆ L corr. Or || 16–17 τῶν –ων τὸ L[2] in ras.

λόγων τὸ προσηνὲς ἀμειβόμενος ἔφη αὐτῷ· "τί οὖν πράσσειν ὀφείλομεν;" ὁ δὲ ἐπομνύμενος ἔλεγεν ὅτι· "καὶ θέλω καὶ σπεύδω τὰς πολιτείας ἐν εἰρήνῃ καθίστασθαι, ἐπεὶ καὶ Χοσρόης οὕτω γε βούλεται. εἴ τι οὖν μοι πείθεσθε, συνεκπέμποιτέ μοι ὡς αὐτὸν τοὺς πρεσβευσομένους. πεισθείη δ' ἂν ἐμοὶ καὶ αὐτὸς εἰρήνην διαιωνίζουσαν κρατῦναι μεθ' ὑμῶν."

7. Ὁ δὲ ὑπέσχετο δώσειν, καὶ ἐν οἷς ἐβουλεύετο συνῄνουν ὅ τε ἱεράρχης καὶ οἱ ἐν τέλει. καὶ ἤδη ἐξελέγοντο Ὀλύμπιος ἔπαρχος πραιτωρίων, Ἀναστάσιός τε ὁ τῶν πραγμάτων τῆς μεγίστης ἐκκλησίας οἰκονόμος, Λεόντιος ὁ τῆς πόλεως ἔπαρχος, οὓς παραλαβὼν Σάϊτος ἐκ Χαλκηδόνος ἀπῆρεν καὶ πρὸς τὰ τῶν Περσῶν ἤθη ἐχώρει. καὶ μέχρι μὲν τῶν μεθορίων τῆς Ῥωμαϊκῆς ἀρχῆς μετὰ τιμῆς ἦγε καὶ θεραπείαν πᾶσαν ἀπένεμεν, τῇ Περσικῇ δὲ εἰσβαλὼν σιδήροις | ἐδέσμει καὶ L28v δεσμώτας πρὸς Χοσρόην ἀπήγαγε. Χοσρόης δὲ ἐπεὶ ἔγνω ὅτι Σάϊτος Ἡράκλειον ὡς βασιλέα ἐτίμησε, καὶ οὐκ αἰχμάλωτον λαβὼν πρὸς αὐτὸν ἀπήγαγεν (ἐν τούτῳ γὰρ αὐτῷ τὰ τῆς ἐλπίδος ἔκειτο) μεγάλα τε ἠγανάκτει κατ' αὐτοῦ καὶ εἰς ἀσκὸν αὐτὸν ἀποδείρας τὴν δορὰν εἶχε, καὶ οὕτως ἀθλίως ἐτελεύτα. τοὺς δὲ Ῥωμαίων πρεσβευτὰς ἰδίᾳ διαστείλας ἕκαστον ἐν φρουραῖς ἀσφαλεστάταις ἀπέθετο καὶ ἐκάκου τὰ μέγιστα.

8. Πολλὴ οὖν δυσθυμία καὶ λύπη τούτων ἕνεκε τὸν βασιλέα εἶχε, καὶ διεβουλεύετο πρὸς Λιβύην ἀποίχεσθαι. καὶ προπέμπει χρήματά τε πλεῖστα καὶ χρυσὸν καὶ ἄργυρον καὶ λίθους πολυτελεῖς ἐκεῖσε· ὧν τὰ πλεῖστα καταίροντα, ναυαγίῳ περιπεσόντα, βρύχια γέγονεν. οἱ οὖν πολῖται αἰσθόμενοι, ὡς δυνατὰ ἦν, διεκώλυον· ὡς καὶ τὸν ἀρχιερέα Σέργιον ὑποθέσθαι ὅρκοις αὐτὸν ἐπὶ τῆς ἐκκλησίας ἐνέγκαντα καταδεσμῆσαι μὴ μεθίστασθαι τῆς βασιλευούσης. λιμὸς μὲν τηνικαῦτα ἐπεκράτει κατὰ τὴν πόλιν (οὐδὲ γὰρ ἡ Αἴγυπτος αὐτοῖς ἐπεσίτιζε λοιπόν) ὅθεν καὶ τὰ πλεῖστα τῶν βασιλικῶν σιτηρεσίων ἐπελελοίπει. ἐν τούτοις καὶ θάνατος τοῖς ἐν τῇ πόλει ἐπενέμετο.

9. Ὑπὸ δὲ τὸν αὐτὸν καιρὸν καὶ ὁ τῶν Οὔννων | κύριος L29r εἰς τὸ Βυζάντιον εἰσῆλθε, καὶ βασιλέα δέχεσθαι αὐτόν τε καὶ τοὺς σὺν αὐτῷ ᾔτησε, καὶ διδόναι τὸν διὰ τοῦ θείου λουτροῦ φωτισμόν· καὶ Θεόδωρος, ὁ τοῦ βασιλέως ἀδελφός, ἐκ τῆς

7: 2 οἱ] τοῖς L corr. Or ex V

ἁγίας κολυμβήθρας ὑπεδέξατο, καὶ ἄρχοντες Ῥωμαίων τοὺς Οὐννικοὺς ἄρχοντας, ὡσαύτως καὶ αἱ τούτων σύζυγοι τὰς ἐκείνων γαμετάς. οὕτω τε φωτισθέντες δώροις βασιλικοῖς ἐτιμήθησαν καὶ ἀξιώματι· πατρίκιον γὰρ τὸν κύριον αὐτῶν πεποίηκε, καὶ πρὸς τὰ αὐτῶν ἀπέπεμπε.

10. Μετὰ τούτου ὁ τῶν Ἀβάρων ἡγεμὼν περὶ εἰρήνης ὡς Ἡράκλειον ἐπικηρυκεύεται. ὁ δὲ πέμπει Ἀθανάσιον τὸν πατρίκιον, εἶτα μετ᾽ αὐτὸν καὶ Κοσμᾶν τὴν ἀξίαν κυαίστορα, καὶ αὐτὸν σὺν δώροις πρὸς αὐτόν. ὁ δὲ τὰ πρὸς φιλίαν ὑποκρινόμενος ἔπειθεν αὐτοὺς ὡς φίλος εἴη τοῦ βασιλέως. οὗτοι ἐκεῖθεν ἀναζεύξαντες τὰ τῆς εὐνοίας τοῦ Ἀβάρου τῷ βασιλεῖ δῆλα ἐποίουν. ὁ δὲ ἡσθεὶς βουλεύεται κατὰ τὴν τῆς Θρᾴκης Ἡράκλειαν τὸν χαγάνον δέχεσθαι, καὶ τήν τε θυμελικὴν σκευὴν προεκπέμπει, ὡς καὶ ἱππικὸν ἀγῶνα ἐπὶ τῇ δοχῇ ἐκείνου θεάσασθαι· στολήν τε αὐτῷ καὶ τοῖς μετ᾽ αὐτοῦ εὐτρέπισεν. αὖθις προπέμπει Κοσμᾶν καὶ Ἀθανάσιον ἀπαγγελοῦντας χαγάνῳ τὴν τοῦ βασιλέως ἔξοδον. ὁ δὲ ἠσμένιζε, | L29v καὶ συντίθεται ἐν Ἡρακλείᾳ καταλαμβάνειν. τοῦ δὲ βασιλέως κατὰ τὴν Σηλυμβρίαν γενομένου ἐφίσταται ὁ χαγάνος τρισὶν ἡμέραις ὕστερον σὺν πλήθει πολλῷ τῶν Ἀβάρων ἐν Ἡρακλείᾳ· ὧν δὴ τοὺς πολλοὺς κατὰ τὰ ὑπερκείμενα τοῦ Μακροῦ Τείχους χωρία διασκεδάννυσι, κρύβδην ἐκεῖσε κατὰ τῶν ὀρῶν χωροῦντας τὰ λάσια, ὡς ἂν κατὰ νῶτον γενόμενοι τοῦ βασιλέως, μέσον αὐτόν τε καὶ τοὺς περὶ αὐτὸν ἀποληψάμενοι χειρώσοιντο. οὓς ὁ βασιλεὺς αἰσθόμενος τὴν στολὴν τὴν βασιλικὴν ἀπαμφιέννυται, ἱμάτιον δὲ ἀλλότριον περιθέμενος καὶ τὸν στέφανον τὸν ἑαυτοῦ τῇ ὠλένῃ περιαψάμενος, πρὸς Βυζάντιον ἔφευγεν ἀνὰ κράτος, ἐντεῦθεν τε εἰσελθὼν μόλις διεσῴζετο. οἱ δὲ βάρβαροι ἐπετίθεντο, καὶ ἔξω πρὸ τῆς πόλεως πεδίον τὸ καλούμενον Ἕβδομον καταλαμβάνουσι, καὶ σκεδάννυνται ἄχρι τῆς καλουμένης γεφύρας τοῦ Βαρβύσσου ποταμοῦ, πολλοὺς Ῥωμαίων ἀναιροῦντες, καὶ τὰ τῇδε χωρία πικρῶς κατεδῄουν, τήν τε βασιλικὴν ἐσθῆτα καὶ τὰς στολὰς παραλαμβάνουσιν, ἔτι δὲ καὶ τὰ θυμελικὰ ὄργανα, πάντας τε τοὺς ταῦτα διακομίζοντας καὶ τῶν δημοτῶν τοὺς

10: 1 an *τοῦτο*? ‖ 3 *κυέστορα* L corr. Or ‖ 10 *αὐτῷ* Or *αὐτοῦ* L ‖ *τοῖς* scripsi *τῆς* L ‖ 14 *Συλυμβρίαν* L corr. Or ‖ 17 *διασκεδάνυσι* L corr. Or ‖ 18 *χωροῦντες* L corr. Or ‖ 19–20 *ἀποληψόμενοι* Or ‖ 21 *ἀλλότριον* scripsi *ἀλλότον* L *ἀλωτὸν* Or ‖ 23 *ἀνακράτως* L corr. Or ‖ 26 *σχεδάννυται* L corr. Or ‖ 27 *πολλοὺς* scripsi *πολλὰ* L an *πολλὰ Ῥωμαίων πλήθη*? ‖ 28 *κατεδίουν* L corr. Or

συνόντας αὐτοῖς. ὁ δὲ ἀριθμός φασι τῶν ἁλόντων | παρ' αὐτοῖς L30r αἰχμαλώτων, οὓς δὴ κατὰ τὴν Ἀβάρων γῆν ἀπεκόμισαν ἀνδρῶν τε καὶ γυναικῶν, εἰς διακοσίας καὶ ἑβδομήκοντα χιλιάδας, ὥς τινες διαδράντες ὡμολόγησαν, συνήκετο.

11. Κατὰ δὲ τὸν αὐτὸν χρόνον ἄγεται Ἡράκλειος εἰς γυναῖκα Μαρτῖναν τὴν ἀνεψιάν, θυγατέρα Μαρίας ἀδελφῆς αὐτοῦ γνησίας, ἣν ἔσχεν ἐκ Μαρτίνου τοῦ πρὸ Εὐτροπίου γεγονότος αὐτῆς γαμέτου, ἐξ ἧς καὶ τίκτει δύο υἱούς, Φάβιον, ὃν καὶ νοβελλήσιμον ἐποίησεν (οὗτος δὲ ἦν βλαμμένος τὸν αὐχένα, ὡς μὴ δύνασθαι ἐπ' οὐθετέρῳ αὐτὸν μέρει περιστρέφειν) καὶ Θεοδόσιον, καὶ αὐτὸν ὄντα κωφόν. διήλεγχον δὲ αὐτοῦ τὴν περὶ τῇ ἀνεψιᾷ παρανομίαν ἐφ' ἱππικοῦ ἀγῶνος καὶ οἱ τοῦ πρασίνου χρώματος δημόται, καὶ κωλύειν τὴν συναφὴν ἐπειρῶντο τὴν ἄθεσμον, οἱ δὲ τοῦ ἀντικειμένου χρώματος συνῄνουν τε καὶ συνέπραττον. [καὶ] Σέργιος δέ, ὁ κατὰ τὸ Βυζάντιον μυσταγωγός, γράμμασιν αὐτὸν ἐνουθέτει καὶ ἐλιπάρει τὴν πρὸς τὸ γύναιον τοῦτο κοινωνίαν ἀπαρνήσασθαι. ὁ δὲ αὐτῷ ἀπελογεῖτο ὡς· "εὖ μὲν ἔχει τὰ παρὰ σοῦ λεγόμενα. ὃ γάρ σοι χρέος ὡς ἀρχιερεῖ καὶ φίλῳ, ἤδη ἀποδέδωκας. ἐφ' ἡμῖν δὲ τὸ λοιπὸν κείσεται τὰ τῆς πράξεως." | L30v κατὰ δὲ τὸν αὐτὸν καιρὸν διεπιπράσκοντο τὰ τῶν ἐκκλησιῶν κειμήλια καὶ εἰς ὑπαγωγὴν φόρων τοῖς βαρβάροις ἐξενεμήθη.

---

31 *ἀλώντων* L corr. Or ‖ 32 *ἀπεκόμησαν* L corr. Or ‖ 33–34 *χηλιάδας* L corr. Or ‖ 34 *διαδράσαντες* L correxi ex V

11: 1 *αὐτὸν*] litt. *–υτ–* in ras. corr. L^2 ut vid. ‖ 4 *γαμετοῦ* L ‖ 9 *δῆμῶτ[αι]* in ras. L^1 corr. Or ‖ 11 *καὶ* secl. Or ‖ 13 *ἐλειπαρει* L corr. Or ‖ 14 *αὐτοῦ* L correxi ex V ‖ *ἔχοι* L corr. Or ‖ 15 *χρεως* L correxi ex V ‖ 16 *κήσεται* L corr. Or ‖ 18 *κειμίλια* L

COMMENTARY

1. Overthrow of Phokas (610)

In addition to Nik., there are three other basic Greek sources for these events: Ioann. Ant., *Exc. de insidiis*, 149–50; *Chr. Pasch.*, 699–701; and Theoph., 297–99. The overlap between Nik. and Theoph. is very slight, being limited to: (1) the *bon mot* about the disastrous nature of the government of Phokas = Theoph., 296.10 (cf. Mich. Syr., II, 378; *Chr. 1234*, 176); (2) the story about the portrait of Priskos = Theoph., 294; but this is also in Ioann. Ant., 149; (3) the alleged pact between Herakleios and Niketas that whoever of them reached Constantinople first would become emperor = Theoph., 297.6–10 (also in Mich. Syr., II, 378; *Chr. 1234*, 177); (4) the mention of Africans and Moors (or Mauritanians) in the armament of Herakleios = Theoph., 298.18. The actual events of the overthrow are, however, related quite differently by Theoph.

It is also clear that Nik. is not dependent here on *Chr. Pasch.* The closest correspondence is with Ioann. Ant., who tells a fuller story, but includes all the basic elements found in Nik. The latter, therefore, must be following either Ioann. Ant. or an intermediary source. Cf. above, pp. 12–14.

20ff. The aberrant form Krispos (for Priskos) reappears in Georg. Mon., 668.3 (from Nik.) and in *Patria*, 273, c. 184, where he is also called a prefect.

31 *ἡ Καισαρίου*: the house or mansion of Kaisarios (perhaps the one who was consul in 397), which gave its name to a quarter and a harbor on the Propontis side of Constantinople. There has been much inconclusive discussion as to whether the harbor of Kaisarios was the same as that of Theodosios or another, to the east or west of it. The identity of the harbor of Kaisarios and that of Theodosios is suggested by *Mir. S. Artemii*, 16. See my *Développement urbain de CP* (Paris, 1985), 55.

47 Marketplace of the Bull or Forum Bovis: exact situation unknown, but approximately corresponding to modern Aksaray. See Janin, *CP*, 69–71.

48 Domentiolos (Domnetziolos, Domnitziolos), brother of Phokas, *magister officiorum*: Theoph., 292.2. Sent to defend the Long Walls (in Thrace) against Herakleios, he promptly returned to the capital: Theoph., 298.29.

49 Bonossos (Bounousos and other spellings), *comes Orientis* (Theoph., 296.22), infamous for his cruel repression of internal disorders at Antioch and else-

where in the East. Unsuccessfully opposed the occupation of Egypt by Niketas before returning to Constantinople. See Kulakovskij, III, 12–13, 20–23; Stratos, I, 186–87, 208–13. His murder was maliciously attributed to the Jew Jacob: *Doctr. Iacobi*, 40.

49 Leontios: named by Ioann. Ant., 150.31 as *sakellarios*. *Chr. Pasch.*, 701 describes him as a Syrian and *ἀπὸ σακελλαρίων*, i.e., former *sakellarios*.

2. Accession of Herakleios (610). Fall of Priskos (612)

No known source.

Recorded dates: coronation of Herakleios, 6 Oct. 610 (*Chr. Pasch.*, 701); birth of Herakleios Constantine, 3 May 612 (*Chr. Pasch.*, 702; Theoph., 300.7); Priskos made a cleric, 5 Dec. 612 (*Chr. Pasch.*, 703).

3ff. Offer of empire to Priskos: The fact or fiction that Herakleios had no intention of becoming emperor and was planning after the overthrow of Phokas to return to Africa is stated in the letter of the Senate to Chosroes: *Chr. Pasch.*, 708.

9ff. Expedition of Priskos: Nik. neglects to say that Caesarea (in Cappadocia) had been taken by the Persians: Theoph., 299.31. This probably happened in 611: cf. W. E. Kaegi in *BZ* 66 (1973), 323. The march of Priskos to Caesarea is confirmed by *V. Theod. Syk.*, c. 153. He is said to have blockaded the city for a year but failed to prevent the Persians' escape (Sebeos, 65). Herakleios went to confer with Priskos at Caesarea (cf. *V. Theod. Syk.*, c. 154) probably in the early months of 612.

24ff. The date of Niketas' arrival at Constantinople is not certain. Theoph., 298.19 implies that he came simultaneously with Herakleios, i.e., in Oct. 610. We know, thanks to *V. Theod. Syk.*, c. 154, that Niketas was in the capital before Herakleios' return from Caesarea (hence by the early part of 612) and was paralyzed, allegedly because he had been poisoned. He was healed by the saint.

44 The rebuke "You have not been a good in-law," etc. is attributed by Mich. Syr., II, 379 to Phokas with respect to Philippikos, brother-in-law of Maurice.

48 Note that L specifically designates Priskos' soldiers as *bucellarii*. On this passage see Haldon, *Praetorians*, 376.

54 On Priskos in the monastery of Chora see F. I. Šmit, *Karie-Džami* = *IRAIK* 11 (1906), 21–22.

57 On the title of *curopalati* (*kouropalates*), held, before Theodore, by Domentziolos, nephew of Phokas, see Bury, *Admin. System*, 33–35. Strictly speaking, it was second in rank to the emperor when there was no Caesar. The text of V, in saying that Theodore (and Philippikos?) was appointed to the command previously occupied by Priskos, creates the incorrect impression that he was made *comes excubitorum*, whereas, in fact, that office was conferred on Niketas: *Chr. Pasch.*,

703; *V. Theod. Syk.*, c. 154.28. It is evident from L that Nik. meant to say merely that Theodore and Philippikos were made generals in the East.

58 Philippikos, *comes excubitorum* under Maurice, became a clergyman and retired to the monastery he had built at Chrysopolis: Theoph., 293.22. On the monastery, which was dedicated to the Virgin Mary, see Janin, *Grands centres*, 24–25. Philippikos led an expedition into Persian Armenia without achieving any notable results. See Kulakovskij, III, 35 and below, c. 6.

3. Death and Funeral of Empress Eudokia (612)

No known source.

Fabia/Eudokia died on 13 Aug. 612 (*Chr. Pasch.*, 702–3) or 14 Aug. (Theoph., 300.9). She was buried the next day in the church of the Holy Apostles.

Note that L provides two details that are absent in V, namely, that the servant girl was a barbarian and that she was burned in the Forum Bovis.

4. Boutelinos (Bizoulinos) story

No known source.

We may suppose that L's Bizoulinos represents the original form of the name, which was probably Thracian. Cf. D. Detschew, *Die thrakischen Sprachreste* (Vienna, 1957), 60ff., 66ff. (Biza, Byza, Bitus, Bithys, Beithys, Vitus, etc.); I. I. Russu, *Die Sprache der Thrako-Daker* (Bucharest, 1969), 112. This lends some support to de Boor's conjecture in line 2 (*ἔν τινι τῶν ἐπὶ Θρᾴκης χωρίων*). The "improvement" of the name may have been inspired by that of the Alamannic chieftain Boutilinos (Buccelin), who is featured prominently by Agathias, I.6.2, etc.

24ff. The factions had special "grandstands" in the Hippodrome, opposite the imperial Kathisma. See R. Guilland, *Etudes de topographie byzantine*, I (Berlin, 1969), 411ff. By joining the "partisans" (*demotai*), Bizoulinos would have made himself visible to the emperor.

5. Coronation of Herakleios Constantine and Eudokia (612–13). Niketas honored with a statue

Coronation of Herakleios Constantine: 22 Jan. 613 according to *Chr. Pasch.*, 703 or 25 Dec. 612 according to Theoph., 300.14. His sister Epiphania/Eudokia had been crowned on 4 Oct. 612 according to both *Chr. Pasch.* and Theoph. Note that V omits the coronation of Eudokia.

The betrothal of Herakleios Constantine to Gregoria and the erection of Niketas' statue are not mentioned elsewhere. Note that V omits the reference to the Tetrakionion, i.e., a group of four columns (a monument not otherwise known to have stood in the Forum) but adds the statement that the statue was an equestrian one. The two epigrams of the Palatine Anthology, XVI, 46, 47, probably pertain to this statue and make it clear that it was erected on behalf of the emperor, the army, the "cities," and the Green faction to commemorate Niketas' victories over the Persians. This circumstance has not been noticed and appears to confirm the tradition that Niketas won a battle near Emesa: Agapios of Menbidj, ed. A. Vasiliev, PO VIII/3, 450. Cf. my remarks in Ἀφιέρωμα στὸν Ν. Σβορῶνο (Rethymno, 1986), I, 30–31.

6. Persian invasion. Interview at Chalcedon (615?)

The account of the Persian invasion is condensed and vague and omits to mention the fall of Jerusalem (614), which is alluded to later, in c. 12. The advance on Chalcedon is placed in *Chr. Pasch.*, 706 in 614/5, but after the mention of a liturgical innovation introduced during Lent of indiction 4 (616). Theoph., 301, has the siege of Chalcedon (Carthage printed by de Boor from Anastasius) in 614/5 and its capture in 615/6. Note that Theoph., too, mentions the conquest of Egypt, including Alexandria, before the march on Chalcedon, whereas modern scholarship holds that the invasion of Egypt began in 616 or 617 and that Alexandria fell in 618 or 619.

V. Anast. Persae, c. 5, a contemporary source, confirms the advance of Shahīn ἕως Καρχηδόνος (surely Chalcedon), adding that he was outflanked by Philippikos, domestic of the Schools, who invaded Persia (εἰσελθόντος ἐν Περσίδι), whereupon Shahīn turned back in an easterly direction. Anastasios, who was serving in the Persian army, proceeded ἕως τῶν μερῶν τῆς ἀνατολῆς, i.e., as far as the diocese of Oriens, where he deserted.

It is difficult to explain why Shahīn (Σαήν in *Chr. Pasch.*, Σάϊν in Theoph.) should be called Saitos by Nik. The confusion may be scribal (e.g., if Σάϊν was written Σάϊ¯), or else Nik. may have been influenced by the Arabic name Saʿīd.

Historians are divided as to whether Egypt was conquered by Shahīn (so Butler, *Conquest*, 70 on the authority of Tabarī) or by Shahrbaraz (so, among others, Kulakovskij, III, 44 and Stratos, I, 277–78 on the authority of Mich. Syr. and other Oriental sources). The argument that Shahīn could not have invaded Egypt because he was busy in Asia Minor (so Stratos) is not necessarily supported by the chronology of the events.

10ff. With regard to the interview, *Chr. Pasch.*, 706 gives more or less the same details as Nik.: Herakleios went by ship to the harbor of Chalcedon taking gifts to Shahīn, and was given a promise of peace if an embassy was sent to the Persian court. The text of the letter addressed by the Senate to Chosroes, which was entrusted to the ambassadors (ibid., 708–9), makes it clear that Shahīn had no authority to negotiate peace, but had his king's assurance regarding the ambassadors' safety.

It may be noted that Sebeos, 77–79, followed by Thomas Artsruni, *History* (trans. R. W. Thomson [Detroit, 1985]), 157, also inserts a long speech at this juncture. It is, however, put in the mouth of Herakleios and takes the form of an abject plea. It would appear, therefore, that some record existed of speeches exchanged on that occasion. The omission of Herakleios' speech, probably motivated by Byzantine *amour propre*, may be ascribed to the source of Nik. Shahīn's rather vacuous oration, as it appears in V, was expanded by Nik. from the shorter version found in L. For another speech by a Persian general in praise of peace see Simok., I.15.3–10.

7. Embassy to Persia (615?). Punishment of Shahīn

The names of the ambassadors are given in the same order by *Chr. Pasch.*, but Anastasios is described as presbyter of the Church of Constantinople (706.19) or as presbyter and *synkellos* (in the text of the letter, 709.11), not as *oikonomos*. Georg. Mon., 668 (who is following Nik.) must be in error in speaking of seventy ambassadors (*μεγιστάνας ο'*). On the fate of the ambassadors see below, c. 15.

The punishment of Shahīn is a fable. He remained in service for another ten or eleven years and is said to have died of grief after being defeated by Theodore in 626. His body, preserved in salt, was brought to Chosroes, who insulted it: Theoph., 315.

8. Famine and plague (c. 619). Herakleios proposes to abandon Constantinople

Note that the order of entries, as given in L, is reversed in V, probably to provide stronger motivation for the emperor's despair.

Famine: *Chr. Pasch.*, 711, without mentioning the loss of Egypt, records that in 618 the beneficiaries of the civic annona were required to pay 3 nomismata per ration; and that in August of the same year the distribution was halted altogether. Even if Alexandria fell in 619, the invasion of Egypt must have disorganized the export of corn.

Plague: A plague in the reign of Herakleios is mentioned in *Mir. S. Artemii*, 52.

Georg. Mon., 669 (who is here following Nik.), after mentioning the famine and plague, adds *καὶ ὁ ἥλιος ἠμαυρώθη, καὶ ἔβρεξε κόνιν*. He may, therefore, have had before him a fuller text of Nik. A partial eclipse of the sun occurred on 24 Oct. 618 and total eclipses on 21 March 619 and 2 Sept. 620: Grumel, *Chronologie*, 461.

Herakleios' plan to withdraw to Libya is not mentioned in any other source. The sinking of the treasure appears legendary.

9. Baptism of Huns

No other source.

It is commonly supposed that the Huns in question were the Onogundurs of

c. 22, whose chief was Organa, uncle of Kuvrat. So, e.g., Gy. Moravcsik, "Byzantinische Mission," *Proc. XIIIth Intern. Congress of Byz. Studies, Oxford 1966* (London, 1967), 21; idem, *Studia byzantina* (Budapest, 1967), 252; Artamonov, *Istorija*, 157–58. Those who favor this view quote in their support the statement of John of Nikiu, Zotenberg, 580 (Charles, 197) to the effect that Kubratos, nephew of Organa, was baptized at Constantinople as a child and brought up in the imperial palace. It appears, however, that the Ethiopic text of John of Nikiu has, not Kubratos and Organa (these forms representing an emendation on the part of the translators), but Qeṭrādes and Kuernāka: see J. Marquart, *IRAIK* 15 (1911), 7 note 5.

Another view is that the Huns in question were the ones to whose land Herakleios withdrew in 625 (Theoph., 310.19) by virtue of previously established friendly relations: so V. Beševliev, *REB* 28 (1970), 157 ff.; idem, *Byzantinobulgarica* 5 (1978), 229–36.

Note that V omits the statement, present in L, that the emperor's brother Theodore acted as baptismal "sponsor" to the lord of the Huns.

The date 619, accepted for this incident by many historians, has no other basis than de Boor's marginal notation.

10. Negotiations with Avars. Avar surprise (623)

There are two other sources for these incidents:

(1) *Chr. Pasch.*, 712–13, which gives the following particulars: In the expectation of concluding a peace treaty with the Avars and impressing them by holding chariot races at Herakleia, the emperor went to Thrace on Sunday 5 June, indiction 11 (= 623), accompanied by a number of dignitaries, landowners, clergymen, shopkeepers, and partisans of both factions. The Chagan "with an infinite multitude" drew near the Long Walls. At the 4th hour of the same day he made a sign with his whip, whereupon his men entered the Long Walls, while he remained outside. The Avars who had entered, starting their depredations in the evening of that Sunday, went on as far as the Golden Gate and captured everyone they found outside the city walls. They desecrated and robbed the church of Sts. Cosmas and Damian at Blachernai and that of St. Michael *πέραν* (i.e., north of the Golden Horn) in the district called *τὰ Προμώτου*. All the captives were removed beyond the Danube. There is no mention of the emperor's flight.

(2) Theoph., 301–2, A.M. 6110 (A.D. 619), who records: An Avar incursion into Thrace (not in Nik.); the dispatch of unnamed ambassadors, who obtained a promise of peace from the Avars; the proposed meeting outside the Long Walls. The account of the actual surprise is very short and contains no particular that is not in Nik. It is possible that both used ultimately the same source, as also suggested by the following verbal similarity:

Nik., 10.24–25: *οὐ μετρίως τῷ παραλόγῳ καταπλαγείς* (not in L)
Theoph., 301.33: *ἐκπλαγεὶς δὲ ὁ βασιλεὺς τῷ ἀπροσδοκήτῳ τοῦ πράγματος*

There has been much debate concerning the date of the Avar surprise. The precise and concordant indications of *Chr. Pasch.* cannot be rejected lightly; but if Herakleios was in Thrace in June 623, he could not at the same time have been on campaign against the Persians, so that the beginning of the major offensive against Persia would have to be moved to 624 (as in *Chr. Pasch.*), and that, in turn, raises further difficulties (see below *ad* c. 12). For this reason N. H. Baynes, *BZ* 21 (1912), 110–28, moved the Avar surprise to 617 (when 5 June also fell on a Sunday), and in this he has been followed by several other historians, including Kulakovskij, III, 53.

13 ff. The reference to chariot races suggests that there was a hippodrome at Herakleia, probably attached to the Tetrarchic imperial palace.

20 Long Walls: see esp. C. Schuchhardt, *JDAI* 16 (1901), 107–15; R. M. Harrison, *Archaeologia Aeliana* 47 (1969), 33–38; idem in *Romah Frontier Studies 1969* (Cardiff, 1974), 245–48; B. Croke, *GRBS* 23 (1982), 59–78; M. Whitby, *Byzantion* 55 (1985), 560–83. The discussion of Stratos, I, 365 ff. is vitiated by his ignorance of the correct situation of the Long Walls (cf. his map facing p. 366), which, in fact, protected Selymbria, where the emperor lodged.

28 Note the criticism of Herakleios implied in his "ignominious flight."

33 Bridge over the Barbysses (at the head of the Golden Horn): presumably the one built by Justinian in 528 (*Chr. Pasch.*, 618). Later called the bridge of St. Kallinikos: *Vita Basilii* in Theoph. Cont., 340, where Βαθύρσου should be corrected to Βαβύρσου. Cf. my remarks in *Studien zur spätantiken und byzant. Kunst F.W. Deichmann gewidmet* (Mainz, 1986), I, 3–4 and below, cc. 13, 25.

38 Captives: the number of 270,000 is incredible. That of 70,000, given by Georg. Mon., though still high, is certainly preferable.

11. Herakleios marries Martina. Alienation of church plate

The marriage of Herakleios to Martina (unfortunately, not mentioned in *Chr. Pasch.*) is generally held to have occurred at the end of 613 or early in 614 on the authority of Theoph., 300, who places it in A.M. 6105, adding that Martina was crowned Augusta by Patriarch Sergios. He records the birth of a Κωνσταντῖνος ἕτερος the following year (A.M. 6106) and, under A.M. 6108 says that on 1 Jan., indiction 5 (= A.D. 617) Herakleios Constantine assumed the consulship and "raised to the rank of Caesar his own brother, the little Constantine, who had been born to Herakleios and Martina." If "the other Constantine" is, as seems probable, Heraklonas (born in Lazica in 626), then Theophanes is in grave error concerning the date of his birth. He is also mistaken as regards the consulship of Herakleios Constantine (the future Constantine III), which occurred in indiction 5 of the next cycle (632): cf. V. Bolotov, *VizVrem* 14 (1907), 74–75. It is thus probable that Theoph. also errs in recording the marriage of Herakleios to Martina in 613/4. A terminus ante quem of March 624 is provided by *Chr. Pasch.*, 713–14. Speck, *Dossier*, 35 ff. places the marriage in 622.

8 Fabius (the reading of L) is in my opinion to be preferred to V's Flavius, which is merely a *gentilicium*. It may be recalled that Herakleios' first wife was called Fabia. Fabius seems to have died in infancy.

8 Theodosios was still alive in 629/30. See below, c. 17.

12 ff. This passage has been discussed (badly) by J. V. A. Fine, *ZRVI* 10 (1967), 34–35 and (sensibly) by Cameron, *Circus*, 339–40. The required reading is conveyed by L. The omission in V is due to homoeoteleuton. There remains the redundant ἐπὶ ταύτῃ of V. I imagine that Nik. in the process of revision wanted to make it clear that the Blues agreed with the Greens *with regard to the marriage* and, having his eye on τὴν συναφήν, added ἐπὶ ταύτῃ. He then changed συναφήν to συνοικέσιον, but forgot to make the necessary adjustment in gender.

21 Alienation of church plate: Theoph., 302–3, mentions it in connection with the Persian campaign of 622. He specifies that Herakleios took money from charitable institutions and melted into coin the *polykandela* and other plate of St. Sophia. Nik. differs in speaking of the sale of plate to pay tribute to the Avars.

12. Persian War. Alliance with Chazars (626)

Nik. (or rather his source) was poorly informed about the conduct of hostilities in the East, with the result that the chronological sequence of this chapter is rather confused.

4 Fall of Jerusalem: This takes us back to 614.

5 Modestos: not strictly true. The bishop of Jerusalem was Zacharias, whom the Persians abducted and who died in captivity. Modestos stood in during the vacancy.

7 Advance on Chalcedon by Shahrbaraz: either in ca. 624 or in 626.

Expedition into Persia: Two separate events appear to be confused. The campaign in question is not the minor one of 622 (known from Pisides, *Exped. persica* and Theoph., 302 ff.) because on that occasion Herakleios traveled across Asia Minor overland and did not make contact with the Chazars, but that of 623 (or rather 624) and its sequel. On the other hand, the entrusting of the government to Bonos refers to 622 (Theoph., 303, who calls him Bonosos), unless the same arrangement was repeated later. *Chr. Pasch.* does not refer to the expedition of 622, but only to that of 624 (assuming it is correctly dated), when Herakleios set out on 25 March

(15 March according to Theoph., 306), celebrated Easter at Nicomedia, then sent his children back to Constantinople and went on with Martina and the magister Anianos (pp. 713–14). A further difficulty is that in 623 Easter fell on 27 March, whereas in 624 it fell on 15 April. See discussion in Stratos, II, 883 ff., who decides for 25 March 624 on the strength of *Chr. Pasch.* and because he believes that in 623 Herakleios returned from the East not before late February. On the latter point he is, however, mistaken. The campaign of 622 had terminated in August and Herakleios did not winter in Pontos: see N. Oikonomides, *GRBS* 1 (1975), 1–9.

14–16 Birth of Herakleios junior: This is the prince commonly called Heraklonas.

17 ff. Alliance with the Chazars: If Theoph., 314–15 is to be trusted, the meeting with the Chazars near Tiflis occurred in 626.

43 ff. Destruction of fire temples: Theoph., 308.8, speaks of the destruction of the fire temple at Thebarmais in the course of the campaign of 623 (as dated by him). On the astral dome see Christensen, *Iran*, 466 ff.; K. Lehmann, *Art Bulletin* 27 (1945), 24–25.

51 ff. Intercepted letter: A similar story, with different details, is told in many sources, Greek, Syriac, and Arabic. See discussion in Stratos, II, 635 ff. and my remarks in *TM* 9 (1985), 107 ff. According to Theoph., 323–24, the letter was addressed to Kardarigas (second in command of Persian forces at Chalcedon) ordering him to put Shahrbaraz to death. It was intercepted in Galatia and delivered to the emperor's son (Constantine), who showed it to Shahrbaraz. The latter concluded an accord with the Romans and withdrew from Chalcedon. Practically the same story is told by Mich. Syr., II, 408–9 and, with some confusions, in Agapios, 461–62. A different account in *Chr. Seert*, 540–41.

13. Siege of Constantinople by the Avars (626)

1 ff. Treaty with the Avars: briefly mentioned by Theoph., A.M. 6111, who alludes to tribute, but gives no further details. Cf. Theod. Synk., 5.30 ff.

5 John/Atalarichos (note the Gothic name): cf. below, c. 24.

6 Stephen: Martina's half-brother. Cf. below, c. 21.

9 ff. The siege: For the events see esp. F. Barišić, *Byzantion* 24 (1954), 371–95. The account of Nik. is independent. The other main Greek sources are:

(1) *Chr. Pasch.*, 716 ff., not an integral part of the Chronicle, but a separate, contemporary document. Note that at 724.9 there is a lacuna caused by the loss of one leaf, between *περάσαι πρὸς τούς* and *ἐπόντισεν*, on which see G. Mercati, *JTS* 7 (1905/6), 409. The lacuna corresponds to the incident on which Nik. lays most stress, namely, the destruction of the Slav flotilla.

(2) A very short account in Theoph., 316.

(3) Pisides, *Bell. avaricum*, a panegyric recited soon after the siege, allusive and imprecise. See P. Speck, *Zufälliges zum Bell. avar. des Georgios Pisides*, Misc. byz. Monac., 24 (1980).

(4) The homily of Theod. Synk., probably delivered in 627.

22 The Pteron: discussed by Speck, op. cit., 34 ff. with plan, whose conclusions I do not entirely share. The Pteron may have been the same as the feature called *βραχιάλιον* in *Chr. Pasch.*, 719.15 (cf. military sense of Latin *bracchium*), which I take to have been an outwork covering the juncture between the land walls and the walls along the Golden Horn, thus preventing access to the stretch of beach outside the latter. I remain unconvinced by the thesis of B. C. P. Tsangadas in *Essays in Memory of B. Laourdas* (Thessaloniki, 1975), 165–75, who locates the *brachialia* on either side of the valley of the Lykos.

40 ff. Extension of Blachernai walls: cf. *Chr. Pasch.*, 726: *ἐκτίσθη τὸ τεῖχος πέριξ τοῦ οἴκου τῆς . . . Θεοτόκου, ἔξωθεν τοῦ καλουμένου Πτεροῦ*. The wall built by Herakleios is usually identified with the stretch running NW from the Greek church of St. Demetrios Kanabou and turning round in the direction of the so-called Prison of Anemas. See esp. Schneider, *Landmauer*, 100 ff. and 156 ff. (sources); Müller-Wiener, *Bildlexikon*, 301.

14. Duel with Razates (627)

The battle of Nineveh (12 Dec.) is described in more detail by Theoph., 318–19, who does not have Razates challenge Herakleios to a duel: it is Herakleios who comes forward and strikes Razates, then a second Persian. A third Persian strikes him with a spear and wounds his lips, but Herakleios kills him. Then, in the fray, the emperor's horse is wounded in the thigh.

15. Death of Chosroes (628). Peace negotiations

Chosroes died on 29 Feb. 628.

Theoph., 325–27 describes in detail how Chosroes intended to bestow the crown on his younger son Merdasan and how the eldest, Siroes (Shiroe), made a plot with the help of Herakleios. In the end Chosroes was bound with fetters and imprisoned in his treasury, *εἰς τὸν οἶκον τοῦ σκότους, ὃν αὐτὸς ὠχύρωσεν ἐκ νέας κτίσας* (surely a borrowing from Pisides). He was then slowly starved and made to witness the execution of Merdasan and his other children. Five days later he was shot to death with arrows. The only common ground with Nik. are the reported words of Siroes, *τὸν χρυσὸν φάγῃ, ὃν συνήγαγε μάτην, δι᾽ ὃν πολλοὺς ἐλιμαγχόνησε καὶ τὸν κόσμον ἠρήμωσεν*.

12 ff. Exchange of letters: *Chr. Pasch.*, 735–37 preserves the mutilated text of the *hypomnestikon* of Siroes (an *ἴσον*, hence an official copy) and a small fragment of the reply of Herakleios. New edition by N. Oikonomides, *Byzantion* 41

(1971), 269 ff. The letter of Siroes expresses the intention of releasing Roman prisoners and the wish to live in peace with the Romans and all other neighbors. It also asks for the release of Persian prisoners held by the Romans. Herakleios is addressed as "brother," i.e., an equal. The reply of Herakleios expresses pleasure at the accession of Siroes and, presumably, at the liberation of prisoners, then breaks off. Oikonomides, op. cit., 278, assumes that Nik. had access to the complete text of *Chr. Pasch.*, and that, therefore, his indications are accurate, but that is unlikely in view of the fact that he shows no knowledge of *Chr. Pasch.* elsewhere. There is thus no confirmation of his statement that Herakleios addressed Siroes as "son" (i.e., as an inferior) and of the further particulars he furnishes.

The corresponding passage in Theoph., 327.10 ff., is very brief and incorrect in stating that Siroes released Patriarch Zacharias and returned the True Cross. Independent account in Sebeos, 86, who names the Roman envoy, Eustathios, perhaps the same as is mentioned in *Cer.*, 629.

25 ff. L's *ἅπερ αὐτῷ κατάφορα γένοιντο* is defensible (such of the *ξύλα* as would be accessible to him). The end of the paragraph seems to lack a verb, unless one adopts de Boor's expedient of placing *ὁ δὲ ὑπέσχετο . . . γένοιτο* in parentheses and changing *ὡς* in line 26 to *ὧν*. In line 28 Oikonomides' emendation of *αὐτόν* to *αὖ τόν* (with reference to the second invasion of Persia in 627) is palaeographically attractive, but does not take into account the fact that Nik. shows no awareness of two successive invasions.

16. Succession of Persian kings

Nik. is greatly confused on this topic. Seiroes and Kaboes were one and the same person (Kavadh II Shiroe), who was succeeded by his infant son Ardashir III. Synkellos, 442 and Theoph., 329 give a more correct sequence:

Siroes, son of Chosroes, 8 months (no length of reign in Theoph.)
Adeser, 7 months
Sarbarazas (–zes, –xas), 2 months
Borane, daughter of Chosroes, 7 months
Hormisdas, who was expelled by the Saracens.

Fuller list in Mich. Syr., II, 410. The accepted sequence (Th. Nöldeke, *Geschichte der Perser und Araber zur Zeit der Sasaniden* [Leiden, 1879], 432 ff.; Christensen, *Iran*, 497 ff.) is:

Kavadh II Shiroe, 25 Feb.–Sept. 628
Ardashir III, Sept. 628–27 April 630
Shahrbaraz, 27 April–9 June 630
Boran, summer 630–winter 631
Various and Hormizd V, 631–32?
Yazdegerd III, last king, 632/3–651/2.

COMMENTARY

The authenticity of the letter to Herakleios is accepted by V. Bolotov, *VizVrem* 14 (1907), 86, who thinks it was sent by Shiroe in Aug./Sept. 628 and concerned his son Ardashir.

17. Negotiations with Shahrbaraz (629). Shahrbaraz king of Persia (630). Dynastic arrangements

2 According to Sebeos, 88, Shahrbaraz came from Alexandria.

5 The required meaning is that Shahrbaraz sought leave to present himself before Herakleios in the guise of a slave. This is conveyed by L: *καὶ παραγενέσθαι ὡς αὐτὸν* (to Herakleios) *ἐξήτησε καὶ ὡς δοῦλον παρίστασθαι*. In revising, Nik. may have wished to avoid the repetition of *ὡς* (in two different senses), but left *αὐτόν*, which now ought to refer to Shahrbaraz. In my text I have followed L, but it would be equally possible to give preference to V with the slight correction of *ἑαυτόν* or *αὑτόν* for *αὐτόν*.

7 I prefer L's *ἧκεν* to V's *ἥκειν*. The meeting, not mentioned in any other Greek source, took place at Arabissos in Cappadocia: *Chr. 724*, 114; cf. Sebeos, 88.

10 It was Ardashir (Shiroe's infant son) who was eventually put to death by Shahrbaraz: *Khuzistan Chr.*, 25; *Chr. Seert*, 556; Strategios Georg., 54.

15 Return of True Cross: see c. 18.

16ff. Dynastic arrangements: On Niketas, son of Shahrbaraz, and the marriage of his sister Nike to Theodosios see my remarks in *TM* 9 (1985), 105ff. The marriage of Constantine III to Gregoria (who was presumably brought from the Libyan Pentapolis) could not have occurred later than Feb. 630, seeing that their son, Herakleios, was born on 7 Nov. of that year (Theoph., 335). The date of the death of the patrician Niketas (Gregoria's father) is not known, and the oft-repeated statement that after the loss of Egypt to the Persians he served as exarch of Africa is open to doubt: see my remarks in *Sitz. Österr. Akad.* 432 (1984), 36.

18. First Arab incursions. Children of the imperial family. Restitution of the True Cross

1 Aithribos, Yathrib = Medina. The incursion in question may refer to the unsuccessful raid of Zayd b. Harithah to Muʾta (E of the S end of the Dead Sea) in A.H. 8 (629): see Elias Nisib., 62, and Donner, *Conquests*, 101, 103. The same event described by Theoph., 335.14ff.

4ff. These details about Eudokia and the four children (two sons and two daughters) who died while Herakleios was in Persia (hence in 624–28) are not found elsewhere. According to a marginal note in V (above, p. 23) the four children were both born in Persia and died there, but it may be doubted that the scholiast had any independent information at his disposal. Fabius may well have been one of those who died; the others cannot be identified.

9 ff. Return of the True Cross to Jerusalem: Various dates have been advanced for this event (628, 629, 630, 631, the last by V. Grumel, *Byz. Forsch.* 1 [1966], 139–49). The one most solidly attested by contemporary sources is 21 March 630, as demonstrated by Kulakovskij, III, 367 ff. The fiction that the Cross was returned inviolate also occurs in Strategios Georg., 55, and must, therefore, have been deliberately circulated at the time. This has been rightly stressed by A. Frolow, *REB* 11 (1953), 88–105, whose explanation of the *mise-en-scène* is, however, unconvincing. Modestos was not patriarch at the time of the restitution: he was ordained in indiction 4, i.e., after 1 Sept. 630: Strategios Georg., 55.

17 ff. This passage raises considerable difficulties. The date of indiction 2, which Nik. must have taken from his chronicle source, corresponds to 628/9. We have seen, however, that the Cross was returned to Jerusalem in 630. It was not conveyed thither via Constantinople, since we are told that it was brought from Persia by the Roman general David to Hierapolis (Mabbug), where Herakleios took possession of it before transporting it to Jerusalem: Mich. Syr., II, 427. Furthermore, it is said to have remained at Jerusalem until Herakleios abandoned the East in 636: Sebeos, 118; Theoph., 337.9. It may be that soon after (as implied by Nik.'s *εὐθύς*) its restoration to Jerusalem the Cross was taken on a triumphal tour to Constantinople, but that would require emending the numeral 2, to say, 5 (631/2), i.e., $\bar{\text{B}}$ to $\bar{\text{E}}$. Furthermore, such a tour is not recorded elsewhere.

According to cod. *Sabait. 366*, fol. 22ᵛ, the "exaltation" under Herakleios corresponded to the liturgical commemoration of 1 Aug., which in the published *Menaia* (vol. VI, [Rome 1902], 277) is called *πρόοδος τῶν τιμίων ξύλων*, and elsewhere the "immersion" (*βάπτισις*) of the True Cross: *Le Typicon de la Grande Eglise*, ed. J. Mateos, I (Rome, 1962), 356; *Synax. CP*, 860.21. For the office see A. Dmitrievskij, *Opisanie liturgičeskikh rukopisej*, II (Kiev, 1901), 165–66. If such, indeed, was the origin of the liturgical commemoration, the "exaltation" may be thought to have occurred on 1 Aug. 629.

19. Triumphal return of Herakleios to Constantinople. Consulship of Constantine III (632)

Theoph., 327–28 describes the emperor's return to Constantinople (but with no mention of a triumph), where he was met at Hieria by his son Constantine, the patriarch, and the people; the following year he proceeded to Jerusalem to restore the True Cross. That would suggest that Herakleios returned to Constantinople in 629, as also argued by Bolotov, *VizVrem* 14 (1907), 94. The same date is accepted by Kulakovskij, III, 112 (after the interview at Arabissos, July 629) and 370–71. A. Pertusi, on the other hand, in his edition of Pisides, 233–34, believes that Herakleios came to Constantinople before 1 Jan. 629 and remained there until the spring, but he is wrong in connecting this visit with the processions described in *Cer.*,

628–30, which must be dated 1 and 4 Jan., indiction 12 (639), not indiction 2 (629) in spite of the reading of the MS. Pertusi may be right, however, in saying that the Novella of 21 March 629, *De clericis conveniendis* (ed. I. Konidaris, *Fontes minores* 5 [1982], 84–94) implies the emperor's presence in the capital.

We have it on the contemporary evidence of *Acta Anastasii Persae* (ed. H. Usener, [Bonn, 1894]), 12–13, that from Jerusalem Herakleios proceeded to Mesopotamia. The monk who undertook to retrieve the saint's relics from Persia accompanied the imperial party as far as Constantina (Tella). After reducing Edessa, Herakleios went to Hierapolis, where he met the Monophysite Patriarch Athanasios (early 631): Mich. Syr., II, 412; cf. Kulakovskij, III, 128–30. A little later he received at Aleppo an embassy from Queen Boran headed by the Persian Katholikos Išoʾyahb: *Chr. Seert*, 557f.; Thomas of Marga, trans. E. A. Wallis Budge, *The Book of Governors* (London, 1893), II, 124–26. Thus, the return to Constantinople could not have occurred before the middle of 631.

It is possible that the triumphal *adventus* described by Nik. is distinct from that in Theoph.

9f. Consulship of Constantine: 1 Jan. 632, as shown by Bolotov, op. cit., 74–75. Theoph., 301 also gives 1 Jan., indiction 5, but mistakenly places it fifteen years too early (A.M. 6108).

20. First Arab successes in Palestine (633–34)

It should be noted that Nik. recounts only the first stage of the Arab advance into Palestine. He is silent about the decisive battle of the Yarmūk (636), the capture of Jerusalem (638), and the conquest of Syria. What he does say in this chapter, which does not shine by its clarity, may be summarized as follows:

(1) Herakleios with his wife and younger son proceed to the East, i.e., from Constantinople.

(2) Theodore (the emperor's brother) is dismissed from his command and replaced by his namesake, Theodore Trithyrios.

(3) A certain Sergios *kata Niketan* (who is not described as having fought a battle) is put to death by the Arabs, that is, the "Roman" Arabs, for denying them their customary commercial dues.

(4) An unnamed subordinate of Theodore Trithyrios, disobeying orders, engages the Arabs at Gabitha and is defeated.

Pace M. V. Krivov, *VizVrem* 43 (1982), 218–25, the above information cannot be easily reconciled with what is known from other sources about an extraordinarily confused sequence of events.

1ff. The Saracens of Arabia could hardly have penetrated to the region of Antioch by this early date; perhaps a local tribe of Arabs is meant. Herakleios is recorded as having resided at Edessa in 633–34: see Kulakovskij, III, 131, 146.

COMMENTARY

4ff. It is generally believed that Theodore (the emperor's brother) was destituted after he had been defeated by the Arabs at Gabitha (presumably in 634) and fled to the emperor at Edessa, and that he was succeeded in his command by Baanes and Theodore the *sakellarios*: so Theoph., 336–37, A.M. 6125 (after the accession of ʿUmar and the conquest of Bostra). Similar story in Mich. Syr., II, 418, who does not specify where the battle was fought.

11ff. The transition is very brusque and the *γάρ* in line 11 is left hanging in the air. A lacuna may be suspected. Theoph., 335–36 also mentions, but with reference to A.D. 631, a financial dispute: the (Roman) Arabs, who used to guard the approaches of the desert, demanded their customary dues, but were rudely dismissed by the imperial paymaster, an unnamed eunuch, as a result of which they joined their fellow-nationals. No trade is, however, involved here.

Sergios *kata Niketan*: For the form of the name, which indicates that Sergios had been in the service of a Niketas (the emperor's cousin?), see A. Cameron in *Glotta* 56 (1978), 87ff. He should probably be distinguished from the commander Sergios, who tried to oppose the Arabs with a small contingent from Caesarea, but was defeated and killed, presumably in 633: Theoph., 336; Mich. Syr., II, 413 (who calls him a patrician and says that in fleeing he fell off his horse three times and was finally put to the sword). The slaying of Sergios (called a *candidatus*, no doubt more correctly) is mentioned in *Doctr. Iacobi*, 86, thus yielding a terminus ante quem of July 634.

14 L's *ἀπειλειμμένος* can be corrected either to *ἀπειλημμένος* (from *ἀπολαμβάνω*) = "shut up" or to *ἀπειλημένος* (from *ἀπειλέω*) = "brought into straits," the latter used by Hdt., II.141, VIII.109.

21 Θεόδωρος, presumably the original reading of V, appears preferable to Θεοδώρῳ (L, V[2]) because it is picked up by *ὑπ' αὐτὸν στρατηγός*, which I understand to mean a commander subordinate to Theodore Trithyrios rather than subordinate to the emperor (an unnecessary qualification). Since, in either case, the order not to engage the Saracens emanated from the emperor (*τὰ κατὰ γνώμην τῷ βασιλεῖ*), the difference in meaning is very slight.

23 *νεώτερα*: cf. Hdt., I.210: *εἰ δέ τις . . . ἀπαγγέλλει παῖδα τὸν ἐμὸν νεώτερα βουλεύειν περὶ σέο*.

27 Gabitha: As we have seen, Theoph. equates the battle of Gabitha with the defeat of Theodore, the emperor's brother. Mich. Syr., II, 420 places the battle of Gabita (on the Yarmūk) in 635 and distinguishes it from the principal battle of the Yarmūk the following year. See also the Syriac fragment, ed. Th. Nöldeke, *ZDMG* 29 (1875), 77, which speaks of Gabitha with reference to the battle of the Yarmūk in 636. The Arabic sources do not mention Gabitha and speak instead of the battle of Ajnādayn.

On the above events see P. Mayerson, *TAPA* 95 (1964), 155–99; Donner,

Conquests, 112ff. (whose statement, p. 144, that Theoph. is dependent on the Arabic tradition is, however, open to doubt).

21. Ransom of hostages held by the Avars

No other source.

For the hostages see above, c. 13. Anianos, *domesticus* and *magister*, is mentioned in *Chr. Pasch.*, 714.7 as accompanying Herakleios on the Persian campaign of 624. Judging by this passage, he may have acted as head of government while Herakleios was in the East.

22. Koubratos throws off Avar yoke

No other source. Cf. above, c. 9 and below, c. 35.

There has been interminable debate concerning Koubratos (Kubrat or Kuvrat), chief of the Bulgarian Onogurs (Onogundurs) and his identity or otherwise with the Kurt of the Bulgarian Princes' List, the Chrobatos of *DAI*, 30.65 (also contemporary with Herakleios, but dwelling in Dalmatia) and the Kouber of *Mir. S. Demetrii*, II.5. The thesis of their identity, most clearly stated by H. Grégoire, *Byzantion* 17 (1944–45), 88ff., has been generally rejected. See, most recently, Beševliev, *Protobulg. Periode*, 149ff., 511ff.; P. Lemerle, *Les plus anciens recueils des Miracles de S. Démétrius*, II (Paris, 1981), 143ff.; idem, in 'Αφιέρωμα στὸν N. Σβορῶνο (Rethymno, 1986), I, 51–58; J. Werner, *Der Grabfund von Malaja Pereščepina und Kuvrat, Abh. Bayer. Akad.*, N.F. 91 (1984).

A further difficulty is posed by Nik.'s statement that Koubratos, who presumably dwelled near the Sea of Azov, rebelled against the Avars, since there is no evidence that the authority of the latter extended that far East in the thirties of the seventh century.

1–2 Note that L has Κούβαρος and 'Αργανᾶ.

5f. The reading of L, *φυλάξει* (sic) and *αὐτοῦ* (instead of *ἑαυτῶν*) would imply that Koubratos kept or promised to keep the peace until the end of *his* life. This makes little difference inasmuch as he died after Herakleios.

23. Arabs in Egypt

This chapter as well as the passage concerning the disgrace of Kyros in c. 26 raise considerable difficulties. In the first place, it is generally held that Herakleios departed from Syria in 636 after the battle of the Yarmūk; hence the appointment of John of Barkaina would pertain to that year at the latest. Yet the Arab invasion of Egypt is believed to have started only in Dec. 639. Another point that does not seem to have been noticed concerns Kyros' alleged plan to offer Eudokia in marriage to ʿAmr. The acclamations recorded in *Cer.*, 630 for 4 Jan. 639 name all the members of the imperial family, but omit Eudokia, thus implying that she was no longer alive at the time.

COMMENTARY

The story told by Theoph., 338, A.M. 6126, if true even in part, would offer some confirmation of the version of events in Nik. Theoph. alleges that, on learning of the Arab advance, Kyros offered to pay a tribute of 200,000 dinars (the passage, lacking in the Greek MSS, is supplied from the Latin trans. of Anastasius, *ducenta milia denariorum*: de Boor mistakenly prints ιβ′ μυριάδας). In this way he kept Egypt untroubled for three years, i.e., from 636 or 637 to 639. Kyros was recalled by the emperor and replaced by the Armenian Manuel as *augustalis*. Manuel refused to pay the tribute, etc. Practically the same story is found in Mich. Syr., II, 425 (and other Syriac chronicles), which proves that Theoph. obtained it from his Syriac source (as also shown by his apparent use of the term *dinars*). Severus of Eschmounein, 229, also speaks, if rather vaguely, of tribute paid to the Muslims for three years.

Butler, *Conquest*, 207–9, 481–82, categorically rejects the accounts of both Theoph. and Nik. In his view the only offer of tribute on the part of Kyros was made during the siege of Babylon (Oct. 640) and this was misconstrued into the story of tribute paid prior to the conquest to purchase immunity from invasion (ibid., 261–63). If so, however, it remains to explain why Nik. and Theoph. = Mich. Syrus, not to mention Severus, being as they are independent sources, converge on the payment of tribute (or the proposal to pay it) in c. 636/7.

2 John of Barkaina: a general by the name of John, who was defeated and killed by the Arabs, is mentioned by John of Nikiu, Charles, 178–80, 184. He seems to have been an imperial appointee, since his body was recovered, taken to Babylon, and thence sent to Constantinople. His identity with John of Barkaina is uncertain. Cf. Butler, *Conquest*, 222 note 1.

4 Marinos, presumably *mag. militum per Thracias*, not recorded elsewhere.

7 Marianos *cubicularius*: A Marianos, who was destroyed by the Muslims, is mentioned by Severus of Eschmounein, 230.

12 Ambros: ʿAmr ibn al ʿAṣī.

15 The emperor's daughters: In addition to Eudokia, these were Augustina and Anastasia. On Kyros' matrimonial schemes see the somewhat questionable study by F. Nau, *Le Muséon* 45 (1932), 1–17. Butler, *Conquest*, 264 rejects the story.

24. Herakleios withdraws to Hieria. Plot against him

No other Greek source. The story of the plot is told in greater detail, but with some confusion of the persons implicated, in Sebeos, 93–94. It involved a number of Armenian noblemen. For the probable date (late in 637) see Stratos, III, 231, note XXIV.

2 Hieria: outside Chalcedon, at modern Fenerbahçe, where Justinian had built a palace. See J. Pargoire, *IRAIK* 4 (1899), 9–78; Janin, *CP*, 148–50; idem, *Grands centres*, 35–36.

10 Theodore *magistros*: mistakenly called the son of Herakleios by Sebeos. He must have succeeded Anianos (above, c. 21) and been followed by Eustathios, attested in 639 (*Cer.*, 629). Theoph., 344.23, 345.1 mentions another son of Theodore (the emperor's brother), viz. Gregory, who was held hostage by Muawiya and died at Heliopolis.

15 Gaudomelete: the island of Gozzo near Malta, mentioned in the Acts of Sts. Peter and Paul, *Acta apostolorum apocrypha*, ed. R. A. Lipsius and M. Bonnet, I (Leipzig, 1891), 178.2, 181.13. Cf. R. A. Lipsius, *Die apokryphen Apostelgeschichten*, II/1 (Braunschweig, 1887), 305.

25. Herakleios returns to Constantinople. Heraklonas crowned emperor (638)

9 For the bridge of the Barbysses see above, c. 10.

11 Heraklonas was crowned on 4 July 638. His brother David was made Caesar the same day. The occasion is described in *Cer.*, 627–28.

26. Death of Patriarch Sergios and ordination of Pyrrhos (638). Disgrace of Kyros

1 Death of Sergios: 13 Dec. 638 according to *Cer.*, 630–31, which specifies that he died on a Sunday. The day in question was, however, a Saturday, so the indication may refer to his funeral rather than to his death. On the other hand, Nik.'s *Χρονογραφικόν*, de Boor, 118, gives him a reign of 28 years, 7 months, 21 days. He was ordained on 18 April 610 (*Chr. Pasch.*, 699, where *η*′ should be corrected to *ιη*′), which would place his death on 8 or 9 Dec. This is accepted by Grumel, *Chronologie*, 435 and Van Dieten, *Patriarchen*, 51.

3ff. Pyrrhos: ordained on 20 Dec. 638. See Van Dieten, *Patriarchen*, 58. Nik.'s *Χρονογραφικόν*, loc. cit., calls him presbyter of St. Sophia, monk, *ἄρχων τῶν μοναστηρίων*, and abbot of Chrysopolis (i.e., of the monastery founded by Philippikos) and gives him a first tenure of 2 years, 9 months, 9 days.

3–4 *ὡς ἡνίκα . . . ἐδέξατο*: This has usually been interpreted to mean that Pyrrhos was the godfather of Herakleios' sister, which from the point of view of chronology appears implausible. See A. Pertusi, *AnBoll* 76 (1958), 19 note 3. The Greek can, however, be understood the other way round, as pointed out by Van Dieten, *Patriarchen*, 57 note 1, who places a comma after *ἐφωτίζετο*.

5 *συνδιαιτώμενον* implies that Pyrrhos had been Sergios' *synkellos*, a fact that is not otherwise recorded.

6ff. This passage appears to be saying that the disgrace of Kyros took place at about the same time (*τηνικαῦτα*) as the ordination of Pyrrhos and that he had been recalled to Constantinople a few years previously. Yet Kyros is known to have been at Alexandria in Nov. 638 (Grumel, *Regestes*, 293) and in 639/40 (PLond 113, *Greek Papyri in the British Museum*, I, ed. F. G. Kenyon [1893], 222–23). It is generally believed that Kyros went to Constantinople in about Nov. 640 to obtain imperial consent for his treaty with ʿAmr, was temporarily banished, and returned to Alexandria only after the death of Herakleios, in Sept. 641: so Butler, *Conquest*, 262ff., Kulakovskij, III, 162–63, and others.

27. Consulship of Heraklonas (639). Death of Herakleios (641)

1ff. Consulship of Heraklonas: presumably 1 Jan. 639. See *Cer.*, 628–29, which describes a πρόκενσος on that date. David had actually been made Caesar on 4 July 638 (above, c. 25), whereas Martinos was named *nobilissimus*, not Caesar, as appears from the acclamations for 4 Jan. 639 (*Cer.*, 630): these are for Herakleios senior and his wife Anastasia Martina, Constantine and Herakleios (Heraklonas) Augusti, Augustina and Anastasia Augustae (daughters of Herakleios), David Caesar and Martinos *nobilissimus*. It is not clear whether Anastasia (daughter) was also called Martina or whether Nik. (or his source) confused her with her mother.

13ff. Nik. implies that Herakleios died on 11 Feb. 641 (counting from 5 Oct. 610), and this has been accepted by most historians. Theoph., 341 gives a March date after a reign of 30 years, 10 months (*recte* 5 months), while the *Chr. Altinate* has 11 Jan. The last has been accepted by P. Grierson, *DOP* 16 (1962), 48. February is, however, confirmed by John of Nikiu, Charles, 184–85, as pointed out by Butler, *Conquest*, 300 note 2. See also Stratos, III, 162 and 231–32, note XXV.

The sarcophagus of Herakleios was placed in Justinian's mausoleum and was of white Dokimian marble, resembling onyx (*Cer.*, 644). It is possibly one of those exhibited in front of the Istanbul Archaeological Museum: see my remarks in *Istanbul Arkeol. Müzesi Yıllığı* 15–16 (1969), 307–9.

Herakleios was presumably afraid of being buried alive, as had allegedly happened to Emperor Zeno, who, for three days, is said to have cried for help from his tomb: Kedr., I, 622; Zonaras, III, 132–33.

28. Opposition to Martina (Feb. 641)

No other source.

For the significance which some historians have attached to this incident see Introduction, p. 8.

16f. It is not clear what is meant by τὸ ἑαυτῆς παλάτιον. Martina would normally have resided in the Imperial Palace next to the Hippodrome rather than in a private palace of her own.

29. Reign of Constantine III (Feb.–May 641)

At his accession Constantine was about twenty-nine. He had married his relative Gregoria in 629/30 and had two sons, Herakleios (born Nov. 630) and Theodosios.

17 Valentinos is mentioned by Sebeos, 103–4 as an Arsacid and commander of forces in the East. Nik.'s statement that he was the adjutant of Philagrios is not clear. For the suggestion that he was *comes obsequii* see Haldon, *Praetorians*, 174.

21–22 Kulakovskij, III, 175, assuming that each soldier would have received a donative of 5 solidi, calculates that the army numbered nearly 44,000 men. The sum of money is incorrectly given as 50,000 plus 16,000 solidi by Stratos, III, 192 and Kaegi, *Unrest*, 155. John of Nikiu, Charles, 192 also says that Valentinos distributed to the army a large sum of money that he had taken from the treasury of Philagrios, but implies a later context. Unfortunately, the sequence of his narrative appears disturbed at this point.

25f. If Herakleios died on 11 Feb., Constantine must have died on 24 May, and this date has been generally accepted. Theoph., 341.14 gives Constantine a reign of four months. The *Chr. Altinate* makes him die on 20 April after a reign of 120 days. See P. Grierson, *DOP* 16 (1962), 48–49 and Stratos, III, 196–97. Note that Nik. does not accuse Martina of having poisoned Constantine and represents his death as having been natural. The allegation that she did so was officially propagated by Constans II (Theoph., 342) and is found in most historical sources, both Greek and Oriental. Pyrrhos is often accused, surely without reason, of having been her accomplice.

30. Accession of Heraklonas. Negotiations with Valentinos (spring–summer 641)

No other Greek source. Brief mention in Sebeos. The account in John of Nikiu, Charles, 191, 196 is fuller, but, unfortunately, confused. He informs us that Heraklonas brought to Constantinople the army of Thrace, a move that enabled him to exile Philagrios to Africa, "where Pyrrhus had previously been in banishment" (see c. 31); that this caused an uprising against Martina because Philagrios was "greatly beloved"; that Valentinos brought his army to Chalcedon and that Heraklonas, accompanied by the clergy, crossed the Bosporos to appeal to him for peace, promising to associate his nephew (Herakleios) to power and to recall Philagrios. For these events see Stratos, III, 200ff.; Kaegi, *Unrest*, 155ff.

6 Kyros returned to Alexandria on the feast of the Holy Cross (14 Sept.) 641: John of Nikiu, Charles, 192. See Butler, *Conquest*, 536ff.

31. Coronation of Herakleios (Constans II). Forced departure of Pyrrhos (Sept. 641)

1ff. The anxiety of the people of Constantinople about their vineyards on the Asiatic side of the Bosporos may indicate an incipient ruralization of the urban economy.

4ff. Coronation of Herakleios: probably in Sept. Cf. E. W. Brooks, *BZ* 4 (1895), 440 note 2, who points out that the Lateran Council of 5 Oct. 649 is dated to the 9th year of Constantine (Mansi, X, 864D).

14 ff. Departure of Pyrrhos: 28/29 Sept. John of Nikiu alleges that Pyrrhos had been banished a first time to an island in the west of Africa (Charles, 185), was brought back on the advice of the Senate (p. 191), and then banished for the second time to Tripoli (p. 197). The first banishment is rejected by T. Kaestner, *De imperio Constantini III*, Diss. Jena (Leipzig, 1907), 14, whereas Van Dieten, *Patriarchen*, 67 is prepared to see in it some kernel of truth. Quite apart from providing a justification for such a move, it is difficult to find a sufficient time span into which a first banishment could have fitted.

25–26 The words attributed to Pyrrhos are interpreted by Van Dieten, *Patriarchen*, 74 as giving the substance of his resignation document (*libellus*). Note that they echo those of Martyrios of Antioch, who was forced out of office by Peter the Fuller: *κλήρῳ ἀνυποτάκτῳ, καὶ λαῷ ἀπειθεῖ, καὶ ἐκκλησίᾳ ἐρρυπωμένῃ ἀποτάττομαι, φυλάττων ἐμαυτῷ τὸ τῆς ἱερωσύνης ἀξίωμα* (Theodoros Anagnostes, ed. Hansen, 110; Theoph., 113.32), thus underlining the unjust treatment of Pyrrhos. A. N. Stratos, *Βυζαντινά* 8 (1976), 11–19 argues that Pyrrhos did not resign.

28 ff. Disputation with Maximos: July 645 (PG 91, 288). Cf. V. Grumel, *EO* 26 (1927), 30. See also Introduction, p. 14.

32. Concessions to Valentinos. Ordination of Paul II (Sept.–Oct. 641)

5 Valentinos' appointment as *comes excubitorum* is confirmed by a seal: Zacos-Veglery, I/1, No. 1087.

8 Coronation of David: exact date unrecorded.

10 Ordination of Paul II: 1 Oct. See E. W. Brooks, *BZ* 6 (1897), 45–46; 7 (1898), 37. Theoph., 342.2, like Nik., gives only the month.

It should be noted that the account of Nik. stops abruptly without rounding off the story: nothing is said about the deposition and mutilation of Martina and Heraklonas, the fate of Valentinos, etc. See Introduction, pp. 14–15.

33. Murder of Constans II (668)

For the circumstances see Theoph., 351–52.

The omission of the reign of Constans II may be explained either by the loss of a folio in the archetype of V and L or by the supposition that Nik. had no materials for the period in question. See Introduction, pp. 14–15.

34. Accession of Constantine IV. Naval attacks on Constantinople (671?–677). Peace treaty with the Arabs

Nik. abridges the same source as that followed by Theoph., A.M. 6164, 6165, and 6169 without giving any additional details. As a result of compression, the peace treaty is attributed to the failure of the Arab attack on Constantinople, whereas Theoph., 355.10 connects it with the incursion of the Mardaites into Lebanon. Note that Theoph. does not preserve the complete text of the source, since the imperial ambassador John Pitzigaudes is described as ὁ πολλαχῶς λεχθεὶς πανεύφημος ἀνήρ (355.29), whereas he had been mentioned only once before.

14 It is now generally held that the "siege" of Constantinople lasted not seven years, but five (674–678) and that the two Greek chroniclers (in fact only one) reckoned from the capture of Kyzikos in 670 (Theoph., A.M. 6162): so, e.g., G. Ostrogorsky, *History of the Byzantine State*, trans. J. Hussey (Oxford, 1968), 124 note 1. In reality, however, there was neither a siege nor a blockade of the capital, merely a succession of engagements in its immediate vicinity. The latest treatment of the subject, by A. N. Stratos, *JÖB* 33 (1983), 89–107, is not entirely satisfactory. For the Arabic sources see E. W. Brooks, *JHS* 18 (1898), 185 ff. These are disappointingly vague and mention Constantinople only under A.H. 54 (673/4) and 56 (676/7). See also Lilie, 75–76, who argues that the Arabs occupied Kyzikos in 671.

30–31 Amount of tribute: the same figures in de Boor's text of Theoph., 355.24, although some MSS read 365,000 (τξε´ instead of τρεῖς) pieces of gold, as in the later treaty between ʿAbd al-Malik and Justinian II (Theoph., 363.9–10). The sum of 3,000 pieces of gold (unless pounds are meant) appears too low: cf. Bury, *LRE*, II, 312. The quotation from Theoph. in *DAI*, 21.15–16 gives 800 (instead of 50) prisoners and 50 horses.

35. The Bulgars settle near the Danube

The account of Theoph., 356.19 ff., which also includes a short geographical excursus (omitted by Nik.), is fuller and closer to the original.

1–2 *Οὔννων καὶ* Βουλγάρων: Seeing that the Onogundurs were a tribe of the Bulgars, V. Beševliev, *REB* 28 (1970), 153–59; Βυζαντινά 13/1 (1985), 48–49, is historically correct in wishing to emend the text to Οὐν(ν)ογουνδούρων Βουλγάρων (as in Theoph.). That Nik. should have written so does not, however, prove that he actually did.

2 ἀρχῆς: I have translated "origin" rather than "dominion" or "empire" in the light of Theoph.'s ἀρχαιότητος.

6 Κοβρᾶτός τις: Nik. forgets that he had already spoken of Κούβρατος at 22.1.

15 μέχρι τοῦ δεῦρο: E. Honigmann, *Nouv. Clio* 4 (1952), 290 note 1, remarks that this comment must come from a contemporary document, viz. the "Chronicle of 713," the alleged direct source of L, which he attributes to Traianos Patrikios. Whether the lost source was or was not by Traianos we have no means of knowing (cf. Introduction, pp. 16–17); but we must resist the suggestion that Traianos is more or less equivalent to L for the simple reason that the Bulgarian

passage is preserved in a fuller version in Theoph., who also has *μέχρι τῆς δεῦρο* (357.21) and, further down (358.11), says that Batbaian continues paying taxes to the Avars *μέχρι τοῦ νῦν*.

18 *τῇ νῦν ὑπὸ Ἀβάροις κειμένῃ*: Theoph., 357.24 has *εἰς Πανονίαν τῆς Ἀβαρίας*. We cannot determine whether *τῇ νῦν* (or something like it) was in the source or was added by Nik. Cf. Introduction, p. 8.

20 Pentapolis: For the circumstances and the western sources concerning these events see A. Guillou, *Régionalisme et indépendance dans l'Empire byzantin au VIIe siècle* (Rome, 1969), 102–3.

23–24 *Ὄγγλον τῇ σφῶν καλούμενον φωνῇ*: a classicizing embellishment, which should not prejudice the derivation of the name Onglos. Concerning the latter commentators are divided: some derive it from Old Slavonic ǫglŭ = "corner," others from Turcic aγul>aul = "court," "fortified enclosure." See Moravcsik, *Byzantinoturcica*, II, s.v. Ὄγγλος and *αὐλή*; N. Bănescu, *Byzantion* 28 (1958), 433–40; M. Vasmer, *Etimologičeskij slovar' russkogo jazyka*, I (Moscow, 1964), 229–30; IV (1973), 145. Theoph., 357.28 ff. makes it clear that the Onglos was to the north of the main course of the Danube. See V. Beševliev, *BZ* 27 (1927), 35, who convincingly transposes the text of Theoph. to read: *τὸν Δάναπριν καὶ Δάναστριν περάσας βορειοτέρους τοῦ Δανουβίου ποταμοὺς καὶ τὸν Ὄγλον καταλαβών, μεταξὺ τούτων κἀκείνων* [or *κἀκείνου*?] *ᾤκησεν*. According to Moses of Chorene, Asparuch established himself on the island of Peuke, i.e., in the Danube delta. See A. Maricq, *Byzantion* 22 (1952), 343.

27 *τὰ δ'οὖν ὄπισθεν κρημνοῖς ἀβάτοις τετειχισμένα*: a confusion. As Theoph., 358.3–4 explains, the Onglos was marshy "in front" and surrounded by rivers (i.e., the Prut, Dniestr, and Danube) on all other sides. The cliffs presumably refer to the second dwelling place of the Bulgars near Varna, described by Theoph., 359.10–12 as being protected at the back by the Danube and on the near side as well as laterally by mountain passes (*διὰ κλεισουρῶν*) and the Black Sea.

29 Bersilia: northern Dagestan. Cf. Simok., VII.8.3 (*Βαρσήλτ*) and Mich. Syr., II, 364 ("le pays d'Alân qu'on appelle Barsâlia"). See Artamonov, *Istorija*, 128, 130–32.

31–32 The text is corrupt and requires radical emendation. Theoph., 358.7–9 has *ἐξῆλθε τὸ μέγα ἔθνος τῶν Χαζάρων ἀπὸ τοῦ ἐνδοτέρου βάθους Βερζιλίας τῆς πρώτης Σαρματίας καὶ ἐδέσποσε πάσης τῆς περατικῆς γῆς μέχρι τῆς Ποντικῆς θαλάσσης*. We may tentatively suggest: *⟨ἐξῆλθε⟩ τὸ τῶν Χαζάρων φῦλον . . . πλείστης ⟨τε⟩ ἀδείας ἐντεῦθεν ⟨ἐπιλαβόμενον⟩* [omit *ἐπέτρεχον* as a gloss on *κατέδραμον*], *τὰ τοιαῦτα πάντα κατέδραμον χωρία τῆς ὑπὲρ Πόντον τὸν Εὔξεινον γῆς* [with a further gloss *τῆς θαλάττης πέραν*].

33 We have emended *ποιησάμενος* to *ποιησάμενον* to agree with *φῦλον*,

but note that Theoph. has the ungrammatical *ἔθνος . . . καταστήσας*. It would appear that Nik. had difficulty in paraphrasing this passage and left several corrections or alternative versions in his MS, thus inducing copyists into error.

36. Failure of Byzantine expedition against the Bulgars (681)

Corresponds to Theoph., 358.11–359.21, who gives a fuller and more precise account. Note that Nik. omits both the derogatory epithet applied by Theoph. to the Bulgars ("the foul nation") and the critical references to the "pusillanimity" and "disgrace" of the Romans (358.26, 359.21).

The expedition is dated 680 or 681 by Kulakovskij, III, 249. Beševliev, *Protobulg. Periode*, 176–77, 182, places it in 680 and the installation of the Bulgars in the Varna region in 681. The crucial piece of evidence is the intervention of the presbyter Constantine of Apamea at the 16th session of the Sixth Council (9 Aug. 681). Having tried to gain a hearing from the start of the Council (7 Nov. 680), he claimed that if he had been heard, "we would not have suffered what we suffered this year (*ἐφέτος*), i.e., the things we suffered in the Bulgarian war" (Mansi, XI, 617). This surely suggests that the Byzantine defeat occurred in 681.

7 *ὀχυρώματα*, cf. 14 *ὀχυρώματι*: It has been suggested that these refer not to the Onglos as such, but to a line of earth ramparts in South Bessarabia. They are described by C. Uhlig, *Prähistorische Zeitschr.* 19 (1928), 197–202; G. Fehér, *Les monuments de la culture protobulgare* = Archaeologia Hungarica VII (Budapest, 1931), 8–12 and fig. 1 on p. 19. See also Beševliev, *Protobulg. Periode*, 177 and note 17.

23f. Neighboring Slavonian tribes: These are the seven tribes mentioned by Theoph., 359.14, on which see I. Dujčev, *Medioevo bizantino-slavo*, I (Rome, 1965), 55–56, 67–82; Beševliev, *Protobulg. Periode*, 179–80.

37. Sixth Ecumenical Council (Nov. 680–Sept. 681). Death of Constantine IV (685)

Corresponds to Theoph., A.M. 6171 from p. 359.25 to the end; 6172 (recording only the Sixth Council); and 6177, p. 361.15–16. Nik. omits the reference to Sergios and Pyrrhos as heretics, the number of bishops present (namely, 289), and the identity of the presidents (emperor and bishops). He adds: (1) a short theological development (*τέλειον αὐτὸν ἐν θεότητι . . . παραπέμψασα*); (2) the statement that Constantine IV was buried in the church of the Holy Apostles. We can be more precise: he was buried in Justinian's mausoleum in a sarcophagus of green Thessalian marble: Leo gramm., 162. Cf. P. Grierson, *DOP* 16 (1962), 50.

The exact date of Constantine's death is uncertain: the *Chr. Altinate* gives 10 July (Grierson, loc. cit.), the *Liber Pontificalis*, ed. Duchesne, I, 366, early September. V. Grumel, *AnBoll* 84 (1966), 254–60, has argued for 3 Sept. on the strength of the commemoration of the "new" or "younger" emperor Constantine in the *Synax. CP*, 12.6, differing from F. Halkin, *Byzantion* 24 (1954), 14–17, who refers it to Constantine, son of Basil I.

2 *ἐκρατύνετο*: not strictly correct. The heresy was in decline at the time.

38. Accession of Justinian II (685). War with Slavonians and Arabs

This paragraph does not add anything to Theoph., who gives much more information spread over several years. The correspondence is as follows:

Justinian assumes power in his sixteenth year: cf. Theoph., 363.26–27, A.M. 6178.

He upsets the treaties concluded by his father; breaks off peace with the Bulgars; conveys cavalry to Thrace: cf. Theoph., 364.5–9, A.M. 6179.

Advances to Thessalonica; takes Slavonian captives, whom he transfers to the theme of Opsikion: cf. Theoph., 364.11–15, A.M. 6180. Note that Nik. omits the statement, which must have come from the same source, that Justinian was ambushed by the Bulgarians on his way back.

Enlists 30,000 Slavonians and names them "The Peculiar People"; Romans defeated at Sebastopolis: cf. Theoph., 365.30–366.20, A.M. 6184. The statement that Justinian broke the treaty that had been concluded by his father (38.14–15) overlooks the fact that the same treaty had been ratified by Justinian himself at the beginning of his reign: Theoph. 363.6ff. The reference to the transfer of the Mardaites ("the armed men who from olden times had been lurking in the mountains of the Lebanon") is misplaced: it resulted from the aforesaid peace treaty (Theoph., 363.14–20; 364.4–5) and was a concession to the Arabs rather than a hostile act against them. Nik. omits the massacre of the remaining Slavonians in Bithynia (Theoph., 366.20–23).

The Arabs intensify their attacks against the Romans: cf. Theoph., 367.1–2, A.M. 6185 (misplaced in Theoph.).

7ff. The expedition to Thessalonica took place in 688–9. The date is confirmed by an inscription, now lost, discovered in 1885 under the pavement of the church of St. Demetrios. See J. M. Spieser, *TM* 5 (1973), 156–59; P. Lemerle, *Les plus anciens recueils des Miracles de S. Démétrius*, II (Paris, 1981), 189–90.

16 The Mardaites: On the controversial problem of their identity see, most recently, H. M. Bartikian in *Byzantium: Tribute to A. N. Stratos*, I (Athens, 1986), 17–39, who considers them to have been Armenian.

17 The engagement at Sebastopolis probably took place in 692/3: it is dated A.H. 73 by Elias Nisib., 73. Among several towns called Sebastopolis the best known was in Armenia I (or II after Justinian's reform), modern Sulusaray, NW of

Sebasteia (Sivas). See *Studia Pontica*, II by F. and E. Cumont (Brussels, 1906), 201 ff.; Ruge, *RE*, Sebastopolis 3. The battle probably took place there. Mich. Syr., II, 470 says it was near Caesarea of Cappadocia. Theoph., 366.6 is mistaken in specifying *ἐν Σεβαστοπόλει τῇ παρὰ θάλασσαν*. The attempt by E. W. Brooks, *BZ* 18 (1909), 154–56, to discover a maritime Sebastopolis in Pontos has been shown to be vain by A. Maricq, *Byzantion* 22 (1952), 350–54.

39. Justinian's cruel ministers

Cf. Theoph., 367.15–29, who gives a fuller story.

2–3 *ταμίας τῶν βασιλικῶν χρημάτων* = *σακελλάριος*.

3 *τοὺς ὑπὸ χεῖρα*: This refers to the workmen and their supervisors who were laboring on Justinian's new buildings in the Imperial Palace.

5 *ἐν σχήματι*: These two words may have been introduced into the text from a marginal scholion drawing attention to the "figure" of speech. Theoph. has *παιδικῶς δι' ἀβηνῶν μαστιγῶσαι*.

10 *τοὺς ὑπ' αὐτόν*: This refers to *διοικηταί*, i.e., collectors of taxes.

Theoph. mentions a third cruel minister, namely, the city prefect. Curiously, Nik. omits two items of local interest, viz. the reconstruction of the Palace and the destruction of the adjacent church of the Virgin Mary *τῶν μητροπολίτου*, which occasioned a famous witticism on the part of Patriarch Kallinikos.

40. Overthrow of Justinian by Leontios (695)

Similar account in Theoph., 368.18–369.30, A.M. 6187, with further details. Nik. adds three particulars: that Leontios was a native of Isauria (1–2), that he spared Justinian's life because of his affection for the latter's father (34), and that Stephen and Theodotos were executed against his wishes (39).

2–3 *τοῦ ἀνατολικοῦ . . . στρατεύματος* = *τῶν* 'Ἀνατολικῶν.

8 Monastery of Kallistratos: at Constantinople, exact situation unknown. See Janin, *Eglises*, 275–76.

10 Monastery of Florus: see Janin, op. cit., 495–96.

17 Praetorium: seat of the city prefect cum prison, on the main street (Mesē), between the Hippodrome and Constantine's Forum: Janin, *CP*, 165–69.

19 *τοῦ πραιτωρίου ὕπαρχος*: The correction is hardly satisfactory but is preferable to the MS reading *τοῦ πραίτωρος*, since the only official at Constantinople bearing the title of praetor was the relatively minor *πραίτωρ τῶν δήμων*, instituted by Justinian and not attested after Maurice. See Bury, *Admin. System*, 72. Of course, Nik. cannot be referring to the praetorian prefect, an office that was defunct at the time. He certainly means the city prefect, and Theoph., 369.7 has simply *τοῦ τηνικαῦτα ὑπάρχου*, identical with the anonymous *ἔπαρχος* at 367.30. There may, therefore, be some justification for bracketing *τοῦ πραίτωρος*.

22 Φόρον: Constantine's Forum.

25–26 *τὸν λουτῆρα*: not the baptistery, but the atrium of the church in the middle of which was a fountain. Cf. J. Ebersolt, *Sainte-Sophie de Constantinople* (Paris, 1910), 5.

28 *κατελθεῖν*: From the Patriarchal Palace situated at the gallery level of St. Sophia.

41 *τοῦ* Βοὸς *ἀγοράν*: see above, *ad* **1.**47.

41. Operations in Africa. Leontios overthrown by Apsimaros (698)

Cf. Theoph., 370.6–371.8, A.M. 6190. Apart from the statement that Leontios was in the 3rd year of his reign when he was dethroned, the only particular in which Nik. diverges from Theoph., except by omission, is at 14–15, *καὶ τὴν* Καρχηδόνα *παραλαμβάνει πάλιν καὶ τὰ περὶ αὐτὴν πολίσματα πάντα*, whereas Theoph. merely says that the Arabs laid siege to Carthage.

The conquest of Roman Africa is known largely from Arabic sources, which are late and generally unreliable. See Ch. Diehl, *L'Afrique byzantine* (Paris, 1896), II, 563 ff.; J. Wellhausen, *Die Kämpfe der Araber mit den Romäern*, Nachr. Kön. Ges. d. Wiss. Gött. (1901), 434–36; *Encyclopaedia of Islam*[1], art. Tunisia (R. Brunschvig), IV, 848; G. Marçais, *La Berbérie musulmane* (Paris, 1946), 29–35; Ch.-A. Julien, *Histoire de l'Afrique du Nord*[2], II (Paris, 1952), 11 ff.; *Encyclopaedia of Islam*[2], art. Ḥassān b. al-Nuʿmān al-Ghassānī (M. Talbi); Stratos, VII, 88 ff.

10 *στρατὸν ὁπλίτην* = Theoph.'s *ταξατιῶνα*.

11 *Σαρακηνῶν βασιλεύς* = *πρωτοσύμβουλος* (ʿAbd Al-Malik).

18 *βουληθείς*: a confusion. As made clear by Theoph., John had decided to return to Constantinople for reinforcements. It was the army officers who were unwilling to come back, fearing punishment for their failure.

21–22 Κουρικιωτῶν . . . *δρουγγάριον*: cf. H. Ahrweiler, *Byzance et la mer*, 50. Antoniadis-Bibicou, *Etudes d'histoire maritime de Byzance*, 85, 96 note 5, supposes that Apsimaros commanded a contingent of men from Korykos (which was no longer within the empire) stationed in the region of Kibyra. For the designation Κουρικιωτῶν *πόλις* cf. F. Halkin, *AnBoll* 72 (1954), 7.

23–24 Plague: According to Theoph., this was caused by the cleansing of the Neorion harbor.

28 Wall of Blachernai: more precisely designated by Theoph. as *τοῦ μονοτείχους* Βλαχερνῶν, i.e., the single wall built by Herakleios after the siege of 626 to protect the church of St. Mary. Cf. above, *ad* **13.**40.

33 Monastery of Delmatos (or Dalmatos): the oldest monastery of Constantinople founded in the late fourth century by St. Isaac in the Psamathia quarter. See Janin, *Eglises*, 82–84.

42. Justinian II regains the throne (705)

Corresponds to Theoph., 372.26–374.8, A.M. 6196; 374.16–23, A.M. 6197; 375.3–28, A.M. 6198, with a number of omissions (of barbarian and other proper names, geographical details and, most notably, the dramatic episode of the storm in the Black Sea). As usual, Nik. classicizes some geographical names (*Φαναγουρία* to *Φαναγώρη*, *Δανοῦβις* to *Ἴστρος*), but *Δόρος* is correct instead of Theoph.'s erroneous *Δαρᾶς*. The following statements, many of them explanatory, are not in Theoph.:

Doros, "which lies in the country of the Goths" (7).

The placing of a Chazar guard "to make sure that he would not escape" (19).

Unnamed archon (Theoph.'s Papatzys) "who was on friendly terms with Justinian" (21).

Tomis, "a coastal place" (29).

Justinian, on his return to Constantinople, "demanded the inhabitants of the City to receive him as emperor" (45–46).

He entered the aqueduct "at night," (47) possibly a substantive addition.

Herakleios, "the brother of Apsimaros, who was *strategos* of the Anatolic army" (*στρατοῦ*) (50). Theoph. says elsewhere (371.9) that Herakleios was appointed by his brother *μονοστράτηγος πάντων τῶν ἔξω καβαλλαρικῶν θεμάτων* and sent to Cappadocia with orders to watch the passes. We may suppose that he was later made *strategos* of the Anatolics.

Apsimaros and Leontios "kept in prison" (54).

The treatment of Tervel (58–64), which Theoph. omits.

Patriarch Kallinikos, "who had cursed him [Justinian] at the proclamation of Leontios" (65).

Kyros foretold to Justinian his second reign "when he [Justinian] was passing through those parts (*ἐκεῖσε*)," i.e., Amastris (68).

Persons promoted to magistracies and then killed (*ἀνῄρει*) (71).

24 *τοῦ πατρὸς οἰκετῶν*: Nik. forgets that Theodora was the Chagan's sister, not his daughter. Curiously, the same mistake occurs in Mich. Syr., II, 478.

34 *Βαρασβακούριον*: All the MSS of Theoph. have *Βασβακούριον*, which de Boor emends to *Βαρισβακούριον* on the strength of "Barisbacurium" in the Latin trans. of Anastasius. On his extant seals he is styled Barasbakourios, patrician and *comes* of Opsikion: Zacos-Veglery, nos. 3080A, 3081. Presumably the same as the Georgian prince Varaz-Bakur described as ex-consul (or proconsul) and patrician: see C. Toumanoff, *Studies in Christian Caucasian History* (Washington, D.C., 1963), 421–22, 424–25, 427.

49 Palace of Blachernai: Attached to the famous church of St. Mary, this imperial residence dated back to the second half of the fifth century. See Janin, *CP*, 123 ff.; Müller-Wiener, *Bildlexikon*, 223, with further bibliography. The aqueduct must have entered the city, as it still does, near the Adrianople Gate.

57 Kynegion: the disused Roman amphitheater between the Seraglio Point and the region of the Mangana. For its condition in the early eighth century see *Parastaseis*, c. 28.

58–64 The conferment on Tervel of the title of Caesar is confirmed by a seal, Zacos-Veglery, I/3, no. 2672 (*Θεοτόκε βοήθει* Τερβελλίου *καίσαρος*). The memory of his "having sat" at the Basilica and received a great amount of tribute lingers on in the *Parastaseis*, c. 37. An obscure passage in the *Suda*, s.v. Βούλγαροι (Adler, I, 483) has been linked with this episode. See Zlatarski, 230; V. Beševliev, *VizVrem* 16 (1959), 8–13. The passage reads: *Ὅτι ἐπὶ Ἰουστινιανοῦ τοῦ Ῥινοτμήτου ἤκμαζεν ὁ* Τέρβελις, *ὁ τῶν* Βουλγάρων *ἀρχηγός· καὶ ὁ αὐτὸς* Ἰουστινιανὸς *καὶ* Κωνσταντῖνος, *ὁ* Ἡρακλείου *υἱός, ὑπόφοροι τούτῳ ἦσαν. τὴν γὰρ ἀσπίδα, ἣν εἶχεν ἐν πολέμῳ, ὑπτίαν ἔθηκε καὶ τὴν ἑαυτοῦ μάστιγα, ᾗ ἐχρῆτο ἐπὶ τοῦ ἵππου, καὶ ἕως οὗ ἐσκέπασεν ἀμφότερα, χρήματα ἐνετίθει. καὶ τὸ δόρυ ἐν τῇ γῇ παρεκτείνας μέχρι τῶν περάτων καὶ ἐς ὕψος πολὺ σηρικὴν ἐσθῆτα ἐτίθει, καὶ κιβώτια πλήσας χρυσοῦ καὶ ἀργυρίου τοῖς στρατιώταις ἐδίδου, τὴν μὲν δεξιὰν χρυσίου πληρῶν, τὴν δὲ λαιὰν ἀργυρίου.* That is: "Terbelis, the chief of the Bulgars, was in his prime at the time of Justinian Rhinotmetos. The same Justinian and Constantine, son of Herakleios [Constantine IV], were tributary to him. Indeed, he laid on its back the shield he carried in war and the whip he used on his horse and piled up coins until he had covered both of them. Laying on the ground his spear, he placed silken cloths upon it from one extremity to the other [reaching up] to a great height. He also filled chests with gold and silver, which he distributed to his soldiers, filling his right hand with gold and his left with silver."

Assuming it was Tervel and not Justinian who did those things (as the sense, if not necessarily the grammar, seems to demand), we may note that the passage refers to a specific occasion that was witnessed by (or reported to) a Byzantine observer. It may be that Tervel, after being admitted to Constantinople and receiving rich gifts, staged such a demonstration outside the walls in the presence of his troops. It would be interesting to know where the passage comes from. Although clumsily worded, it aims at an elegant style (note, e.g. the ἐς), which we do not associate with the common source of Nik. and Theoph.

43. Justinian defeated in Bulgaria (708)

Does not add anything to the fuller account of Theoph., 376.13–29.

For the events see Beševliev, *Protobulg. Periode*, 196.

44. Siege and fall of Tyana (707–8). Arab raid reaches Chrysopolis

1–18 corresponds to Theoph., 376.31–377.14, but with notable differences.

According to Theoph., the Arab commanders were Masalmas (Maslama) and Abas (Al-ʿAbbas, son of Caliph Al-Walid); the attack was launched in retaliation for the slaughter of Maiouma's army by Marianos (not mentioned previously in Theoph.: the person in question was Maimum the Mardaite); the partial destruction of the walls of Tyana is omitted; the commanders sent by Justinian are named as Theodoros Karteroukas and Theophylaktos Salibas (the same who had taken part in the Cherson episode, 373.19) and they quarrel among themselves; the lack of provisions applies to the Arabs, not to the besieged; Tyana remains uninhabited "until now" (which probably refers to the date of the source rather than to the time of Theoph.'s writing).

For the events see E. W. Brooks, *JHS* 18 (1898), 192; Stratos, VI, 156–58; Lilie, 116–18. Cf. also the account of Mich. Syr., II, 478, who dates the fall of Tyana to March 708 after a siege of nine months.

18–24 The raid on Chrysopolis is not in Theoph. or any other source. Theoph., A.M. 6202 records an invasion led by Abbas, but does not specify its destination. Cf. Lilie, 118 note 43, who believes that Nik. is in error.

45. Punitive expeditions against Cherson. Downfall of Justinian (711)

Cf. Theoph., 377.22–381.6, with the following differences:

Theoph. mentions a second commander of the armament, namely, the patrician Mauros (who reappears in both Theoph. and Nik. in connection with the third expedition).

Theoph. omits the unlikely figure of 100,000 men. Nik. appears to have misunderstood the source: as may be deduced from Theoph., the ships, great and small, were requisitioned from (or collected with the help of contributions by: *ἀπὸ διανομῆς*) senators, shopkeepers, ordinary citizens, and various dignitaries—these men were not sent on the expedition.

Bardanes is mentioned at a later point by Theoph. (378.24). He had been banished to Kephalenia by Apsimaros on suspicion of aspiring to the throne (372.7, A.M. 6194).

Theoph. adds that Toudounos was the Chagan's representative and that Zoilos was first citizen by reason of his descent; but he does not qualify as administrators of other towns (21–22) the 20 men who were drowned in a boat.

Theoph. omits the indication that the drowned bodies were washed up between Amastris and Herakleia (Pontica).

In naming the commanders of the second expedition Theoph. specifies that George was logothete *tou genikou*. He adds a third name, that of Christopher, turmarch of the Thrakesians.

Theoph. explains that Toudounos died while he was on his way to the Chagan and that the Chazars killed the turmarch (Christopher) and the three hundred soldiers *εἰς δοχὴν αὐτοῦ*, i.e., in his honor. Nik. is guilty of a nonsense in implying that Toudounos was killed by the Chazars.

Theoph. omits the statement (probably a mere elaboration) that the Indian cook was ugly (56).

Theoph. adds that Mauros was a Bessos (Thracian) and that he was equipped with siege engines, with the help of which he threw down a tower of Cherson called Kentenarion and another tower called Syagros.

Theoph. omits the recourse to the Bulgarian Tervel and the mention of Damatrys as the point of concentration (which he names later at 380.9, 13, 31), but adds to the Opsikians a part of the Thrakesian army. Instead of the obscure village Gingilissos he names Sinope.

Theoph. has more detail about the death of Justinian and his son Tiberios.

4 [*εἰδότας*]: de Boor's conjecture *ἰδιώτας* can hardly be right, since, according to Nik., the men in question included both soldiers and senators, who could not have been described as "ordinary people."

11 *δορυφόρον* = *σπαθάριον*. Also at 93.

16 Toudounos: a Turcic title (*tudun* = viceroy), not a proper name. See Moravcsik, *Byzantinoturcica*, II, s.v.

19 *σὺν γυναιξὶ καὶ παισί* renders Theoph.'s *συνφαμίλους* (378.6).

20 *ὀβελοῖς* renders *σούβλας* (Theoph., 378.8).

37 *ἐν αὐτοῖς*: I have corrected to *ἐν αὐταῖς* to agree with *τῶν χωρῶν*, but Nik. may have had *τῶν κάστρων* in his source (as in Theoph., 378.21) and so inadvertently used the neuter.

42 *Ἠλίαν*: Nik. forgets to explain that Helias had turned traitor (Theoph., 378.24).

51 *δυσφημήσαντες καθύβριζον* = *ἀνέσκαψαν* (Theoph., 379.13).

57 Mauros: Theoph. 379.18 calls him a Thracian (Bessos). Probably the same as the Bulgarian chieftain Mauros, who hatched a plot to seize Thessalonica, was prevented from doing so, and finally joined the emperor at Constantinople and was given a title: *Mir. S. Demetrii*, II.5. According to Lemerle, the date of this incident falls between 678 and 685, perhaps in 682–4. The identity of the Bulgarian Mauros and Mauros the patrician is established by a seal, Zacos-Veglery, no. 934. Other seals of Mauros the patrician ibid., nos. 1552, 2168. See Lemerle's commentary on *Mir. S. Demetrii*, vol. II, 152ff.

65 *ἀπηναίνοντο* = *ἀνέσκαψαν* (Theoph., 379.28).

100 *τοῦ ὑπερκειμένου τείχους πυλίδα*: Theoph., 380.25 has *ἐπὶ τῷ ἄνω τῶν Καλλινίκης παραπορτίῳ*. The text of L helps to resolve a small topographical puzzle. Following a suggestion of Mordtmann, *Esquisse topographique de Constantinople* (Lille, 1892), 37, no. 60, accepted by A. van Millingen, *Byzantine Constantinople* (London, 1899), 173–74, and, apparently, by Janin, *CP*, 286, the postern of Kallinikos (sic) was the same as the Xyloporta, known from fourteenth–fifteenth-century sources, the latter being an opening in the short wall connecting

the north extremity of what is usually regarded as the Heraclian Wall to the shore of the Golden Horn. The Xyloporta was destroyed in 1868: A. G. Paspatis, *Βυζαντιναὶ μελέται* (Constantinople, 1877), 61, who says that its ancient name had survived to his days. It is, however, evident from our text that the postern was "in the wall that rises above," which can only refer to the old Theodosian Wall. The latter evidently passed a short distance east of the church of Blachernai and remained standing (on higher ground than the church) after the Heraclian extension had been built. Regarding the name of the postern, it evidently had nothing to do with St. Kallinikos, for in that case it would have been called *τοῦ ἁγίου Καλλινίκου*. If Theoph. preserves the correct form (in the fem.), it may have been called after the Blachernai Virgin, *τῆς καλλινίκου* (or –*ης*) in memory of her "victory" over the Avars in 626; but if Nik.'s *τῶν Καλλινίκων* is to be preferred, it may have adjoined a church dedicated to certain saints who "brought victory."

102 Church of the Anargyroi (Kosmas and Damian): This is the famous church at Kosmidion, on which see Janin, *Eglises*, 286–89, who fails to note the fem. form of the name, *τῶν Παυλίνης*, both in Nik. and Theoph.; elsewhere *τὰ Παυλίνου*. If *τῶν Παυλίνης* is the correct form, the church had nothing to do with Paulinus (*mag. off.* in 430), the well-known companion of Theodosios II and alleged lover of the empress Eudokia, as stated in the *Patria*, 261, c. 146 (note that all the MSS of the *Patria* but one read *Παυλίνης*).

46. Philippikos revives the Monothelete heresy

Combines the source of Theoph., 381.20ff., A.M. 6203, and 382.10–21, A.M. 6204 (much fuller) without introducing any further information.

1 *ἀσέμνως καὶ ῥᾳθύμως*: cf. Theoph., 381.29, *ἀσέμνως καὶ ἀνικάνως*.

5 *Ἰωάννην τὸν τηνικαῦτα*: This is misleading. Nik. neglects to say that John VI was the new emperor's appointee (ordained in Dec. 711). The word *τηνικαῦτα* applies in Theoph., 382.16 to Germanos. For the circumstances see Van Dieten, *Patriarchen*, 166ff.

6 Germanos: Nik. does not explain that he was the future patriarch of Constantinople.

7 "Other priests and many senators": Some of them are named by Theoph. (Andrew of Crete, the quaestor Nicholas, Elpidios deacon of the Great Church, Antiochos the chartophylax).

47. Bulgarian and Arab raids

Corresponds to Theoph., 382.22–30, A.M. 6204. According to Agathon the deacon, Mansi, XII, 193B, the Bulgarian raid was in reprisal of non-payment of tribute.

2 The addition of *κατά* is not imperative, since *ἐπεισπίπτω* can govern the acc. as in Euripides, *Herc.*, 34.

4 *τέρψεως καὶ ἡδυπαθείας*: Theoph. is more specific in saying that the Bulgars, who had come by way of Philea (Derkos), surprised many inhabitants of Constantinople, who had crossed the Golden Horn (*περαματίζοντας*) to celebrate sumptuous wedding parties al fresco. This explains the reference to silver vessels.

10 *μετὰ δὲ ταῦτα*: perhaps an arbitrary addition. It need not imply that the Arab raid was actually subsequent to the Bulgarian one. Tabarī records in A.H. 93 (Oct. 711–Oct. 712) the capture of Samastiyya by Al-ʿAbbas: Brooks, *JHS* 18 (1898), 193 note 3. Cf. Lilie, 120.

48. Fall of Philippikos (June 713)

Cf. Theoph., 383.5–21, who has more detail, but omits the reference to the Bulgarian danger in Thrace, which is also mentioned by Agathon the deacon, Mansi, XII, 193B. Cf. c. 42, where Theoph. omits the honors bestowed on Tervel.

There can be little doubt that Philippikos was deposed on 3 June 713, which corresponds to the Saturday before Pentecost Sunday. The date is confirmed by Agathon the deacon, loc. cit. Theoph., 386.14 must, therefore, be in error in assigning to Philippikos a reign of 2 years, 9 months instead of 1 year, 9 months: see Brooks, *BZ* 6 (1897), 52; G. V. Sumner, *GRBS* 17 (1976), 287–89. There remains a difficulty as regards the circus games on the "birthday of the city," i.e., 11 May. Kulakovskij, III, 312 states that the games were held on the emperor's birthday, but that is surely incorrect. Now, Nik. implies that the games and the insurrection took place on the same day, whereas Theoph. is somewhat more ambiguous. He says that after the victory of the Greens at the *γενέθλιον ἱππικόν* Philippikos decided (*ἔδοξε τῷ βασιλεῖ*) to make a ceremonial procession to the baths of Zeuxippos on Whitsun Saturday, which does not mean that the procession was to be the same day as the games. It is a little odd, however, that he should have wished to celebrate the victory of the Greens on 11 May by a procession three weeks later. The difficulty cannot be resolved by shifting the year to 714, as does P. Grierson, *DOP* 16 (1962), 51–52, when Pentecost Sunday fell on 27 May, quite apart from Agathon's testimony. Whatever the solution of this little puzzle, Nik. has certainly obscured in his paraphrase the sequence of events.

Irrespective of the above, the precision of the dates in Theoph. ("birthday" games, Saturday before Pentecost, Pentecost Sunday, the following Saturday, the Saturday after that) suggests a contemporary account.

As already noted in the Introduction, above, p. 6, the termination of L at line 15, in the middle of a connected narrative, must be considered accidental.

3–4 *ὕπνον . . . μεσημβρινόν*: *μεσημβρίζειν* in Theoph., indicating the practice of the afternoon siesta.

6 *τοῦ Ὀψικίου στρατοῦ ἡγούμενος*: renders *κόμητος τοῦ Ὀψικίου* in Theoph.

8 *γνώμῃ*: Theoph., probably rightly, says that the coup was launched at the

instigation of *both* George and Theodore Myakios (or rather Myakes). The latter had been an attendant of Justinian II: Theoph. 373.23.

9–10 *τῶν ὑπηρετῶν τινα*: renders *πρωτοστράτωρ τοῦ Ὀψικίου*.

13–14 *πρὸς τὸν τοῦ ἱπποδρομίου χῶρον* instead of the more precise *εἰς τὸ ὀρνατώριον τῶν Πρασίνων*.

15 *δεύτερον ἔτος . . . διάγοντα*: more accurate than Theoph.'s *διετοῦς δὲ χρόνου . . . παραδραμόντος* (383.5–6).

18–19 *γραμματέα . . . ἀσηκρῆτις*: *πρωτοασηκρήτης* in Theoph.

22 *τοῦτον*: according to Theoph. both men were exiled to Thessalonica.

49. Anastasios prepares to withstand Arab attack

Cf. Theoph. 383.29–384.14, A.M. 6206, who is more specific.

3–5 The text, as given by V, if a little awkward, is grammatically defensible. It would mean, however, that the caliph, on learning of the emperor's preparations and wise appointments, decided to launch an expedition against the Romans; thereupon, the emperor (the subject of *ἀποστέλλει*) sent Daniel on an embassy. Comparison with Theoph. shows that the source must have said the opposite, namely, that Anastasios, on becoming aware of Arab preparations, dispatched a peace mission to Syria. I have emended accordingly. The possibility remains that Nik. misunderstood his source and that the V text should be maintained.

12 It is noteworthy, as already pointed out by de Boor, that both Nik. and Theoph. should present at this point the same small lacuna, a lacuna, furthermore, that could easily have been filled from the context, as was done by Anastasius, who in his Latin translation of Theoph. adds *tum ille praecipit*. Hence the lacuna must have been in the source, and it appears likely that both Nik. and Theoph. had before them the same MS of it. If Theoph. was copying the source more or less mechanically, his inadvertence may be excused. It is rather more surprising that Nik., who was paraphrasing the source, should have paid so little attention to its sense as to leave out the verb.

14 Repair of sea walls: ascribed to Apsimar in *Parastaseis*, c. 3.

50. Operations at Phoenix; Theodosios proclaimed emperor (spring 715)

Cf. Theoph. 385.5–24, A.M. 6207.

2 Phoenix: This could have been the Phoenix of the Rhodian Peraea (modern Fenaket) opposite Symi rather than the better-known Phoenix (Finike) on the south coast of Lycia. On the former see F. Durrbach and G. Radet, *BCH* 10 (1886), 246ff.; T. A. B. Spratt, *Archaeologia* 49 (1886), 359–60; P. M. Fraser and G. E. Bean, *The Rhodian Peraea and Islands* (Oxford, 1954), 58.

4 *στρατόν*: renders *ταξάτους*, Theoph. 385.7.

4 *χώρας*: renders *θέματος*, Theoph. 385.8.

9–10 *ὑπάρχοντα . . . καθιστάμενον*: This explanatory amplification is not in Theoph., who does, however, have *τὸ τηνικαῦτα λογοθέτην γενικὸν ὑπάρχοντα*. The pleonastic *ὑπάρχοντα*, which seems to have crept in from the source, should perhaps be deleted.

15 *δεδοίκεσαν*: *οὐ κατεδέξαντο* in Theoph. 385.16.

16 *ἐδυσφήμουν* renders *ἀνέσκαψαν*.

19 Adramyttion: On the coast of Asia Minor, opposite Lesbos. The spelling *'Αδραμύντιον*, if it is not due to corruption, is peculiar. It cannot be explained as a more classical form, since Adramytt(e)ion (Atramyteion or –tteion) occurs in Herodotus, Thucydides, Xenophon, etc.

21 *πράκτορα*: *ἐκλήπτορα*, Theoph. 385.21.

21 *ἀπράγμονά τινα καὶ ἰδιώτην τυγχάνοντα*: *ἀπράγμονά τε καὶ ἰδιώτην* in Theoph. Cf. Plato, *Rep.* 620c, *βίον ἀνδρὸς ἰδιώτου ἀπράγμονος*. The precise connotation of *ἀπράγμων* in this context is not immediately clear. It may mean "fond of quiet," "uninvolved in politics," hence a positive characterization (*ἀπραγμοσύνη* being a virtue) or possibly "out of service." The same uncertainty applies to *ἰδιώτης*: is it a judgment ("an ordinary fellow") or does it mean a private citizen? If the latter, Theodosios must have been a retired tax collector. He was later represented as a gentle emperor, *Θεοδόσιος ὁ πραότατος βασιλεύς* in *Epist. ad Theophilum*, PG 95, 357, and his tomb at Ephesus, in the church of St. Philip, was believed to work miracles: Kedr., I, 787–88; *Chr. Altinate*, 109 (*in templo Sancti Phylippi, in antiqua urbe iuxta portum*). For his role in oracular literature see my remarks in *RSBS* 2 (1982), 312–13.

G. V. Sumner, *GRBS* 17 (1978), 291–92 argues that Theodosios was the son of Apsimaros. This theory does not appear entirely convincing.

51. Downfall of Anastasios (715)

Cf. Theoph. 385.24–386.13, A.M. 6207, who is more coherent.

4 *τοῦ 'Οψικίου στρατόν*: *τὸ θέμα τοῦ 'Οψικίου καὶ τοὺς Γοτθογραίκους* in Theoph. 385.28–29. On the latter see Bury, *LRE*, II, 344; Kulakovskij, III, 414 ff.

7 *ἐφ' ἑκάστου*: *καθ' ἑκάστην ἡμέραν*, Theoph. 386.1. Nik. fails to explain that the fleet of Anastasios was first stationed at St. Mamas, on the European shore of the Bosporos, and then moved to the Neorion, thus enabling Theodosios to cross over to Thrace.

9 Neorion harbor: on the Golden Horn, near modern Galata bridge. See Janin, *CP*, 235–36, 396–97.

13 Wall of Blachernai: see above, *ad* **13.** 40 and **41.**28.

16 Germanos: ordained on 11 August 715 (Theoph. 384.20). G. V. Sumner, *GRBS* 17 (1976), 290–91, suggests this may have happened on 11 Aug. 714 be-

cause in Aug. 715 Constantinople was under naval blockade, which would have impeded the transfer of Germanos from Kyzikos to the capital. This would not have been necessarily so, since the engagements were taking place in the Bosporos.

52. Arab invasion. Abdication of Theodosios (716–7)

No corresponding passage in Theoph., who has instead (A.M. 6208) a detailed account, clearly due to an eyewitness, of Leo's maneuvers in Asia Minor in the face of the advancing Arabs, with whom he evidently had a prior understanding. Another interesting account in Mich. Syr., II, 484–85. For the Arabic sources see Brooks, *JHS* 19 (1899), 19ff.

3–4 *ἡ τῶν λόγων ἠφανίζετο παίδευσις*: Theoph. 405.12–14 tendentiously connects the decline of education with the iconoclastic measures of Leo III.

11 1,800 ships: same figure in Theoph. 395.25 (under the command of Sulayman).

17 *ὑπεχώρει*: for the abdication cf. also *Vita Stephani iun.*, PG 100, 1084B; *Epist. ad Theophilum*, PG 95, 357C.

17 *ἐνιαυτὸν ἕνα*: rounded off (from c. Nov. 715 to March 717).

18 *εἰς ψῆφον ἐληλυθότων*: if there was a ballot, it must have been purely pro forma, since Leo was already holding hostage Theodosios' son and had advanced to Chrysopolis.

21–22 Leo's entrance through the Golden Gate is not mentioned elsewhere. The date was 25 March 717 (Theoph. 412.24–25).

53. Fall of Pergamon (winter 716–7)

Corresponds to Theoph. 390.26–391.2, A.M. 6208, with trivial differences. *Chr. 846*, 177, A.G. 1027 and Mich. Syr., II, 483, state that Sardis and other towns were also captured.

7 *ἐπὶ λέβητος* renders *ἐπὶ κακκάβου*.

9 *χειρίδας* renders *μανίκια*.

10–12 *αἱ γὰρ χεῖρες . . . ἀμαχητί*: probably a rhetorical amplification.

54. Constantinople besieged by the Arabs (717–8)

Corresponds to Theoph. 395.15–396.10, 21–23, 24–397.15, A.M. 6209, with many omissions. The only addition made by Nik. is that the siege lasted thirteen months: yet, according to Theoph. 395.18, 399.6, it started on 15 Aug. and ended on 15 Aug., hence continued for exactly one year.

For the sources and the events see Brooks, *JHS* 19 (1899), 19–31; M. Canard, *Journal asiatique* 208 (1926), 80ff.; R. Guilland, *Etudes byzantines* (Paris, 1959), 109–33; Lilie, 128–32. A homily by the patriarch Germanos on the deliverance of Constantinople is edited by V. Grumel, *REB* 16 (1958), 183–205. The source of Theoph. and Nik. appears to be due to an eyewitness, who was in Constantinople during the siege and so was unaware of what was happening beyond the Arab camp. Note that Theoph. does not mention any fighting along the walls. This is confirmed by Germanos, who says that the Arabs never used their siege engines and never shot an arrow against the city (ed. Grumel, 194, 196). The explanation is provided by Mich. Syr., II, 485: the Arabs were continually harassed by the Bulgars (cf. Nik. c. 57), whom they feared more than the Romans and in fact found themselves surrounded in their own camp. That is why the Arabs suffered from famine and why, in the end, their expedition failed. Cf. Beševliev, *Protobulg. Periode*, 200–201.

4 *χάρακα*: Theophanes speaks of a ditch and a breastwork of dry stone; Mich. Syr. of a double ditch, one facing the city and another in the rear to guard against the Bulgars.

7–8 According to Theoph., the fleet under Sulaymān (b. Muʿād̲) arrived on 1 Sept. and put in at the Hebdomon. Two days later, when a south wind blew, it sailed past the city and up the Bosporos.

24 Σοφιάμ: Σουφιάμ in Theoph. (Sufyān). This and the following commander do not appear in the Arabic sources: Canard, op. cit., 83 note 3, 90.

28 Ἰέζιδος: Ἰζίδ in Theoph. (Yazīd).

33–34 *λέμβους τῶν νηῶν*: *κατηνῶν σανδάλους* in Theoph. 397.6–7.

55. Revolt in Sicily (718)

Corresponds to Theoph. 398.7–399.4, A.M. 6210, with some omissions and the following differences:

The *strategos* Sergios has the title protospatharios in Theoph., that of patrician in Nik.

Nik. implies that Paul was patrician before being sent to Sicily, whereas Theoph. (probably correctly) says that he was the emperor's chartulary and was given both the title of patrician and the office of *strategos* of Sicily at the time of his dispatch.

George (line 16) probably corresponds to the anonymous *μονοστράτηγος* in Theoph. 398.29.

1 Τούτῳ τῷ χρόνῳ: Τούτῳ τῷ ἔτει in Theoph. Note the retention of a "chronicle" entry. The expedition to Sicily took place before the departure of the Arabs from Constantinople, in the spring or early summer of 718.

2–3 *καὶ οἱ τὰ ἑσπέρια . . . ἀπογνόντες*: an amplification.

4–5 *τῶν ὑπηρετῶν τινα*: *ἐκ τῶν ἀνθρώπων αὐτοῦ* in Theoph.

8–9 *ἅτε πιστόν . . . ἔμπειρον*: an amplification.

11 Λογγουβάρδους: Λογγιβάρδους in Theoph.

12 *γράμματα*: *τῆς σάκρας* in Theoph.

56. Birth of Constantine V. Arabs shipwrecked on their homeward journey (718)

Theoph. records the withdrawal of the Arabs under A.M. 6210 and the birth of Constantine under A.M. 6211, i.e., in reverse order. He was baptized on 25 Dec. (400.2). Nik. omits the insulting epithets applied by Theoph. to Leo and Constantine as well as the famous incident of the fouling of the baptismal font.

6 "as far as Cyprus": not in Theoph. The miraculous destruction of the Arab fleet is also mentioned by Germanos, *REB* 16 (1958), 197. The fiery "hail" and the boiling of the sea must have been due to volcanic activity in the Aegean, which culminated in the eruption of Thera (c. 59).

57. Artemios attempts to regain the throne (719?)

The account of Theoph. 400.18–401.3, A.M. 6211, is shorter and presents notable differences. The initiative for the plot is ascribed to Niketas Xylinites, who writes to Artemios at Thessalonica urging him to go to Tervel and ask for Bulgar help. Artemios does so and obtains an army and 5,000 lbs. of gold. With this force he comes to Constantinople, but is not admitted by the inhabitants of the city. The Bulgars surrender Artemios to Leo, are rewarded by him, and return home. Leo beheads Artemios and Niketas and confiscates the latter's estate. The Bulgars have in the meantime beheaded Sisinnios Rhendakis (who had accompanied Artemios), and they deliver to Leo the archbishop of Thessalonica, who is likewise beheaded. Other conspirators who are executed include Isoes, patrician and *comes* of Opsikion, Theoktistos the *protoasekretis*, and Niketas Anthrax, commander of the Wall.

For once, the account of Nik., though omitting a few details (the mention of Tervel, the 5,000 lbs. of gold, etc.) is both fuller and appears more coherent. Since it is unlikely that two separate sources are involved, we must conclude that Theoph. abbreviated the source in an absentminded manner. We have seen on other occasions (above, c. 42, 45) that he was reluctant to speak of events that showed the empire as being indebted to the Bulgars, perhaps as a reaction to the disasters of 811 and the years following.

There is also a chronological difficulty. If Sisinnios was sent to Bulgaria to obtain help against the Arabs, this must have happened well before the withdrawal of the latter in Aug. 718. Indeed, Mich. Syr., II, 485 reports that when Maslama had crossed the Dardanelles and was marching through Thrace to Constantinople (June/July 717), he was harassed by the Bulgars, "que Léon avait engagés." Hence the mission of Sisinnios must have taken place in the spring of 717 at the latest. Perhaps he remained in Bulgaria (as also suggested by Nik.'s *διατρίβοντα*), being unable to return to Constantinople. The advance to Herakleia was certainly after Aug. 718 and may have occurred in 719 if Theoph. places it in the correct year, but presumably before the death of Tervel, the date of which is uncertain.

For these events see G. Cankova-Petkova, *BSL* 24 (1963), 41–53, who argues that the Bulgarians in question were not the Danubian ones, but those settled near Thessalonica, and that Tervel was no longer alive at the time; Kaegi, *Unrest*, 211–12; Beševliev, *Protobulg. Periode*, 201–2. P. A. Giannopoulos, *ΕΕΒΣ* 39–40 (1972–73), 579–93, wishes to identify Sisinnios Rhendakis with Sisinnios *strategos* of the Anatolics in ca. 683/4, mentioned by Georg. Mon., 737, Leo gramm., 175, and the *Epist. ad Theophilum*, PG 95, 357. The Rhendakis/Rhentakios family appears here for the first time. We find it established in Boeotia in the ninth and tenth centuries. Other officials of the seventh/eighth centuries named Sisinnios include the commander of the imperial fleet (*στρατηγὸς τῶν καράβων*), who was sent to Thessalonica, perhaps in 682–4, and a Sisinnios, patrician and *magistros*, whose seal is published by W. Seibt, *Die byzant. Bleisiegel in Österreich*, I (Vienna, 1978), no. 78. Cf. ibid., no. 136 and Zacos-Veglery, no. 2370. See also P. Lemerle's commentary on *Mir. S. Demetrii*, vol. II, 154–55.

A seal of Niketas, patrician and *magistros* (presumably Xylinites) is published by Zacos-Veglery, no. 437.

12 *πρώτιστον τῶν βασιλικῶν γραμματέων* = *πρωτοασηκρήτην*.

13–14 *ἄρχοντα τειχῶν*: *τειχίου* (sing.) in Theoph., 401.1. This is the earliest attestation of the office, named *κόμης* or *δομέστικος τῶν τειχέων* (or *τοῦ τείχους*) or simply *ὁ τειχιώτης* in the ninth–tenth centuries. See Bury, *Admin. System*, 67–68, who is probably mistaken in connecting this command with the Anastasian Long Walls (which appear to have been no longer operational in the eighth century); R. Guilland, *Byzantion* 34 (1964), 17–25. Oikonomides, *Listes*, 336–37 believes that the count (or domestic) was initially in charge of the palace walls and that in the ninth century he was mainly responsible for the prison of the Chalke Gate.

58. Coronation of Constantine V (720)

Cf. Theoph. 401.9–12, A.M. 6212, who gives Easter day, indiction 3. Easter fell that year on 31 March, so that Nik.'s 25 March is incorrect.

59. Volcanic eruption in the Aegean (726)

Cf. Theoph. 404.18–29, A.M. 6218, with the date of indiction 9. Nik. adds the explanation that Thera and Therasia lie in the Cretan sea as well as the last sentence (the sea water was too hot to touch).

60. Beginning of Iconoclasm. Revolt in Greece (727)

1–7 Cf. Theoph. 405.1–2, A.M. 6218, who, however, places in the previous year, i.e., A.D. 725/6, the beginning of Leo's pronouncements against icons (404.3–

4). There has been much discussion as to whether there was or was not an iconoclastic edict in 726. The case against is stated by G. Ostrogorsky, *Mélanges Ch. Diehl*, I (Paris, 1930), 238–42; the case for by M. V. Anastos, *ByzF* 3 (1968), 5–41.

8–18 Revolt of the Helladics: cf. Theoph. 405.14–24, with the exact date of the arrival of the rebel fleet before Constantinople, 18 April, indiction 10. Theoph. is more precise: he specifies that the expedition was commanded by Agallianos, turmarch of the Helladics, and that many rebels were drowned *περὶ τὸν λάκκον*, whatever exactly that may mean. A vague memory of the turmarch Agallianos survives in *Patria*, 257.

61. Nicaea besieged by the Arabs (727)

Cf. Theoph. 405.25–406.2, A.M. 6218, who has more detail and adds a story about one Constantine, *strator* of Artabasdos, who threw a stone at an icon of the Virgin and was killed. The Arabic sources do not mention the attack on Nicaea. *Chr. 1234*, 241–42 dates the siege A.G. 1040 (729) and says it lasted forty days. Misdated A.G. 1042 by Mich. Syr., II, 501. The failure of the Arabs is mentioned in an inscription of the walls of Nicaea put up in the reign of Leo III, ed., e.g., A. M. Schneider and W. Karnapp, *Die Stadtmauer von Iznik (Nicaea)* (Berlin, 1938), 49, No. 29 and pl. 50.

3 *Ἄμερος*: *Ἄμερ* in Theoph. (ʿAmr), not mentioned in the Arabic sources. *Μανίας*: Muʿawiya b. Hisham, named as the leader of numerous raids into Byzantine territory from 725/6 onward: Brooks, *JHS* 18 (1898), 198 ff.

62. Iconoclastic silention (January 730)

Cf. Theoph. 408.31–409.14, 19–21, A.M. 6221, who is fuller and gives the exact date of the meeting, namely, 7 Jan., a Tuesday, indiction 13.

1 *ἀθροίζει πλεῖστον λαόν* renders *σελέντιον . . . ἐκρότησεν*.

2 *περὶ τὰ βασίλεια* instead of the more specific *ἐν τῷ τριβουναλίῳ τῶν ιθʹ ἀκουβίτων*.

3–4 *συγγράφειν κατὰ τῶν εἰκόνων*: *ὑπογράψαι κατὰ τῶν ἁγίων εἰκόνων* in Theoph. The words *τῆς καθαιρέσεως*, which I have bracketed, probably entered the text from a marginal title like *περὶ τῆς καθαιρέσεως τῶν εἰκόνων*.

6 *ἔγγραφον πίστιν οὐκ ἐκτίθεμαι*: Nik.'s paraphrase misses the point and shows a surprising lack of understanding of ecclesiastical terminology. Of course, Germanos was entitled to present a written declaration of (correct) faith without recourse to a council. What he is reported to have said was quite different, namely, "If I am [another] Jonah, cast me in the sea. For without an ecumenical council I find it impossible to change (*καινοτομῆσαι*) the faith (or doctrine), O Emperor."

7 *πατρικὸν οἶκον*: Theoph. adds that his ancestral house was at a place

called Platanion, which later tradition identifies with the monastery of Chora. See *Passio X martyrum* (composed after 869), Acta Sanctorum, Aug. II, 441B: *ἀπελθὼν ἐν τῷ λεγομένῳ Πλατωνίῳ, ἤτοι ἐν τῇ μονῇ τῇ νῦν καλουμένῃ Χώρᾳ, ἐκεῖσε ἡσύχασεν*. The *Synodicon vetus*, c. 147, ed. J. Duffy and J. Parker (Washington, D.C., 1979), 122, has two stages of confinement, first in his house, then in the monastery of Chora, where the emperor allegedly had him hanged. Three stages in the *Vita Germani*, cc. 27, 31, ed. L. Lamza, *Patriarch Germanos I. von Konstantinopel* (Würzburg, 1975), 232, 238: Germanos withdraws to his house; the emperor exiles him; he is recalled and placed incommunicado *ἐν τῷ Πλατωνίῳ . . . τῇ χώρᾳ* (sic). The *Vita Stephani iun.*, PG 100, 1085B, says he became a monk after his deposition. He seems to have lived on after 733, the date usually given for his death. For scholarly opinion concerning the latter see Lamza, op. cit., 178–79.

8 Anastasios, who had been *synkellos*, was ordained patriarch on 22 Jan. (Theoph., 409.11).

63. Marriage of Constantine V (732). Earthquake (740)

1–4 Cf. Theoph., 409.30–31, who, for once, is more "classical" in referring to *τῶν Σκυθῶν δυνάστου*. Theoph. adds that the princess was made a Christian, renamed Eirene, and that she lived in piety.

4–16 Cf. Theoph., 412.6–16, who gives the exact date (26 Oct., a Wednesday, in the 8th hour, indiction 9) and more detail, but omits the damage to St. Eirene and the statement that people left Constantinople and dwelt in huts. According to Theoph. various towns in Thrace as well as Nicomedia, Prainetos, and Nicaea were also devastated.

9 St. Eirene: Most of the upper part of the structure, as it stands today, was rebuilt after the earthquake. See W. S. George, *The Church of Saint Eirene at Constantinople* (Oxford, 1912), 5–6, 70; U. Peschlow, *Die Irenenkirche in Istanbul* (Tübingen, 1977), 212–13.

11 ff. Column of Arkadios: On this monument, which survived until the eighteenth century and whose pedestal is still extant, see, e.g., G. Becatti, *La colonna coclide istoriata* (Rome, 1960), 151 ff.

64. Accession of Constantine V (June 741). Usurpation of Artabasdos

1–3 Death of Leo III: cf. Theoph. 412.24–26, 413.1–4, A.M. 6232, giving the exact date (18 June, indiction 9 after a reign of 24 years, 2 months, 25 days), but not naming the disease.

4–42 Cf. Theoph. 414.18–415.22, A.M. 6233, with similar details but a tendentious interpretation. The story told by Theoph. is as follows. On 27 June, indiction 10 (742) Constantine set out against the Arabs and came to Krasos in the Opsikian theme. He sent word to Artabasdos, who was encamped with his army at

Dorylaion, to convey to him his two sons (his own nephews), pretending to be anxious to see them, but in fact intending to keep them as hostages. Driven to despair, Artabasdos raised a rebellion and killed the "Saracen-minded" patrician Beser, who had come forward to meet him (the looting of Constantine's camp is not mentioned). Constantine found a saddled horse and escaped to Amorium, where he was well received by Langinos, *strategos* of the Anatolics. He also obtained the support of Sisinnakios, *strategos* of the Thrakesians. A civil war ensued. Artabasdos, using as messenger the *silentiarios* Athanasios, wrote an account of what had happened to Constantine's *locum tenens* at Constantinople, the patrician and *magistros* Theophanes. The latter, who was sympathetic to Artabasdos, gathered the people in the gallery of St. Sophia and convinced everyone that Constantine had been killed. The news was received with joy, even by the "false" patriarch Anastasios, and Artabasdos was acclaimed emperor. Thereupon Monōtēs (the same as Theophanes) instructed his son Nikephoros, who was *strategos* of Thrace, to muster his troops so as to guard the city. He secured the gates and imprisoned Constantine's supporters. Artabasdos entered Constantinople with the Opsikian army and set about restoring the icons. Constantine, meanwhile, advanced to Chrysopolis with the Anatolics and Thrakesians, but being unable to achieve anything, returned to Amorium for the winter.

For an exhaustive discussion of the events described in cc. 64–66 see Speck, *Artabasdos*.

4 Theophanes writes Ἀρτάνασδος, which is also the spelling of the contemporary Nicaea inscription (above, *ad* c. 61). He was married to Leo's sister Anna (Theoph. 414.1).

6–7 Niketas and Nikephoros: named later by Theoph. (417.23–25).

8–9 Nik. makes it clear that Artabasdos rebelled as soon as he had heard of Leo's death, i.e., in June 741, not the following year as stated by Theoph. This is confirmed by Chronicle 2 in *Die byzant. Kleinchroniken*, ed. P. Schreiner, I (Vienna, 1975), 47. See Speck, op. cit., 72ff.

13 Krasos: Clearly close to Dorylaion (Eskişehir), but apparently not identified.

17 Βίσηρος: Βησήρ in Theoph. A. Syrian(?), who had allegedly converted to Islam, this man is identified as Leo's evil genius: Theoph. 402.9–15, 405.3–5. Cf. L. Bréhier, "Beser," *DHGE* 8 (1935), 1171–72; P. J. Alexander, *Nicephorus*, 235 note E; S. Gero, *Byzantine Iconoclasm during the Reign of Leo III*, CSCO, Subs. 41 (1973), 189–98.

20–21 τῇ χώρᾳ τῶν Ἀνατολικῶν = τῷ θέματι τῶν Ἀνατ. (Theoph. 414.29).

23–24 ὡς μέχρις αἵματος . . . κίνδυνον: probably an amplification.

25 Σισίννιον: Σισιννάκιον in Theoph. 414.31.

29–30 *τὴν βασιλέως χρείαν . . . ἀποπληρῶν* = *ἐκ προσώπου ὄντα ἐν τῇ πόλει* (Theoph. 415.3).

35 *ὑπηρετῶν*: corresponds to *τοὺς φίλους Κωνσταντίνου* (Theoph. 415.16).

39–40 *ἐπίνειον . . . διακείμενον*: an amplification. Nik. forgets that he had already explained the situation of Chrysopolis (**44**.22–23).

65. Civil war. Reverses of Artabasdos (743)

Cf. Theoph. 417.23–418.11, A.M. 6234, with more detail and exact dates: Artabasdos sets out for Asia in May, battle of Modrine August, indiction 11.

2 *στρατηγὸν . . . τῶν Ἀρμενιάκων*: in Theoph., probably correctly, he is said to have been appointed *μονοστράτηγος*, i.e., supreme commander in Asia Minor, and sent to the theme of the Armeniacs. Cf. Speck, *Artabasdos*, 88.

7–9 *τόν τε ὑπόντα λαόν . . . εἰσποιησάμενος*: not in Theoph.

9–10 Theoph. 417.31 also has the words *τὴν Κύζικον καταλαβών*.

12 Modrine: east of Nicaea, modern Mudurnu. It was a bishopric, subject to Nicaea. Cf. Ramsay, *Hist. Geogr.*, 459–60; *RE*, Modra (W. Ruge).

14 Among the killed Theoph. mentions the patrician Tiridates, cousin of Artabasdos.

14–20 The moralizing comment, differently expressed, is also in Theoph.

66. Constantine regains the throne (743)

Cf. Theoph. 419.7–421.6, A.M. 6235, who is much fuller and provides dates: Constantine crosses to Thrace in Sept., indiction 12 (743), captures Constantinople on 2 Nov. The following particulars are not in Theoph. or are given differently:

Theoph. does not say that some inhabitants of Constantinople threw themselves down from the walls and others bribed the guards; not does he say that Constantine received them with open arms. Instead, he says that some disguised themselves as women or monks and so were able to slip away.

Markellinos is described by Theoph. as a *curator* and former bishop (*ἀπὸ ἐπισκόπων κουράτορι*), not as metropolitan of Gangra.

Theoph. omits the flight of Artabasdos to Nicaea and his recruiting of soldiers there(?).

The blinding of Artabasdos and his sons is placed by Theoph. immediately after their capture and before their exhibition in the Hippodrome.

Theoph. does not say that Sisinnios hatched a plot. Instead, his blinding is represented as an act of gratuitous wickedness, the more so as he was Constantine's cousin and had done so much to help him. This is another example of tendentiousness on the part of Theoph.

16–18 A difficult passage. Note that the MS reading is *οἴκοι*, which is not impossible. Artabasdos may have announced at Nicaea that he was going to recruit soldiers "at home" or "in his own country" and, after surrounding himself with a force "there" (ἐκεῖ), would come back. The alternative, reading ἥκοι, would be that Artabasdos announced that he was on his way to raise a contingent, presumably at or near Nicaea, which would further imply that the Opsikians he had with him at Constantinople did not constitute the totality of the locally available manpower. The lacuna, indicated by Speck and accepted by us, makes it impossible to decide on the correct interpretation. Cf. Speck, *Artabasdos*, 93 ff. and 306 note 67 with further references as regards recruitment.

20–21 *ἀπόμοιραν . . . ἐκπέμψας*: not in Theoph. Possibly supplied from the context.

27–29 Theoph. does not explain what happened to Artabasdos after his blinding, except to say that he was buried in the monastery of Chora and that thirty years later his wife (Anna) was obliged by Constantine to dig up his bones and throw them in the charnel pit called *ta Pelagiou*. The *Life* of St. Michael Synkellos, ed. F. Šmit, *IRAIK* 11 (1906), 251, says that Artabasdos, Anna, and their nine children were banished to the monastery of Chora and were buried there.

67. Capture of Germanikeia. Plague at Constantinople (747–48)

1–4 Capture of Germanikeia: cf. Theoph. 422.11 ff., A.M. 6237, who adds that Constantine took the city by capitulation; that he found there his maternal relatives, whom he transferred to Constantinople along with many Monophysite Syrians, who were settled in Thrace. Cf. Brooks, *JHS* 18 (1898), 207.

4 ff. Plague: cf. Theoph., 422.29 ff., A.M. 6238, who specifies that it started in Sicily and Calabria and moved by way of Greece and the islands in the course of indiction 14; reached Constantinople in indiction 15 (de Boor mistakenly prints 5), and attained its peak in the spring/summer of indiction 1 (748). Theodore the Studite, *Laud. Platonis*, PG 99, 805D, says that the climax of the plague (of which Plato's parents died) lasted two months. For further details see above, Introduction, p. 10. Spread of the plague to Syria and Mesopotamia: Mich. Syr., II, 506, 508.

10 Cruciform markings: "oily" crosses in Theoph., 423.7 and Theodore Studite, op. cit., 805C.

12 Doors and door posts: not in Theoph.

16 *ξένοις τισὶ συνοδεύειν καὶ εἰδεχθέσιν ἀνθρώποις*: *ξένοις τισίν, ὡς ἐδόκουν, καὶ βριαροῖς προσώποις συνοδεύειν* Theoph., 423.17.

19–21 Phantastic apparitions: cf. Procopius, *Bell.* II.22.10 (concerning the plague of 542); *Mir. S. Demetrii*, c. 37.

20 *ξίφεσιν ἀλλήλους τινὰς βάλλοντας*: a clumsy paraphrase. Theoph., 423.16–17 is clearer: the apparitions entered houses and either killed the inmates or wounded them with a sword.

24–25 *σεσαγμένοις . . . ζῴοις*: *διὰ ζώων σαγματουμένων* Theoph., 423.22.

31 *τὰς ἀνύδρους τῶν δεξαμενῶν*: *κινστέρνας ἀνύδρους* Theoph., 423.26.

33 *κῆποι*: Theoph., 423.28 specifies that these orchards were within the "old," i.e., Constantinian walls.

36–37 One year's duration and abatement: not in Theoph. except by implication.

68. Repopulation of Constantinople. Naval victory off Cyprus

Repopulation: The corresponding passage in Theoph., 429.22 ff., is placed several years later (A.M. 6247). He specifies that the new settlers were brought from Greece and the islands together with their families.

Naval victory: cf. Theoph., 424.3 ff. (same year as the plague). He states that the Arab fleet was surprised in the harbor *τῶν Κεραμαία* whose mouth the Byzantines occupied; and that of 1,000 Arab ships only three escaped. The situation of Keramaia is unclear: see Sir George Hill, *A History of Cyprus*, I (Cambridge, 1940), 262 note 5.

69. Birth of Leo IV (January 750). Earthquake in Syria

Cf. Theoph., 426.14 ff. Leo was born on 25 Jan., indiction 3.

Earthquake: The account in Theoph. shows a close verbal similarity to that of Nik. with the following slight differences: Theoph. has *ζῶον μουλικόν* without indication of sex, and has it foretell *ἔθνους* (unnamed) *ἐπιδρομὴν ἐκ τῆς ἐρήμου κατὰ τῶν Ἀράβων*, without any mention of the slaughter caused by it. This passage appears to be based on vague reports exploited by imperial propaganda, and has no exact equivalent in the eastern sources. Cf. Mich. Syr., II, 507, A.G. 1056 (earthquakes in the desert of Arabia; mountains move closer together; villages swallowed up); 509–10 (earthquake damage in Syria/Palestine; a village near Mt. Tabor shifted four miles without damage; a source of water near Jericho displaced by six miles).

70. Coronation of Leo IV (Pentecost 751). Capture of Melitene. Death of Augusta Maria

Coronation of Leo IV: cf. Theoph., 426.26 ff., who gives exact date (Pentecost, indiction 4) and specifies it was performed by Patriarch Anastasios.

Capture of Melitene: Theoph., 427.14 ff., A.M. 6243, records briefly the taking of Theodosioupolis and Melitene, without referring to a siege, captives, or booty. Arab sources place the capture of Melitene, by capitulation, in A.H. 133 (9 Aug. 750–29 July 751). See Brooks, *EHR* 15 (1900), 731; 16 (1901), 88 and note 204, arguing that the siege of Melitene took place at the latest in autumn of 750. Mich. Syr., II, 518 has it in A.G. 1063; likewise *Chr. 1234*, 263.

Death of Maria: not in Theoph. Maria must have been Constantine's second wife, since the first was certainly the Chazar Eirene (above, c. 63) and the third was Eudokia. She appears to have died childless after a very short marriage. Cf. Bury, *LRE*, II, 458–59; A. Lombard, *Constantin V*, 102–3, and my remarks in *AnBoll* 100 (1982), 407–8. Mich. Syr., II, 517 must be mistaken in stating that Eirene died in A.G. 1063 and that Constantine remained celibate three years after her death. *Chr. 1234*, 262 records the death of an unnamed wife.

71. Celestial prodigy

Theoph., 435.5 ff. records it in one sentence in March 764; date confirmed by Chronicle 2 in *Die byzant. Kleinchroniken*, ed. Schreiner, I, 48. The prodigy was considered to presage the end of the world. For the corresponding passage in the *Megas Chronographos* (where it is made contemporary with the birth of Leo IV, i.e., 25 Jan. 750), see above, Introduction, p. 17. Mich. Syr., II, 507–8 records various celestial signs in A.G. 1056–58.

If Nik. is indeed speaking of the phenomenon of 764, his chronological error would be hard to explain.

72. Death of Patriarch Anastasios. Iconoclastic council (754)

Cf. Theoph., 427.25 ff., who is more specific: Anastasios died of a disease of the guts, vomiting excrement through his mouth; the council, held in the palace of Hieria (modern Fenerbahçe) was presided by Theodosios of Ephesos (son of Apsimar) and Pastillas of Perge, without representation from other patriarchates; it lasted from 10 Feb. to 8 Aug.; the new patriarch of Constantinople (Constantine II) was appointed in the church of Blachernai; a public proclamation was made in Constantine's Forum on 27 Aug.

The Definition (*horos*) of the council is preserved. See M. V. Anastos in *Late Classical and Mediaeval Studies in Honor of Prof. A. M. Friend, Jr.* (Princeton, 1954), 177–88.

15 George of Cyprus: hero of The Admonition of the Old Man concerning the Holy Images, written in 750–54 by his disciple Theosebes. Ed. B. M. Melioranskij, "Georgij Kiprianin i Ioann Ierusalimljanin," *Zap. Ist.-Fil. Fak. Imp. St. Petersb. Univ.* 59 (1901). Cf. Alexander, *Nicephorus*, 11–12.

73. Syrians and Armenians transferred to Thrace. War with Bulgaria

1–9 Transfer of population and Bulgarian reprisals: cf. Theoph., 429.19 ff., A.M. 6247, who states that the new settlers caused the spread of the Paulician heresy; that the Bulgarians demanded tribute with respect to the *kastra* that had been built; when their emissary had been dismissed insultingly, they invaded Byzantine territory, took many captives, and returned safely home. The construction of fortifications in Thrace was considered a great achievement: Nik., *Antirrh.* III, PG 100, 512B.

8 Long Walls: see above, c. 10.20.

9ff. Bulgarian war: Nik. appears to be speaking of two distinct operations: (1) a successful punitive raid; (2) some time later (*μετ' οὐ πολύ*) an important expedition by land and sea culminating in a victory at Markellai. The first appears to correspond to Theoph., 430.21–22, A.M. 6250, who says it was directed against the Slavs "and others" in Macedonia. With regard to the second, Theoph., 431.6ff., A.M. 6251, speaks of a defeat at the pass of Verigava, where the Byzantine army was surprised and suffered heavy casualties. The disagreement between Nik. and Theoph. is discussed by Lombard, *Constantin V*, 43–45, who suggests that the defeat at Verigava was a minor episode of a war that ended in the victory of Markellai. Beševliev, *Rev. ét. sud-est europ.* 9 (1971), 363–67; *Etudes Balkaniques* 7/3 (1971), 5–9; *Protobulg. Periode*, 209–10, argues that Nik., as distinct from Theoph., is here following the "official" version put out by the organs of imperial propaganda. He dates the second campaign to 760.

17 Markellai: a fort on the Byzantine-Bulgarian border, situated near the valley between Goloe and Diampolis (Jambol) according to Anna Comnena, ed. Leib, II, 105. Identified by K. Škorpil with Karnobatski Hisar, whose ruins are described by him, *IRAIK* 10 (1905), 513–14, 564; pl. CXIII, 4–5. See also I. Dujčev, *Rev. ét. sud-est europ.* 4 (1966), 371–75. Markellai was rebuilt by Constantine VI: Theoph., 467.28.

74. Severe winter (763–4)

Cf. Theoph., 434.6ff., who gives more precise geographical indications and dates: the cold started in early Oct.; the ice split in Feb., indiction 2.

10–11 *τὴν ὑπερπόντιον τοῦ Εὐξείνου θάλασσαν* corresponds to *τὴν ἀρκτῴαν τοῦ Πόντου παραλίαν*, Theoph., 434.9.

14 Medeia: modern Midye.

31 Daphnousia: A small island off the northern coast of Asia Minor, west of the mouth of the Sangarios. See Ramsay, *Hist. Geogr.*, 182–83, 196; *RE*, II/xi (1936), 718–20, s.v. Thynias 2 (K. Ziegler).

45–46 Fort of Galata: first mentioned in connection with the siege of 717–8 (Theoph., 396.2), the *kastellion* of Galata served as the northern point of attachment of the chain that barred the mouth of the Golden Horn (Leo Diaconus, 78–79). The *Patria* (p. 265, c. 157) ascribes its construction to Tiberius, but that may be fanciful. Its vaulted undercroft is occupied by the Ottoman Yeraltī (or Kurşunlu Mahzen) Camii, a short distance east of Karaköy bridge. See A. M. Schneider and M. I. Nomidis, *Galata* (Istanbul, 1944), 6, 31–32.

49 *ἐνθένδε ἀπηλλάσσοντο* corresponds to *οἴκοι ἀνέκαμπτον*, Theoph., 435.4.

A difficulty is posed by the personal aside in Theoph., 434.23–25: "Of this I was myself an eyewitness, for I climbed on one of those icebergs and played on it together with some thirty boys of the same age. Some of my wild and tame animals also died." Since Theoph. himself was about four years old at the time it is unlikely that he would have been allowed to climb on an iceberg with a band of other boys. If the reminiscence derives from the common source of Theoph. and Nik., and assuming that its subject was about ten years old in 763–4, we would have to conclude that the common source could hardly have been written before c. 780. It is not impossible that the aside is due to George Synkellos, who provided Theoph. with most of the latter's historical material.

For the freezing of the Black Sea cf. P. de Tchihatchef, *Le Bosphore et Constantinople*[2] (Paris, 1866), 268ff.

75. Migration of Slavs

Cf. Theoph., 432.27–29, A.M. 6254, who omits the number of the Slavs and their crossing of the Euxine.

1 Nik. appears to be mistaken in stating that the migration took place several years after the winter of 763–4. Theoph. connects it with the usurpation of Teletz, which, according to Zlatarski, I, 276, occurred late in 761. Constantine's Bulgarian expedition described in the next paragraph is, in any case, firmly dated to 763.

4 The accuracy of the figure is defended by Ostrogorsky, *History*, 168 note 2, against P. Charanis, *Byzantion* 18 (1948), 76–77, who considered it exaggerated. B. A. Pančenko, *IRAIK* 8 (1903), 35 had argued that it applied only to men able to bear arms, excluding women and children.

76. Teletz, ruler of Bulgaria. Battle of Anchialos (763)

Cf. Theoph., 432.25–433.14, who gives exact dates: Constantine marches into Thrace on 16 June; battle of Anchialos on Thursday, 30 June, indiction 1, from the 5th hour of the day until evening. Theoph. omits the following details: (1) Thrace overrun by Teletz; (2) Byzantine fleet sent to the Danube; (3) capture of *prominent* Bulgarians; (4) Bulgarian prisoners handed over to citizens *and members of the circus factions*; (5) the Sicilian basins.

14–15 "Many of the enemy fell on both sides" is, of course, nonsense, unless Nik. understood *πολέμιοι* to mean "belligerents," which is not its classical connotation. Theoph., 433.7 has *κόπτουσιν ἀλλήλους ἐπὶ πολύ*. In his *Antirrhet.* III, PG 100, 508B Nik. refers to the heavy casualties suffered: the bones of the fallen could still be seen in the plain round Anchialos.

77. Sabinos, ruler of Bulgaria (763). Feigned peace

1–9 Cf. Theoph., 433.14ff., who is more precise: Sabinos is described as the *γαμβρός* of former King Kormesios; he flees to Mesembria and is succeeded by Paganos. All of this before the winter of 763/4. Sabinos appears to correspond to Vinekh of the Bulgarian List of Princes: J. B. Bury, *BZ* 19 (1910), 143–44; Beševliev, *Protobulg. Periode*, 212 note 3.

9–11 Not in Theoph. The subject of the sentence is presumably Constantine.

11–18 Cf. Theoph., 436.9ff., 21ff., A.M. 6256, who gives the following sequence: (1) Paganos, the lord of Bulgaria, seeks and obtains an interview with the emperor; feigned peace concluded. Note verbal overlap: *ὠνείδισε τὴν ἀταξίαν αὐτῶν καὶ τὸ κατὰ Σαβίνου μῖσος* (436.13); (2) emperor sends agents to Bulgaria and kidnaps Sklavounos, chief of the Severoi, and Christianos, chief of the Skamaroi; (3) emperor makes a sudden attack on Bulgaria while the passes are unguarded. He sets fire to the Bulgarian *αὐλαί* and returns home. Constantine's success won by taking advantage of dissension among the Bulgarians is mentioned by Nik., *Antirrhet.* III, PG 100, 508C. For these events see Beševliev, *Protobulg. Periode*, 216–17.

78. Birth of Niketas. Arab attack on Sicily

Not in Theoph.

1 The chronological indication (indiction 1 = 762/3) need not apply to all the events described in c. 77.

2 Niketas, third son of Constantine and Eudokia, made *nobilissimus* on 2 April 769 (below, c. 87). Mentioned in Edirne inscription: C. Mango and I. Ševčenko, *BZ* 65 (1972), 385, 390.

2ff. Attack on Sicily: An attack is recorded in A.H. 135 (752/3). See M. Amari, *Storia dei Musulmani di Sicilia*, ed. C. A. Nallino, I (Catania, 1933), 299–301; E. Eickhoff, *Seekrieg und Seepolitik zwischen Islam und Abendland* (Berlin, 1966), 38–39.

79. Expedition into Bulgaria (765)

Not in Theoph., but presumably refers to the raid mentioned by him at 436.21ff. (above, c. 77).

3 Oumaros: Oumor is mentioned in the Bulgarian List of Princes with a reign of 40 days: Moravcsik, *Byzantinoturcica*, II, 353.

4 Toktos: not mentioned elsewhere. It is not altogether clear whether Baianos is the same as Theoph.'s Paganos or whether the latter is to be identified with Nik.'s Kampaganos. Beševliev, *Protobulg. Periode*, 219, 505 ff. opts for the second alternative and explains that Kampaganos was a title, not a name. He believes that Toktos was the senior and Baianos the junior khan.

80. Iconoclastic persecution intensified

Not in Theoph., but perhaps merely a rhetorical expansion of 436.27, *ἐκμανὴς γενόμενος ὁ δυσσεβὴς καὶ ἀνόσιος βασιλεὺς κατὰ παντὸς φοβουμένου τὸν θεόν*. Note that Nik.'s father Theodore, who was *asekretis*, was banished at about this time: Alexander, *Nicephorus*, 55–56.

81. Martyrdom of St. Stephen the Younger (Nov. 765). General persecution

1–17 Cf. Theoph., 436.26–437.9, who gives the date as 20 Nov., indiction 4. This has generally been preferred to the chronology of *Vita Stephani iun.*, which dates the martyrdom to 28 Nov. in the saint's 53rd year, i.e., 767 (PG 100, 1177D). See G. Huxley, *GRBS* 18 (1977), 97–108; M.-F. Rouan, *TM* 8 (1981), 421. The erroneous date 764 often given to this event is due to Ch. Diehl, *CRAI* 1915, 147 ff.

10 Prison: the Praetorium in which, according to the *Vita*, 1160B, 1164B, Stephen was confined for eleven months.

12 *τῶν βασιλικῶν . . . περιβόλων*: Theoph., 437.4 says more accurately that Stephen was dragged from the Praetorium to ta Pelagiou. Similarly *Vita*, 1176B.

13–14 The *Vita*, 1177A specifies that at the Forum Bovis a tavernkeeper split the saint's skull (he had already died). The situation of ta Pelagiou has been the subject of debate: Janin, *CP*, 405, maintains that it was the same as the area called Krisis in the western part of the city, whereas P. Franchi de' Cavalieri, *AnBoll* 64 (1946), 157 ff. denies this. I believe Janin is right, or nearly so, because *Vita Stephani*, 1177B makes it clear that the saint's body was dragged along the main street from Forum Bovis past the nunnery *τοῦ* Μ*ονοκιονίου* before being thrown in the charnel pit called ta Pelagiou. The nunnery in question, probably named after the Exokionion, may well have been the same as the church of St. Andrew en Krisei (Koca Mustafa Paşa Camii), in which case ta Pelagiou should be sought some distance to the west of it. Janin, *Eglises*, 396–96 points out that there was no St. Pelagios (as stated in the sources) and believes that the place was named after St. Pelagia. On the analogy of other Constantinopolitan toponyms it is more likely that the area was called after a former owner Pelagios, e.g., the one recorded as patrician in 490: *PLRE*, II, Pelagius 2.

17 ff. Cf. Theoph., 437.9–15, who adds that the emperor persuaded Patriarch Constantine to eat meat and listen to music at table.

82. Disaster of Byzantine fleet (766)

Cf. Theoph., 437.19–25, who specifies that the expedition set out on 21 June, indiction 4, and that the emperor returned on 17 July. Details not in Theoph.: (1) that Constantine encamped near pass of Verigava; (2) that the fleet was ordered to approach Mesembria and Anchialos; (3) that the Bulgarians sued for peace.

3–4 Pass of Verigava: probably the Riš Pass. The name is Thracian, not Slavonic according to V. Beševliev, *Recherches de géographie historique* = Studia Balcanica, I (Sofia, 1970), 69–75; *Protobulg. Periode*, 180 and note 28.

8 Anchialos: Theoph. has *εἰς Ἀχελόν*, presumably a popular form of the name. Cf. N. Bănescu, *BZ* 26 (1926), 114–15 and already T. L. F. Tafel, *De Thessalonica* (Berlin, 1839), 485–86, who point out that the famous battle of the Achelôos (in 917), as it is called in our classicizing sources, must have been fought near Anchialos, not on the river in Aetolia.

12 *ἀλίμενος* applies not to the coast between Mesembria and Sozopolis, but to that between Mesembria and Varna. See Beševliev, *Protobulg. Periode*, 222.

83. Monks ridiculed. Conspiracy against the emperor. Patriarch Constantine deposed (Aug. 766)

1–8 Monks ridiculed: cf. Theoph., 437.25 ff., who gives the date as 21 Aug., indiction 4. He says that each monk was made to hold a woman (not a nun) by the hand.

8–21 Conspiracy: cf. Theoph., 438.2 ff., who says that nineteen dignitaries were paraded in the Hippodrome on 25 Aug. He names eight of them, starting with Constantine Podopagouros, patrician and logothete of the course, and his brother Strategios, *spatharios* and domestic of the excubitors. The two of them were considered the leaders of the plot. Theoph. names Antiochos in third place and describes him as former (*γεγονώς*) logothete of the course—correctly, because the office was then held by Constantine—and *strategos* of Sicily. Theophylaktos comes fifth and is described as *protospatharios* (not patrician) and *strategos* of Thrace.

21–28 Deposition of Patriarch Constantine: cf. Theoph., 438.26 ff., with the date 30 Aug., indiction 4. He was exiled first to Hieria, then to the island of Prinkipos.

τῇ ὑστεραίᾳ: presumably after the execution of the conspirators for which Theoph. does not give an exact date.

28 Appointment of Niketas: 16 Nov. 766 according to Theoph., 440.11, who calls him *ἀπὸ Σκλάβων εὐνοῦχος*, but omits to say that he was a presbyter of the

church of the Holy Apostles. For his other titles see F. Fischer, "De patriarcharum Const. catalogis," *Comment. philol. jenenses* 3 (1884), 290. The appointment is mentioned here out of sequence in order to round off the story without regard to the August date (line 31).

84. Execution of ex-Patriarch Constantine (Oct. 767)

Out of sequence with regard to next paragraph.

Cf. Theoph., 441.5–442.12 with much fuller detail and the dates 6 Oct. for the scene in St. Sophia and 15 Oct. for Constantine's interrogation by the patricians and(?) his execution.

1–2 It seems that Nik. began by writing down the date, then decided to omit it for stylistic reasons.

4 *τινά . . . τῶν βασιλικῶν γραμματέων* = *ἀσηκρήτης*.

8 *καθαιροῦσι*: not clear seeing that Constantine had already been deposed. Theoph., 441.17 says that he was made to give up his omophorion, which suggests that he had retained the episcopal dignity.

8–9 Why was the new patriarch reading the same accusations in a low voice? Theoph., 441.14–15 has simply *ἐν τῷ συνθρόνῳ καθεζομένου καὶ θεωροῦντος*.

85. Drought. Aqueduct of Valens repaired (766–7). Artificial abundance of foodstuffs

1–12 Cf. Theoph., 440.14ff., who is more detailed, but omits the reference to the workmen's allowances (lines 10–11).

12–21 Cf. Theoph., 443.18–22 under the year 767–8. New Midas: see above, Introduction, p. 10. Theoph. omits the important indication of prices.

86. Birth of Anthimos (768–9). Repairs of St. Sophia. Captives ransomed

1–2 Birth of Anthimos not in Theoph. Anthimos is mentioned on the Edirne inscription, but his title is unfortunately lost: C. Mango and I. Ševčenko, *BZ* 65 (1972), 385, 391.

2–8 Work in St. Sophia: cf. Theoph., 443.22ff. (under the year 767–8), who has no mention of repairs but records with greater precision the removal of mosaics and frescoes. For the identification of the two *secreta* and the archaeological evidence for the destruction of their earlier decoration see C. Mango, *The Brazen House*, 53; idem, *Materials for the Study of the Mosaics of St. Sophia at Istanbul* (Washington, D.C., 1962), 94; R. Cormack and E. J. W. Hawkins, *DOP* 31 (1977), 200f., 205ff.

8 *κηροχύτου ὕλης* = *ὑλογραφίας*.

8–15 Ransom of prisoners not in Theoph.

87. Coronation of Eudokia (1 April 769)

Cf. Theoph., 443.28 ff., who adds that Constantine was married for the third time; gives the venue as the Tribunal of the Nineteen Accubita; specifies that the children were Eudokia's and supplies additional details about the ceremony.

6–7 *ὑπατείαν ἐποίησαν καὶ . . . χρήματα διένειμαν* is a tautology. Theoph. specifies that the coins distributed were *τριμίσια καὶ σημίσια καὶ νομίσματα καινούργια*.

88. Eirene crowned Augusta (17 Dec. 769)

Cf. Theoph., 444.15 ff., who is more detailed: Eirene arrives from Athens by way of Hieria on 1 Nov.; betrothal on 3 Nov. in the church of the Pharos; marriage and coronation on 17 Dec. in the palace hall named Augusteus and the chapel of St. Stephen of Daphne.

INDICES

CP = Constantinople
emp. = emperor
patr. = patriarch
+ indicates words and names restored by emendation
[ ] indicates words and names bracketed in our edition

1. INDEX NOMINUM

All entries pertaining to Constantinople (but not its suburbs) are listed under Κωνσταντινούπολις, although Nikephoros seldom uses that name, preferring Βυζάντιον (q.v.) or various periphrastic locutions.

2. INDEX GRAECITATIS